D1523319

TERM PAPER RESOURCE GUIDE TO NINETEENTH-CENTURY U.S. HISTORY

TERM PAPER
RESOURCE GUIDE
TO NINETEENTH-CENTURY
U.S. HISTORY

Kathleen W. Craver

Greenwood Press
Westport, Connecticut · London

Library of Congress Cataloging-in-Publication Data

Craver, Kathleen W.
   Term paper resource guide to nineteenth-century U.S. history / Kathleen W. Craver.
      p. cm.
   Includes bibliographical references and index.
   ISBN-13: 978–0–313–34810–5 (alk. paper)
   1. United States—History—19th century—Chronology. 2. United States—History—19th century—
Bibliography. 3. Report writing—Handbooks, manuals, etc. I. Title.
   E337.5.C73 2008
   016.9735—dc22   2008004508

British Library Cataloguing in Publication Data is available.

Library of Congress Catalog Card Number: 2008004508
ISBN-13: 978–0–313–34810–5

First published in 2008

Greenwood Press, 88 Post Road West, Westport, CT 06881
An imprint of Greenwood Publishing Group, Inc.
www.greenwood.com

Printed in the United States of America

The paper used in this book complies with the
Permanent Paper Standard issued by the National
Information Standards Organization (Z39.48–1984).

10 9 8 7 6 5 4 3 2 1

Contents

Acknowledgments

I wish to thank my husband, Charlie, for his enthusiasm and encouragement while I worked on this book. I gratefully acknowledge the advice, interest, and support that my editor, Wendi Schnaufer, gave me throughout this exciting project. I would also like to express my appreciation to Chip Chase for his patience with reformatting the manuscript and my copy editor, Kathy Breit, for her highly professional assistance.

Introduction

Research into nineteenth-century American history has become gratifying and enriching because students have access to a wealth of resources not only in print but also online. History students have the opportunity to select almost any topic for a term paper with the full expectation that their information searches will be rewarded with sufficient materials. If there is a problem now for history students, it rests with the myriad of potentially excellent topics available to them. Educators and historians have long endeavored to stimulate high school and undergraduate interest in American history. They have also sought to hone students' critical thinking skills by instructing them how to effectively interpret and evaluate historical evidence from a variety of primary and secondary sources. This book assists students and the faculty and librarians who help them in selecting appropriate research topics and in finding relevant, term-paper-related resources.

Selecting one hundred significant historical events from the nineteenth century is a daunting challenge because there were so many important social, political, cultural, literary, and scientific developments that occurred between 1800 and 1899 in the United States. The guiding philosophy underlying the choices for inclusion is to ensure that events, people, inventions, wars, and technological advances that are considered totally reflective of the country's nineteenth-century character and experience were included. As well, I have tried to select topics that would engage students' interest. Although there were a number of important Supreme Court decisions that affected nineteenth- and even twentieth-century history, many are excluded because student interest in them is usually minimal at best. Instead, every attempt has been made to provide a list of topics that students will find exciting and intellectually challenging to research.

The topics cited in the book are listed chronologically, but not all include specific dates. While the election of 1824 took place within the indicated year, the rise of the "Robber Barons" during the Gilded Age occurred throughout the 1880s and well into the 1890s. Fortunately, the study of American history is no longer restricted to the study of events and developments that affected white men and women and their respective cultural and political institutions. Many recent historians have shed new light on nineteenth-century events, particularly those involving African Americans and American Indians. They have also provided researchers with provocative evidence and interpretations of many nineteenth-century events, people, and trends that were previously seen only through a Eurocentric perspective. The connection between Thomas Jefferson and his slave, Sally Hemings, for example, must be reconsidered in light of recently performed DNA tests on their descendants. Giving more exposure to topics concerning African Americans, American Indians, immigrants, and Mexican Americans is deliberately designed to provide students with the opportunity to avail themselves of so many of the new multicultural print and online resources.

The audience for *Term Paper Resource Guide to Nineteenth-Cenury U.S. History* is twofold. The book is written for high school and college students who are searching for appropriate topics for history assignments. They may read the extensive annotations, browse through the summarized primary and secondary sources and Internet sites, or make arrangements to access or purchase some of the relevant cited multimedia sources. A second audience consists of faculty and librarians who are charged with the task of assisting students with locating relevant research topics that their students will find sufficiently exciting and stimulating to complete history assignments. These may consist of term papers, online timelines, legal analyses, or other alternative term paper formats.

Every attempt has been made to cite recent materials that are readily accessible in local academic, public, and school libraries. All materials listed are available for purchase through Amazon.com. If students initiate their research with sufficient planning, many works can be purchased through Amazon.com's used book sellers or other online used book vendors such as Alibris.com. Cited periodical articles are available in JSTOR, which is accessible as an online database in many public, school, and academic libraries, and also are available for purchase through Internet searches.

Many bibliographic guides are written to serve the research needs and interests of historians and scholars. This guide, however, specifically targets high school and undergraduate students who are searching for suitable term paper topics that are interesting and researchable. Most secondary sources cited are recent publications, making them readily available for purchase or borrowing from local school, academic, and public libraries.

USING THE GUIDE

Each of the entries provides a short overview of the event that is designed to pique student interest in the topic. The overview is followed by a *Term Paper Suggestions* section that features six traditional research questions that students may either adopt or adapt for possible term paper topics. Two questions listed under the category *Alternative Term Paper Formats* furnish students with an opportunity to present their research product in the form of, for example, a Web site, podcast, legal brief, time-line, series of letters, or an iMovie. The remaining categories in an alpha-betized order of sequence are delineated as follows:

Primary Sources—Whenever possible digital primary sources are cited because of their availability and ready access. The range of relevant primary sources is extremely broad and may take the form of oral histories, period books and newspaper articles, diary entries, letters, interviews, photographs, maps, car-toons, eyewitness accounts, laws, and census records. For each entry, two or three relevant primary sources are included.

Secondary Sources—These materials include books and periodical articles that give an overview of the topic, biographies that shed light on a specific aspect of a person's life, and titles that assist in answering one or more of the posed term paper questions.

World Wide Web—Seven relevant Internet sites are provided for each entry. All are considered valid and reliable and were operative at the time of publication. As many students initiate research by searching the Internet, some sites are introductory, whereas others are relevant to specific questions.

Multimedia Sources—At least one multimedia source is furnished for each entry. Although most sources are videocassettes or digital videos, some take the form of streaming Internet videos, Internet audio clips, or CD-ROM databases that contain audio and visual components.

1. Presidential Election of 1800

Mudslinging, attacks, counterattacks, personal insults, and scandalous newspaper articles are not just the province of contemporary elections. They were the *de rigueur* of the presidential election of 1800. The election of 1800 even threatened the country's survival as states vowed to secede or ready their militias to fight a civil war. At stake was a philosophical struggle that had enormous implications for America's foreign, social, and economic policies in the years to come. In 1800, America was facing threats from Great Britain and France, constitutional issues over the powers of government branches, and a tenuous economy that was dependent upon many imports. Two parties with strong-willed leaders and philosophies emerged. President John Adams, a Federalist who believed in a strong central government, squared off against his own vice president, Thomas Jefferson, a Republican who favored individual freedoms over a federalized approach. Adams was eliminated, but Jefferson and his vice-presidential running mate, Aaron Burr, tied in the Electoral College with 73 votes each, throwing the decision into the House of Representatives. After thirty-six votes, Jefferson and Burr became president and vice president respectively, but not before almost tearing the country apart and causing the Twelfth Amendment to the Constitution to be written to ensure that such a political debacle never occurred again.

TERM PAPER SUGGESTIONS

1. The Constitution of the United States stated that state legislatures were to choose electors to vote for the president. Describe how the Federalists tried to manipulate this rule to their advantage and why a twelfth amendment to the Constitution was needed after the election of 1800.

2. In her book, *Affairs of Honor: National Politics in the New Republic,* Joanne B. Freeman cites the use of newspapers, pamphlets, and broadsides as a weapon in the election of 1800. Jefferson's platform was the *National Gazette* and Hamilton's was the *Gazette of the United States.* Compare press pieces from any of these sources and describe each party's position based on them.

3. Some New England states threatened to secede and/or call out their militias to fight in a civil war during the election. Discuss the differences in issues that brought these states to the brink of either secession or civil war.

4. Read President Jefferson's first inaugural address at http://www.pbs.org/jeffer son/enlight/social.htm. In it he declared that "we are all Republicans, we are all Federalists." Discuss how far his efforts toward conciliation transpired.

5. In this election, politics truly became personal. Cite examples of the enmities among various politicians and give an opinion regarding the resulting political damage in terms of public trust and faith in government.

6. The founding fathers genuinely feared the development and entrenchment of rival political parties in America. Analyze the pros and cons of a bi-cameral legislature. How can they serve as an in-house series of checks and balances?

ALTERNATIVE TERM PAPER SUGGESTIONS

1. Assume you are a political consultant for Thomas Jefferson, who has indicated that he desperately wants to win the election of 1800. Develop a Web site for Jefferson based upon his views concerning individual freedoms, slavery, the right to bear arms, etc.

2. Political cartoons were also used as a weapon during the election of 1800. Draw ten cartoons accompanied by appropriate explanations that either humorously or satirically depict an issue or politician.

SUGGESTED SOURCES

Primary Sources

"A Profession of Political Faith to Elbridge Gerry." http://www.positive atheism.org/hist/jeff1055.htm. Supplies the full text of what is known as Jefferson's platform for the election of 1800.

Cunningham, Noble E., Jr. *Jefferson vs. Hamilton: Confrontations That Shaped a Nation.* Boston, MA: St. Martin's Press, 2000. Provides excerpts from the papers of Thomas Jefferson and Alexander Hamilton about the election of 1800.

Wilentz, Sean. *Major Problems in the Early Republic, 1787–1848: Documents and Essays.* Lexington, MA: D.C. Heath, 1992. Contains primary source documents in the form of essays about Thomas Jefferson concerning the election of 1800.

Secondary Sources

Building the Nation. 1791–1832. (Debatable Issues in U.S. History). Westport, CT: Greenwood Press, 2004. Chapter 3 is devoted to a discussion of the controversial issues surrounding the election of 1800.

Campbell, Tracy. *Deliver the Vote: A History of Electoral Fraud, an American Political Tradition 1742–2004.* New York: Carroll and Graf, 2005. Discusses the culture of corruption that the author claims has been present in American political elections, including the election of 1800.

Dunn, Susan. *Jefferson's Second Revolution: The Election Crisis of 1800 and the Triumph of Republicanism.* Boston, MA: Houghton Mifflin, 2004. Describes the 1800 election as probably the most vicious in terms of mudslinging and personal attacks on the candidates and compares it to present-day elections.

Ferling, John. *Adams vs. Jefferson: The Tumultuous Election of 1800.* New York: Oxford University Press, 2005. Gives a scholarly yet exciting account of one of the most contested elections in American history.

Freeman, Joanne B. *Affairs of Honor: National Politics in the New Republic.* New Haven, CT: Yale University Press, 2002. Freeman contends that the founding fathers used three weapons as a means of reputation protection that would preserve their legacies in history: theater, gossip, and the press. All were used during the exciting election of 1800.

Gumbel, Andrew. *Steal This Vote: Dirty Elections and the Rotten History of Democracy in America.* New York: Nation Books, 2005. Traces the history of unsavory politics from early nineteenth-century elections up to the one in 2004. Includes recommendations for direct elections and same-day registrations as a means to reduce voter fraud and other dirty tricks.

Hakim, Joy. *A History of the U.S.: The New Nation.* 3rd ed. New York: Oxford University Press, 2003. Chapter 3 is devoted to a discussion of the development of the Federalist and Republican parties that were to oppose each other in the election of 1800. Chapter 10 provides information about how Thomas Jefferson represented the Republican viewpoint.

Horn, James P., Lewis, Jane Ellen, and Onuf, Peter S., eds. *The Revolution of 1800: Democracy, Race, and the New Republic.* Charlottesville, VA: The University of Virginia Press, 2002. Describes the revolutionary potential of the election of 1800 and the constitutional changes that were necessary for reform.

Keyssar, Alexander. *The Right to Vote: The Contested History of Democracy in the United States.* New York: Basic Books, 2001. Written by a Duke University historian, this academic work shows how the election of 1800 was just one part of America's necessary evolutionary process to resolve basic constitutional issues.

Larson, Edward J. *A Magnificent Catastrophe: The Tumultuous Election of 1800, America's First Political Campaign.* New York: Simon & Schuster, 2007. Written for non-historians, this is a well-researched account of the election of 1800.

Sharp, James Roger. *American Politics in the Early Republic: The New Nation in Crisis.* New Haven, CT: Yale University Press, 1995. Provides an historian's viewpoint about the real crisis that America faced in its first party dispute over a national election.

World Wide Web

"The Election of 1800: Teaching about a Critical Moment in the History of American Constitutional Democracy." http://www.ericdigests.org/2000-2/1800.htm. Although this site is directed to teachers, it contains an excellent overview of the issues involved in the election of 1800, including a set of appropriate external links.

"The Gilder Lehrman Institute of American History—Hamilton vs. *The Partisan Press.*" http://www.gilderlehrman.org/collection/docs_print/print_partisan.html. Contains the full text of a letter written by Alexander Hamilton threatening a slander suit against the newspaper, *Aurora,* for accusations of corruption.

"The Gilder Lehrman Institute of American History—Jefferson in My View Is Less Dangerous Than Burr." http://www.gilderlehrman.org/collection/docs_archive/docs_archive_ham3.html. Furnishes the full text of a letter that Hamilton wrote to his fellow Federalists urging them to break the deadlock by voting for Jefferson rather than Burr.

"History Now—The Presidential Election of 1800: A Story of Crisis, Controversy, and Change." http://www.historynow.org/09_2004/historian4.html. Written by Joanne B. Freeman of Yale University, this site places the election of 1800 in historical perspective and compares it to some contemporary elections.

"HistoryCentral.com—Election of 1800." http://www.multied.com/elections/1800.html. Provides graphs, the history behind the election, and state-by-state voting results.

"PBS—Thomas Jefferson: The Revolution of 1800." http://www.pbs.org/newshour/inauguration/lesson_jefferson.html. Contains historical background information, activities, and the full text of Jefferson's inaugural speech.

"Voting Rights and Citizenship—Jefferson and the Election of 1800." http://www1.cuny.edu/portal_ur/content/voting_cal/jefferson.html. Described as a "peaceful transition of power," this site gives an overview of the politicians and issues at stake in the election of 1800.

Multimedia Sources

Adams vs. Jefferson: The Election of 1800. West Lafayette, IN: C-Span Video.org, 2004. 1 DVD. 58 minutes. John Ferling, author of *Adams vs. Jefferson*

The Tumultuous Election of 1800, speaks about the political leaders of the Federalist and Republican parties and contrasts their platforms on a variety of positions that were essential to nineteenth-century America.

The Making of a Nation #35—October 23, 2003: Election of 1800. Washington, DC: Voice of America, 2003. 2 minutes. Click on this audio link: http://www.voanews.com/specialenglish/archive/2003-10/a-2003-10-22-1-1.cfm. Sponsored by the Voice of America, this site features the text and audio of a reenactment of some of the issues involved in the great differences between the parties during the election of 1800.

2. Barbary Pirate Wars (1801–1815)

Nominally under the Ottoman Empire the Barbary States (Morocco, Algeria, Tunis, and Tripolitana) were relatively self-governing. Pirates from these states prowled the Mediterranean Sea and the Atlantic Ocean even as far as Iceland, capturing ships and enslaving and ransoming their crews and passengers. When they were not seizing ships, they busied themselves exacting tribute against future piracy. Although Britain's powerful navy could have wiped them out, they chose to use them as a threat against their maritime rivals by paying a small annual protection fee. As part of the British Empire, the United States was covered. After independence was attained, President Thomas Jefferson negotiated tribute payments and treaties with individual Barbary States until 1801 when the Pasha of Tripoli raised the amount and declared war against the United States. War officially broke out in 1803 when President Jefferson sent warships to the Mediterranean to successfully recapture the ship, *Philadelphia,* and to blockade the coast of Tripolitana. During the War of 1812, Algiers declared war on America because of insufficient tribute. On May 10, 1815, U.S. warships responded by capturing two pirate ships and forcing Algiers to sign a treaty that ended any future payments. Similar treaties were achieved with Tunis and Tripolitana.

TERM PAPER SUGGESTIONS

1. Discuss why European countries such as Spain, France, and Britain used the Barbary pirates in a system of political and economic checks and balances.
2. Describe the initial attempts by the United States to appease the Barbary pirates by paying tribute and making treaties with them.

3. Analyze the pros and cons of President Jefferson's proposed league of nations to patrol pirate waters. What would have been the advantages and disadvantages?

4. When the American ships *Maria* of Boston and the *Dauphine* of Philadelphia were captured in Algeria, President Jefferson requested $1 million from Congress for their release. Discuss the implications of a government yielding to the pirates' demands.

5. Was the United States justified in waging war against nations that harbored the Barbary pirates?

6. Trace the parallel between the actions of the Barbary pirates and modern-day state-sponsored terrorism.

ALTERNATIVE TERM PAPER SUGGESTIONS

1. Using documents and film clips from the DVD, *Battle of Tripoli,* create a five-minute iMovie of the event. Conclude with a summary of its historical significance.

2. Assume that you are President Jefferson announcing the foreign capture of two American ships to the nation and Congress. Prepare a series of podcasts requesting $1 million for their release. Structure your oral argument based upon President Jefferson's own words.

SUGGESTED SOURCES

Primary Sources

Lane-Poole, Stanley. *The Barbary Corsairs with Additions by Lieut. J. D. J. Kelley.* Boston, MA: Adamant Media Corporation, 2001. This book is a facsimile of the 1894 edition. It places the depredations of the Barbary pirates in a historical context as retaliation by Moslems for the loss of Spain and parts of Europe in 1492.

"Naval History: Account of the Operations of the America Squadron, under Commodore Decatur, against Algiers, Tunis, and Tripoli," *The Analectic Magazine* 7 (February 1816): 13. (Available in JSTOR.) Gives a one-page description and account of visiting Lepatis, an ancient Tripolitan city where Commodore Stephen Decatur concluded a treaty on behalf of the United States.

Secondary Sources

Clissod, Stephen. *The Barbary Slaves.* Totowa, NJ: Rowman & Littlefield, 1977. Provides an historical account of the life of captives under Islamic pirates.

Earle, Peter. *The Pirate Wars*. New York: St. Martin's Griffin, 2006. Gives a succinct overview of the Barbary Pirate Wars.

Fremont-Barnes, Gregory. *The Wars of the Barbary Pirates: To the Shores of Tripoli: The Rise of the US Navy and Marines*. Oxford: Osprey Publishing, 2006. Discusses the role of the newly formed U.S. Marines and the establishment of America's first navy as a result of the Barbary Wars.

Lambert, Frank. *The Barbary Wars: American Independence in the Atlantic World*. New York: Hill and Wang, 2005. Provides the rationale for the United States to wage war with the Barbary pirates.

Lane, Kris E. *Pillaging the Empire: Piracy in the Americas, 1500–1750*. Armonk, NY: M. E. Sharpe, 1998. Discusses the history of privateering and piracy in the previous centuries that helps place the Barbary Wars within an historical perspective.

Leiner, Frederick C. *The End of Barbary Terror: America's 1815 War against the Pirates of North Africa*. New York: Oxford University Press, 2006. Supplies a scholarly account of the second Barbary Pirate War.

London, Joshua. *Victory in Tripoli: How America's War with the Barbary Pirates Established the U.S. Navy and Built a Nation*. Hoboken, NJ: Wiley Publications, 2005. Summarizes how the need to build warships to protect American shipping from piracy actually aided the United States in defending herself in the War of 1812.

Vivian, Herbert. "Tunisia and the Modern Barbary Pirates." *Journal of the American Geographical Society of New York* 31 (May 1899): 507–508. (Available in JSTOR.) Contains excerpts from Vivian's book where he declares the Arab pirates to be gentlemen and Americans to be impudent vulgarians.

Wheelan, Joseph. *Jefferson's War: America's First War on Terror, 1801–1805*. New York: Carroll & Graf Publishers, 2003. Depicts the Barbary Pirate War as America's first clash with Moslem countries and terror.

Wilson, Gary E. "American Hostages in Moslem Nations, 1784–1796: The Public Response." *Journal of the Early Republic* 2 (Summer 1982): 123–141. (Available in JSTOR.) Gives an historical perspective to the captive life, ransoming by religious groups, and conversion to Islam of American hostages in the seventeenth century.

Zacks, Richard. *The Pirate Coast: Thomas Jefferson, the First Marines, and the Secret Mission of 1805*. New York: Hyperion, 2005. Furnishes information about the role that the Marines played in boarding and capturing Tripolitan frigates during the first Barbary War.

World Wide Web

"British Slaves on the Barbary Coast." http://www.bbc.co.uk/history/british/ empire_seapower/white_slaves_01.shtml. Written by historian Rees Davies, this six-page summary describes the depredations by Barbary pirates on British subjects in prior centuries.

"Congressional Resolution." http://www.yale.edu/lawweb/avalon/diplomacy/ barbary/barmenu.htm. Contains the full text of the Congressional acknowledgements of U.S. Naval Officers Preble's and Decatur's conduct in sinking a Tripolitan frigate and a letter thanking the Danish consul for assistance when Captain Bainbridge and his crew were in captivity in Tripoli.

Gawalt, Gerard W. "America and the Barbary Pirates: An International Battle against an Unconventional Foe." Available in *The Thomas Jefferson Papers,* http://memory.loc.gov/ammem/collections/jefferson_papers/ mtjprece.html. Provides an excellent synopsis of the Barbary pirate depredations on American ships.

"Treaty with Tripoli June 4, 1805." http://www.yale.edu/lawweb/avalon/ diplomacy/barbary/barmenu.htm. Provides the full text of the treaty negotiated with Tripoli that ended tribute and guaranteed the safety of American ships.

"Treaty with Algeria June 30 and July 3, 1805." http://www.yale.edu/lawweb/ avalon/diplomacy/barbary/barmenu.htm. Furnishes the full text of a treaty concluded with Algeria to end pirates preying on American ships.

"Treaty with Algeria December 22 and 23, 1816." http://www.yale.edu/lawweb/ avalon/diplomacy/barbary/barmenu.htm. Gives the full text of another treaty drawn up between the United States and a Barbary State to end Algerian countenanced piracy of American ships.

"United States Statutes." http://www.yale.edu/lawweb/avalon/diplomacy/ barbary/barmenu.htm. Provides the full text of all statutes enacted by Congress that authorized payments for war with Tripolitan subsequent treaties with various Barbary States.

Multimedia Sources

The Barbary Wars: Lessons from America's First Foreign War. Carlisle, PA: Army Heritage Educational Center, 2006. 1 DVD. 52 minutes. Features a public lecture by Franklin T. Lambert, a Professor at Purdue University, as a case study for future dealings with adversarial middle eastern leaders.

The Battle of Tripoli. New York: A&E Television Networks, 2004. 1 DVD. 50 minutes. Filmed on location in Morocco, this DVD includes period documents, reenactments, and interviews with leading scholars about the role the Marines played in the Barbary Pirate Wars.

3. Innovations and Inventions (1801–1807)

Early in the nineteenth century a series of design innovations and inventions helped propel the United States forward to become a manufacturing colossus. The designs at the time seemed innocuous: a small wooden clock and a mechanical device that separated seeds from cotton. Each, however, employed power machinery, interchangeable parts, or a division of labor that would help lay the foundation for the American industrial revolution. Eli Whitney (1765–1825), inventor of the cotton gin, and Eli Terry (1772–1852), a clockmaker, shared similar first names and origins. Both were from Connecticut. Although Whitney applied for a patent for his cotton gin in 1794, it was not granted until 1807. Terry, on the other hand, received the first patent for a clock mechanism by the U.S. Patent Office in 1801. Terry's innovation involved the use of jigs and fixtures that allowed him to produce a significant number of interchangeable parts in an assembly line format rather than handcraft each clock. Whitney's cotton gin also revolutionized southern agriculture and reenergized the use of slavery in the South because farmers needed additional labor to supply more cotton to northern U.S. and British textile towns and cities.

TERM PAPER SUGGESTIONS

1. Discuss the market value of cotton after the invention of the cotton gin.
2. Whitney and Terry were early pioneers in the development of interchangeable mechanisms. Describe how their inventions and innovations were important to the development of a powerful American manufacturing base.
3. Describe how Terry's standardization of parts in his wooden clocks decimated the British clockmaking industry.
4. Whitney and his partner Phineas Miller chose not to sell cotton gins, but instead sold access to them at harvest time. Discuss why this decision was a recipe for their financial disaster and infringement of their patent rights.
5. Analyze how the invention of the cotton gin revitalized slavery in the South.
6. Examine how the development of northern manufacturing cities based on textiles and other industries helped the North win the Civil War.

ALTERNATIVE TERM PAPER SUGGESTIONS

1. Eli Whitney did not win the right to renew his patent for the cotton gin. Using his testimony before a Congressional panel, prepare a podcast consisting of his oral argument and some of the questions that were posed by panel members.

2. Assume that you are a lawyer representing Southern planters who are concerned that the firm of Whitney and Miller will establish a monopoly if their cotton gin patent is renewed. Write a legal brief on their behalf arguing the law and citing the power of the U.S. Congress to pass laws related to patents.

SUGGESTED SOURCES

Primary Sources

"Cotton Gin Petition." http://www.pbs.org/wgbh/aia/part3/3h1517t.html. Provides a full text copy of Eli Whitney's letter to then Secretary of State Thomas Jefferson requesting a patent for his invention of the cotton gin. The patent would not be granted until 1801.

Olmstead, Denison. *Memoir of Eli Whitney, Esq.* New Haven, CT: Durne & Peck, 1846. http://openlibrary.org/details/memoirofeliwhitn00olms rich. Furnishes the full text of a memoir first published in 1832 about the trials and tribulations of Eli Whitney as he tried to obtain financing for his numerous inventions, including the manufacture of firearms.

"Teaching with Documents: Eli Whitney's Patent for the Cotton Gin." http://www.archives.gov/education/lessons/cotton-gin-patent/#documents. Contains the full text of Article I, Section 8, Clause 8 of the Constitution concerning Congress and patent law, Eli Whitney's cotton gin petition and drawing, and an analysis of the patent problems he personally experienced.

Terry, Henry. *American Clock Making: Its Early History. Also, Illustrated Catalogue of Clocks, Manufactured by the Terry Clock Company, Pittsfield, Mass.* Bristol, CT: American Clock and Watch Museum, 1974. Written by one of Eli Terry's sons, this book describes his father's successful attempts to mass-produce affordable wooden clocks with interchangeable parts.

Secondary Sources

Britton, Karen Gerhardt. *Bale O' Cotton: The Mechanical Art of Ginning Cotton.* College Station, TX: Texas A&M University, 1993. Chapter 2 provides information about Eli Whitney's cotton gin and its legacy within the cotton industry.

Church, R. A. "Nineteenth Century Clock Technology in Britain, the United States, and Switzerland." *The Economic History Review* 28 (November 1975): 616–630. (Available in JSTOR.) Compares the course of innovation in a single industry in three countries and shows how the failure to employ American innovative techniques of systematic production destroyed the British preeminence in an entire industry.

Clouette, Bruce, and Matthew Roth. *Bristol, Connecticut: A Bicentennial History, 1785–1985*. Canaan, NH: Phoenix Publishing, 1984. Contains a brief description of the opening of Eli Terry's first clock factory in Bristol, Connecticut.

Green, Constance McLaughlin. *Eli Whitney and the Birth of American Technology*. Boston, MA: Longman, 1997. Describes, in an easy-to-understand format, the impact on society of Eli Whitney's invention of the cotton gin.

Hoke, Donald R. *Ingenious Yankees: The Rise of the American System of Manufactures in the Private Sector*. New York: Columbia University Press, 1990. Scholarly account of the increased efficiencies of American production, including Eli Terry's manufacture of affordable wooden clocks and refuting the assertion that these new innovations should be attributed to Eli Whitney's work.

Latham, Jean Lee. *The Story of Eli Whitney: Invention and Progress in the Young Nation*. New York: Aladdin Books, 1953. Provides a biography of Eli Whitney that traces his long legal journey to win rights over his pirated cotton gin and to fulfill his government contract for ten thousand muskets with interchangeable parts.

Lawet, Angela. *Inventing the Cotton Gin: Machine and Myth in Antebellum America*. Baltimore, MD: The Johns Hopkins University Press, 2003. This book disputes the myth that the invention of the cotton gin was inextricably linked to the expansion of slavery.

Murphy, John Joseph. "Entrepreneurship in the Establishment of the American Clock Industry." *The Journal of Economic History* 26 (June 1966): 167–189. (Available in JSTOR.) Describes how the clock industry was a forerunner for industries with interchangeable parts and mass marketing.

Mussey, June Barrows. *Young Father Time: A Yankee Portrait*. New York: Newcomen Society in North America, 1950. Summarizes the contribution and legacy that Eli Terry made to modern manufacture systems when he developed an affordable wooden clock constructed of interchangeable parts.

Roberts, Kenneth D. *Eli Terry and the Connecticut Shelf Clock*. Fitzwilliam, NH: Ken Roberts Publishing Co., 1994. Furnishes information about Eli Terry and the methods and interchangeable parts he used to mass-produce wooden clocks in the early nineteenth century.

Yafa, Stephen. *Big Cotton: How a Humble Fiber Created Fortunes, Wrecked Civilizations, and Put America on the Map.* New York: Viking Press, 2004. Discusses the role that the cotton crop played in American history, including the invention of the cotton gin by Eli Whitney.

World Wide Web

"Connecticut—Eli Terry." http://www.netstate.com/states/peop/people/ct _et.htm. Provides a brief overview of Eli Terry's life and his contribution to early American industrialization with his mass production system for wooden clocks.

"Eli Whitney Inventor of the Cotton Gin." http://www.whitneygen.org/ archives/biography/eli.html. Contains an excellent overview biography of Eli Whitney.

"Eli Whitney Museum & Workshop." http://www.eliwhitney.org/test/ index2.htm. Features an extended biographical sketch of Eli Whitney plus illustrations, explanations, and diagrams of all of his inventions, including the cotton gin.

"Engines of Our Ingenuity—No. 383: Wooden Clocks." http://www.uh.edu/ engines/epi383.htm. Furnishes a brief biographical sketch of Eli Terry and discusses how and why his manufacture of wooden clocks with interchangeable parts was so significant to the industrialization of America.

"Product Design and Cost considerations: Clock, Watch, and Typewriter Manufacturing in the 19th Century." http://www.h-net.org/~business/ bhcweb/publications/BEHprint/v018/p0119-p0128.pdf. This paper by Donald Hoke looks at wooden movement clocks, watches, and typewriters to prove how their product design helped give rise to the American system of manufacturing by taking into account cost effectiveness, and mass production techniques.

"United States Resource Center—Eli Whitney's Cotton Gin." http://college. hmco.com/history/us/resources/students/primary/cottongin.htm. Provides an easy-to-understand animation of how the cotton gin actually worked, along with questions concerning its application in agriculture and manufacturing.

"Virtual American biographies—Eli Terry." http://famousamericans.net/eliterry/. Furnishes a short biography of Eli Terry and discusses his contribution to early American industrial design.

Multimedia Sources

Eli Whitney. Wynnewood, PA: Schlessinger Media, 2001. 1 DVD. 23 minutes. Discusses the events that led to the invention of the cotton gin and the enormous economic changes that resulted, while also addressing its unforeseen impact on slavery in America.

4. The Sally Hemings and Thomas Jefferson Connection (1802)

Although Thomas Jefferson's affair with a young slave girl named Sally Hemings supposedly took place in the late 1700s, it was not until 1802 when he was a U.S. president that it became public. The spark was the publication of several articles written for *The Richmond Recorder* by journalist James Thompson Callender. The articles reported the presence of a slave boy at Jefferson's home in Charlottesville, Virginia, who bore such a remarkable resemblance to him that people were actually gossiping about it. For years various notable historians debunked the articles as vengeful because Callender was turned down by President Jefferson after seeking a position in his administration. The controversy came to light again in the twentieth century with the publication of two books, *Jefferson: An Intimate Biography* (1974) by Fawn Brodie and *Sally Hemings* (1979) by Barbara Chase Riboud. Both books claimed that the relationship was real and that the boy's name was Thomas Jefferson Hemings. Defenders of Jefferson jumped into the fray, claiming that Jefferson had an affair with Maria Cosway, the wife of a painter while he was an envoy in Paris and not Sally Hemings. It was not until 1998 that science weighed in on the matter with the publication of a short article in *Nature* that proved through DNA analysis of Jefferson's descendants that Hemings youngest child, Eston, was actually a direct descendant of Thomas Jefferson.

TERM PAPER SUGGESTIONS

1. Historian John Chester Miller in his book, *Wolf by the Ears,* stated that if the Sally Hemings story was true then "Jefferson deserves to be regarded as one of the most profligate liars and consummate hypocrites ever to occupy the presidency." Do you think that the DNA and other historical evidence support this assertion?

2. Sally Hemings was officially Jefferson's chambermaid, and her room was adjacent to Jefferson's bedroom through a covered passageway. She was never officially freed by Jefferson, perhaps because of a law that freed slaves had one year to leave the state. Many historians have argued that the story of

Thomas Jefferson and Sally Hemings is a great romance akin to Heloise and Abelard. Examine the affair from this standpoint, showing that Jefferson was a human being with all the strengths and failings that accompany that condition.

3. Jefferson's life was a series of contradictions on the subject of slavery. He claimed to be a dedicated foe of the slave trade, yet he bought and sold slaves when necessary. He believed that "all men are created equal," yet he tracked one of his runaway slaves down twice. Use his writings and his deeds concerning slavery to show how these contradictions existed in the same person.

4. Why did historians dismiss the charges against Jefferson or fail to mention them at all in their scholarly treatment of him? Do you think that there was a double standard with respect to such a prominent American?

5. In light of the most recent evidence of Jefferson's affair, how might his legacy as the father of liberty be affected?

6. W. E. B. Du Bois in "The Propaganda of History" wrote that "What we have got to know, as far as possible, is what actually happened in the world." Is the continued discussion of the Hemings-Jefferson affair important to the study of history, or is it just salacious gossip that really belongs in the dustbin of history?

ALTERNATIVE TERM PAPER SUGGESTIONS

1. Design a Web quest including links to all the DNA evidence and follow-up reports. Present conclusions about their significance to the historical record concerning President Thomas Jefferson.

2. Pose a series of ethical questions and host a forum comprised of pro and con advocates about how Thomas Jefferson should be viewed by historians because of his alleged affair with Sally Hemings.

SUGGESTED SOURCES

Primary Sources

Bear, James A., Jr. *Jefferson at Monticello.* Charlottesville, VA: University Press of Virginia, 1967. Provides the full text of the recollections of Edmund Bacon, Jefferson's overseer.

Durey, Michael. "With the Hammer of Truth: James Thompson Callender and America's Early Heroes." *The William and Mary Quarterly* 50 (April 1993): 462–464. (Available in JSTOR.) Includes extensive excerpts from the articles that James Thompson Callender published in the *Richmond Recorder* in 1802.

Flower, Milton E. *James E. Parton: The Father of Modern Biography.* Durham, NC: Duke University Press, 1951. Features the full text of a letter by Jefferson's biographer Henry S. Randall to James Parton, June 1, 1868, which discusses the Heming connection to Thomas Jefferson.

Gordon-Reed, Annette. *Thomas Jefferson and Sally Hemings: An American Controversy.* Charlottesville, VA: University Press of Virginia, 1997. Contains the complete text of many primary source documents, including letters written by Jefferson's children on both sides of the family tree, former slaves, and more.

Lander, Eric S., and Joseph J. Ellis. "Founding Father." *Nature* 396 (November 5, 1998): 13–14. Reignites the controversy that has smoldered for so long in American history by confirming via DNA analysis that Thomas Jefferson was the father of at least one of Sally Heming's children.

Lewis, Jan Ellen, and Peter S. Onuf. *Sally Hemings & Thomas Jefferson: History, Memory, and Civic Culture.* Charlottesville, VA: University Press of Virginia, 1999. Furnishes James Callender's reports, memoirs of slaves from Monticello, and documentation of interracial sex in the Chesapeake and the British Atlantic world about 1700–1820.

Secondary Sources

Adair, Douglass. "The Jefferson Scandals." In *Fame and the Founding Fathers,* edited by Trevor Colburn. New York: Norton, 1974. Devotes pages 160–191 to the connection between Thomas Jefferson and Sally Hemings.

Brodie, Fawn. "The Great Jefferson Taboo." *American Heritage* 22 (June 1972): 49–57, 97–100. Gives a complete account of the Jefferson-Hemings affair.

Brodie, Fawn. *Thomas Jefferson: An Intimate Biography.* New York: Norton, 1974. One of the first psychobiographies to analyze the inner motivation behind some of Jefferson's political and personal decisions regarding the government and his personal life.

Jordon, Winthrop D. *White Over Black: American Attitudes toward the Negro 1550–1812.* Chapel Hill, NC: University of North Carolina Press, 1968. Contains a twenty-page discussion of the affair and the reasons why this behavior was not only accepted but also hidden from the public.

Kukla, John. *Mr. Jefferson's Women.* New York: Knopf, 2007. Presents a flattering portrait of Jefferson with regard to his affairs with women, including Sally Hemings.

Lanier, Shannon, and Jane Feldman. *Jefferson's Children: The Story of an American Family.* New York: Random House, 2000. Details the meeting among the black and white descendants of Sally Hemings and Thomas Jefferson and discusses the legacy of a unique American family.

Malone, Dumas. *Jefferson the President: First Term 1801–1805*. Charlottesville, VA: University of Virginia Press, 2005. Provides several pages about the Jefferson-Hemings connection and defends Jefferson because this act would have been considered inconsistent with his character and proposed ideals.

Malone, Dumas, and Steven Hochman. "A Note on Evidence: the Personal History of Madison Hemings." *Journal of Southern History* XLI (November 1975): 523–528. (Available in JSTOR.) Provides a brief overview of the evidence given by Madison Hemings, a son of Sally Hemings, regarding his mother's relationship with Thomas Jefferson.

Miller, John Chester. *The Wolf by the Ears: Thomas Jefferson and Slavery*. Charlottesville, VA: University Press of Virginia, 1991. Addresses every issue of slavery involving Thomas Jefferson. Several chapters are devoted to the Sally Hemings story.

O'Brien, Conor Cruise. "Thomas Jefferson: Radical and Racist." *Atlantic Monthly* 278 (October 1996): 53–72. Based on the new DNA evidence, Conor argues that Jefferson's "flaws are beyond redemption."

Woodson, Bryon W. *A President in the Family: Thomas Jefferson, Sally Hemings and Thomas Woodson*. Westport, CT: Praeger Publishers, 2001. Discusses the post DNA legacy of the Sally Heming and Thomas Jefferson connection.

World Wide Web

"Jefferson Digital Archive." www.etext.virginia.edu/jefferson/texts/. Provides 1,590 documents and letters by and from Thomas Jefferson, including several about civic duty and the shaping of the American character.

"Report of the Research Committee on Thomas Jefferson and Sally Hemings." www.monticello.org/plantation/hemingscontro/hemings_report.html. Includes the analyses by top genetic scientists about the DNA study performed by Eric Lander and Joseph Ellis that was published in *Nature.*

"Sally Hemings: Mistress of Thomas Jefferson?" http://womenshistory.about .com/od/hemingssally/a/sally_hemings.htm. Furnishes background information surrounding the connection between Hemings and Jefferson.

"Sally Hemings (1773–1835)." http://www.monticello.org/plantation/lives/ sallyhemings.html. Supplies a brief biographical sketch of Sally Hemings that refers to her connection to Thomas Jefferson.

"The Thomas Jefferson–Sally Hemings Myth and the Politicization of American History." http://www.ashbrook.org/articles/mayer-hemings.html. An America History professor takes issue with the DNA results and other evidence indicating that Sally Hemings was the mother of some of Jefferson's children.

"Thomas Jefferson and Sally Hemings: A Brief Account." http://www.monti cello.org/plantation/hemingscontro/hemings-jefferson_contro.html. Furnishes a valid overview of the controversy and evidence linking Thomas Jefferson romantically to his slave, Sally Hemings.

"Thomas Jefferson–Sally Hemings DNA Study." http://www.angelfire.com/va/ TJTruth/. Includes links to all the DNA evidence and genetic studies that support the connection between Thomas Jefferson and Sally Hemings.

Multimedia Sources

Jefferson's Blood. Alexandria, VA: PBS Home Video, 2000. 1 videocassette. 87 minutes. Narrated by African American historian Shelby Steele, this film examines Thomas Jefferson's life and follows the descendants of Jefferson and his slave Sally Hemings as they search their family history and sort out their places along America's blurred color line.

Sally Hemings: An American Scandal. Santa Monica, CA: Artisan Home Entertainment, 2000. 1 DVD. 171 minutes. Dramatizes the story of the thirty-eight-year affair between Thomas Jefferson and his slave mistress, Sally Hemings.

5. Robert Fulton and the Steamboat (1803)

Robert Fulton is associated with the steamboat, but he did not invent it. His brilliance was in designing and building a commercially successful one. Fulton foresaw the transportation and military potential for a steam-powered vessel as early as 1793 when he learned of other builders' attempts. In 1796 he published *A Treatise on the Improvement of Canal Navigation* and used the text to interest the U.S. and French governments in steam-powered boat projects. When neither government responded positively, in 1797 he moved to France where he continued working on plans for not only a steamboat but also a submarine that was commissioned by Napoleon. Christened *The Nautilus,* Fulton's submarine would have revolutionized naval warfare, but he was unable to convince the French government of its possibilities. Still undaunted, Fulton turned his energies back to the steamboat and, with financing from Robert Livingston, American Minister of France, successfully powered a steamboat on the Seine River. Fulton returned to the United States in 1807 where he launched a twenty-eight–horsepower steam engine made by James Watt. It steamed up the Hudson River from New York City to Albany in thirty-two hours. With Fulton's invention, the transportation revolution was truly underway.

TERM PAPER SUGGESTIONS

1. England and France were engaged in the Napoleonic Wars when Fulton presented Napoleon with his prototype of a practical submarine. Discuss how this invention might have been used to counteract a superior British Navy.

2. Fulton did not invent the steamboat. Discuss the contributions and designs made by James Rumsey, William Symington, and the Marquis Claude de Jouffroy.

3. Discuss how the use of the steamboat expanded commercial markets along eastern lakes and rivers in the United States.

4. Study Fulton's design for a steamboat and those of his predecessors. Analyze why he succeeded and they failed to create a commercially successful steamboat.

5. Demonstrate how the use of steamboats changed the prices of goods and services for people living in the western part of the country.

6. As soon as canals were built, there was a rush to construct additional ones in other parts of the country. Describe how steamboat design changed to adapt to shallower canal waters and rivers.

ALTERNATIVE TERM PAPER SUGGESTIONS

1. Assume you are a safety engineer who has been called to testify before a Congressional Steamboat Committee that is concerned over the increasing number of steamboat fires and risk to the public. Prepare a PowerPoint presentation showing committee members how steamboats are vulnerable to fires and conclude with a list of recommended safety procedures.

2. Robert Fulton may have been more of a businessman than inventor. He had a vision for the use of steamboats before they were even functional. Produce a contemporary Web-based marketing plan that Fulton could have taken to Britain and France to persuade both countries to fund his plans.

SUGGESTED SOURCES

Primary Sources

Fulton, Robert. *A Treatise on the Improvement of Canal Navigation.* London: I and J. Architectural Library, 1796. http://fax.libs.uga.edu/TC744x F97/1f/canal_navigation.pdf. Contains the full text of Fulton's proposal on the construction of canals and special boats to speed up transportation on existing and future canals throughout the world.

Thurston, Robert H. *A History of the Growth of the Steam-Engine.* New York: Appleton and Company, 1878. http://www.history.rochester.edu/steam/thurston/1878/. Provides a biography of Fulton, his original drawings, illustrations, and diagrams of steamboats, including plans for their use on canals and rivers.

Secondary Sources

Brockman, R. John. *Exploding Steamboats, Senate Debates, and Technical Reports: The Convergence of Technology, Politics, and Rhetoric in the Steamboat Bill of 1838.* Amityville, NY: Baywood Publishing Company, 2002. Addresses the safety problems of exploding steam engines on steampowered vessels and the Senate's attempt to legislate a solution.

Chapelle, Howard Irving. *Fulton's Steam Battery: Blockship and Catamaran.* Washington, DC: Smithsonian Institution, 1964. Includes an easy-to-understand description of Fulton's innovation, along with pictures and design diagrams.

Dickinson, W. H. *Robert Fulton, Engineer and Artist, His Life and Works.* Freeport, NY: Books for Libraries, 1971. Robert Fulton was also a professional artist. This work discusses both aspects of his career.

Dohan, Mary Helen. *Mr. Roosevelt's Steamboat.* Gretna, LA: Pelican Publishing Company, 2004. Describes the maiden voyage of the steamboat *New Orleans,* built by Robert Fulton's colleague, Nicholas Roosevelt.

Fox, Stephen. *Transatlantic: Samuel Cunard, Isambard Brunel, and the Great Atlantic Steamships.* New York: HarperCollins Publishers, 2003. Provides a history of Fulton's steamboat and how it evolved into large, commercially successful oceangoing vessels that presaged the contemporary ocean liner.

High, Mike. *The C & O Canal Companion.* Baltimore, MD: The Johns Hopkins University Press, 2001. Part of this book is devoted to describing John Rumsey's attempts to build a steamboat to navigate the Chesapeake and Ohio Canal in the eighteenth century.

Hutcheon, Wallace S. *Robert Fulton: Pioneer of Undersea Warfare.* Annapolis, MD: Naval Institute Press, 1981. Describes and analyzes Fulton's design and development of a workable submarine that could have transformed naval warfare during the nineteenth century had France and Great Britain understood its applications.

McCabe, James Dabney. *Great Fortunes and How They Were Made.* Freeport, NY: Books for Libraries Press, 1972. Also available at http://www.gutenberg .org/etext/15161#CHAPTER_XIII. Chapter 13 is devoted to Robert Fulton and how he was able to successfully commercialize his design for a steamboat.

Sale, Patrick. *The Fire of His Genius: Robert Fulton and the American Dream.* New York: Free Press, 2001. Sale readily admits that Fulton did not invent the steamboat, but did know how to build a commercially successful one. In doing so, he credits Fulton with helping to open up the West for expansion.

Shagena, Jack L. *Who Really Invented the Steamboat? Fulton's Clermont Coup.* Amherst, NY: Humanity Books, 2004. Describes all the other inventors and innovators who contributed to Fulton's successful launch of a steam-powered vessel on the Seine and Hudson rivers.

Sutcliffe, Andrea. *Steam: The Untold Story of America's First Great Invention.* New York: Palgrave MacMillan, 2004. Provides an excellent overview of the development of the steamboat, including attempts by Symington, Rumsey, and Fitch plus information about its strategic importance to westward expansion.

World Wide Web

"Chapter 18 Upriver in a Teakettle." http://www.hrmm.org/diglib/carmer/ chapter18.html. Chapter 18 from *The Hudson,* by Carl Cramer (New York: Farrar & Rinehart, 1939), describes Robert Fulton's first steamboat voyage from New York City to Albany.

"Old Steamboat Days on the Hudson River." http://www.hrmm.org/diglib/ oldsteam/chapter2.html. Chapter 2 of this 1907 online book documents the first 100 years of steamboats beginning with Robert Fulton's celebratory trip up the Hudson River in 1807.

"Robert Fulton and His Life's Work." *Scientific American* (September 25, 1909). http://www.hrmm.org/diglib/sciamer/rfulton/rfulton.htm. This lengthy *Scientific American* article provides a biographical sketch of Robert Fulton and information about his development of the steamboat.

"Robert Fulton Commercial Steamboat." http://web.mit.edu/invent/iow/ fulton.html. Provides a historically accurate biographical sketch of Robert Fulton, including information about his contribution to the building of a commercially successful steamboat.

"Robert Fulton Steamboats of the Hudson River The First Steamboat of 1807." http://www.hrmm.org/steamboats/fulton.html. This site from the Hudson Maritime Museum furnishes diagrams and illustrations, plus biographies of other people involved with the steamboat's development.

"Steaming Along." http://memory.loc.gov/ammem/today/aug26.html. Gives an overview, accompanied by primary source illustrations, of the prototype steamboats designed by James Rumsey, Ben Campbell, and John Fitch prior to Robert Fulton's design.

"William Symington." http://www.gsk58.dial.pipex.com/symington/index.shtml. Provides a biographical sketch of William Symington and many primary sources in the form of diagrams and illustrations of his steamboat, which he successfully patented and floated on the canals of Glasgow, Scotland, in 1801.

Multimedia Sources

The Fire of His Genius. West Lafayette, IN: C-Span Archives, 2001. 1 videocassette. 61 minutes. Contains an interview with Patrick Sales concerning his book, *The Fire of His Genius,* in which he researched how Robert Fulton's invention of the steamboat helped spur technological growth in nineteenth-century America.

19th Century Turning Points in U.S. History. New York: Ambrose Video Publishing, 2002. 1 DVD. 23 minutes. Part of this digital video contains reenactments, illustrations, and documents about the significance of Robert Fulton's construction of a steamboat.

6. The Lewis and Clark Expedition (1803–1806)

Several months before the Louisiana Purchase, President Thomas Jefferson requested $2,500 from Congress to finance an expedition into the West. He asked Congress to prepare a bill that would appropriate money for the expedition to "extend the external commerce of the United States." To lead the trip, he chose his private secretary and former army veteran, Meriwether Lewis (1774–1809). President Jefferson had a keen interest in every aspect of the expedition, and he expected Lewis to not only explore uncharted territory but also serve as the group's resident botanist, zoologist, mineralogist, geographer, and negotiator with Native Americans. Lewis wisely chose fellow Virginian and Indian Wars veteran

William Clark (1770–1838) to share the administrative burdens. Using Canadian author and explorer Alexander Mackenzie's published account of his trip from Montreal to the Pacific Coast as a guide, Lewis and Clark departed in 1803 with some forty soldiers and civilians from St. Louis, Missouri, in three boats. Paddling upstream in the winter, they reached North Dakota in the autumn of 1804 and constructed Fort Mandan. While waiting for spring to arrive, they ran out of provisions and were saved by a French Canadian trapper named Toussaint Charbonneau and his companion, a Shosone/Hidata woman named Sacagawea, who continued to guide them for the rest of the journey. After reaching the Pacific, Lewis and Clark formed two groups to explore alternate routes back and successfully reunited in St. Louis in 1806. Their meticulous journals filled with the beauty and excitement of their 3,700 mile journey challenged and tantalized Americans who were eager to expand to the West.

TERM PAPER SUGGESTIONS

1. Thomas Jefferson felt that Alexander Mackenzie's rapid expedition was terribly negligent because he failed to neither map the route nor note its distinguishing features. Read President Jefferson's written instructions to Captain Lewis and discuss the president's overall contribution to the expedition.

2. William Clark took his slave, York, on the expedition as a cook and orderly. Describe some of his adventures. How was he received by various Indian tribes? Argue that York, as a full member of the expedition, had more freedom than he would have had back in Virginia.

3. In most history books Sacagawea is depicted as a guide for Lewis and Clark. Read portions of Lewis and Clark's journals and discuss Sacagawea's additional roles as a translator among the Shoshone and a procurer of indigenous, edible, and medicinal foods.

4. Lewis and Clark encountered several different Indian tribes, but followed a fairly set formula based on past Indian policy for dealing with them. Read the portions of their journals where they encountered Indians and analyze their approaches.

5. Many Indians believe that the Lewis and Clark expedition spelled the "beginning of the end" for their way of life, lands, and heritage. Discuss the negative aspect of the expedition from an Indian point of view.

6. Expeditions throughout history have been used to establish legal claims on uncharted territory. Discuss how the United States used this one to lay claim to the Pacific Northwest.

ALTERNATIVE TERM PAPER SUGGESTIONS

1. Using maps, video clips from Lewis and Clark digital videos, and diary excerpts, create a Web site that highlights the dangers that Lewis and Clark faced from the environment and local Indian tribes.

2. Imagine that you are in charge of this expedition today. Prepare a PowerPoint presentation to brief the Corps of Discovery about the problems they will face geographically, environmentally, and demographically. Base the presentation solely on the beliefs held by President Jefferson and other naturalists at the time of the original expedition.

SUGGESTED SOURCES

Primary Sources

Ambrose, Stephen E. *Lewis & Clark Voyage of Discovery*. Washington, DC: National Geographic Society, 1998. Contains original illustrations of the portions of the Lewis and Clark Trail, photographs of equipment, weapons, maps, and other artifacts.

Chuinard, E. G. *Only One Man Died: The Medical Aspects of the Lewis and Clark Expeditions*. Glendale, CA: The Arthur H. Clark Company, 1979. Furnishes excerpts from the journals concerning the illness and role of Sacagawea in aiding the expedition.

Moulton, Gary E., ed. *The Definitive Journals of Lewis and Clark*. Vols. 1–13. Lincoln, NE: University of Nebraska Press, 1986–2001. Contains the unexpurgated journals of Lewis and Clark in thirteen volumes.

Secondary Sources

Ambrose, Stephen E. *Undaunted Courage: Meriwether Lewis, Thomas Jefferson and the Opening of the American West*. New York: Simon & Schuster, 1996. Quotes extensively from the Lewis and Clark journals and provides explanations of President Jefferson's motivation for the journey.

Betts, Robert B. *In Search of York: The Slave Who Went to the Pacific with Lewis and Clark*. Boulder, CO: Colorado Associated Press, 1985. Describes the life of York, the only African American slave, on the Lewis and Clark expedition.

Buckley, Jay H., and James J. Holmberg. *By His Own Hand? The Mysterious Death of Meriwether Lewis*. Norman, OK: University of Oklahoma Press, 2006. Written by two historians, this book discusses the evidence that Meriwether Lewis committed suicide in 1809.

Clarke, Charles G. *The Men of the Lewis and Clark Expedition: A Biographical Roster of the Fifty-one Members and a Composite Diary of their Activities from All Known Sources*. Lincoln, NE: University of Nebraska Press, 2002. This book almost fits into the primary sources category because of its extensive excerpts about every member of the Lewis and Clark party.

Cutright, Paul Russell. *Lewis and Clark, Pioneering Naturalists*. Urbana, IL: University of Illinois, 1969. Discusses the many flora and fauna on the trail as first seen and documented by Lewis and Clark in their journals.

Duncan, Dayton. *Lewis & Clark: an Illustrated History*. New York: Knopf, 1997. Accompanies the documentary film that Ken Burns made of the Lewis and Clark expedition. Provides facsimiles of journal entries, historic and present photographs, and maps.

Hawke, David Freeman. *Those Tremendous Mountains: The Story of the Lewis and Clark Expedition*. New York: Norton, 1980. Supplies a solid overview of the events, people, and places of the Lewis and Clark expedition.

Holloway, David. *Lewis & Clark and the Crossing of North America*. New York: Saturday Review Press, 1974. Furnishes an easy-to-understand overview of the expedition.

Jones, Landon Y. *William Clark and the Shaping of the West*. New York: Hill and Wang, 2004. Tells the story of William Clark, who was overshadowed by the more educated and well-connected Meriwether Lewis.

Ronda, James P. *Lewis and Clark Among the Indians*. Lincoln, NE: University of Nebraska, 2002. Devotes the entire book to Lewis and Clark's interactions with the Indians.

Schmidt, Thomas. *National Geographic Guide to the Lewis & Clark Trail*. Washington, DC: National Geographic Society, 2002. Contains lavish illustrations of the trail, plus information about the past and present conditions of the Indian tribes that Lewis and Clark encountered.

World Wide Web

"Discovering Lewis & Clark." http://www.lewis-clark.org/content/content-article.asp?ArticleID=513. Contains journal excerpts, maps, equipment illustrations, and Indian tribal information.

"The Journals of the Lewis and Clark Expedition." http://lewisandclark journals.unl.edu/v02.appendix.a.html. Click on the year to find specific journals of the expedition. This site is also replete with images and maps of the trip.

"Lewis & Clark." http://www.pbs.org/lewisandclark/. Site contains information to accompany the PBS film, plus interactive trail maps, classroom resources, expert historian testimony, descriptions of encounters with Indians, and more.

"Lewis & Clark Mapping the West." http://www.edgate.com/lewisandclark/. An excellent site from the Smithsonian Institution that features original maps that Lewis and Clark used as guides, information about their pattern of Indian treatment and tribes encountered, and legacy of the expedition.

"National Archive Photographs Dating from 1860s through the 1890s of Native Cultures the Expedition Encountered." http://lewisandclarkjournals. unl.edu/images2.html. The original photographs at this site are useful for researching question No. 5.

"National Geographic Lewis & Clark." www.nationalgeographic.com/lewisand clark/. Provides information about the explorers' discovery of flora and fauna, geological wonders, plus journal entries from both men.

"Rivers, Edens, and Empires Lewis & Clark and the Revealing of America." http://www.loc.gov/exhibits/lewisandclark/lewis-landc.html#56. Provides Jefferson's instructions to Captain Lewis concerning the purpose of the expedition plus a host of other primary sources.

Multimedia Sources

Lewis & Clark: Great Journey West. Washington, DC: National Geographic Society, 2003. 1 videocassette. 40 minutes. Brings to life the great expedition replete with scenic footage and all its dangers and challenges.

Jefferson's Enlightenment (A Lewis & Clark Doc-Series). Vol. One. Minot, ND: Communications Corp/Eagle One Media Distribution, 2004. 1 DVD. 52 minutes. Contains forty-five short stories about the trail and explores the preparations during the year prior to leaving. Selected by the National Council for the Lewis and Clark Bicentennial as an official documentary to celebrate the Bicentennial of the Corps.

Lewis & Clark: The Journey of the Corps of Discovery. Santa Monica, CA: PBS Home Video, 1997. 2 videocassettes. 240 minutes. Skillfully combines journal excerpts, photographs, and interviews with noted historians to recreate Lewis and Clark's majestic journey west.

7. Louisiana Purchase (1803)

The largest area ever purchased by the United States consisted of lands that today encompass Arkansas, Iowa, Missouri, Minnesota west of the Mississippi River, the Dakotas, and parts of Kansas, Colorado, Montana, Wyoming, and Louisiana. Originally owned by France, it passed to Spain following the Seven Years' War in 1763 and was returned to France following a secret treaty in 1800. If France ever relinquished the territory, it was supposed to revert to Spain. In 1802 relations between France and the United States deteriorated when France decided to lay siege to New Orleans and ban the storage of U.S. goods in New Orleans for transshipment. The French, under Napoleon, needed monies after a disastrous campaign to regain control over the Caribbean island of St. Domingue (present-day Haiti and the Dominican Republic). Napoleon's failure and lack of interest in the New World opened the door for President Thomas Jefferson to approach France. President Jefferson sent James Monroe and Robert Livingston to negotiate with Charles Maurice de Talleyrand-Perigord ("Talleyrand"), the French Foreign Minister, for the purchase of an area that doubled the size of the United States at a cost of $15 million, or approximately four cents per acre.

TERM PAPER SUGGESTIONS

1. Negotiations between France and the United States were protracted because there were four alternatives. These were as follows: (a) to purchase Florida and New Orleans; (b) to purchase New Orleans by itself; (c) to purchase all of the land on the east bank of the Mississippi River on which an American port could be constructed; and (d) acquire perpetual rights of navigation and deposit. Analyze and discuss the political, military, and economic implications of any of the alternatives that were not adopted.

2. At first the negotiations between the United States and France were unsuccessful. Discuss the role that the Haitian Revolution had in changing Napoleon's mind to sell the Louisiana Territory.

3. In 1804 President Jefferson commissioned George Hunter and William Dunbar to explore the southern unmapped area of the Louisiana Purchase. Read portions of their journal and geographically trace their route. Describe some of the natural wonders that they encountered.

4. The Louisiana Purchase was made using U.S. bonds that were the result of Alexander Hamilton's U.S. bank initiative. President Jefferson resisted the bank initiative as unconstitutional. Discuss the hypocrisy of President Jefferson's decision.

5. Analyze the reasons that President Jefferson had for making the Louisiana Purchase, and comment on the legacy of that decision.

6. President Jefferson also enlisted the assistance of Pierre Samuel du Pont de Nemours to negotiate the Louisiana Purchase. Discuss the significant role he played in the negotiations.

ALTERNATIVE TERM PAPER SUGGESTIONS

1. Create a virtual field trip of the Louisiana Purchase and highlight the major geographic areas. Include information concerning the flora and fauna, as well as the Indian tribes living in this vast area at the purchase time.

2. Design a timeline of the negotiations process between the United States and France, indicating specific events that may have served as tipping points in the favor of the United States.

SUGGESTED SOURCES

Primary Sources

Adams, Henry. *The History of the United States during the Administrations of Jefferson and Madison.* New York: Charles Scribner's Sons, 1889–1891. Describes President Jefferson's role in the Louisiana Purchase.

Berry, Trey, et al. *The Forgotten Expedition, 1804–1805: The Louisiana Purchase Journals of Dunbar and Hunter.* Baton Rouge, LA: Louisiana State University, 2006. Features the journals of the two expeditionaries.

Secondary Sources

Brecher, Frank W. *Negotiating the Louisiana Purchase: Robert Livingston's Mission to France, 1801–1804.* Jefferson, NC: McFarland & Company, 2006. A former U.S. Foreign Service officer analyzes the complex negotiations for the Louisiana Purchase.

Cerami, Charles A. *Jefferson's Great Gamble: The Remarkable Story of Jefferson, Napoleon and the Men Behind the Louisiana Purchase.* Naperville, IL: Sourcebooks, 2003. Contains a readable account of the geopolitical and diplomatic implications of the purchase.

Chidsey, Donald Barr. *Louisiana Purchase.* New York: Crown, 1972. Gives a good overview of the key people and motivations surrounding the Louisiana Purchase.

Duke, Marc. *The du Ponts: Portrait of a Dynasty,* pp. 77–83. New York: Saturday Review Press, 1976. Provides information about Samuel du Pont's role in the negotiations.

Fleming, Thomas. *The Louisiana Purchase.* New York: Wiley, 2003. Includes a wealth of details concerning the complex negotiations between France and the United States.

Keats, John. *Eminent Domain; the Louisiana Purchase and the Making of America.* New York: Charterhouse, 1973. This excellent text details the relations between France and the United States over the Louisiana Purchase.

Kennedy, Roger G. *Mr. Jefferson's Lost Cause: Land, Farmers, Slavery, and the Louisiana Purchase*. New York: Oxford University Press, 2004. Analyzes the purchase from the standpoint of its role in solidifying slavery in the south.

Kluger, Richard. *Seizing Destiny: How America Grew from Sea to Shining Sea*. New York: Knopf, 2007. Traces the expansion of America, beginning with the Louisiana Purchase.

Phelan, Mary Kay. *The Story of the Louisiana Purchase*. New York: Crowell, 1979. Gives an excellent overview of the people and events of the Louisiana Purchase.

Rand, Clayton. *Stars in Their Eyes; Dreamers and Builders in Louisiana*. Gulfport, MS: Dixie Press, 1953. Contains centennial celebration material including maps and documents.

Sanford, Levinson. *The Louisiana Purchase and American Expansion, 1803–1898*. Landham, MD: Rowman & Littlefield Publishers, 2005. Provides a scholarly account of the decision to purchase the Louisiana Territory and the role it played in western expansion.

World Wide Web

"The Cabildo the Louisiana Purchase." http://lsm.crt.state.la.us/cabildo/cab4.htm. Provides an overview of the Louisiana Purchase, including portraits of all the politicians and negotiators involved with transaction.

"Jefferson's Big Deal: The Louisiana Purchase." www.monticello.org/jefferson/lewisandclark/louisiana.html. Furnishes a timeline, confidential letters by Jefferson concerning the purchase, maps, a biographical sketch of Jefferson, and more.

"Louisiana Purchase Bicentennial 1803–2003." www.louisianapurchase2003.com/history/documents/index.htm. Features the Treaty of Cession, First Convention, Second Convention, and several scanned originals of the various signers' signatures.

"The Louisiana Purchase Exhibit." http://www.sos.louisiana.gov/purchase-index.html. Contains a set of historical maps detailing the Louisiana Territory and the bank documents describing the financial transactions.

"Louisiana Purchase Treaty and Related Resources at the Library of Congress." www.loc.gov/rr/program/bib/ourdocs/Louisiana.html. Provides a wealth of documents in the form of correspondence, nineteenth-century articles, presidential papers, maps, and more.

"Napoleon Letter to Toussaint Louverture (1801)." http://www.thelouvertureproject.org. Contains the text of Napoleon's letter to Toussaint Louverture threatening to expel his children from Haiti if Toussaint does not agree to French demands.

"Text of the Louisiana Purchase Treaty." www.archives.gov/exhibits/american _originals/louistxt.html. Includes the treaty of cession and two conven tions dealing with the payments to be made to France.

Multimedia Sources

The Louisiana Purchase. New York: Arts & Entertainment Video, 2005. 1 DVD. 50 minutes. Useful for understanding the background and negotiations for the Louisiana Purchase.

You Are There—Jefferson Makes a Difference/The Vote That Makes Jefferson President/The Louisiana Purchase. Chatsworth, CA: Woodhaven Entertainment, 2004. 1 DVD. 50 minutes. Focuses on the presidency of Thomas Jefferson and his daring decision to purchase the Louisiana Territory without funding from Congress.

8. *Marbury v. Madison* (1803)

Termed "the most famous case ever decided by the United States Supreme Court" by former Chief Justice William Rehnquist, *Marbury v. Madison* is replete with legerdemain legal maneuvers. In 1801, the Federalists under President John Adams were about to relinquish power to Thomas Jefferson and the Republicans. The power transfer took from December 1800 to March 1801, enabling Adams, under the 1801 Judiciary and Justice of the Peace Acts, to appoint sixteen circuit court judges and forty-two justices of the peace, most of whom were strong Federalists. John Marshall, as Sec-retary of State, was empowered to deliver the commissions and neglected to deliver one to William Marbury. After Jefferson took office, he told his new Secretary of State, James Madison, to withhold the commission. Marbury brought suit to be made a judge in a case that went to the U.S. Supreme Court. It was presided over by none other than Supreme Court Justice John Marshall, a cousin of Thomas Jefferson and the same man who neglected to deliver Marbury's commission. Marshall subsequently used Marbury as a pawn in a series of legal ploys that enabled him to rule a section of the 1789 Judiciary Act unconstitutional and void. The decision was the first time that the Supreme Court had overturned an act of Congress, and it stated that "a law repugnant to the constitution is void. . . ." The implica-tions of *Marbury v. Madison* resonate to this day because it established a basis for judicial review of Congressional acts and reinforced the principle of "checks and balances" within the Constitution.

TERM PAPER SUGGESTIONS

1. Read the language of Marshall's opinion and analyze how the justice avoided a direct confrontation with President Jefferson over the issue of judicial review. How did Marshall think that the Constitution should be interpreted?
2. Citing the language of the decision, formulate an argument that the judicial branch should have total authority over constitutional interpretation.
3. Marbury's climb up the judicial ladder to have his case heard has always been a legal mystery. After losing in the Supreme Court, Marbury could have availed himself of the Circuit Court of the District of Columbia for relief. Explain why he did not choose this route and why he did not elect it as a first step in the legal process.
4. Reconcile how Marshall stated that Marbury was entitled to his judgeship while simultaneously stating that he was unable to order James Madison to deliver Marbury his commission.
5. Use language from the decision to show how Marshall's opinion might be used against the executive branch in cases of undeclared wars.
6. The case of *Marbury v. Madison* carries a legacy implying judicial independence. Argue the dangers that are inherent in judicial independence.

ALTERNATIVE TERM PAPER SUGGESTIONS

1. Citing parts of the Constitution and other documents, write a legal brief on behalf of Marbury arguing that he is entitled to his judgeship.
2. Draft an argument showing how the principles decided in *Marbury v. Madison* can be employed by the Supreme Court to confront presidents over undeclared wars such as Vietnam and Iraq.

SUGGESTED SOURCES

Primary Sources

Graber, Mark A., and Michael Perhac. *Marbury versus Madison: Documents and Commentary.* Washington, DC: CQ Press, 2002. Uses various primary source excerpts to comment on the case.

"Marbury v. Madison, Opinion by John Marshall (1803)." In *100 Key Documents in American Democracy,* edited by Peter B. Levy. Westport, CT: Greenwood Press, 1994. Gives a brief introduction of the case followed by the written opinion.

Secondary Sources

Beveridge, Albert Jeremiah. *The Life of John Marshall*. Boston, MA: Houghton Mifflin, 1919. This four-volume set is a definitive biography about the life of John Marshall. Substantial parts are dedicated to Marshall's role in the *Marbury v. Madison* case.

Bickel, Alexander. *The Least Dangerous Branch*. Indianapolis, IN: Bobbs-Merrill Company, 1962. Written by a legal scholar, this definitive work gives a thorough analysis of *Marbury v. Madison*.

Clinton, Robert Lowry. *Marbury v. Madison and Judicial Review*. Lawrence, KS: University Press of Kansas, 1989. Provides a detailed legal and scholarly analysis of the case.

DeVilliers, David. *Marbury v. Madison: Powers of the Supreme Court*. Springfield, NJ: Enslow Publishers, 1998. Written for secondary school students, this easy-to-understand text gives the who, what, where, when, and how of *Marbury v. Madison*.

Mountjoy, Shane. *Marbury v. Madison: Establishing Supreme Court Power*. New York: Chelsea House, 2006. Written for secondary school students, this book provides not only an overview but also a thorough analysis of the case.

Naden, Corinne J. *Marbury v. Madison: The Court's Foundation*. Tarrytown, NY: Benchmark Books, 2005. Furnishes a brief, comprehensible explanation of the case and its dynamic role in constitutional law.

Nelson, William Edward. *Marbury v. Madison: The Origins and Legacy of Judicial Review*. Lawrence, KS: University Press of Kansas, 2000. Explains why *Marbury v. Madison* was a foundation case for U.S. constitutional law.

Randolph, Ryan P. *Marbury v. Madison: The New Supreme Court Gets More Power*. New York: Rosen Publishing Group, 2004. Gives an understandable analysis of how this case gave the Supreme Court additional power within the system of checks and balances.

Smith, Jean Edward. *John Marshall: Definer of a Nation*. New York: Henry Holt & Company, 1996. Integrates a variety of primary sources seamlessly into a nonlegal text about Marshall and his role in shaping the Supreme Court's decisions.

World Wide Web

"Article III, U.S. Constitution." www.pbs.org/wnet/supremecourt/democracy/sources_document1.html. Contains Article III of the U.S. Constitution that establishes the nation's judicial branch, including one Supreme Court and lower federal courts.

"Debate from the Constitutional Convention Regarding the Function of the Judiciary (July 21, 1787)." www.pbs.org/wnet/supremecourt/democracy/sources_document5.html. Outlines the basic duties of the judicial branch as seen by the constitutional framers.

"Hamilton, Alexander. Federalist No. 78." http://thomas.loc.gov/home/histdox/fed_78.html. Provides an analysis of the judiciary department and the procedures for appointing judges.

"John Marshall's Statement to the Virginia Ratifying Convention (June 20, 1788)." www.pbs.org/wnet/supremecourt/democracy/sources_document6.html. Furnishes Marshall's rationale for the Constitution's plan to improve the powers of the judiciary.

"The Judiciary Act of 1789." http://www.constitution.org/uslaw/judiciary_1789.htm. Includes the full text of one of the acts that was instrumental in initiating the case.

"Marbury v. Madison." www.law.cornell.edu/supct/html/historics/USSC_CR_0005_0137_ZS.html. Contains a helpful syllabus and the opinion of the Supreme Court decision.

"Marbury v. Madison." www.pbs.org/wnet/supremecourt/democracy/landmark_marbury.html. Contains an excellent overview of the case complete with biographies and several primary sources.

Multimedia Sources

A DVD History of the US Constitution (1619–2005). New York: Ambrose Video Publishing, 2005. 4 DVDs. 224 minutes. Disc 1 analyzes the significance of the *Marbury v. Madison* case.

The Judicial Branch. Wynnewood, PA: Schlessinger Media, 2006. 1 videocassette. 44 minutes. Examines the landmark case, *Marbury v. Madison*.

Standard Deviants American Government. Haymarket, VA: Cerebellum Corp., 2003. 1 DVD. 242 minutes. Part 2 explores the judicial powers of the U.S. government and the significance of the *Marbury v. Madison* decision.

9. Fall of Aaron Burr (1804–1807)

Although Aaron Burr (1756–1836) had a distinguished career as an American Revolutionary soldier, lawyer, U.S. senator, and the third vice president of the United States, he was always considered an opportunist by his peers as well as being fond of political machinations rather than the democratic process. After showing tremendous courage as a soldier during the American Revolution, Burr went on to finish his law degree, serve in the New York State Assembly, become New York State's attorney general, and become a U.S. senator. In 1798 he returned to the New York legislature where he became the primary politician involved in getting Thomas Jefferson elected president by raising his campaign funds. He tied for electoral votes with Jefferson and became the vice president by a House of Representatives vote. It was as vice president that Aaron Burr fell from grace when he killed Alexander Hamilton, one of the nation's founding fathers and the creator of America's first political party, the Federalists, in a duel. Burr then became involved in a scheme to organize a force to invade Mexico and establish a new nation in the West. He was captured and placed on trial for treason, but acquitted. About to be retried on the same charge, he fled the country for Europe and returned twelve years later to New York where he lived until his death in 1826.

TERM PAPER SUGGESTIONS

1. Aaron Burr was reported to have an aristocratic demeanor that was carefully cultivated by his reading of *Lord Chesterfield's Letters* (London: Oxford University Press, 1992). Click on "Lord Chesterfield's Letters" at http://books.google.com/books?hl=en&id=280MAAAAYAAJ&dq=lord+chesterfield%27s+letters&printsec=frontcover&source=web&ots=hePCFw-NsQ&sig=vGGcVksQJjlRHTFYR83vtTWEpfk&prev=http://www.google.com/search?hl=en&rlz=1T4ADBR_enUS204US213&q=lord+chesterfield%27s+letters&btn=Search&sa=X&oi=print&ct=result&cd=1&cad=bottom-3results#PPP1,M1. Describe how Burr violated the essence of these letters by dueling with Alexander Hamilton.

2. Thomas Jefferson and James Madison enlisted Aaron Burr's help for the election of 1800. Analyze Burr's political moves for funding Jefferson's campaign. How did he use Tammany Hall to obtain the necessary New York votes to clinch Jefferson's election?

3. The duel between Burr and Hamilton was the explosive result of a ten year enmity. Trace the slights and betrayals that are considered evidence of their mutual dislike.

4. Chief Justice John Marshall, a Federalist, presided over the trial of Aaron Burr. Discuss the legal rulings that he used to ensure Burr's acquittal.

5. Historians are not sure whether Burr really conspired to invade Mexico and form a separate nation because one of the witnesses against him was on the payroll of Spain. Discuss the questionable testimony of General James Wilkinson as it related to the Burr case.

6. George Washington had several encounters with Aaron Burr and was quoted as saying "Colonel Burr is a brave and able officer, but the question is whether he has not equal talents for intrigue." Cite examples from Burr's life that support this summation of Burr's character. How did it contribute to Burr's downfall?

ALTERNATIVE TERM PAPER SUGGESTIONS

1. Use iMovie to create one version of the duel between Alexander Hamilton and Aaron Burr.
2. Design a Webography of the life and times of Alexander Hamilton that emphasizes his long simmering feud with Aaron Burr.

SUGGESTED SOURCES

Primary Sources

Adams, Henry. *History of the United States of America.* 7 vols. New York: Charles Scribner's Sons, 1890–1891. Provides a factual, detailed description of Burr's conspiracy.

Kline, Mary-Go, and Joanne Wood Ryan, eds. *Political Correspondence and Public Papers of Aaron Burr.* 2 vols. Princeton, NJ: Princeton University Press, 1983. Contains nearly one thousand letters, reports, memoranda, and other assorted papers that shed light on the political life of Aaron Burr.

Lomask, Milton. *Aaron Burr.* 2 vols. New York: Farrar, Straus & Giroux, 1979. Furnishes extensive excerpts and quotes from Burr's correspondence and his peers such as Alexander Hamilton, George Washington, Thomas Jefferson, and James Madison.

Parton, James. *The Life and Times of Aaron Burr.* 2 vols. Boston and New York: Houghton Mifflin and Company, 1892. Presents a nineteenth-century perspective concerning the life of Aaron Burr.

Secondary Sources

Abernathy, Thomas Perkins. *The Burr Conspiracy.* New York: Oxford University Press, 1954. Provides a scholarly yet readable account of the conspiracy charges and subsequent trial of Aaron Burr.

Faulkner, Robert K. "John Marshall and the Burr Trial." *Journal of American History* 53 (September 1966): 247–258. (Available in JSTOR.) Quoting extensively from the trial, the author describes how Justice Marshall effectively argued against guilt in the Burr trial.

Fleming, Thomas. *Duel: Alexander Hamilton, Aaron Burr, and the Future of America*. New York: Basic Books, 1999. Places the duel in the context of the political factions that were lobbying for power and influence during the early 1800s.

Isenberg, Nancy. *Fallen Founder: The Life of Aaron Burr*. New York: Viking Press, 2007. Examines Burr's life as a founding father, showing the idealistic, democratic, nonpartisan aspect of his personality.

Kennedy, Roger G. *Burr, Hamilton, and Jefferson: A Study in Character*. New York: Oxford University Press, 2000. Seeks Burr's redemption as a founding father despite the duel and trial.

McCaleb, W. F. *The Aaron Burr Conspiracy*. New York: Dodd, Mead and Company, 1903. Furnishes an academic accounting of the Burr conspiracy and the convoluted events that led up to it.

Melton, Buckner F., Jr. *Aaron Burr: Conspiracy to Treason*. New York: John Wiley, 2002. Depicts Burr as a nineteenth-century Machiavelli whom Jefferson, Washington, Adams, and Hamilton heartily disliked.

Parmet, Herbert S., and Marie B. Hecht. *Aaron Burr: Portrait of an Ambitious Man*. New York: Macmillan, 1967. Prolific biographers Parmet and Hecht paint Burr as a man with specific personal and political goals, which he was bent on achieving at whatever cost.

Rogow, Arnold A. *A Fatal Friendship: Alexander Hamilton and Aaron Burr*. New York: Hill and Wang, 1998. Rogow understands that the duel may have been personal because Burr and Hamilton came from totally different backgrounds and were vying for similar offices and political rewards.

Wheelan, Joseph. *Jefferson's Vendetta: The Pursuit of Aaron Burr and the Judiciary*. New York: Carroll & Graf Publishers, 2004. The author sees Thomas Jefferson very much as a villain as he tries to use the judicial system to destroy a political rival.

Wood, Gordon S. *Revolutionary Characters: What Made the Founding Fathers Different?* New York: Penguin Press, 2006. Proposes that Aaron Burr differed from peers like Jefferson, Hamilton, and Madison because he pursued politics for personal and pecuniary interests rather than serving society.

World Wide Web

"The Aaron Burr Trial 1807." http://www.law.umkc.edu/faculty/projects/ftrials/burr/burrtrial.html. This outstanding site features copies of the indictment, trial testimony, arguments, and Jefferson's letter's involving the case.

Davis, Matthew L. *Memoirs of Aaron Burr with Miscellaneous Selections from His Correspondence*. 2 vols. http://www.gutenberg.org/etext/7852. Provides Aaron Burr's recollections from his childhood and political life as well as letters and interrogatories about the election of 1800. There are references to Alexander Hamilton, but not to the duel.

"The Duel." http://www.pbs.org/wgbh/amex/duel/. Contains a timeline, maps, and a teacher's guide about the duel between Burr and Hamilton.

"Duel at Dawn, 1804." http://www.eyewitnesstohistory.com/duel.htm. Provides accounts of the duel by the participants' seconds who witnessed it.

"Opinion of Chief Justice Marshall in the Burr Trial." http://www.law.umkc .edu/faculty/projects/ftrials/burr/burropinion.html. Gives the ruling opinion of Justice Marshall, who presided over Burr's trial for conspiracy and treason.

"The Thomas Jefferson Papers." http://memory.loc.gov/ammem/collections/ jefferson_papers/. Contains many letters and other correspondence between Thomas Jefferson and Aaron Burr, including one written by Jefferson's secretary of the treasury, Albert Gallatin, about the Burr conspiracy.

"The Treason Trial of Aaron Burr." http://jurist.law.pitt.edu/trials21.htm. Furnishes excellent background material and an analysis of one of the most exciting nineteenth-century trials.

Multimedia Sources

Alexander Hamilton. Santa Monica, CA: PBS Paramount, 2007. 1 DVD. 120 minutes. Re-creates the life of Alexander Hamilton as a gifted founding father with some tragic character flaws.

The American Experience—The Duel. Alexandria, VA: PBS Home Video, 2000. 1 videocassette. 60 minutes. Using re-creations and interviews with subject experts, this excellent documentary presents two distinct versions of the duel between Burr and Hamilton.

10. Slave Trade Act (1807)

Even though slavery would continue until 1865 in the United States, one of the major blows toward its abolishment was struck in 1807 with the passage of the Slave Trade Act. The United States cannot claim sponsorship for the act because its principal proponent was a heroic Englishman named William Wilberforce. The subject of a 2007 feature-length film entitled *Amazing Grace,* Wilberforce, along with Thomas Clarkson and a coalition of Quakers and evangelical Protestants, lobbied, cajoled, persuaded, badgered, and finally shamed the British House of Parliament into passing a law that banned the slave trade in the British

Empire, allowed for the search and seizure of ships suspected of transporting enslaved people, and provided compensation for the freedom of slaves on March 25, 1807. Guided by economic self-interest, Britain persuaded the U.S. Congress to pass the same act in March 1807. The latter became law on January 1, 1808. Enforcement of the law by the British was more effective with other European nations than it was with the United States. The American government refused to comply with British search and seizure orders, and many slave traders took advantage of this maritime loophole to continue smuggling slaves into the United States. The Slave Trade Act also resulted in an expansion of an interstate slave trade because it was unregulated by any U.S. laws.

TERM PAPER SUGGESTIONS

1. After the British passed the Slave Trade Act of 1807, they felt obligated by economics to pressure other nations, but particularly the United States, to abolish the slave trade. Discuss the economic considerations of the Slave Trade Act for Britain.

2. During the nineteenth century, abolitionists resided on both sides of the Atlantic Ocean. Discuss the possible reasons why the Slave Trade Act was initiated by a British evangelist/legislator and not an American one.

3. Describe how the arguments and activities that led to abolishing slavery in Britain were instrumental to similar ones in the United States.

4. Despite the passage of the Slave Trade Act in the United States, many American slave traders continued to smuggle slaves into the country. Research examples like the slave ship, *The Wanderer*, and others as historical evidence of continued violations of the law.

5. Examine the heroic efforts and sometimes questionable methods of William Wilberforce, Thomas Clarkson, the Quakers, and evangelical Protestants to abolish the slave trade.

6. The beginning of anti-slave-trade agitation among Quakers and other groups occurred in the 1680s. Trace the early legal attempts, including the Constitutional Convention of 1787, to abolish slavery in the United States.

ALTERNATIVE TERM PAPER SUGGESTIONS

1. After passage of the Slave Trade Act, slavery not only flourished but even expanded in the new southern territories. Create an interactive map showing these areas, and analyze and discuss the possible reasons for the expansion.

2. Assume you are the British captain of an interdiction squadron who has been commanded to search and seize ships suspected of carrying slaves. Write a Web-based ship's log describing your encounters with suspected American slave ships that refused under U.S. law to permit you to board.

SUGGESTED SOURCES

Primary Sources

British and Foreign Anti-Slavery Society. *The First Annual Report of the British and Foreign Anti-Slavery Society for the Abolition of Slavery and the Slave Trade throughout the World: presented...Exeter Hall on Wednesday, June 24th, 1840.* Ithaca, NY: Cornell University Library, 2006. Provides a platform about how the British Anti-Slavery Society planned to conduct a public campaign to raise awareness of the continuing problem of slavery in the United States and other parts of the world.

Curtin, Philip D. *The Atlantic Slave Trade: A Census.* Madison, WI: University of Wisconsin Press, 1969. This classic primary source provides all the necessary quantitative data concerning the numbers of slaves transported from Africa via the Atlantic passageway from the fourteenth through nineteenth centuries. Chapter 8 is devoted solely to the nineteenth century.

Wilberforce, William. *A Practical View of Christianity.* Peabody, MA: Hendrickson Publishers, 2006. This primary source can be used to discern the Christian rationale for the strength and fortitude to conduct a forty-year crusade to end slavery in Britain and the rest of the world.

Secondary Sources

Calonius, Erik. *The Wanderer: The Last American Slave Ship and the Conspiracy That Set Its Sails.* New York: St. Martin's Press, 2006. Relates the history of *The Wanderer,* a black-market slave trade ship that illegally transported four hundred slaves from Africa to sell on Jekyll Island, Georgia, well after the Slave Trade Act had been passed.

Deyle, Steven. *Carry Me Back: The Domestic Slave Trade in American Life.* New York: Oxford University Press, 2004. Historian Deyle outlines the hard, economically driven cause of slavery and how it continued to function well after it was officially banned in 1808 because of the people who profited so highly from the trade.

Diouff, Sylviane. *Dreams of Africa in Alabama: The Slave Ship Clotilda and the Story of the Last Africans Brought to America.* New York: Oxford University Press, 2007. Relates the story of an Alabama businessman who, in 1860, took a bet that he could bring a slave ship of 110 men, women, and children from Africa to Mobile, Alabama, in defiance of all existing U.S. laws.

Gumstead, Robert H. *A Troublesome Commerce: The Transformation of the Interstate Slave Trade.* Baton Rouge, LA: Louisiana State University Press, 2003. Furnishes reasons why, after Congress outlawed international trade in slaves in 1808, the practice of selling slaves from one state to another actually expanded.

Johnson, Walter, ed. *The Chattel Principle: Internal Slave Trades in the Americas.* New Haven, CT: Yale University Press, 2005. Contains a scholarly account of how the slave trade continued in Brazil, the West Indies, and the southern United States despite passage of the Slave Trade Act.

Jordan, Michael. *The Great Abolition Sham: The True Story of the End of the British Slave Trade.* Thrupp, Stroud, U.K.: Sutton Publishing, 2007. Examines the personalities and issues behind the abolition movement in Britain and the internal quarrels that went on for eighteen years prior to the passage of the act abolishing slavery. Both sides did not hesitate to use whatever method they could to win their cause.

Klein, Herbert. *The Atlantic Slave Trade.* New York: Cambridge University Press, 1999. Written for nonacademic researchers, this book quantifies, in a comprehensible way, the economic and political impact that the Atlantic slave trade had on America, the West Indies, and Africa.

McMillin, James A. *The Final Victims: Foreign Slave Trade to North America, 1783–1810.* Columbia, SC: University of South Carolina Press, 2004. Using primary source data in the form of cargo and slave manifests, this work establishes the extent to which the slave trade continued in the United States after it was officially abolished by an act of Congress in 1807.

Metaxas, Eric. *Amazing Grace: William Wilberforce and the Heroic Campaign to End Slavery.* New York: HarperCollins Publishers, 2007. This book was written to accompany the feature length film, *Amazing Grace,* commemorating a man who dedicated his life to ending slavery in Britain.

Rediker, Marcus. *The Slave Ship: A Human History.* New York: Viking Press, 2007. Brings to life the terrible history of trafficking in human cargo that resulted in 10 to 15 million Africans being brought to America as slaves from the late 1400s through the 1800s.

Rothman, Adam. *Slave Country: American Expansion and the Origins of the Deep South.* Cambridge, MA: Harvard University Press, 2007. Provides documentation about how slavery actually expanded in Alabama, Mississippi, and Louisiana, particularly after the passage of the 1807 abolishment act.

Thomas, Hugh. *The Slave Trade: The Story of the Atlantic Slave Trade: 1440–1870.* New York: Simon & Schuster, 1999. This monumental tome covers the economics and politics of the slave trade from a personal and governmental involvement viewpoint.

Tomkins, Stephen. *William Wilberforce.* Grand Rapids, MI: Eerdmans, 2007. Provides a balanced biography of the life and times of William Wilberforce and the valiant role he played in the early abolition movement.

World Wide Web

"About.com—The Trans-Atlantic Slave Trade." http://africanhistory.about.com/library/weekly/aa080601a.htm. Gives an excellent overview of the Atlantic slave trade complete with maps, demographic data, and analysis.

"Africans in America." http://www.pbs.org/wgbh/aia/part1/1narr4.html. Produced by PBS, this outstanding four-part site is replete with interactive maps, charts, census data, primary sources, illustrations, and more. Parts 1 and 2 encompassing 1450–1805 are especially relevant to the abolition act of 1807.

"An Act for the Abolition of the Slave Trade." http://www.pdavis.nl/Legis_06.htm. Provides the full text of the act abolishing the slave trade in Britain and eventually the United States.

"Historic Figures—William Wilberforce (1759–1833)." http://www.bbc.co.uk/history/historic_figures/wilberforce_william.shtml. Contains a biographical sketch of Wilberforce along with a set of related links, interactive maps of slave trade routes, articles, and a timeline of events in the slave trade and early Abolitionist Movement.

"Parliament and the British Slave Trade 1600–1807." http://slavetrade.parliament.uk/slavetrade/explore/documents/. Sponsored by the British Parliament, this site features facsimiles of petitions for and against passage of the act, a copy of the act, and commentaries by noted British historians in commemoration of the 200th anniversary of the Slave Trade Abolition Act.

"Part III: African Slave Trade & European Imperialism AD/CE 15th–early 19th Centuries." http://web.cocc.edu/cagatucci/classes/hum211/timelines/htimeline3.htm. Supplies a useful, annotated timeline of events, countries, and people involved in the African slave trade and the role that the British and other empires played in it.

"Understanding Slavery." http://www.understandingslavery.com. Contains selected artifacts from museum collections and historical information organized into eight chronological themes along with lesson plans about slavery.

Multimedia Sources

Amazing Grace. Beverly Hills, CA: 20th Century Fox Home Entertainment, 2007. 1 DVD. 111 minutes. This inspirational dramatized version of William Wilberforce's life shows his mighty struggles against the institutional powers of slavery and his professional triumph with the successful passage of the Slave Trade Abolition Act of 1807.

Eltis, David, et al., eds. *The Trans-Atlantic Slave Trade: A Database on CD-ROM.* New York: Cambridge University Press, 2000. Contains the records of 27,233 transatlantic slave ship voyages made between 1595 and 1866 from all over Europe. The software allows users to process data by time periods and geographic areas and allows the downloading of data in SPSS formats for use in other programs. Interactive maps showing specific geographic points are also included. An accompanying data set has 226 fields of information for each voyage. A teacher's and user's manual are also included.

William Wilberforce. Worcester, PA: Gateway Films, 2006. 1 DVD. 30 minutes. Uses original paintings and historical art to tell the story of William Wilberforce's heroic struggle to end slavery in Britain and other parts of the world. A free guide can be downloaded at www.visionvideo.com.

11. War of 1812 Catalysts (1807–1809)

The War of 1812 had two catalysts: seizures of U.S. ships by the British and the impressments of sailors from American ships, also by the British. England and France were at war from 1803 to 1814 and Britain had the superior navy, which required a great many seamen. To crew their warships, they relied upon a quasi-legal sanction called impressments. On June 22, 1807, a crisis occurred when the British ship *Leopard* fired on the *U.S. Chesapeake,* killing three Americans and wounding eighteen. The British overcame the *Chesapeake,* boarded her, and removed four Royal Navy sailors, charging them with desertion. President Thomas Jefferson's response to these maritime depredations was to request that Congress pass a series of Embargo Acts barring exports to Europe until England and France ceased their unlawful acts against American ships and her seamen. The United States had a healthy economy by shipping goods to both combatants. The acts backfired on the United States, causing a serious economic depression accompanied by significant unemployment. Protests against the acts and flouting of them by U.S. captains were vociferous until the acts were repealed in 1809. Their failure to halt the capture of

American ships and impressment of seamen by the British, however, directly led to the War of 1812.

TERM PAPER SUGGESTIONS

1. Describe the reaction of the American public to the *Chesapeake-Leopard* Incident.

2. Was President Jefferson wise in attempting diplomacy and economic pressure via the Embargo Acts to keep America neutral during the Napoleonic Wars?

3. How did the British use the 1795 Jay Treaty and a disregard for U.S. citizenship to impress American seamen into the British Navy?

4. Analyze why President Jefferson's "cordon sanitaire" solution via the Embargo Acts jeopardized the American economy.

5. The Embargo Acts were so economically devastating that they caused a booming smuggling business as merchants and seamen tried to circumvent them. Compare the passage of the Embargo Acts to the passage of the Volstead Act of 1919 that prohibited the manufacture, sale, and transportation of alcoholic beverages. What was it about both acts that made Americans so readily violate them?

6. President Jefferson's secretary of the treasury, Albert Gallatin, was the only cabinet member to oppose passage of these acts. He did so because he thought them unenforceable. Should President Jefferson have taken Secretary Gallatin's advice?

ALTERNATIVE TERM PAPER SUGGESTIONS

1. Read the poem *Embargo* by William Cullen Bryant: http://www.4literature.net/William_Cullen_Bryant/Embargo/. Write a satirical poem in his style that makes fun of President Jefferson and the Embargo Acts.

2. Assume you are a New England shipping magnate whose business has been devastated by the Embargo Acts. Prepare a podcast, accompanied by appropriate nineteenth-century music or protest voices to tell your fellow New Englanders how and why the Embargo Acts are so dangerous to the New England economy.

SUGGESTED SOURCES

Primary Sources

Adams, Henry. *History of the United States of America.* 7 vols. New York: Charles Scribner's Sons, 1890–1891. Provides a factual, detailed description of

Thomas Jefferson's attempt at neutrality through the use of the Embargo Acts.

Calhoun, John C. *Report, or Manifesto of the Causes and Reasons of War with Great Britain, Presented to the House of Representatives by the Committee of Foreign Relations.* June 3, 1812. Washington, DC: A & G. Way, 1812. Furnishes a rationale for waging war with Britain based on ship seizures and impressment of American seamen.

Emerson, John Cloyd. *The Chesapeake Affair of 1807; an Objective Account of the Attack by HMS Leopard upon the U.S. Frigate Chesapeake off Cape Henry, Va. June 22, 1807 and its Repercussions.* Portsmouth, VA: unknown publisher, 1954. Includes newspaper accounts, official documents, and other authoritative sources of the event.

Gallatin, Albert. *The Writings of Albert Gallatin.* 3 vols. Philadelphia: J. B. Lippincott & Company, 1879. Gives a detailed rationale for why Secretary of the Treasury Gallatin opposed the passage of the Embargo Acts.

Ingersoll, Charles Jared. *A View of the Rights and Wrongs, Power and Policy, of the United States of America.* Philadelphia: Doubleday, 1808. Argues that the weak foreign policy of the United States should not continue and that the United States should retaliate against England and France.

Secondary Sources

Cray, Robert E., Jr. "Remembering the *USS Chesapeake:* The Politics of Maritime Death and Impressment." *Journal of the Early Republic* 25 (Fall 2005): 445–474. Provides a scholarly description of the events and aftermath of the Leopard-Chesapeake Affair.

Debatable Issues in U.S. History. Westport, CT: Greenwood Press, 2004. Includes a chapter on the Embargo Acts and their failure to stop British seizure of American ships and impressment of U.S. seamen.

Sears, Louis M. *Jefferson and the Embargo.* New York: Octagonal, 1967. Discusses Jefferson's attempt to maintain America's neutrality through the use of an ineffectual series of Embargo Acts.

Steel, Anthony. "Impressment in the Monroe-Pinkney Negotiation, 1806–1807." *The American Historical Review* 57 (January 1952): 352–369. (Available in JSTOR.) Poses that the impressment problem was somewhat exaggerated and was not of that much importance as a causus belli for the War of 1812.

Taylor, George Rogers. *The War of 1812; Past Justifications and Present Interpretations.* Boston, MA: D.C. Heath, 1963. Devotes one essay to the causes of the War of 1812.

Tucker, George Holbert. *Norfolk Highlights, 1584–1881.* Norfolk, VA: Norfolk Historical Society, 1972. Also available at http://norfolkhistorical.org/

highlights/contents.html. Devotes a chapter to the naval skirmish between the *Leopard* and the *Chesapeake.*

Usher, Roland G., Jr. "Royal Navy Impressment during the American Revolution." *The Mississippi Valley Historical Review* 37 (March 1951): 673–688. (Available in JSTOR.) Through the use of newly acquired materials, the author quantifies the impressment problem that helped precipitate the War of 1812.

Watson, Paul Barron. *The Tragic Career of Commodore James Barron, U.S. Navy (1769–1851).* New York: Coward-McCann, 1942. Tells the tale of Commodore Barron who gave up his ship to the *HMS Leopard* much to the disgrace of the U.S. Navy.

Zimmerman, James Fulton. *Impressment of American Seamen.* New York: Columbia University Press, 1925. Furnishes a scholarly account of the problem that impressment presented during war time.

World Wide Web

Bryant, William Cullen. "Embargo." http://www.4literature.net/William _Cullen_Bryant/Embargo/. This is just one of many poems written by various satirists and columnists as political satire against President Jefferson and the passage of the Embargo Acts.

"Cause of the War of 1812." http://library.thinkquest.org/22916/excauses.html. Contains a history of the causes of war, including a timeline, description of battles, biographical sketches of the main participants, several quizzes, tours of the battle sites, and more.

"The Causes of the War of 1812." http://www.globalsecurity.org/military/ library/report/1989/HWW.htm. Furnishes a lengthy analysis of the causes of the War of 1812, including a chronological outline of the events leading up to it.

"The Impress Service." http://www.nelsonsnavy.co.uk/broadside7.html. Features a facsimile of a press warrant issued to British ship captains that authorized them to impress seamen.

"Key Events & Causes: War of 1812." http://home.earthlink.net/~gfeldmeth/ chart.1812.html. Provides an annotated chronology of the causes and events of the War of 1812.

"Thomas Jefferson to Congress, March 22, 1808." http://memory.loc.gov/ cgi-bin/query/r?ammem/mtj:@field(DOCID+@lit(tj110015)). Indicates President Jefferson's intention to pursue diplomatic solutions with Britain over the *Leopard-Chesapeake* Affair.

"War of 1812: People & Stories." http://www.galafilm.com/1812/e/people/ index.html. Contains several firsthand accounts of key British, American,

Indian, and Canadian citizens who were involved in orchestrating the War of 1812.

Multimedia Sources

America under Thomas Jefferson, 1800–1809. Evanston, IL: United Learning, 2003. 1 videocassette. 15 minutes. Includes narrated visuals, dramatic recreations, photos, maps, and documents. Part of the video is devoted to the Embargo Acts and their effect on New England.

The War of 1812. New York: Arts and Entertainment Home Video, 2005. 1 DVD. 280 minutes. Contains narration and character portrayal of every aspect of the 1812 war, including information about battles, political negotiations, and the aftermath.

12. John Jacob Astor and the Fur Trade (1808)

John Jacob Astor (1763–1848) was one of America's first monopolists and philanthropists. In 1808, by an act of Congress that barred foreigners from participating in the fur trade south of the Canadian border, Astor cornered the market on the fur trade. He began his career as a fur trader in the eighteenth century and by 1800 had initiated a brisk business with China, trading furs, teas, sandalwood, and opium. John Jacob Astor was the classic immigrant "rags to riches story." He arrived from Germany in 1784 determined to seek his fortune. He married Sarah Todd from an Old Dutch family. Her dowry gave him the funds to open a store selling musical instruments and trading furs. With each trip to the frontier, Astor made connections throughout the Northwest Territories. By 1800 he had monopolized the American side of the fur trade business by using modern corporate practices such as division of labor and vertical integration. His vision, however, was always on world trade. He tried to establish routes and trading forts through the Pacific Northwest that would improve his efficiency in trading with China. Astor was also interested in New York real estate. He purchased large tracts of land in New York City and leased the land to businesses. After leaving his business, Astor began a career in philanthropy by sponsoring artists and writers. He also gave the funds to construct the New York City Public Library. He died in 1848, the richest man in America, with an estate worth approximately $20 million.

TERM PAPER SUGGESTIONS

1. Discuss John Jacob Astor's role in opening up the West through the establishment of forts and trails.
2. Discuss the historical evidence that John Jacob Astor was involved in the opium trade during his business with China.
3. How did the writer Washington Irving influence John Jacob Astor?
4. John Jacob Astor was the recipient of the U.S. government's first federal subsidy of an industry. Discuss the implications of the decision by Congress and President Jefferson to exclude other people from entering the same business.
5. Analyze the philanthropic contributions that John Jacob Astor made to New York and his sponsorship of writers and artists.
6. America has always resisted a formal class system. Discuss how monopolies similar to Astor's can create an aristocracy based on wealth. What are the inherent dangers of a formal class system?

ALTERNATIVE TERM PAPER SUGGESTIONS

1. After dealing in furs and foreign trade, John Jacob Astor turned his business to acquiring huge tracts of land in New York City. Using Google Earth and historical maps of Manhattan, show Astor's impact and influence on the development of New York City.
2. At the time of his death, John Jacob Astor was the richest man in America. Use "Inflation Calculator" at http://www.westegg.com/inflation to compare his wealth to other American monopolists from the nineteenth, twentieth, and twenty-first centuries. Are the scales similar or dissimilar? You may wish to consider monopolists such as Andrew Carnegie, John D. Rockefeller, and Bill Gates.

SUGGESTED SOURCES

Primary Sources

Astor, John Jacob. *Business Letters, 1813–1828*. Benson, VT: Chaldize Publications, 1991. Includes 134 letters of business correspondence showing how Astor created and expanded the fur trade westward.

Irving, Washington. *Astoria: Adventure in the Pacific Northwest*. London: Kegan Paul International, Ltd., 1987. Reprint ed. Astor hired Irving to write the story of his business-sponsored fur trading expedition that established trading posts and a fort named Astoria to further trade with China via access to the Pacific Northwest.

Ross, Alexander. *Adventures of the First Settlers on the Oregon or Columbia River, 1810–1813*. Corvallis: Oregon State University Press, 2000. Furnishes the narrative of the expedition sponsored by Astor to create the Pacific Fur Company and also gives an account of the Pacific Northwest Indian tribes encountered by the expedition.

Secondary Sources

Brannon, Gary. *The Last Voyage of the Tonquin: An Ill-Fated Expedition to the Pacific Northwest*. Waterloo, ON: Escart Press, 1992. Astor funded several expeditions to the Pacific Northwest in the hope of establishing a Pacific trade route. This work discusses the sinking of one of his ships.

Bryce, George. *Remarkable History of the Hudson's Bay Company including that of the French Traders of North-Western Canada and of the North-West, XY, and Astor Fur Company*. Boston, MA: Adamant Media, 2000. While Chapter XXII is devoted solely to the Astor Fur Company, the rest is a historical treasure trove of information about Astor's competitors and the nature of the business.

Haeger, John D. *John Jacob Astor: Business and Finance in the Early Republic*. Detroit, MI: Wayne State University Press, 1991. Presents a scholarly financial analysis of how Astor monopolized the fur trade.

Homberger, Eric. *Mrs. Astor's New York: Money and Power in a Gilded Age*. New Haven, CT: Yale University Press, 2002. Written by a scholar, this book traces the history of the Astor family and their evolution into an American aristocratic family similar to ones in Europe.

Jones, Robert F. *Annals of Astoria: The Headquarters Log of the Pacific Fur Company on the Columbia River, 1811–1813*. New York: Fordham University Press, 1999. Gives the most accurate description of the trading fort that Astor attempted to establish in the Pacific Northwest.

Kaplan, Justin. *When the Astors Owned New York: Blue Bloods and Grand Hotels in a Gilded Age*. New York: Viking Press, 2006. Beginning with John Jacob Astor, this book examines several generations of Astors and their impact on New York real estate.

Kavaler, Lucy. *The Astors: A Family Chronicle of Pomp and Power*. Dallas, TX: Backinprint.com, 2000. Furnishes a family history of the Astors beginning with John Jacob and his business dealing in furs, with China, and in New York property.

Madsen, Axel. *John Jacob Astor: America's First Multimillionaire*. New York: John Wiley, 2001. Shows how Astor's careful attention to every business detail propelled him to monopolize the fur trade and to obtain further success in other business ventures.

Minnigerode, Meade. *Certain Rich Men, Stephen Girard, Jacob Astor, Jay Cooke, Daniel Drew, Cornelius Vanderbilt, Jay Gould, and Jim Fisk*. Freeport, NY: Books for Libraries Press, 1970. Contains biographical sketches of the some of the richest men and monopolists of nineteenth-century America.

Parker, Lewis K. *John Jacob Astor and the Fur Trade*. New York: PowerKids Press, 2003. Written for the secondary student, this easy-to-understand work gives an overview of Astor's business success in the fur trade.

Smith, Arthur D. Howden. *John Jacob Astor, Landlord of New York*. Philadelphia, PA: J. B. Lippincott & Company, 1929. Traces the business dealings of Astor and shows how he dominated the New York City real estate market.

Terrell, John Upton. *Furs by Astor: The Full Story of the Founding of a Great American Fortune*. New York: William Morrow & Company, 1963. Provides the details on how Astor came to monopolize the American fur trade industry.

World Wide Web

"Exploration the Fur Trade and Hudson's Bay Company." http://www.canadiana.org/hbc/sources/sources_e.html#fur_trade. Features government documents, eyewitness accounts, and U.S. trade and land claims between Canada and the Hudson Bay Trading Company, Astor's main competitor in the fur trade industry.

"The Fur Trade: Beaver Powered Mountaineering." http://xroads.virginia.edu/~hyper/HNS/Mtmen/furtrade.html. An excellent overview of the ups and downs of the fur trade and Astor's attempts to establish a trade route to the Pacific Northwest and China.

"John Jacob Astor." http://www.linecamp.com/museums/americanwest/western_names/astor_john_jacob/astor_john_jacob.html. Provides a hyperlinked short biography of Astor with links to the names of famous fur trappers/explorers.

"John Jacob Astor and the Fur Trade: Testing the Role of Government." http://www.fee.org/publications/the-freeman/article.asp?aid=4866. Questions the act by Congress that gave Astor a virtual fur trade monopoly south of Canada.

"John Jacob Astor—Pacific Fur Company Astorians—Tonquin—Fort Astoria." http://www.thefurtrapper.com/astorians.htm. An excellent site showing Astor's role and influence on the development of the Oregon Trail.

"John Jacob Astor: Wealthy Merchant and Fur Trader." http://www.historynet.com/magazines/american_history/3027641.html. Gives a historically

accurate biographical sketch of John Jacob Astor and his role in monopo-
lizing the fur trade.

"Library of Western Fur Trade Historical Source Documents, Diaries, Narratives,
and Letters of Mountain Men." http://www.xmission.com/~drudy/
mtman/mmarch.html. Provides accounts of the Rocky Mountain fur
trade during the early 1800s, including an online version of *Astoria* by
Washington Irving.

Multimedia Sources

Biography—The Astors: High Society. New York: A&E Home Entertainment
Video, 2006. 1 DVD. 60 minutes. Beginning with John Jacob Astor, this
film traces his monopolization of the fur trade and continues to follow
the family's fortunes to present day.

13. Tecumseh and "the Prophet" (1811)

Internecine warfare among various Indian tribes and their willingness to
serve the interests of competing invaders were two causes of their exile to
remote areas of the United States and the loss of their lands. Tecumseh, a
Shawnee chief, and his brother Tenskwata, also known as "the Prophet,"
were exceptional warriors who tried to unite various Indian tribes to prevent the theft of their ancestral lands in what was considered the Northwest
Territory (currently Ohio, Indiana, Illinois, Michigan, Wisconsin, and the
eastern part of Minnesota). While Tenskwata spoke to Indians of his vision
for reviving Indian ways, Tecumseh campaigned vigorously all throughout
the northwestern territories to unite them in a confederation that would be
strong enough to battle with U.S. troops and repel settlers. After his brother's poorly timed attack on General William Henry Harrison's troops at the
confluence of the Tippecanoe and Wabash Rivers, Tecumseh blamed his
brother for the defeat and exiled him. Tecumseh formed an alliance with
the British in Canada who were warring with the United States over
impressments and ship seizure issues. After capturing Fort Dearborn in
the village of Chicago, Tecumseh was killed at the Battle of the Thames
in 1813. He was the first Indian chief to propose that Indians held
land communally and that no tribe "owned" land that it could sell to
settlers. His death ended any Indian resistance to stop the settlement of
the northwestern territories.

TERM PAPER SUGGESTIONS

1. How did "Tecumseh's War" provide the United States with ammunition to go to war with Britain?
2. Describe Tenskwata's vision. What part of it may have contributed to the Indians' defeat at Tippecanoe?
3. How did Tecumseh transform Tenskwata's vision from a religious movement into a political one?
4. Analyze Tecumseh's philosophy about land ownership. Why might it have appealed to Indians and not Americans?
5. Tecumseh was admired by friend and foe. How did he lead his life so that even his enemies admired and respected him?
6. Tecumseh urged other Indian tribes to form a confederacy to halt the usurpation of their lands by settlers. What would have been the benefits to such a union for the purposes of negotiation and treaties with the U.S. government?

ALTERNATIVE TERM PAPER SUGGESTIONS

1. Tecumseh traveled widely to proselytize to various Indian tribes about the need to stop American expansion westward. Use Google Earth and historical maps of the Northwest Territory to show where those tribes were in the 1800s and what has happened to their lands in the twenty-first century.
2. Scan illustrations, maps, and other primary source documents, and use them to create a two minute iMovie biography of Tecumseh.

SUGGESTED SOURCES

Primary Sources

Smith, David. *Presidents from Adams through Polk, 1825–1849: Debating Issues in Pro and Con Primary Documents*. Westport, CT: Greenwood Press, 2005. This text is helpful for documents concerning U.S. policy toward American Indian tribes.

Sonneborn, Liz. *War of 1812: A Primary Source History of America's Second War with Britain*. New York: Rosen, 2004. Provides historical evidence of Tecumseh's alliance with the British at the beginning of the War of 1812.

Secondary Sources

Calloway, Colin G. *The Shawnees and the War for America*. New York: Viking Penguin, 2007. Examines the history of the Shawnee tribe from the eighteenth century through repeated removals by the U.S. government in the nineteenth century. The author devotes parts of the book to the role of Tecumseh and Tenskwata in trying to stave off the Diaspora of the Shawnees.

Dowd, Gregory Evans. *A Spirited Resistance: The North American Indian Struggle for Unity, 1745–1815.* Baltimore, MD: The Johns Hopkins University Press, 1992. Contains a well-researched and documented review of the struggles that the Indian tribes had against western expansion and their last organized attempt to halt it.

Drake, Benjamin. *Life of Tecumseh and of His Brother the Prophet, with a Historical Sketch of the Shawanoe Indians.* Salem, NH: Ayer Company Publishers, 1988. Originally published in 1858, this title relates the story of the role both brothers played in trying to establish an Indian confederacy.

Eckert, Allan W. *A Sorrow in Our Hearts, The Life of Tecumseh.* New York: Bantam, 1992. A blend of fact and fiction based on twenty-five years of research that recreates Tecumseh's conversations and thoughts on land ownership and various other topics.

Edmunds, R. David. *The Shawnee Prophet.* Lincoln, NE: University of Nebraska Press, 1983. Relates the story of Tenskwata and the role he played with his brother in an attempt to unify the Indians in the Ohio Valley.

Edmunds, R. David. *Tecumseh and the Quest for Indian Leadership.* New York: Pearson Longman, 2007. This second edition is a well-researched biography of Tecumseh and his attempt to form an Indian nation to stop the erosion of Indian lands.

Immell, Myra. *The Importance of Tecumseh.* San Diego, CA: Lucent Books, 1997. Provides an easy-to-understand biography of Tecumseh and the significance of his attempt to unite the Indians against further incursion into the Northwest Territory.

Moss, Joyce. *Profiles in American History: Significant Events and the People Who Shaped Them.* Vol. 2. Detroit, MI: Gale Research, 1994. Discusses Tecumseh's life as a leader who tried to prevent the great Indian Diaspora from the Ohio Valley.

Sugden, John. *Tecumseh: A Life.* New York: Henry Holt & Company, 1998. Considered the definitive biography of Tecumseh's life and also furnishes a great deal of information about the Shawnees.

Sugden, John. *Tecumseh's Last Stand.* Normal, OK: University of Oklahoma Press, 1990. Supplies a detailed analysis of the last campaign of Tecumseh that culminated with his death at the Battle of the Thames.

Tucker, Glen. *Tecumseh: Vision of Glory.* New York: Russell & Russell, 1973. Presents an empathetic view of Tecumseh's goal for an Indian nation.

Warren, Stephen. *The Shawnee and Their Neighbors, 1795–1870.* Urbana, IL: The University of Illinois Press, 2005. Furnishes a scholarly account of the trials and tribulations of the Shawnee as their lands were breached by Americans expanding westward.

World Wide Web

"Act Creating Indiana Territory, 1800." http://www.in.gov/history/6214.htm. Includes the full text of the act that created the territory of Indiana as a prelude to statehood and the loss of part of the northwestern territory that belonged to several Indian tribes.

"Harrison Land Act—1800." http://www.in.gov/history/6209.htm. Contains the full text of the act that reduced the amount of acreage needed and gave monetary credit to settlers so that they could expand into the Northwest Territory.

"Tecumseh: 'Sell a Country! Why not Sell the Air?'" http://www.phschool .com/atschool/california/why_we_remember/amer_rev_to_1914/primary _sources/WWR_1914_PS5.html. Furnishes a speech by Tecumseh in response to the proposal that the Indians sell their lands to the U.S. government.

"Tecumseh's Speech at Machekethie in the Spring of 1812." http://www.galafilm. com/1812/e/people/tec_speach2.html. Provides the full text of Tecumseh's plea to the Huron tribe to join the confederacy before it was too late.

"Tecumseh's Speech of August 11, 1810, to Governor William Henry Harrison, Indiana Territory." http://www.geocities.com/SouthBeach/Cove/ 8286/harrison.html. Provides the full text of Tecumseh's speech to Governor Harrison indicating his exasperation and despair over the government purchase of Indian lands and his promise to fight to stop it.

"Tecumseh's Speech to the Osages in the Winter of 1811–1812." http:// www.galafilm.com/1812/e/people/tec_speaches.html. Gives the full text of his persuasive speech to the Osage tribe beseeching them to join the confederation and fight to halt the erosion of their ancestral lands.

"The Treaty of Grenville, August 3, 1795." http://www.law.ou.edu/ushistory/ greenvil.shtml. Contains the full text of the treaty among many Indian tribes including Tecumseh's Shawnee that began the dispersal of their lands to the U.S. government.

"Treaty with the Delawares, Etc., 1809." http://www.in.gov/history/6164.htm. Furnishes the full text of the treaty that ceded one-third of Indiana to the government and finally aroused Tecumseh and his brother, "the Prophet," to try to form an Indian nation to halt government acquisition of Indian property.

Multimedia Sources

Tecumseh: The Last Warrior. Atlanta, GA: Turner Home Entertainment, 1995.
1 DVD. 64 minutes. Gives a somewhat glamorized portrait of Tecumseh
and his quest to unite American Indians to halt westward expansion and
the loss of their ancestral lands.

14. War of 1812

Neither Britain nor the United States distinguished herself in this war that
was fought on and off from 1812 to 1815, ostensibly over British interference with American shipping interests. Battles were waged on land and
sea throughout Canada, the Great Lakes, and the Middle Atlantic states,
but the results were inconclusive for both sides. America tried to conquer
Canada and burned York (present-day Toronto), while the British retali-
ated by burning the White House, Capitol, and other government buildings. At sea the *U.S.S. Constitution* ("Old Ironsides") won several
victories, but they did not change the outcome of the war. The largest
battle occurred two weeks after Britain and America signed The Treaty of
Ghent (1814). It was led by General Andrew Jackson who realized instant
fame when his troops killed more than two thousand British soldiers while
suffering few casualties. The Treaty of Ghent resolved the boundaries
between the United States and Canada, demilitarized the great Lakes,
and established British and American control of The Oregon Territory in
the Pacific Northwest until 1824.

TERM PAPER SUGGESTIONS

1. Analyze how the War of 1812 was America's "second war of independence."
2. Argue that the War of 1812 was really a war for material gain and not patrio-
tism.
3. Indians were caught in the middle during the War of 1812. Describe the
role they played in the war. Should they have sided with the United States
or Britain?
4. New England was in a paradox during the war. Discuss how New Englanders
demanded a resolution to the shipping and impressment problem with
Britain while simultaneously desiring to make a profit by continuing to trade
with Britain.

5. Although the British impressed and seized the most American sailors and ships, the French also seized many. Why did the United States fight Britain and not France over these issues?

6. Discuss what the Americans, British, and Canadians wanted to accomplish by going to war in 1812.

ALTERNATIVE TERM PAPER SUGGESTIONS

1. Look carefully at "The American in Caricature 1765–1865" Web site. http://www.indiana.edu/~liblilly/cartoon/war.html. Choose several issues surrounding the War of 1812 and draw six caricatures that would be similar and representative of the caricatures during those times.

2. Using maps and other relevant documents, design a Web site showing how General Andrew Jackson won the Battle of New Orleans against superior British forces.

SUGGESTED SOURCES

Primary Sources

Bozonelis, Helen Koutras. *Primary Source Accounts of the War of 1812*. Berkeley Heights, NJ: Enslow Publishers, 2006. Includes entries from soldiers' journals and other documents from the National Archives and various state historical societies.

Dudley, William S. *The Naval War of 1812: A Documentary History*. 3 vols. Washington, DC: Naval Historical Center, 1985. Contains correspondence, military orders, maps, and other primary sources about maritime operations during the 1812 war.

Fredriksen, John C. *War of 1812 Eyewitness Accounts: An Annotated Bibliography*. Westport, CT: Greenwood Press, 1997. Provides a summarized list of first-person accounts of the War of 1812.

Secondary Sources

Beirne, Francis F. *War of 1812*. New York: Dutton, 1949. Contains a well-researched text on the causes, events, and consequences of the war between the United States and Britain.

Berton, Pierre. *The Invasion of Canada: 1812–1813*. Boston, MA: Little Brown, 1980. Gives the Canadian perspective of the War of 1812.

Borneman, Walter R. *1812: The War That Forged a Nation*. New York: HarperCollins Publishers, 2004. Features an Americanized account of the war.

Forester, C. S. *The Age of Fighting Sail: The Story of the Naval War of 1812*. New York: Doubleday, 1956. Analyzes how Britain's powerful Navy did not win the day during the War of 1812 because of the construction of more maneuverable American ships.

Hickey, Donald R. *The War of 1812: A Forgotten Conflict*. Urbana, IL: University of Illinois Press, 1989. Gives a scholarly account of the war, including the causes and aftermath.

Hickey, Donald R., and Donald R. Graves. *Don't Give Up the Ship!: Myths of the War of 1812*. Urbana, IL: University of Illinois Press, 2006. Exposes the patriotic myths surrounding the war.

Hitsman, J. Mackay. *The Incredible War of 1812*. Toronto, Canada: University of Toronto Press, 1965. Provides a scholarly account of the war by a Canadian author.

Langguth, A. J. *Union 1812: The Americans Who Fought the Second War of Independence*. New York: Simon & Schuster, 2006. Gives a broad, brush-stroked account of the war, including how it was implicated in America's westward expansionists' dreams.

Marrin, Albert. *1812, The War Nobody Won*. New York: Athenaeum, 1985. Describes the causes and leading events of the early nineteenth-century conflict between Great Britain and the United States.

Roosevelt, Theodore. *The Naval War of 1812: The History of the United States during the Last War with Great Britain to which Is Appended an Account of the Battle of New Orleans*. New York: Charles Scribner's Sons, 1926. This title is Volume VI in *The Works of Theodore Roosevelt* series. Written when he was the U.S. secretary of the navy, this is former President Roosevelt's account of the causes of the War of 1812 and its significant battles.

Tucker, Glenn. *Poltroons and Patriots: A Popular Account of the War of 1812*. New York: Bobbs-Merrill Company, 1954. A Washington journalist, Tucker furnishes a military version of the War of 1812.

World Wide Web

"American in Caricature 1765–1865. The War of 1812." http://www.indiana.edu/~liblilly/cartoon/war.html. Contains several nineteenth-century caricatures concerning the 1812 war.

"The Avalon Project at Yale Law School: The War of 1812." http://www.yale.edu/lawweb/avalon/diplomacy/britain/br1814m.htm. Provides documents such as the declaration of war, the cartel for exchanging prisoners of war, and more.

"Clark Historical Library." http://clarke.cmich.edu/nativeamericans/mphc/warof1812.htm. Contains more than fifty original sources pertaining to the war, including many letters, addresses and speeches regarding the position of various Indian tribes, and progress of the war in Canada.

"Correct Map of the Seat of War 1812." http://memory.loc.gov/ammem/ gmdhtml/gmdhome.html. Furnishes an 1812 map of the states and territories involved in the War of 1812.

"Debate on the Naval Establishment 1812." http://www.shsu.edu/~his_ncp/ Nav1812.html. Features the debate in the House of Representatives between the Federalists who wished to establish a naval force in 1812 and the Republicans who desired to keep it at minimum strength.

"Transcript of Treaty of Ghent." http://www.ourdocuments.gov/doc.php? doc=20&page=transcript. Provides the full text of the Treaty of Ghent that ended the war between Britain and the United States.

"The War of 1812 Website." http://www.warof1812.ca/1812art.htm. Contains hundreds of articles, letters, and legal acts from the time period.

"Winfield Scott in the War of 1812." *Harper's New Monthly Magazine* 23 (September 1861): 451–467. http://memory.loc.gov/cgi-bin/query/ r?ammem/ncps:@field(DOCID+@lit(ABK4014-0023-72))::. Details General Winfield Scott's role in improving the military capabilities of the army during the War of 1812.

Multimedia Sources

Battle of New Orleans. Huntsville, TX: Educational Video Network, Inc., 2005. 1 DVD. 25 minutes. Gives a detailed description of the Battle of New Orleans and how it was successfully waged by General Andrew Jackson.

The History Channel Presents the War of 1812. New York: A&E Home Video, 2000. 1 DVD. 280 minutes. Contains information about the dangerous declaration of war by President James Madison, the writing of the "Star Spangled Banner," the Battle of New Orleans, and the first use of ironclad ships to wage war by the United States.

15. Hartford Convention (1814)

The United States was only thirty-eight years old when opposition to national economic and military policies affecting the states of Connecticut, New Hampshire, Vermont, Rhode Island, and Massachusetts drove them to consider secession at a convention held in Hartford, Connecticut. Prior to the War of 1812, New England was thriving as it exported goods to Britain and other European countries that were engaged in the Napoleonic Wars. Despite a state of war, New England continued to sell supplies to British troops quartered in Canada and to British troops offshore. The loss of this trade through federal government embargoes and the War of 1812 jeopardized New England's economy, causing serious unemployment and economic hardship. When President James Madison was elected, Massachusetts and Connecticut were asked to send militias to aid the federal government without any offer of compensation. Governor Caleb Strong of Massachusetts, outraged at the federal government's failure to reimburse his state, believed that the time had come for Massachusetts and other similarly situated states to look after their own interests. They held a convention that rejected secession, but recommended several amendments to the Constitution that called for drastic changes in the relationship between the federal government and individual states. Even though the delegates never seriously considered secession, the convention set a future precedent for states who were at odds with national policies.

TERM PAPER SUGGESTIONS

1. The Hartford Convention was composed of Federalist delegates who held certain beliefs about the role of a central government. Discuss how their convention hastened their demise as a political party.

2. Delegates at the convention proposed several constitutional amendments that they believed would increase states' autonomy. Argue the pros and cons of these amendments.

3. One of the reasons for the Hartford Convention was the dire straits of the New England economy. Cite facts and figures from trade and the fishing industry to support the idea that the poor economy was a major impetus for the convention rather than states' rights.

4. Harrison Gray Otis, a delegate from Massachusetts, played a pivotal role in preventing the delegates from voting for secession. Analyze his reasons for blocking the radicals' proposals.

5. Since the convention was held as a closed session for three weeks, many of its deliberations remain a secret. President Madison, however, stationed Army Officer Thomas Sydney Jessup to observe the proceedings. Discuss what fears President Madison held about the convention.

6. Argue that the Hartford Convention was a formal state-sponsored form of dissent against an unpopular and poorly planned and managed war.

ALTERNATIVE TERM PAPER SUGGESTIONS

1. Research the economic conditions in New England and correspondence from Hartford Convention delegates. Create a podcast that urges New Englanders to vote to secede from the Union.

2. Write a series of letters as Army Officer Thomas Sydney Jessup telling President Madison what you have seen and heard about the Hartford Convention. Give your personal opinion about whether the President should or should not be fearful of a Union dissolution.

SUGGESTED SOURCES

Primary Sources

Adams, Henry. *The History of the United States during the Administrations of Jefferson and Madison*. New York: Charles Scribner's Sons, 1889–1891. Discusses the causes and aftermath of the Hartford Convention.

Lyman, Theodore. *A Short Account of the Hartford Convention: Taken from Official Documents, and Addressed to the Fair Minded and the Well Disposed; To Which Is Added an Attested Copy of the Secret Journal of the Body*. Boston, MA: O. Everett, 1823. Contains a summary of the convention along with secret journal documents.

Morison, Samuel Eliot. *The Life and Letters of Harrison Gray Otis, Federalist, 1765–1848*. Boston, MA: Houghton Mifflin Company, 1913. Noted historian provides an account of the role played by Federalist Otis at the convention.

Secondary Sources

Anderson, Frank Maloy. *A Forgotten Phase of the New England Opposition to the War of 1812*. Cedar Rapids, IA: n.p., 1913. Provides an understandable account of New England's reaction to the Embargo Acts and the subsequent War of 1812.

Banner, James M., Jr. "A Shadow of Secession? The Hartford Convention, 1814." *History Today* 38 (September 1988): 24–30. (Available in Ebsco Host.) Written for secondary school students, this article explains the Hartford Convention in clearly understandable terms.

Banner, James M., Jr. *To the Hartford Convention: The Federalists and the Origins of Party Politics in Massachusetts, 1789–1815*. New York: Random House, 1970. Discusses the political machinations involved with the Hartford Convention.

Buckley, William Edward. *The Hartford Convention.* New Haven, CT: Yale
University Press, 1934. Provides a scholarly perspective of the Hartford
Convention.

Carey, Mathew. *Olive Branch, or Faults on Both Sides, Federal and Democratic.*
Plainview, NY: Books for Libraries, 1969. Attempts to give an unbiased
rendering of the Hartford Convention.

Clarke, Jack Alden. "Thomas Sydney Jessup: Military Observer at the Hartford
Convention." *The New England Quarterly* 29 (September 1956):
393–399. (Available in JSTOR.) Discusses Jessup's reporting role
to President Madison who, fearing a civil war, dispatched him to
report confidentially to him about the proceedings of the Hartford Convention.

Coles, Harry L. *The War of 1812.* Chicago, IL: University of Chicago Press,
1965. Presents a scholarly view of the War of 1812 and the rationale
for the Hartford Convention.

Dwight, Theodore. *History of the Hartford Convention with a Review of the Policy
of the United States Government which Led to the War of 1812.* New York:
Da Capo Press, 1833. Furnishes a Federalist's account of the U.S.
economic policies that led to the War of 1812.

Gannon, Kevin M. "Escaping Mr. Jefferson's Plan of Destruction: New England
Federalists and the Idea of a Northern Confederacy, 1803–1804."
Journal of the Early Republic 21 (Autumn 2001): 413–443. (Available in
JSTOR.) Shows how the seeds for the Hartford Convention were sown
as early as 1803 through the policies of the Federalists.

Hickey, Donald R. "New England's Defense Problem and the Genesis of the
Hartford Convention." *The New England Quarterly* 50 (December
1977): 587–604. (Available in JSTOR.) Explains how the purpose of
the Hartford Convention was to provide for the military defense of
New England against Britain.

Morison, Samuel Eliot. *Harrison Gray Otis, 1765–1848, the Urbane Federalist.*
Boston, MA: Houghton Mifflin, 1969. Furnishes a biography of one of
Massachusetts's leading representatives at the Hartford Convention.

World Wide Web

"Amendments to the Constitution Proposed by the Hartford Convention,
1814." http://www.yale.edu/lawweb/avalon/amerdoc/hartconv.htm.
Provides the full texts of the Hartford Convention's planned changes to
the U.S. Constitution.

"The Hartford Convention." http://www.ctheritage.org/encyclopedia/
ct1763_1818/hartconv.htm. Contains a well-written synopsis of the

events surrounding the Hartford Convention, including additional reading suggestions.

"The Hartford Convention: Dec. 15, 1814–Jan. 4, 1815." http://www.bare footsworld.net/hartford.html. Contains a summary of the Hartford Convention, including the full text of the resolutions passed by the delegates.

"Nathan Dane's Role in the Hartford Convention of 1814–1815." http://www .primaryresearch.org/PRTHB/Dane/Norton/journal.htm. Describes Nathan Dane's contribution as a Federalist Massachusetts delegate to the Hartford Convention and includes links to the secret journal.

"Secession Crisis." http://civilwar.bluegrass.net/secessioncrisis/hartford convention.html. Furnishes an overview and the voting results concerning secession.

"Secret Journal of the Hartford Convention." http://www.primaryresearch.org/ PRTHB/Dane/Norton/journal.htm. Provides the full text of the proceedings of the 1814 Hartford Convention.

"War of 1812–1814 Hartford Convention." http://war1812.tripod.com/ hartford.html. Contains a brief overview of the causes and events surrounding the Hartford Convention.

Multimedia Sources

First Invasion: The War of 1812. New York: A&E Home Entertainment Video, 2004. 1 videocassette. 280 minutes. Includes a reenactment of the Hartford Convention.

16. Francis Cabot Lowell and Early Industrialization (1815)

Francis Cabot Lowell was thirty-six years old and a successful wealthy Boston area tradesman when he traveled to the textile towns of England and Scotland to study how their power looms worked. At the time Britain was jealously guarding the machine's design to prevent industrial espionage and competition from the United States and elsewhere. At night, Lowell carefully traced the designs of machines that he had observed in the factories during the day. He returned to America, enlisted the help of Paul Moody to make several technological enhancements to the power loom, and opened the Boston Manufacturing Company in 1815. Lowell's second innovation involved a change in the labor force. Instead of sending out yarn to local weavers, Lowell hired young, single women to tend his power looms. By mechanizing the entire process, Lowell pioneered the first American manufacturing company. His system was so successful that the company opened more textile mills along the Merrimack River (Massachusetts). Although Lowell died within three years after constructing his first textile mill, his partners named the new textile town Lowell in honor of his achievement.

TERM PAPER SUGGESTIONS

1. Research how Britain attempted to protect its textile factories from industrial espionage and what was at stake if other countries could replicate Britain's designs and production methods.
2. Describe all the steps that Lowell took to ensure a continuous, cost effective manufacturing process beginning with innovations to the power loom and an on-site carefully managed work force.
3. Explore how the Lowell factory system fostered the building and growth of public schools.
4. The textile industry was to become the North's economic power base. Analyze how the South contributed to it by supplying the northern factories with cheap, raw material.
5. At first the housing for the mill girls was considered so superior that it inspired poetry by John Greenleaf Whittier and praise by author Charles Dickens and politician Henry Clay. Trace how the living and employment conditions declined over time, resulting in strikes by the employees.
6. Discuss the pros and cons of being a "mill girl."

ALTERNATIVE TERM PAPER SUGGESTIONS

1. Assume you are a Lowell mill house girl. Write a blog where you and your fellow workers describe the living conditions and strict rules you must follow to keep the job. Include appropriate references and research on opportunities for recreation and financial independence.
2. Create a PowerPoint presentation and import online textile mill engravings and illustrations. Describe what the images convey about the working and social conditions in the factory and boarding house.

SUGGESTED SOURCES

Primary Sources

Dublin, Thomas. *Farm to Factory.* New York: Columbia University Press, 1993. Written for secondary school students, this source is filled with primary sources in the form of first-person accounts and letters by women about their experiences making the transition from farm girls to mill girls in the 1800s.

Eisler, Benita. *The Lowell Offering: Writings by New England Mill Women (1840–1845).* New York: W. W. Norton, 1997. Furnishes first-person accounts of what it was like to tend looms and perform other work in the Lowell textile mills during the mid-nineteenth century.

Robinson, Harriet Hanson. *Loom and Spindle or Life among the Early Mill Girls.* Kailua, HI: Press Pacifica, 1976. Documents life in the early mill town period and the eventual investigation concerning the working conditions of the factories.

Secondary Sources

Bruland, Kristine. *British Technology and European Industrialization: The Norwegian Textile Industry in the Mid-Nineteenth Century.* New York: Cambridge University Press, 2003. Discusses how Britain and other European countries acquired the technology to establish a profitable textile industry and how they needed the United States as an export market for their product.

Chandler, Alfred D. *Samuel Slater, Francis Cabot Lowell, and the Beginnings of the Factory System in the United States.* Cambridge, MA: Harvard Business School, 1984. Provides a scholarly account of the groundbreaking contributions that Samuel Slater and Francis Cabot Lowell made to the early industrialization of America, particularly in the textile industry.

Corrick, James A. *The Industrial Revolution.* San Diego, CA: Lucent Books, 1998. Provides an excellent, easy-to-understand overview of the birth of the industrial revolution in America beginning with the power loom and business prowess of Francis Cabot Lowell.

Deane, Phyllis. *The First Industrial Revolution.* New York: Cambridge University Press, 1987. Chapter 6, devoted to the cotton industry, details how it propelled the rest of the industrial revolution because of the market need and constant innovations in the machines.

Deitch, Joanne Weisman. *The Lowell Mill Girls: Life in the Factory.* Carlisle, MA: Discovery Enterprises, 1998. This short work contains letters written by mill girls and a listing of the strict rules and regulations that governed not only their working lives but also their social ones.

Dublin, Thomas. *Transforming Women's Work: New England Lives in the Industrial Revolution.* Ithaca, NY: Cornell University Press, 1995. Chapters 2 and 3 are devoted to the social and employment conditions of the women who worked in the Lowell textile factories.

Dublin, Thomas. *Women at Work.* New York: Columbia University Press, 1981. Describes how the invention of the power loom and other machines permanently changed the employment, educational, and social conditions of women.

Isaacs, Sally Senzell. *Life in a New England Mill Town.* Chicago, IL: Heinemann, 2002. Written for secondary school students, this book depicts what it was like to live, work, and play in a nineteenth-century textile town.

Moran, William. *The Belles of New England: The Women of the Textile Mills and the Families Whose Wealth They Wove.* New York: St. Martin's Press, 2004. Written by a journalist, this work traces the history of the textile industry beginning with Francis Cabot Lowell's first mill that liberated young women from the drudgery of farming only to replace it with mind-numbing work on a machine until the industry's demise in the twentieth century.

O'Connor, Thomas H. *Lords of the Loom, the Cotton Whigs and the Coming of the Civil War.* New York: Charles Scribner's Sons, 1968. Documents the connection between the need for cheap labor in the South to feed the maw of northern textile mills.

Selden, Bernice. *The Mill Girls: Lucy Larcom, Harriet Hanson Robinson, Sarah G. Bagley.* New York: Athenaeum, 1983. Discusses the lives of three "mill girl" women who went on to become distinguished for their writing and speaking about the conditions in New England textile mills.

Stearns, Peter N. *The Industrial Revolution in World History.* San Francisco, CA: Westview Press, 1993. Provides a scholarly history of the spread of the industrial revolution from Europe to other parts of the world. Chapter 4, devoted to the social impact of the industrial revolution, discusses the rise of New England mill towns.

World Wide Web

"Center for Lowell History." http://library.uml.edu/clh/index.Html. Furnishes a bibliography of primary and secondary sources on the history of Lowell, including information about the textile industry, exhibits containing photographic images, maps, descriptions of the town's buildings and locations, and a list of Internet and genealogical resources.

"Francis Cabot Lowell." http://www.economicadventure.org/decision/lowell.pdf. Furnishes one of the better accounts of Francis Cabot Lowell's life and his contribution to the American industrial revolution.

"The History of Mills." http.//inventors.about.com/library/inventors/blmills .htm. Accompanied by a clear illustration of mill power drives, this site includes information about Lowell's innovation and how he used his business acumen to make a fortune with one of the first integrated manufacturing systems.

"Mill Girls and Immigrant Video." http://www.nps.gov/lowe/photosmulti media/mgi.htm. Narrated by a Lowell National Historical Park Service officer, this short online video narrates the story of what it was like to work in a nineteenth-century mill town. The site also features photographs and an online lesson plan for teachers about the textile industry.

"Modern History Sourcebook: Harriet Robinson: Lowell Mill Girls." http:// www.fordham.edu/halsall/mod/robinson-lowell.html. Provides a significant passage from Harriet Hanson Robinson's autobiography describing her earlier life as a mill girl from 1834 to 1848, including her observation of the 1836 strike.

"Spindle, Loom, and Needle—History of the Textile Industry." http://inventors .about.com/cs/inventorsalphabet/a/textile_2.htm. Furnishes a short history of the early nineteenth-century textile industry and the role that Slater, Moody, and Lowell played in it.

"Who Made America? Francis Cabot Lowell." http://www.pbs.org/wgbh/they madeamerica/whomade/lowell_hi.html. Provides an outline biographical sketch of Francis Cabot Lowell that discusses his legacy as an inventor of integrated manufacturing systems.

Multimedia Sources

So Far From Home. New York: Scholastic, 1999. 1 videocassette. 30 minutes. Uses a diary format to describe the longing for Ireland and the conditions in the textile mills by a 14-year-old Lowell textile worker.

17. African Methodist Episcopal Church Founded (1816)

Many churches are formed when differences over religious practices, doctrines, or rites become irreconcilable. The African Methodist Episcopal Church (AME Church), however, was founded in 1816 for people of African descent who were seeking spiritual refuge from racial discrimination. The impetus was a decision by church officials to segregate the congregation at St. George's Methodist Episcopal Church (Philadelphia, PA) and create a gallery section solely for African American worshipers. In November 1876, three black members, Richard Allen, Absalom Jones, and William White, mistakenly sat in the wrong gallery and were forcibly removed while praying. Their humiliation and that of other black worshipers led to a mass exodus from the church and a movement to create not only a separate church but also a Free African Society dedicated to addressing concerns such as emancipation and employment discrimination. Allen and Jones, tireless evangelists and proselytizers for these causes, preached in churches and homes all along the seaboard states. By 1816 the AME was an officially recognized and formally established church with thousands of members that played a significant role with abolition, the War of 1812, the Civil War, Reconstruction, and the Civil Rights Movement. Now open to members of any race, it continues to address important social concerns.

TERM PAPER SUGGESTIONS

1. Describe how the AME Church's independence from other Methodist and Episcopal denominations created a haven for African Americans during the long period of racial discrimination.

2. Trace the contributions that the AME Church made to black education from 1816 to 1954, ending with the *Brown v. Board of Education (Topeka, Kansas)* Supreme Court Case of 1954.

3. Examine and explore the reasons why the AME Church protested the plans of the American Colonization Society for immigration of free blacks back to Africa.

4. By 1812, Britain had a strong abolitionist movement and seemed to be making better progress toward emancipation of all slaves. Discuss the possible self-destructive action behind the AME Church's recruitment of three thousand members for the Black Legion to fight the British during the War of 1812.

5. Explore how the AME Church improved social and economic conditions for all African Americans throughout the nineteenth century.

6. Investigate the role that AME Church Bishop Morris Brown may have played in the Denmark Vesey slave rebellion.

ALTERNATIVE TERM PAPER SUGGESTIONS

1. Create an online, hyperlinked biographical sketch of Richard Allen. Place an emphasis on his role as founder of the AME Church.

2. Gospel and hymn singing are integral parts of AME Church worship. Richard Allen compiled a collection of sixty-four hymns for his congregation in 1801. Create a podcast interspersed with some of those hymns and commentary that illustrate their essential role as part of the AME Church's services.

SUGGESTED SOURCES

Primary Sources

Allen, Richard. "Letters of Richard Allen and Absalom Jones." *Journal of Negro History* 1 (October 1916): 436–443. (Available in JSTOR.) Provides the correspondence between the two leaders of the AME Church.

Allen, Richard. *The Life Experience and Gospel Labors of the Rt. Rev. Richard Allen*. Reprint ed. Nashville, TN: Abingdon Press, 1983. Presents an accounting of Allen's religious life and the role he played in founding the AME Church.

Secondary Sources

Angell, Stephen W., and Anthony B. Pinn, eds. *Social Protest Thought in the African Methodist Episcopal Church 1862–1939*. Knoxville, TN: University of Tennessee Press, 2000. Examines the role of the AME Church during the Civil War and its aftermath.

Campbell, James T. *Songs of Zion: The African Methodist Episcopal Church in the United States and South Africa*. Chapel Hill, NC: University of North Carolina Press, 1998. Traces the founding of the AME Church and its decision to open a mission in South Africa in 1896 as well as the interaction between the two churches over the years.

Dickerson, Dennis C. "African Methodist Episcopal Church." In *Encyclopedia of African-American Culture and History*. Vol. 1, edited by Jack Salzman et al. New York: Macmillan, 1996. Furnishes an excellent, accurate overview of the origins and development of the AME Church in 1816.

Dodson, Jualynne E. *Engendering Church: Women, Power, and the AME Church*. Landham, MD: Rowman & Littlefield, 2002. Provides information about the history of the church along with the important role that women have played in it.

Dvorak, Katharine L. *An African American Exodus*. Brooklyn, NY: Carlson, 1991. Gives a history of the AME Church and analyzes the theological concepts underpinning it.

George, Carol V. R. *Segregated Sabbaths: Richard Allen and the Rise of Independent Black Churches, 1760–1840*. New York: Oxford University Press, 1973.

Traces the development of the independent African American churches and the role of Richard Allen in fostering them.

Lincoln, C. Eric, and Lawrence H. Mamiya. *The Black Church in the African American Experience*. Durham, NC: Duke University Press, 1990. Filled with statistical data and other primary sources, this scholarly work provides information about the origins and development of the AME Church.

Lutz, Norma Jean. *The History of the Black Church*. Philadelphia, PA: Chelsea House, 2001. Secondary school students will find this text useful for an overview of the AME Church and the role it played not only in the Civil War but also in the Civil Rights Movement.

Newman, Richard F. *Freedom's Prophet: Bishop Richard Allen, the AME Church, and the Black Founding Fathers*. New York: University Press, 2008. Provides a scholarly biography of Richard Allen that sheds light on his role as a founding member of the AME Church and Supporter of abolition and the Black community.

Rasmussen, R. Kent. *Farewell to Jim Crow: The Rise and Fall of Segregation in America*. New York: Facts on File, 1997. Written for secondary school students, this book places the founding of the AME Church within the broader perspective of African American history.

Roboteau, Albert J. *A Fire in the Bones: Reflections on African-American Religious History*. Boston, MA: Beacon Press, 1995. Contains brilliantly written essays by a noted Princeton scholar on the beginnings of the AME Church, the role of Richard Allen, and the development of African American churches.

World Wide Web

"African Methodist Episcopal (AME)." http://etext.lib.virginia.edu/relmove/nrms/ame.html. Furnishes a history, set of beliefs, issues and controversies, a bibliography and related links about the AME Church.

"AMEC African Methodist Episcopal Church." http://www.ame-church.com/. This is the official online site of the AME Church. It includes a short history of the AME Church, its mission, and links to other church-related news organizations.

"Denmark Vesey." http://www.gale.com/free_resources/bhm/bio/vesey_d.htm. Provides an extensive biographical sketch of Denmark Vesey, his position in the church, and his unsuccessful attempt at leading a slave rebellion in Charleston, South Carolina, in 1822.

"The Greater Allen A.M.E. Cathedral of New York." http://www.allencathedral.org/. Gives a succinct overview of Richard Allen's life and his founding father role in the AME Church.

"History of the African Methodist Episcopal Church." http://www.camelot castle.org/history.htm. Contains an extensive history of the AME Church together with pictures and biographical sketches of the founding fathers and mothers.

"Richard Allen and African-American Identity." http://earlyamerica.com/ review/spring97/allen.html. Summarizes Allen's life and the effect his actions had on the growth and development of African American culture.

"Welcome to AME Today." http://www.ame-today.com. This site provides additional historical information about the AME Church and news of its current social activities.

Multimedia Sources

Religions, African and African American. Wynnewood, PA: Schlessinger Media, 1998. 1 videocassette. 50 minutes. While this video, narrated by academy-award winner Ben Kingsley, also discusses Islam, Buddhism, and other religions, it focuses on the unique part that African culture has played on the evolution of African American religions and within the AME Church. A guide includes a timeline, vocabulary list, focus and discussion questions, and a bibliography.

18. Erie Canal (1817)

A canal linking the Great Lakes with the Atlantic Ocean was proposed as early as 1724. It failed to materialize because the project was so huge that it required public financing. Finally, public support and funds came in the form of a farsighted New York governor named DeWitt Clinton. In 1817 he persuaded the New York legislature to authorize monies to con- struct a canal forty feet wide by four feet deep that would run 363 miles between Albany on the Hudson River to Buffalo on Lake Erie. The canal was a nineteenth-century civil engineering feat that included a double set of locks built into a granite escarpment at Lockport and an aqueduct 802 feet long mounted on stone arches that carried the canal across the Genesee River. Finished in 1825, it promoted trade with the Midwest and Europe and created boom towns and cities such as Syracuse, Rochester, Utica, Buffalo, and Albany. In its heyday, it inspired songs and was the setting for works by Nathaniel Hawthorne, Mark Twain, Harriet Beecher Stowe, and Francis Trollope.

TERM PAPER SUGGESTIONS

1. Jesse Hawley, Joseph Ellicott, and Governor DeWitt Clinton were strong proponents of building the Erie Canal. Discuss what motivated each of them.

2. The geological and engineering problems involved with the construction of the Erie Canal were formidable. Using topographical maps and original Erie Canal construction maps, describe and analyze these challenges.

3. James Geddes, Benjamin Wright, and Nathan Roberts supervised the initial construction. Research their qualifications for overseeing such a massive building project. Describe some of the construction problems they faced, including the Montezuma Swamp problem.

4. Describe why it was economically necessary for the city of Buffalo to widen and deepen local creeks, create a harbor, and fund a public relations effort to become the terminus town for the Erie Canal.

5. The Erie Canal not only created an economic boom for western New York cities, it also opened up eastern markets to Midwestern agricultural products and increased trade to Europe. Analyze the benefits of the Erie Canal in terms of types of products and trade volume.

6. The Erie Canal was a massive six-year-long construction project that required many skilled and unskilled laborers. Find evidence about the extent of immigration, and discuss its impact on western New York cities and towns.

7. The building of the Erie Canal inspired many writers including Herman Melville, Francis Trollope, Mark Twain, and Harriet Beecher Stowe to write tales and incorporate aspects of the canal into their books or short stories. All were not positive that the Erie Canal represented progress. Research their writings and describe how the canal was depicted in their literature.

8. The canal generated surplus revenues that were deposited in local banks adjacent to the canal line. Describe how the Canal Fund became a type of development bank for New York State.

ALTERNATIVE TERM PAPER SUGGESTIONS

1. Assume you are an Erie Canal travel guide. Design a Web-based brochure with an itinerary for tourists, mentioning towns they will visit, inns they will stay in, and the local cuisine they will sample while they cruise the canal in total comfort and leisure.

2. The Erie Canal was responsible for a large population surge in western New York. Use the Historical Census Browser at http://fisher.lib.virginia.edu/

collections/stats/histcensus/ and Excel to chart and graph the population surges in towns and cities adjacent to the canal construction. Discuss its historical implications for future construction projects.

SUGGESTED SOURCES

Primary Sources

Garrity, Richard. *Canal Boatman: My Life on Upstate Waterways*. Syracuse, NY: Syracuse University Press, 1977. Contains a personal account of a man who grew up along the Erie Canal and spent his life working on barge canals.

Holtham, Herbert. *An Englishman's Journey Along America's Eastern Waterways: The 1831 Illustrated Journal of Herbert Holtham's Travels*. Rochester, NY: University of Rochester Press, 2000. Provides Holtham's account of his travels in parts of the eastern United States, particularly along the Erie Canal, only six years after its final construction phase. It also includes his pen and ink drawings of the canal and surrounding area.

Morganstein, Martin, and Joan H. Cregg. *Images of America: Erie Canal*. Mount Pleasant, SC: Arcadia Publishing Company, 2001. Provides historical photographs of boats, barges, and constructions aspects of the Erie Canal.

Secondary Sources

Bernstein, Peter L. *Wedding of the Waters: The Erie Canal and the Making of a Great Nation*. New York: W. W. Norton, 2005. Discusses in depth how the building of the Erie Canal changed U.S. history.

Coleman, Wim, and Pat Perrin. *The Amazing Erie Canal and How a Big Ditch Opened Up the West*. Berkeley Heights, NJ: Myreportlinks.com, 2006. Written for secondary students, this title gives an excellent overview of the construction of the Erie Canal and its significance in the expansion of the United States.

Finch, Roy G. *The Story of the New York State Canals: Historical and Commercial Information*. Albany, NY: J. B. Lyon Company, 1925. Provides the history of the canal system written by the state engineer. Renewed in 1998, this work is also available at the New York Canal site at http://www.nyscanals.gov/cculture/history/finch/index.html.

Hawthorne, Nathaniel. "The Canal Boat." *New England Magazine* 9 (December 1835): 398–409. Text available at http://www.history.rochester.edu/canal/bib/hawthorne/canalboat.htm. Describes Hawthorne's trip on the canal and his poor impression of what the canal had done to the environment and the economy.

Hecht, Roger W. *The Erie Canal Reader, 1790–1950.* Syracuse, NY: Syracuse University Press, 2003. Provides poems, essays, travelogues, and fiction written by Hawthorne, Stowe, Twain, Trollope, and other writers who were either inspired or disappointed by the construction of the Erie Canal.

Klees, Emerson. *The Erie Canal in the Finger Lakes Region: The Heart of New York State.* New York: Friends of the Finger Lakes Publishing, 1996. Includes a history of the canal together with accounts of life along it, a history of adjacent towns and villages, and biographical sketches of the primary people who planned, funded, and constructed it.

Larkin, F. Daniel. *The New York State Canals: A Short History.* Fleischmanns, NY: Purple Mountain Press, 1998. Discusses the great competition to construct other canals after the Erie Canal was finished, which helps put this first engineering feat in a historical perspective.

Riley, Kathleen L. *Lockport: Historic Jewel of the Erie Canal.* Mount Pleasant, SC: Arcadia, 2005. The town of Lockport features a double Erie Canal lock built into a granite escarpment. This work traces the construction challenges and the town's history from the moment it became part of the Erie Canal.

Shaw, Ronald E. *Erie Water West: A History of the Erie Canal, 1792–1854.* Lexington, KY: University of Kentucky Press, 1966. Furnishes a scholarly account of the early attempts to build a canal and the use of the canal's profits to establish a development bank for New York State.

Sheriff, Carol. *The Artificial River: The Erie Canal and the Paradox of Progress, 1817–1862.* New York: Hill and Wang, 1996. Cites primary sources to document the environmental, economic, and sociocultural impact that the Erie Canal had not only on western New York State but also America.

World Wide Web

"The Erie Canal." http://www.eriecanal.org/index.html. Provides historical information, images, illustrations, an annotated bibliography, and construction diagrams about the Erie Canal.

"The Erie Canal: A Journey Through History." http://www.epodunk.com/routes/erie-canal/index.html. Features songs, historical information, postcards, photographs, maps, and community profiles about the canal and its national impact.

"Erie Canal—175th Anniversary." http://www.union.edu/News/Events/Celebrations/Erie/. An engaging site with information about how locks work, the history of the Erie Canal, and more.

"Guide to Canal Records." http://www.archives.nysed.gov/a/research/res_topics
_trans_recrds.shtml. Provides surveying and engineering records from
the original construction of the Erie Canal.

"History of the Erie Canal." http://www.history.rochester.edu/canal/. Furnishes
information primarily about the construction of the Erie Canal in and
around Rochester, New York, including nineteenth-century maps, demographic data, and diagrams of barge boats.

"Marco Paul's Travels on the Erie Canal: An Educational Voyage." http://
memory.loc.gov/ammem/ndlpedu/lessons/00/canal/. Sponsored by the
Library of Congress American Memory Project, this site contains
primary sources, questions for possible term papers, and lesson plans.

"New York State Canals." http://www.nyscanals.gov/index.html. Supplies up-to-
date information about the present-day Erie Canal sponsored by the
New York State Canal Corporation.

Multimedia Sources

Canal Towns. Rochester, NY: Public Broadcasting Council, 2000. 1 videocassette. 62 minutes. Includes a 19 minute clip on the legacy of the Erie
Canal.

The Era of the Erie Canal. Lockport, NY: Low Bridge Productions, 2005.
1 DVD. 30 minutes. Features five episodes that show the present-day
Erie Canal, along with the history involved in its construction and completion.

The Erie Canal: Albany to Buffalo. Manlius, NY: Media Artists, 2002. 1 DVD. 75
minutes. Gives a history of the Erie Canal but dwells on its attraction for
tourists today.

Modern Marvels: The Erie Canal. New York: A&E Television Network, 2000.
1 videocassette. 50 minutes. Provides a re-creation of the construction
of the Erie Canal and its significance to the western expansion of the
United States.

19. Seminole Wars (1817–1858)

The Seminole Wars, also known as the Florida Wars, numbered three, and
historians have never been able to agree on their exact dates. They involved
a group of Indian tribes who were not united, but were collectively known
as Seminoles. In 1816 the United States built Fort Scott between Georgia
and Florida, which was then under Spanish control. Across the river, Chief
Neamathla of the Mikasuki settlement headed a village called Fowlstown,

which he used as a staging place for raids into the southeastern United States and a refuge for runaway slaves. His continued hostilities caused Brigadier General Edmund P. Gaines to send several hundred men to attack Fowlstown, igniting the first Seminole War of 1817–1818. Major General Andrew Jackson, soon to be president of the United States, was also commissioned by President James Monroe to wage war. Jackson reached Fort Scott in 1818 with a force of 1,500 men and 2,000 Creek Indians. He trailed the Indians, destroying their villages, and then turned his forces against the remaining Spanish outposts. President Monroe had to return the conquered property to the Spanish, and they in turn deeded it to the United States in 1821. In 1830, Congress passed the Indian Removal Act, which transplanted all eastern Indians somewhere west of the Mississippi River. This act triggered the second Seminole War, which was led by Chief Osceola to resist the loss of ancestral lands and removal to present-day Oklahoma. After seizing Osceola, the United States fought a pitched battle on December 25, 1837, near Lake Okeechobee during which many Indians were killed or captured. By the third war, there were less than four hundred Seminoles living in Florida. It was relatively easy for a superior, well-armed force of Florida volunteers and U.S. troops to force or persuade the remaining Indians to leave their homeland for transportation west. By 1858 there were approximately 125 Seminoles left in Florida.

TERM PAPER SUGGESTIONS

1. Florida had become a refuge for runaway slaves. Discuss why this safety haven posed a threat to people living in the southeastern United States.

2. Throughout Indian history other tribes were manipulated by the United States and Britain not only to achieve military objectives but also to confiscate other tribes' ancestral lands. Analyze how the U.S. policy of divide and conquer enabled the government to succeed in almost extinguishing the indigenous population.

3. How did the forcible removal of the Seminoles help fulfill what was known as America's policy of Manifest Destiny?

4. Discuss the international repercussions of Major General Andrew Jackson's decision to capture a Spanish garrison and invade and seize West Florida.

5. In 1823, the government signed the Treaty of Moultrie Creek with the Seminoles. Analyze the terms, protections, and compensation due the Seminoles. Why was the treaty never really implemented?

6. Discuss the role of Chief Osceola and the Treaty of Payne's Landing in the Seminole War.

ALTERNATIVE TERM PAPER SUGGESTIONS

1. The Seminole Wars are complicated because they raged on and off for so many years and involved many different U.S. government and Indian leaders. Design a Web-based chronology with hyperlinks regarding significant events, battles, and people who played major roles in the wars.

2. Assume you are a negotiator for the government after the first war and have been sent to Florida to settle the Seminole problem. Based upon historical accounts, describe some of the Indians you will need to meet and the promises and the threats that you may make to them to achieve your objectives. Prepare a series of podcasts that will be broadcast to Indian villages telling them what the government is offering to do for them.

SUGGESTED SOURCES

Primary Sources

Bemrose, John. *Reminiscences of the Second Seminole War.* Tampa, FL: University of Tampa Press, 2001. Provides an eyewitness account of an eighteen-year-old enlisted man who served in the Second Regiment of Artillery during the second Seminole War.

Missall, John, and Mary Lou Missall. *The Seminole Wars: America's Longest Conflict.* Gainesville, FL: University Press of Florida, 2004. Replete with diaries, military reports, and archival newspaper articles, this work succinctly describes the three Seminole Wars and their impact on the American Indian population.

Prince, Henry, and Frank Laumer. *Amidst a Storm of Bullets: The Diary of Lt. Henry Prince in Florida, 1836–1842.* Tampa, FL: University of Tampa Press, 1998. Furnishes an eyewitness account of the guerilla war strategies employed by the Seminoles in 1836 at Fort King and Camp Izard.

Wilentz, Sean. *Major Problems in the Early Republic, 1787–1848: Documents and Essays.* Boston, MA: D. C. Heath, 1992. Provides primary source documents about President Jackson and the Indian Removal Act.

Secondary Sources

Elder, John. *Everlasting Fire: Cowokoci's Legacy in the Seminole Struggle Against Western Expansion.* Edmond, OK: Medicine Wheel Press, 2004. Describes how slavery played a major part in the Seminole Wars.

Heidler, David Stephen, and Jeanne Heidler. *Old Hickory's War: Andrew Jackson and the Quest for Empire*. Baton Rouge, LA: Louisiana State University, 2003. Relates the story of Major General Andrew Jackson's defeat of the Creeks and Seminoles as an example of the Manifest Destiny policy of the U.S. government.

Johansen, Bruce E., and Barry M. Pritzker, eds. *Encyclopedia of American Indian History*. New York: ABC CLIO, 2007. This four-volume encyclopedia provides an overview and up-to-date resources about the history of the American Indian, including information about the Seminole Wars.

Knetsch, Joe. *Florida's Seminole Wars 1817–1858*. Mount Pleasant, SC: Arcadia Publishing, 2003. Describes the military tactics of the Seminoles and how they were able to keep the U.S. Army and militias at bay for forty-one years through the use of guerilla warfare.

Laumer, Frank. *Dade's Last Command*. Gainesville, FL: University Press of Florida, 1995. Recounts a successful Indian attack in 1835 on Major Francis Drake's column of soldiers.

Mahon, John K. *History of the Second Seminole War, 1835–1842*. Gainesville, FL: University Press of Florida, 1991. Contains one of the best overviews of the second Seminole War.

Meltzer, Milton. *Hunted Like a Wolf: The Story of the Seminole War*. Sarasota, FL: Pineapple Press, 2004. Provides a well-researched account of the motives, leaders, and legacy of the Seminole Wars.

Milanich, Jerald, and Samuel Proctor, eds. *Tacachale: Essays on the Indians of Florida and Southeastern Georgia during the Historic Period*. Gainesville, FL: University Press of Florida, 1994. Ten authors write essays about the Seminoles and other tribes of the Southeastern United States and describe their circumstances during the early nineteenth century.

O'Brien, Sean Michael. *In Bitterness and in Tears: Andrew Jackson's Destruction of the Creeks and Seminoles*. Guilford, CT: The Lyons Press, 2005. Gives the U.S. government and Indian sides of the Seminole Wars.

Remini, Robert V. *Andrew Jackson and His Indian Wars*. New York: Penguin, 2002. Argues that Jackson's policy of removing the Indians from their ancestral lands may have saved them from complete annihilation.

Sprague, J. T. *The Origin, Progress, and Conclusion of the Florida War*. Tampa, FL: University of Tampa Press, 2000. Includes an excellent overview of a complicated forty-one year conflict that resulted in the hunting down and forcible removal of thousands of Florida Indians.

World Wide Web

"American Military Strategy in the Second Seminole War." http://www.global security.org/military/library/report/1995/WJC.htm. Features a 1995

Master's thesis written by Marine Corps Major John C. White Jr. It includes military lessons and strategies that are applicable to other jungle conflicts such as Vietnam and Cambodia, an annotated bibliography, a chronological list of commanders, and treaty information.

"Judgment Day People & Events: Indian Removal 1814–1858." http://www .pbs.org/wgbh/aia/part4/4p2959.html. Outlines Andrew Jackson's role in Indian removal in terms of costs and hardships. Other tribes are mentioned in addition to the Seminoles.

"Osceola: A Brief Account and Evaluation of His Life." http://www.geocities .com/bigorrin/osceola.htm. This three-part site gives information about Osceola's childhood, military career, death, and legacy.

"Seminole War Chiefs." http://www.afn.org/~micanopy/chiefs.html. Contains an annotated chronology of the Seminole War Chiefs and their respective military campaigns.

"Seminole Wars." http://www.georgiaencyclopedia.org/nge/Article.jsp?id =h-842. Includes a hyperlinked article of the Seminole Wars.

"Seminole Wars Timeline." http://www.tampabayhistorycenter.org/semwars .htm. Provides an annotated chronology of the Seminole Wars, including a list of relevant U.S. military and Indian commanders.

"Wars and Battles, Third Seminole War 1855–58." http://www.u-s-history.com/ pages/h1156.html. Gives a brief, hyperlinked history of the third Seminole War along with links to three other sites with additional information.

Multimedia Sources

America under James Monroe and John Quincy Adams, 1817–1828. Culver City, CA: Social Studies School Service, 2003. 1 videocassette. 15 minutes. Provides information about the first of the Seminole Wars along with other events in both presidents' administrations.

How the West Was Lost. Bethesda, MD: Discovery Channel, 1995. 8 videocassettes. 50 minutes each. Episode three, *Seminole: The Unconquered,* relates the story of the Seminole Wars.

20. *McCulloch v. Maryland* (1819)

Throughout American history there has always been an inherent tension between the rights and powers of individual states and those of the federal government. In 1819 this strain manifested itself in a lawsuit between the State of Maryland and the federal government over the establishment of the Second National Bank of the United States. Maryland did not want federal banks within the state because it believed federal bank managers were corrupt, federal banks created unwanted competition, and federal banks prevented Maryland banks from issuing more paper money than could be redeemed. Maryland decided to levy a high annual tax on each federal bank to discourage their establishment. John McCulloch was the cashier at the Baltimore branch of the Bank of the United States. When he refused to pay the tax, Maryland took him to court. McCulloch was convicted by a Maryland court, but he appealed. His case was heard by the U.S. Supreme Court, which found that federal laws are supreme over state laws and that Congress, by having the ability to tax and spend, can charter a bank as a place to enable the government to collect and disburse revenue.

TERM PAPER SUGGESTIONS

1. One of the reasons Maryland opposed the Bank of the United States was that their managers were corrupt. Find evidence of their corruption and apply it as a rationale for Maryland's imposition of a tax on all federal banks.

2. Alexander Hamilton (Secretary of the Treasury, 1790) and Thomas Jefferson (Secretary of State, 1790) were diametrically opposed to the establishment of a national bank. Choose either cabinet member's viewpoint and defend it, citing their letters, speeches, and correspondence as historical evidence.

3. Federal banks were viewed as competitors by state banks. Discuss how the Federal Bank could threaten state banks.

4. Explain how the chartering of a national bank helped the functioning of the federal government and Congress.

5. The Supreme Court agreed to hear this case because the justices believed that a constitutional principle was at stake. Discuss these issues by citing parts of the Supreme Court's opinion and the Constitution.

6. The Second Bank of the United States (1816) was created to resolve serious national economic problems. Analyze these problems and their implications for the United States.

ALTERNATIVE TERM PAPER SUGGESTIONS

1. Assume that you are a Supreme Court clerk advising Justice John Marshall about the merits of hearing this case. Using the facts and the U.S. Constitution, write a legal memo giving Justice Marshall the pros and cons of accepting the case for argument.

2. Create one chapter of an online graphic nonfiction book that features panels concerning the socioeconomic impact of the Panic of 1819. (You may want to use "Comic Life" software available from the Plasq.com Company.)

SUGGESTED SOURCES

Primary Sources

Hamilton, Alexander. *Alexander Hamilton: A Biography in His Own Words*. New York: Harper & Row, 1973. Edited by Mary Jo Kline, this biography comprises Volumes 1–19 of *The Papers of Alexander Hamilton,* including his financial plans for the creation of a national bank.

Marshall, John. *The Papers of John Marshall: Vol. III: Correspondence, Papers and Selected Judicial Opinions, March 1814–December 1819*. Chapel Hill, NC: University of North Carolina Press, 1995. Includes the text of the *McCulloch v. Maryland* case and essays penned by Marshall in response to questions regarding *McCulloch v. Maryland.*

Marshall, John. *The Papers of John Marshall: Vol. IX: Correspondence, Papers and Selected Judicial Opinions, January 1820–December 1823*. Chapel Hill, NC: University of North Carolina Press, 1998. Provides additional information about *McCulloch v. Maryland* and sheds light on Marshall's concerns about the powers of the Supreme Court.

Secondary Sources

Bowers, Claude Gernade. *Jefferson and Hamilton: The Struggle for Democracy in America*. Boston, MA: Houghton Mifflin, 1925. Outlines the differences these two founding fathers had relating to the financial structure of the country.

Brannen, Daniel E. *Supreme Court Drama: Cases that Changed America*. 4 vols. Detroit, MI: U.X.L., 2001. Volume 4 discusses *McCulloch v. Maryland* and its impact on the financial structure of nineteenth-century America.

Brown, Marion A. *The Second Bank of the United States and Ohio (1803–1860): A Collision of Interests*. Lewiston, NY: Edwin Mellen Press, 1998. Gives an historical account of the tension caused by Federal Banks not only in Maryland but also in Ohio.

Catterall, Ralph C. *The Second Bank of the United States*. Chicago, IL: University of Chicago Press, 1903. Furnishes a scholarly economic account of the establishment of the second Federal Bank, including reasons for its creation.

Crompton, Samuel Willard. *McCulloch v. Maryland: Implied Powers of the Federal Government*. New York: Chelsea House, 2007. Provides an easy-to-understand overview of the historic significance of the case.

Cunningham, Noble E. *Jefferson vs. Hamilton: Confrontations that Shaped a Nation*. Boston, MA: Bedford/St. Martin's Press, 2000. Discusses the great philosophical differences that Hamilton and Jefferson had regarding the creation of a national bank.

Gold, Susan Dudley. *McCulloch v. Maryland: State v. Federal Power*. Tarrytown, NY: Benchmark, 2007. Presents a comprehensible overview of the case and its consequential strengthening of the federal government.

Hall, Kermit L. *The Oxford Companion to the Supreme Court of the United States*. New York: Oxford University Press, 1992. Gives a comprehensible overview of the facts, impact, and influence surrounding the *McCulloch v. Maryland* case.

Killenbeck, Mark Robert. *McCulloch v. Maryland: Securing a Nation*. Lawrence, KS: University Press of Kansas, 2006. Furnishes a scholarly account of the vital importance of this Supreme Court case to establishing a strong federal government.

Rosen, Jeffrey. *The Supreme Court: The Personalities and Rivalries That Defined America*. New York: Henry Holt and Company, 2007. This companion to the PBS television series on the Supreme Court devotes many pages to the role of John Marshall on shaping the powers of the federal government and the significance of the *McCulloch v. Maryland* case.

Taylor, George Rogers. *Jackson Versus Biddle: The Struggle over the Second Bank of the United States*. Boston, MA: D. C. Heath, 1965. Furnishes the reasons relating to the Panic of 1819 that may account for the charges of corruption against the Second Bank of the United States.

World Wide Web

"Hamilton, Alexander—Report of the Secretary of the Treasury to the House of Representatives, Report on the Public Credit, January 9, 1790." http://www.gwu.edu/~ffcp/exhibit/p13/p13_3.html. Describes Alexander Hamilton's plans and reasons for the establishment of a national bank of the United States.

"Landmark Cases of the Supreme Court—*McCulloch v. Maryland*." http://www.landmarkcases.org/mcculloch/home.html. Provides lesson plans, additional resources, and the full text of the case.

"*McCulloch v. Maryland*, 1819." http://www.lectlaw.com/files/case15.htm. Gives the full text of the case, along with excellent explanatory hyperlinks of various legal terms.

"*McCulloch v. Maryland* (1819)." http://usinfo.state.gov/infousa/government/overview/10.html. Furnishes a lengthy analysis of this important Supreme Court case, including its constitutional law implications.

"*McCulloch v. Maryland* (1819)." http://www.ourdocuments.gov/doc.php ?doc=21. Presents a short overview of the case along with images of the original pages of the Supreme Court decision.

"*McCulloch v. Maryland,* 17 U.S. 316 (1819)." http://www.law.cornell.edu/ supct-cgi/get-us-cite?. Provides the full text of the Supreme Court decision.

"Supreme Court History the First Hundred Years." http://www.pbs.org/wnet/ supremecourt/antebellum/landmark_mcculloch.html. This PBS site dedicated to the *McCulloch v. Maryland* Supreme Court case contains primary source excerpts as well as background material related to the case.

Multimedia Sources

Equal Justice under the Law: McCulloch v. Maryland. Capitol Heights, MD: National Audiovisual Center, 1987. 1 videocassette. 30 minutes. Provides a dramatization of the *McCulloch v. Maryland* Supreme Court case.

21. Missouri Compromise (1820)

Although there were two previous debates about slavery—the Constitutional Convention of 1787 and the Slave Trade Act of 1808—slavery reared its ugly head again in 1819 when Missouri requested statehood. The nation was equally divided by eleven northern states that wished to abolish slavery and eleven southern states that did not. Congress called upon Senator Henry Clay of Kentucky to fashion a compromise amenable to both sections of the country. Clay's first attempt involved a Senate bill admitting Maine as a nonslave state, admitting Missouri as a slave state, and limiting slavery in future western states. The first compromise narrowly passed the House of Representatives. Clay drafted a second compromise when Missouri wrote a constitution that banned freed slaves from entering their state. Clay's second provision confirmed Missouri's admission as a state only if Missouri's legislature refused to pass any law that restricted the rights and privileges of the citizens of other states. The debate sparked by the slavery issue raged from December 1819 to March 1820. The compromise held the union together for another thirty years until it was negated by the Kansas-Nebraska Act (1854), which established local choice on the issue of slavery.

TERM PAPER SUGGESTIONS

1. Senator Henry Clay owned many slaves, yet he professed to be against slavery. Site primary sources in the forum of speeches and other correspondence that reveal Clay's ambivalence toward slavery and his participation in an organization that proposed to repatriate African slaves to Africa.

2. Discuss President James Monroe's initial decision to veto any bill that would place limits on slavery in Missouri and his subsequent decision to sign the compromise.

3. Former President Thomas Jefferson was quoted as saying that the Missouri Compromise debate "came like a fire bell in the night." Presented with the same set of circumstances, create a third compromise that may have been acceptable to both sections of the country.

4. The Missouri Compromise was also a debate about politics. The "Three-Fifths" compromise written in the Constitution allowed slaves to be counted as part of the total population for the purposes of allocating congressional representation. Analyze how this provision gave slave states a political advantage over free states.

5. There were economic aspects to the Missouri Compromise. Wage-paying northerners were forced to compete against slave labor in the South. Discuss the implications for employment, productivity, and profit in both sections of the country.

6. The second Missouri Compromise tipped the balance of power in favor of the slave-free northern states. Analyze how the arrangement would affect the South.

ALTERNATIVE TERM PAPER SUGGESTIONS

1. Obtain an online 1816 pre–Missouri Compromise map and a post–Missouri Compromise one. Design a series of hyperlinks that outline and explain both compromises and the potential for violations, especially in territory north of 36°30′.

2. Many Northerners viewed the issue of slavery in Missouri and the western territories in moral terms. Write an online pamphlet complete with graphic illustrations describing how slavery violates the Preamble to the Constitution and fundamental human rights. Site the opinions of Senator Rufus King of New York in support of the cause of abolishment.

SUGGESTED SOURCES

Primary Sources

Finkelman, Paul. *Defending Slavery: Proslavery Thought in the Old South: A Brief History with Documents*. New York: St. Martin's Press, 2003. Cites the

Constitution, Supreme Court cases, and other national documents that the South used to support its position on slavery.

Frohen, Bruce. *The American Republic: Primary Sources.* Indianapolis, IN: Liberty Fund, 2002. Includes hundreds of uninterpreted documents from the American Revolution to shortly before the Civil War, including the Missouri Compromise and documents leading up to it.

Lowance, Mason, ed. *Against Slavery: An Abolitionist Reader.* New York: Penguin, 2000. Contains speeches, lectures, and essays that were used in the abolitionist crusade against slavery including pieces by Harriet Beecher Stowe, Frederick Douglass, Wendell Phillips, and Ralph Waldo Emerson.

Secondary Sources

Baxter, Maurice G. *Henry Clay the Lawyer.* Lexington, KY: University Press of Kentucky, 2000. Provides a scholarly account of the life of Henry Clay with an emphasis on his great abilities as an attorney and negotiator.

Brown, Richard Holbrook. *The Missouri Compromise: Political Statesmanship or Unwise Evasion?* Boston, MA: D. C. Heath, 1964. This classic book describes how the United States simply postponed the inevitable civil war when it settled on the Missouri Compromise as a solution to the slavery problem.

Burgan, Michael. *The Missouri Compromise.* Minneapolis, MN: Compass Point Books, 2006. Written for secondary school students, this easy-to-understand text provides a useful overview of the main points of the Missouri Compromise.

Cawardine, Richard J. *Evangelicals and Politics in Antebellum America.* Nashville, TN: University of Tennessee, 1997. Discusses the powerful role that evangelicals played in formulating moral arguments and raising the level of consciousness concerning the slavery issue.

Fehrenbacher, Don Edward. *Sectional Crisis and Southern Constitutionalism.* Baton Rouge, LA: Louisiana State University Press, 1995. Describes and analyzes the court decisions and parts of the Constitution that the South relied upon to maintain its position on slavery.

Forbes, Robert Pierce. *The Missouri Compromise and Its Aftermath: Slavery and the Meaning of America.* Chapel Hill, NC: University of North Carolina Press, 2007. Delves into the negotiations and trade-offs that were necessary between northern and southern states to effect a compromise that would hold the union together for another thirty years.

King, Charles, ed. *The Life and Correspondence of Rufus King Comprising his Letters, Private and Official, his Public Documents, and his Speeches.* New York: Da Capo Press, 1971. Contains Rufus King's speeches, letters, and relevant documents related to his antislavery position on the Missouri Compromise.

Remini, Robert V. *Henry Clay: Statesman for the Union*. New York: W. W. Norton, 1993. Furnishes an academic biography of Henry Clay complete with primary sources that describes his role in fashioning the Missouri Compromise.

Schurz, Carl. *Life of Henry Clay*. Vols. 1 and 2. Boston, MA: Adamant Media Corporation, 2001. Furnishes the definitive biography of Henry Clay and the role he played in drafting the Missouri Compromise.

Shoemaker, Floyd. *Missouri's Struggle for Statehood, 1804–1821*. New York: Russell & Russell, 1969. Traces the background of the problems about slavery that became the center of the problem facing Missouri when it requested admission into the Union.

Stewart, James B. *Holy Warriors: The Abolitionists and American Slavery*. New York: Hill and Wang, 1997. Provides the background about how abolitionists became such a great force in the North. Chapters 2 and 3 are devoted to a history of the movement prior to the Missouri Compromise.

World Wide Web

"Africans in America—Missouri Compromise 1820." http://www.pbs.org/wgbh/aia/part3/3h511.html. Provides an excellent, brief overview of the Missouri Compromise and a copy of the actual document.

"The Law that Ripped America in Two." http://www.smithsonianmag.com/history-archaeology/law.html. Ross Drake makes history come alive in this online article from *Smithsonian Magazine* about the motives, machinations, and legacy of the Missouri Compromise.

"The Library of Congress—Missouri Compromise." http://www.loc.gov/rr/program/bib/ourdocs/Missouri.html. Includes Missouri's request for admission into the Union, Congressional information related to the Missouri Compromise, correspondence from former President Thomas Jefferson about the Missouri Compromise, and other related primary source documents.

"Library of Congress—Today in History June 29." http://memory.loc.gov/ammem/today/jun29.html. Provides numerous primary source documents about Henry Clay's role in the Missouri Compromise of 1820 and the Compromise of 1850 as well as speeches and other correspondence.

"Map of the United States Free/Slave Soil Map—1820 the Missouri Compromise." http://tah.cusd.com/tah/exhibitions/8th/0809/primarysources.htm. Furnishes a color copy of the map that shows the new boundaries regarding slave and free states after the Missouri Compromise.

"The Missouri Compromise—Cross Tab." http://www.princeton.edu/~vote view/xtabmap.html. Shows the cross tab of the two votes on the Missouri Compromise and how the voting affected whether states and territories were considered free or slave states as part of the Compromise.

"The Missouri Compromise (1820)." http://www.historycentral.com/docu ments/Miscompromise.html. Provides a substantive overview of the Missouri Compromise and discusses its consequences for the Union in the future.

"National Archives—Missouri Compromise." http://www.archives.gov/ historical-docs/todays-doc/index.html?dod-date=306. Contains the committee report transcripts, the transcript of the Missouri Compromise, Congressional Committee reports, slavery records, ideas for further research, questions about the Missouri Compromise, and suggested lesson plans.

Multimedia Sources

Causes of the Civil War. Wynnewood, PA: Schlessinger Media, 2003. 1 DVD. 30 minutes. Part of the series, *The United States History DVD Collection,* shows how the interests of the industrial North and agricultural South were to clash over the request by Missouri for entrance into the Union. The program also covers other explosive events precipitating the Civil War.

Slavery and the Making of America. New York: Ambrose Video Publishing, 2004. 4 DVDs. 60 minutes each. Volume 3, *Seeds of Destruction,* contains reenactments of the events leading up to and concluding with the Missouri Compromise, as seen through the eyes of the enslaved.

22. Land Act of 1820

In the early nineteenth century the federal government had only two sources of income: tariffs and land sales receipts. The tariffs were a constant problem to the South because they increased the price on imported goods that southern states needed to maintain an agricultural economy. Land sales, however, were doubly blessed. They provided revenue to a country saddled with huge debts from the War of 1812, and they furnished a way to expand and settle the West. The act's legislative history originated with such men as Alexander Hamilton, Secretary of the Treasury (1789–1795), who recommended applying the profit generated from land sales to reducing the national debt; Albert Gallatin, Secretary of the Treasury

(1801–1814), who established a system of Land Offices; William Henry Harrison (1811), who after winning the Battle of Tippecanoe expanded settlement into contemporary Indiana; and Anthony Wayne (1745–1796), who was one of the first Army generals to force Indians to cede large tracts of the Old Northwest. Initially land sales were disappointingly slow because land cost $2 per acre and the minimum size was 160 acres. In 1800, however, William Henry Harrison persuaded Congress to modify the sales rules. Buyers were permitted to purchase smaller plots of land and were also allowed to pay on an installment plan. Sales boomed between 1812 and 1819, but also revealed a flaw in the system. Credit purchases were difficult to supervise, and there were almost no time limits on credit payments. In 1820, Congress passed the Land Act, which outlawed credit purchases and reduced the price of land from $2 to $1.25 per acre.

TERM PAPER SUGGESTIONS

1. Examine how the Land Act of 1820 disenfranchised the Indians by making it financially attractive for Euro-Americans to settle in the West.

2. The Land Act of 1820 increased the population in western states. Analyze how it changed the political balance of power among the northern and southern states, especially regarding the slavery issue.

3. The Land Act reduced the minimum acreage requirement from 160 to 80 acres; reduced the price from $1.65 to $1.25 per acre; required a down payment of $100; and extended the time creditors had to finish payments. Discuss how these incentives paved the way for increased settlement of the West.

4. Examine how the Land Act of 1820 assisted President James Polk's speech about "Manifest Destiny."

5. The United States went through many formal treaty arrangements that forced Indians to cede their lands to settlers. Why did they find it necessary to use such legal means when they were simply taking the Indian's property without any real recourse?

6. Describe some of the problems encountered with tribes of the Old Southwest (contemporary states of Alabama, Mississippi, and parts of western Georgia) in gaining their acceptance for ceding their ancestral lands to settlers.

ALTERNATIVE TERM PAPER SUGGESTIONS

1. Prepare a hyperlinked map of the areas that opened for settlement as a result of the Land Act of 1820.

2. Assume you have been hired to prepare a series of brochures that encourage people to purchase land and settle parts of the Old Southwest and Northwest territories. The brochures should include information about the Land Act's purchase requirements but also might downplay possible encounters with hostile Indian tribes and lack of government services and support.

SUGGESTED SOURCES

Primary Sources

"1820—Map: Western Exploration." http://www.lib.utexas.edu/maps/united _states/exploration_1820.jpg. This map shows the areas that were potentially open to western expansion as a result of the Land Act of 1820.

Hart, Albert Bushnell. "The Acquisition and Disposition of the Public Lands." *The Quarterly Journal of Economics* 1 (January 1887): 251–254. (Available in JSTOR.) Presents tabulated census data concerning how much land was acquired by the United States from 1783 to 1883. The tables are useful for calculating the amount of land acquired prior to and after passage of the Land Act of 1820.

Secondary Sources

Cartensen, Vernon, ed. *The Public Lands: Studies in the History of the Public Domain.* Madison, WI: University of Wisconsin Press, 1963. Provides a scholarly account of the most controversial issues surrounding the public land acts.

Clark, Thomas D., and John D. W. Guice. *Frontiers in Conflict: The Old Southwest, 1795–1830.* Albuquerque, NM: University of New Mexico Press, 1989. Relates the problems with the tribes of the Old Southwest in getting them to cede their lands by treaty or forcibly removing them from the land.

Gates, Paul W. *History of Public Land Law Development.* Washington, DC: Zenger, 1968. Contains information about all the land laws that the United States passed during settlement of its territories prior to statehood.

Hurt, Douglas. *The Ohio Frontier: Crucible of the Old Northwest, 1726–1830.* Bloomington, IN: Indiana University Press, 1996. Provides a comprehensive history of the early settlement of Ohio, a major territory affected by the Land Act of 1820.

Junkin, Elizabeth Darby. *Lands of Brighter Destiny: The Public Lands of the American West.* Golden, CO: Fulcrum, 1986. Analyzes how the lure of cheap land tantalized people to settle the West in the hope of a better economic future.

Lebergott, Stanley. "The Demand for Land: The United States, 1820–1860." *The Journal of Economic History* 45 (June 1985): 181–212. (Available in JSTOR.) Traces the insatiable demand for land by immigrants and farmers to inherited attitudes about the creation of wealth and government policies, including passage of the Land Act of 1820.

McCluggage, Robert W. "The Senate and Indian Land Titles, 1800–1825." *The Western Historical Quarterly* 1 (October 1970): 415–425. (Available in JSTOR.) Analyzes how the Senate systematically controlled the titles to Indian lands through a series of limiting agreements that they assumed the Indians would have little knowledge of or voice in.

North, Douglas, and Andrew R. Rutten. "The Northwest Ordinance in Historical Perspective." In *Essays on the Economy of the Old Northwest,* edited by David C. Klingaman and Richard K. Vedder. Athens, OH: Ohio University Press, 1968. Contains a useful history of the problems associated with the Land Act of 1820, specifically in the Old Northwest.

Rezneck, Samuel. "The Depression of 1819–1822, A Social History." *The American Historical Review* 39 (October 1933): 28–7. (Available in JSTOR.) Discusses the panic and subsequent depression of 1819 and its resulting depreciation of land values. This slump may have been a factor in the U.S. government's passing the Land Act of 1820 to gain needed revenue and make land affordable despite an economic recession.

Rohrbough, Malcolm J. *The Land Office Business: The Settlement and Administration of American Public Lands, 1789–1837.* New York: Oxford University Press, 1968. Gives a scholarly account of how the business of surveying, selling, and collecting revenues for public lands functioned and malfunctioned.

Sword, Wiley. *President Washington's Indian War: The Struggle for the Old Northwest, 1790–1795.* Norman, OK: University of Oklahoma Press, 1985. Details the confrontations and hostilities that President Washington had with Indians east of the original thirteen colonies in an effort to free up the territory for settlers.

World Wide Web

"About.com—A History of American Agriculture 1776–1879." http://www.publiclands.org/museum/story/story09.htm. Provides a useful chronology that shows how the government passed numerous land acts and other measures to ensure westward expansion and the eventual union of all the states.

"Georgia's Land Lottery." http://ngeorgia.com/history/lotteries.html. Furnishes a short history about how the largest land lotteries of 1805 and 1820 robbed the Creek and Cherokee Indians of their ancestral lands.

"A History of American Agriculture." http://www.agclassroom.org/gan/timeline/
1820.htm. This site is not in exact chronological order, but it does give a
timetable for other events that may have impacted passage of the Land
Act of 1820.

"Land Act of 1820." http://www.ohiohistorycentral.org/entry.php?rec=1473.
Discusses the impact and legacy of the Land Act of 1820 in relation to
the development and growth of the State of Ohio.

"Library of Congress—American State Papers, Senate, 19th Congress, 1st Session Public Lands: Volume 4, pages 769 through 770, No. 520. Opera-
tion of the act to provide for the extinguishment of the debt due the
United States by the purchasers of public lands prior to July 1, 1820."
http://memory.loc.gov/. Type the words "land act of 1820" and click
on this citation. Provides the full text of the law that relieved land owners
of prior land debts.

"Relief Act of 1821." http://www.ohiohistorycentral.org/entry.php?rec=1441.
Details the reasons that the government needed to pass the Relief Act
to enable Ohioans to return land they had bought, reduce the price per
acre, and provide other stopgap measures to assist citizens in dealing with
the depression caused by the Panic of 1819.

"The Story of Public Lands." http://www.publiclands.org/museum/story/
story09.htm. Furnishes a timetable of important acts and decisions in
the disposition and management of government public lands from
1785 to 1879.

Multimedia Sources

America's History in the Making. Washington, DC: Annenberg Media, 2007.
1 DVD. 59 minutes. Program No. 7, "Contested Territories." Furnishes
an exploration of America's contested territories during the western
expansion. The unit also comes with a facilitator's guide and additional
teacher's materials that are available at http://www.learner.org/resources/
series208.html.

23. Survival on the *Essex* (1820) and Mutiny on the *Globe* (1824)

Although these maritime disasters are four years apart, they share a
common origin. Both were Nantucket whaling ships on voyages to hunt
whales for their oil to light homes and businesses. The *Essex* left Nantucket
in 1819. About 2,000 miles off the coast of Ecuador, on November 20,

1820, the ship was rammed by an eighty-foot sperm whale and sunk. Initially twenty sailors survived in three open boats. After landing on Henderson Island (a modern-day island in the Pitcairns), the sailors began to die from dehydration and malnutrition. They eventually resorted to cannibalism. When they were rescued on April 5, 1821, there were only eight survivors.

The *Globe*'s misfortunes, on the other hand, were planned by a demented, delusional man named Samuel Comstock. In 1824, two years out on the voyage, he organized a mutiny and killed the *Globe*'s officers. Comstock intended to found his own island kingdom on an atoll in the Marshall Islands. Within days of landing, he was killed by his fellow conspirators. George Comstock, who was Samuel's brother, and six other men retook the *Globe,* while most of the others were killed by islanders. The U.S. schooner, *Dolphin,* made a daring land rescue of the remaining survivors, some of whom wrote first-person accounts of their trials and tribulations.

TERM PAPER SUGGESTIONS

1. Read selections from the first-person accounts of Owen Chase, Thomas Nickerson, and others who survived the *Essex* sinking. Analyze why they might have been able to survive while others did not.

2. The remaining crew of the *Essex* had a terrible fear of making landfall in a place where there might be hostile islanders who would practice cannibalism. Examine some of the locations they considered and show how their final decision to sail south was a fatal one for some of them.

3. The *Essex* was twenty years old when she was struck by the sperm whale. Research the upkeep on the *Essex* and decide whether her owners should be held liable because her maintenance was inadequate.

4. Although Samuel Comstock was considered demented, he was still able to convince a majority of the *Globe*'s crew to seize the ship and kill her officers. Describe the living and working conditions on the *Globe* and the crews' lack of success at hunting whales as possible causes for mutiny.

5. Assume you are a surviving *Globe* crewmember with little knowledge of the Pacific Ocean and navigation. Discuss how the crewmembers might have made their decision to sail to Valparaiso, Chile. Research and establish the correct navigation course.

6. One reason both ships traveled to the Pacific Ocean was that the eastern Atlantic right whale population had been seriously overhunted by 1820.

Trace the history of this depletion and discuss its legacy for the present-day population of eastern Atlantic right whales.

ALTERNATIVE TERM PAPER SUGGESTIONS

1. Write a series of historically accurate online, illustrated letters using the prose style of Herman Melville to describe the *Essex* encounter with the sperm whale.

2. Assume you are a public relations consultant who has been hired by the owners of the *Globe* for damage control purposes. Provide a detailed plan for handling the press and bad publicity about the mutiny.

SUGGESTED SOURCES

Primary Sources

Chase, Owen. *The Wreck of the Whaleship* Essex. San Diego, CA: Harcourt Brace, 1999. Written in 1821, this book relates the experience of First Mate Owen Chase when his ship, *The Essex,* was rammed and sunk by a huge sperm whale. Owen's son passed a copy of his father's book to Herman Melville where it became the inspiration for his sea classic, *Moby Dick.*

Chase, Owen, et al. *The Loss of the Ship* Essex *by a Whale*. New York: Penguin, 2000. Contains more than Chase's personal account of the *Essex* disaster. It also features first-person accounts by Thomas Nickerson, a fifteen-year-old cabin boy, plus period newspaper and magazine articles that described the event.

Gibson, Gregory. *Demon of the Waters: The True Story of the Mutiny on the Whaleship* Globe. Reprint ed. Boston, MA: Little, Brown, 2003. Using the 1827 notebook of a seventeen-year-old sailor named Augustus Strong, who was on a rescue ship searching for the remaining *Globe* crew, the author tells the entire mutiny tale along with information about the Nantucket whaling industry.

Secondary Sources

Busch, Briton Cooper. *Whaling Will Never Do for Me: The American Whaleman in the Nineteenth Century*. Lexington, KY: University of Kentucky Press, 1994. Describes the harsh and usually short life of American seamen in the nineteenth-century whaling industry.

Dolin, Eric Jay. *Leviathan: The History of Whaling in America*. New York: W. W. Norton & Company, 2007. Provides an exciting, well-researched history of centuries of American whaling, including information about the *Globe* mutiny and the sinking of the *Essex.*

Ellis, Richard. *Men and Whales*. New York: The Lyons Press, 1999. Traces the physical and mythical relationship between man and whales back to the time of Alexander the Great and how man's fascination led to his hunting of them and the destruction of some of the species.

Heffernan, Thomas Farel. *Mutiny on the* Globe: *Fatal Voyage of Samuel Comstock*. New York: W. W. Norton & Company, 2002. Heffernan makes this grisly moment on the high seas come alive by skillfully weaving primary sources about Samuel Comstock and the *Globe* into a narrative of terror on the high seas replete with mutineers, belligerent natives, and delusion.

Heffernan, Thomas Farel. *Stove by a Whale: Owen Chase and the* Essex. Middletown, CT: Wesleyan University Press, 1990. Cites primary source books, ships' logs, court records, and ships' and museums' records to document what exactly transpired when the *Essex* was sunk 2,000 miles west of Ecuador by a sperm whale.

Hoyt, Edwin. *The Mutiny on the Globe*. New York: Random House, 1975. Provides an overview and historical account of what transpired during the *Globe* mutiny.

Kraus, Scott D., and Rosalind Rolland, eds. *The Urban Whale: North Atlantic Right Whales at the Crossroads*. Cambridge, MA: Harvard University Press, 2007. Provides historical background about how the right whales living in the North Atlantic were hunted almost to extinction in addition to information about 300 presently residing on the east coast of North America.

Murphy, Jim. *Gone A-Whaling: The Lure of the Sea and the Great Whale*. New York: Clarion, 1998. Written for secondary school students, this exciting history uses diaries and other primary sources to bring alive the whaling industry in the nineteenth century.

Philbrick, Nathaniel. *In the Heart of the Sea: The Tragedy of the Whaleship* Essex. New York: Penguin, 2001. Using primary sources, Philbrick recounts the sinking of the whaling ship *Essex* by an eighty-foot sperm whale in the Pacific Ocean as well as the grim details about the survivors' ordeal in an open boat for ninety-three days with little water, food, or hope.

Philbrick, Nathaniel. *The Revenge of the Whale: The True Story of the Whaleship* Essex. New York: Puffin, 2000. Written for secondary school students, this work provides an excellent overview of the event together with excerpts from primary sources.

Severin, Timothy. *In Search of Moby Dick: The Quest for the White Whale*. New York: Basic Books, 2000. To separate fact from fiction regarding Herman Melville's great sea classic, *Moby Dick,* Severin visits the little known island of Lamarala where they still hunt whales with spears.

World Wide Web

"History of Whaling and Estimated Kill of Right Whales, Balaena glacialis, in the Northeastern United States, 1620–1924—Statistical Data Included." http://findarticles.com/p/articles/mi_m3089/is_3_61/ai_65344736. Available through FindArticles.com, this site contains the full text statistical table of an article by Edward D. Mitchell published in the Summer 1999 issue of *Marine Fisheries Review.* The statistics tell the sorry tale of how Nantucket whalers killed the local right whales and had to venture after larger whales in the Pacific Ocean.

"Moby Dick." http://www.pbs.org/odyssey/class/mobydick.html. Provides information about how Herman Melville served on a whaleship and obtained the information that inspired him to write his great sea classic, *Moby Dick.*

"Mutiny on the Globe: The Fatal Voyage of Samuel Comstock." http://books.google.com. Contains the table of contents and the full text, with the exception of pages 7–12, of Chapter 1 from Thomas Heffernan's book about the *Globe* mutiny.

"Nantucket and Whaling." http://www.pbs.org/odyssey/class/nantucket.html. Furnishes information about Nantucket and their domination of the global whale oil business in the nineteenth century.

"Overview of American Whaling." http://www.whalingmuseum.org/library/index.html. Compiled by the New Bedford (MA) Whaling Museum, this site provides an excellent summary of the history of the American whaling industry, including separate links about hunting whales, varieties of whales, ships, ship life, and the inspiration for *Moby Dick.*

"Whaleship *Essex.*" http://www.pbs.org/odyssey/class/essex.html. The contemporary ship *Odyssey* revisits the events and scene of the wreck of the *Essex.* The site also includes external links about Nantucket and the whaling industry as well as artifacts from Nickerson's and Chase's first-person accounts.

"The Wreck of the Whaleship *Essex.*" http://www.bbc.co.uk/dna/h2g2/classic/A671492. Provides an excellent overview of the entire event presented in outline form.

Multimedia Sources

"*Globe* Mutiny." Contains a "Talking History" program with Eileen Dugan interviewing Gregory Gibson, author of *Demon in the Waters: The True Story of the Mutiny on the Whaleship* Globe. Available in MP3 format at http://talkinghistory.oah.org/arch2003.html. Airdate: September 29, 2003.

"The History of Whaling in Albany, Australia." http://www.pbs.org/odyssey/
class/albany.html. Provides Australian news footage from the 1950s
showing how use of the modern-day harpoon gun brought so many
whale species, including the sperm whale, to the brink of extinction.

24. Santa Fe Trail (1821)

It was not "gold in them thar hills" that led William Becknell and
his band of thirty men to find an overland trade route from Franklin,
Missouri, to Santa Fe, New Mexico, in 1821; it was to trade fabricated
goods in exchange for Mexican silver dollars and furs. Long the province
of Spain, which vigorously defended any attempt to settle Santa Fe by
confiscating traders' goods and imprisoning wagoners, Santa Fe officially
became a northern province of the Republic of Mexico in 1821 when
Becknell and his men blundered into an encampment of Mexican soldiers. Mexico's economy was in a shambles after a ten-year revolution
against Spain and the U.S. economy was recovering from the Panic of
1819, so trade was mutually beneficial. Becknell returned to Missouri
laden with silver dollars. One of his investors realized a $900 profit on a
$60 investment. Becknell returned to map the official route and improve
methods of travel. Wagons loaded with manufactured goods left Franklin,
Missouri, traveled up the Arkansas River Valley, then southwest through
the Raton Pass in Colorado to Santa Fe. It was a difficult and dangerous
route with many traders encountering hostile Comanche and Kiowa
Indians and harsh weather when crossing the Great Plains and Cimarron
Desert. In 1822, Becknell pioneered a more direct route through the
desert known as the Cimarron Cutoff that no longer required wagoners
to ascend the Raton Pass with heavy loads. Trade was brisk for almost
six decades until the Atchison, Topeka, and Santa Fe Railroad displaced
the famous trail in 1880.

TERM PAPER SUGGESTIONS

1. For years Mexico had suffered from currency depletion because its
   mineral wealth was being shipped to Spain. At the same time, the Panic of
   1819 worsened the currency shortage in the United States. Investigate the
   mutual advantages for trade between the United States and Mexico during
   this period.

2. Examine how the Santa Fe Trail served as a conduit for social and economic exchanges between Mexico and the United States.

3. Smuggling was rife along the trail because Mexico lacked the personnel to regulate the borders. Analyze how Mexico lost wealth because officials were either unable to collect trail taxes or traders bribed officials to let them avoid payment.

4. Describe the role that William Becknell played in discovering, marking, and developing the Santa Fe Trail including the Cimarron Cutoff.

5. Use of the Santa Fe Trail brought traders into contact with the Comanche and Kiowa tribes who resented their homelands being invaded. Examine the impact of the Santa Fe Trail on both tribes.

6. Traders who used the Santa Fe Trail soon realized that Mexico's military was not up to par with that of the United States. Discuss how this knowledge provided the United States with military intelligence that encouraged them to take over the region.

ALTERNATIVE TERM PAPER SUGGESTIONS

1. Refer to the map of the Santa Fe Trail at http://en.wikipedia.org/wiki/Image:1845_trailmap.gif. Use Google Earth to compare settlement in the area from that time to present day. Conclude with a discussion of the Santa Fe Trail's legacy.

2. Refer to the Historical Census Browser at http://www.sscnet.ucla.edu/issr/da/index/techinfo/M10141.HTM. Obtain census data for the counties and towns along the trail from 1821 to 1880. Use Excel to graph changes in population along the trail. Discuss the implications for growth and development.

SUGGESTED SOURCES

Primary Sources

Coues, Elliot, eds. *The Journal of Jacob Fowler, 1821–1822*. New York: Frances P. Harper, 1898. Describes how Jacob Fowler and Hugh Glen traced the route of the Arkansas River and obtained permission to trap and trade in Mexican territory in 1821. Their work laid the foundation for Becknell's success in mapping the trail.

Gregg, Josiah. *Commerce of the Prairies*. Reprint. Harrisburg, PA: Stackpole Books, 2001. Provides a riveting account of the author's four trips on the Santa Fe Trail during the 1830s and 1840s, including his encounters with Indians.

"Trail West Maps." http://www.nps.gov/archive/safe/fnl-sft/maps/map6n/map6 n.htm. Provides maps of the various Santa Fe Trail routes along with names of cities and towns, trail photographs, weather forecasts, and an interpretative history.

Secondary Sources

Albert, Lieutenant James William. *Expedition to the Southwest: An 1845 Recon-naissance of Colorado, New Mexico, Texas, and Oklahoma*. Lincoln, NE: University of Nebraska Press, 1999. The writer was commissioned in 1845 to survey the Southwest, which was part of Mexico. His firsthand encounters with the Kiowa and Comanche tribes, who viewed him with total suspicion, are very enlightening.

Beachum, Larry M. *William Becknell: Father of the Santa Fe Trade*. El Paso, TX: Texas Western Press, 1982. Furnishes an outstanding overview of the role William Becknell played in the growth and development of the Santa Fe Trail.

Dary, David. *The Santa Fe Trail: Its History, Legends, and Lore*. Reprint. New York: Penguin Books, 2002. Contains a well-written and exciting account of the complete history of the Santa Fe Trail.

DuBuys, William. *Enchantment and Exploitation: The Life and Hard Times of a New Mexico Mountain Range*. Albuquerque, NM: University of New Mexico Press, 1985. Gives useful information about the social and economic changes of the lower Rockies after the opening of the Santa Fe Trail.

Gardner, Mark L. *Wagons for the Santa Fe Trade: Wheeled Vehicles and Their Makers, 1820–1880*. Albuquerque, NM: University of New Mexico Press, 2001. Provides a lavishly illustrated volume of the types of wagons used to carry freight from Missouri to New Mexico that satisfied the weight and tax requirements of the Mexican government.

Hall, Thomas D. *Social Change in the Southwest, 1350–1880*. Lawrence, KS: University Press of Kansas, 1989. Contains an analysis of the impact of marriage and trade on families in the Santa Fe area.

Hyslop, Stephen G. *Bound for Santa Fe: The Road to New Mexico and the American Conquest, 1806–1848*. Norman, OK: University of Oklahoma Press, 2002. Provides a thorough history of the Santa Fe Trail replete with primary source narratives. Hyslop also deals with the cultural differences that existed then and continue today between Americans and Mexicans.

Simmons, Marc, ed. *On the Santa Fe Trail*. Lawrence, KS: University Press of Kansas, 1986. Contains a collection of first-person accounts by people who traveled the Santa Fe Trail during the nineteenth century.

Simmons, Marc. *Yesterday in Santa Fe: Episodes in a Turbulent History.* Santa Fe, NM: Sunstone Press, 1989. Furnishes an exciting history of Santa Fe up until the coming of the railroad in 1880.

Young, Otis. *The First Military Escort on the Santa Fe Trail, 1829.* Glendale, CA: Arthur H. Clark, 1952. Describes the attacks on the wagon trains by hostile Kiowa and Comanche Indian tribes.

World Wide Web

"Best of Wagon Tracks." http://www.santafetrail.org/wagontracks/Hiram_Young .pdf. Relates the story of African American Hiram Young's business adventures on the Santa Fe Trail.

"Kansas Collection: Kansas Historical Quarterlies—A Robbery on the Santa Fe Trail, 1827." http://www.kancoll.org/khq/1955/55_3_covington.htm. Contains an article with the full text of a letter to Congress by several tradesmen who were robbed of their goods by Pawnee Indians while on the Santa Fe Trail. In the letter, they request protection and support from the U.S. government.

"The Old Santa Fe Trail: The Story of a Great Highway by Colonel Henry Inman." http://www.kspatriot.org/library/khnsantafetrail.htm. Contains an outstanding online book giving an account of the development and events of the Santa Fe Trail. The following chapters are particularly useful: Chapter 3 relates the founding of the trail and Becknell's role; Chapter 4 recounts the trials and tribulations of the caravans; and Chapter 5 tells the story of a battle with the Comanches.

"Santa Fe Trail." http://www.bicknell.net/sftrail.htm. Provides an excellent overview of the founding of the Santa Fe Trail by William Becknell, including his encounters with various Indian tribes.

"The Santa Fe Trail." http://www.sangres.com/history/santafetrail/index.htm. Features trail maps, illustrations of caravans, a history of the trail, and more.

"Santa Fe Trail Links." http://www.over-land.com/santafe.html. Includes links to maps, articles, routes, and histories of the trail.

"The Topic: Santa Fe Trail." http://www.42explore2.com/santafe.htm. Contains many links to maps, routes, and the history of the Santa Fe Trail.

Multimedia Sources

The West. Santa Monica, CA: PBS Home Video, 1996. 5 DVDs. 70 minutes each. Disc 2, *Empire upon the Trails.* Includes information about the Santa Fe Trail. Click on http://www.pbs.org/weta/thewest/program/ to obtain a multimedia-guided tour of each episode in the series along with selected documentary materials, archival images and commentary, and links to background information and other resources of the Web site.

25. American Colonization Society and the Founding of Liberia (1822)

In the nineteenth century, as more people came to regard slavery as a moral wrong, abolitionists, religious leaders, and politicians sought solutions to the problems of emancipated slaves and incompatibility of the races. In 1816, Charles Fenton Mercer, a Virginia legislator, proposed the idea of black colonization. His brother-in-law, Presbyterian minister Robert Finley, founded an organization whose full name was the American Society for Colonizing the Free People of Color of the United States (ACS). The ACS had many prominent members, including Francis Scott Key, Henry Clay, and John Randolph. They raised funds by selling memberships and successfully lobbied Congress for funds to support their cause. President Abraham Lincoln was also a proponent of the ACS's cause and tried on numerous occasions to arrange resettlements. In 1820, the ACS obtained sufficient funds from Congress, purchased a ship, and with eighty-eight emigrants set sail for West Africa. Their first attempt failed, but, after negotiations with African chiefs, they were able to purchase land in the Cape Mesurado area, now the site of Monrovia, Liberia. Between 1821 and 1867 the ACS helped ten thousand African Americans, together with several thousand Africans from interdicted slave ships, resettle in Africa. Although support for resettlement ceased after the U.S. Civil War, the ACS continued to fund educational and missionary activities for African Americans until 1964.

TERM PAPER SUGGESTIONS

1. Another motivation for resettlement of freed slaves may have been the rebellion of one thousand slaves led by Gabriel Prosser from Virginia in 1800. Discuss the fears of states that had significant slave populations. What may have motivated them to support colonization of freed slaves?

2. Some members of the ACS were abolitionists and others were slave owners. Both groups, however, held similar beliefs about the inability of freed African Americans to assimilate within the white population. Discuss whether the society's doubts were justified or unjustified.

3. After the Civil War, many African Americans wished to emigrate to Liberia. Explore the reasons why neither the government nor the ASC was interested in paying their passage.

4. Ironically the treatment of African tribal chiefs by African Americans was similar to the treatment that Native American chiefs suffered under white settlers. Discuss the role that Jehudi Ashmun played in enlarging Liberia at the expense of native Africans.

5. From the beginning there was mutual mistrust between the newly arrived and indigenous Liberians. Discuss how their mutual mistrust and hostility toward one another manifested itself in employment discrimination, participation in government, and land ownership. Examine how this bifurcation in society may have contributed to the 1989 and 1999 Liberian Civil Wars.

6. Outline what would have been lost to American culture if all free persons of color had chosen to emigrate to Liberia. Be sure to include contributions to American music, art, dance, diet, science, and literature.

ALTERNATIVE TERM PAPER SUGGESTIONS

1. Prepare an online pamphlet addressed to freed African Americans that would encourage them to emigrate to Liberia. Describe the climate and economic and social potential of the country.

2. Assume you are a nineteenth-century demographer who has been asked to use census data to analyze how many free persons of color might consider emigrating to Liberia. Use the Historical Census Browser to determine the numbers for the years 1821–1867. Investigate the economic implications of paying to transport this population to Liberia.

SUGGESTED SOURCES

Primary Sources

Garrison, William Lloyd. *Thoughts on African Colonization: Or an Impartial Exhibition of the Doctrines, Principles and Purposes of the American Colonization Society.* Boston, MA: Adamant Media Corporation, 2005. Presents the thoughts of William Lloyd Garrison, noted nineteenth-century abolitionist and editor of *The Liberator,* an antislavery newspaper, on the idea of resettlement of free persons of color to Africa.

Hall, Richard L. *On Africa's Shore: A History of Maryland in Liberia, 1834–1857.* Baltimore, MD: Maryland Historical Society, 2005. Contains first-person accounts of freed slaves who were repatriated to Liberia by the Maryland Colonization Society in 1834.

Stebbins, Giles Badger. *Facts and Opinions Touching the Real Origin, Character and Influence of the American Colonization Society: Views of Wilberforce, Clarkson and Others and...Free People of Color of the United States.* New York: Negro Universities Press, 1969. Provides the opinions of British abolitionists, William Wilberforce, Thomas Clarkson, and others, about the motivation for the ACS.

Secondary Sources

Barnes, Kenneth C. *Journey of Hope: The Back-to-Africa Movement in Arkansas in the Late 1800s.* Chapel Hill, NC: University of North Carolina Press, 2004. Relates the history of delegates who met at a Baptist church in Arkansas on November 23, 1877, to make plans to emigrate to Liberia. All were suffering from the enactment of Jim Crow laws and segregation in schools, housing, and employment.

Beyan, Amos Jones. *The American Colonization Society and the Creation of the Liberian State: A Historical Perspective, 1822–1900.* Landham, MD: University Press of America, 1991. Traces the history of the ACS from its initial stage of resettlement to one of missionary and educational work.

Burin, Eric. *Slavery and the Peculiar Solution: A History of the American Colonization Society.* Gainesville, FL: University Press of Florida, 2005. Provides an objective history of the ACS from historians who portray it as a proslavery movement to those who envisioned it as an abolitionist movement.

Ellis, Stephen. *The Mask of Anarchy: The Destruction of Liberia and the Religious Dimension of an African Civil War.* New York: New York University Press, 2006. Traces the ethnic, political, and cultural roots of the Liberian civil wars and details how these problems still persist.

Fox, Early Lee. *The American Colonization Society, 1817–1840.* New York: AMS Press, 1971. Contains an overview of the ACS movement from the early to mid-nineteenth century.

Hyman, Lester S. *United States Policy Towards Liberia, 1822–2003: Unintended Consequences.* Cherry Hill, NJ: Africana Homestead Legacy, 2006. Chapter 1 is devoted solely to tracing the settlement of Liberia by free persons of color and its consequences for the future of Liberia.

Levitt, Jerry. *The Evolution of Deadly Conflict in Liberia: From "Paternaltarianism" to State Collapse.* Durham, NC: Carolina Academic Press, 2005. Contains scholarly support for the historical causes of contemporary anarchy in Liberia, some of which were based on initial authoritarianism by repatriated settlers from America.

Pham, John-Peter. *Liberia: Portrait of a Failed State.* New York: Reed Press, 2004. Gives a scholarly account of how the seeds for Liberia's failed attempts at democracy may have been sown in the past because of Western intervention and colonization efforts.

Sawyer, Amos. *The Emergence of Autocracy in Liberia: Tragedy and Challenge.* San Francisco, CA: Institute for Contemporary Studies, 1992. Discusses the colonial history of Liberia and how it contributed to its failure to achieve a true democracy in the twentieth century.

Tyler-McGraw, Marie. *An African Republic: Black and White Virginians in the Making of Liberia.* Chapel Hill, NC: University of North Carolina Press, 2007. Provides demographic data and a discussion of why the repatriation of thousands of free persons of color to Liberia could never have been accomplished.

Yarema, Allen E. *The American Colonization Society: An Avenue to Freedom?* Landham, MD: University Press of America, 2006. Examines how the decision by free persons of color to emigrate to Liberia may have been a passport to disaster for them and their descendants.

World Wide Web

"American Colonization Society." http://www.loc.gov/rr/print/coll/007.html. Presents selected holdings and images from the reports of the ACS, which donated them in 1913, 1964, and 1965.

"American Colonization Society." http://www.pbs.org/wgbh/aia/part3/3p1521.html. Provides a brief overview that answers the basic questions concerning the founding and development of the American Colonization Society.

"American Colonization Society: A Memorial to the United States Congress." http://www.pbs.org/wgbh/aia/part3/3h483t.html. Contains the full text of a letter from the ACS to the U.S. Congress, summarizing its aims to colonize Liberia with free persons of color and simultaneously promote antislavery positions.

"Colonization—The African-American Mosaic—The Library of Congress." http://www.loc.gov/exhibits/african/afam002.html. This mega site features primary source documents in the form of letters, images, maps, and oral histories of the settlement of Liberia by free persons of color from the United States.

"Douglas Egerton on the Black Support for the ACS." http://www.pbs.org/wgbh/aia/part3/3i3132.html. Contains a short question and answer session by historian Douglas Egerton on the economic motivations behind the ACS's decision to support emigration by free persons of color to Liberia.

"Introduction to the Liberian Letters." http://etext.lib.virginia.edu/subjects/liberia/intro.html. Contains the full text of two collections of letters written by former Virginia slaves who settled in Liberia from 1834 to 1866.

"Liberia." http://www-sul.stanford.edu/depts/ssrg/africa/liberia.html. Furnishes an outstanding webography of links, ranging from the early colonization of Liberia to the present-day political situation.

"Library of Congress—History of Liberia: A Timeline." http://memory.loc.gov/ammem/gmdhtml/libhtml/liberia.html. Presents a useful, annotated chronology from 1815 to 1997 of the major events, people, and issues about the founding of Liberia.

Multimedia Sources

Africans in America. Alexandria, VA: PBS Home Video, 1998. 2 DVDs. 180 minutes. Part 3, *Journey through Slavery (1791–1831),* of this six-part series contains information about the American Colonization Society.

"The Colonization of Liberia." http://www.english.ilstu.edu/students/sekoca/repurposingsite/liberiahistory.html. Provides a valid PowerPoint presentation replete with maps and other images of the early settlement of Liberia by free persons of color and the legacy of that decision for Liberia's indigenous population.

"Maryland Historical Society Library—American Colonization Society/Liberia Collection." http://www.mdhs.org/library/fotofind/PP0161lnk.html. Contains twenty-six photographs of Liberian immigrants and buildings and places in Liberia from 1827 to 1871.

26. Monroe Doctrine (1823)

On December 2, 1823, President James Monroe delivered an address to Congress that proclaimed that the United States would not tolerate intervention in the Americas (North, Central, and South America) by European nations and that it would not interfere with already established colonies or with governments in Europe. Crafted by Secretary of State John Quincy Adams, the speech became known as the Monroe Doctrine and is still considered a cornerstone of the foreign policy of the United States. Its impetus arose from a Russian czar who declared an area north of the fifty-first parallel and one hundred miles into the Pacific Ocean to be off-limits to non-Russians and revolutions for independence in South American colonies that were threatening to reassert European rule in the area by Spain and France. The United States was feeling confident when it announced this policy. The nation was expanding westward, the northeastern part of the country was beginning to industrialize, and a series of treaties after the War of 1812 had helped to solidify its boundaries and remove the threat of another war with Britain. Initially the doctrine was viewed as an act of isolationism on the part of the United States and a desire to withdraw from the constant wars in Europe. It was also viewed as a strong statement of independence from any interference or domination by a foreign power and America's willingness to defend herself militarily against such threats. As time passed, however, the Monroe Doctrine was also interpreted to justify the annexation of Texas from Mexico, as well as military interventions in Central and South America.

TERM PAPER SUGGESTIONS

1. Revolutions for independence were already occurring in South America when British Foreign Secretary George Canning approached Secretary of State John Quincy Adams to propose that Britain and the United States write a joint proposal warning France and Spain to desist intervening in these burgeoning South American republics. Examine the pros and cons of the United States formulating a foreign policy with Britain. Be sure to cite Adams's objections to the proposal.

2. Explain how America almost immediately violated the principle of the Monroe Doctrine by cooperating with European powers when they reasserted their control in Hispaniola (contemporary Haiti and the Dominican Republic). Investigate why our economic interests outweighed the invocation of the Monroe Doctrine.

3. Cite passages of the Monroe Doctrine to demonstrate that it was America's true statement of independence as a nation that was finally freed from the yoke of dependence upon any foreign power for foreign imports, military protection, and financial aid.

4. Investigate why the United States did not invoke the doctrine against European powers when they militarily intervened in various Latin American republics.

5. Some political scientists view the Monroe Doctrine as a rationale for opportunistic intervention whenever the self-interest of the United States was threatened. Choose three events from the nineteenth century that support this viewpoint and analyze the dynamics of American self-interest.

6. Discuss how President John Tyler used the Monroe Doctrine to justify the seizure of Texas from Mexico in 1842.

ALTERNATIVE TERM PAPER SUGGESTIONS

1. In 1861, Secretary of State William H. Seward attempted to use the Monroe Doctrine as a diversionary tactic by initiating a drive to liberate Cuba from Spain in the hope of avoiding the Civil War. Prepare a PowerPoint presentation of his proposal that will be shown to President Abraham Lincoln.

2. Assume you are an editor of a nineteenth-century Venezuelan newspaper. Write several online op-ed pieces warning your fellow Latin American citizens how the Monroe Doctrine is being used to establish U.S. hegemony throughout the continent.

SUGGESTED SOURCES

Primary Sources

"The Avalon Project at Yale Law School—Monroe Doctrine; December 2, 1823." http://www.yale.edu/lawweb/avalon/monroe.htm. Furnishes the complete text of the Monroe Doctrine.

"Library of Congress—Primary Documents in American History." http://www.loc.gov/rr/program/bib/ourdocs/Monroe.html. Includes the text of the Monroe Doctrine, broadsides discussing it in relation to the events of 1800, copies of Monroe's seventh annual message found in the House and Senate Journals, a letter to former President Thomas Jefferson seeking foreign policy advice, nineteenth-century periodical articles, and more.

Monroe, James. *The Political Writings of James Monroe*. Washington, DC: Regnery Publishing, 2002. Includes the writings of James Monroe about the presidency, politics, and the Monroe Doctrine.

Secondary Sources

Alvarez, Alejandro. *The Monroe Doctrine: Its Importance in the International Life of the States of the New World*. Buffalo, NY: W. S. Hein, 2003. Presents the significance of the Monroe Doctrine in relation to the growth and development of new republics in Central and South America.

Borgens, Victor G. *Background of the Monroe Doctrine*. New York: Vantage Press, 2004. Gives a brief, easy-to-understand history of the Monroe Doctrine.

Dangerfield, George. *The Era of Good Feelings*. Norwalk, CT: Easton Press, 1986. This standard work covers the period after the Treaty of Ghent (1814), which ended the War of 1812 and helped establish America's independence vis-à-vis European powers.

Hunt, Michael. *Ideology and U.S. Foreign Policy*. New Haven, CT: Yale University Press, 1988. Provides a scholarly analysis of how the Monroe Doctrine has been used for different foreign policy purposes that at various times actually opposed each other.

Murphy, Gretchen. *Hemispheric Imaginings: The Monroe Doctrine and Narrative History of U.S. Empire.* Durham, NC: Duke University Press, 2005. Discusses how the Monroe Doctrine has been used both to isolate the United States and to provide the political justification to interfere in the affairs of sovereign states within Latin America.

Perkins, Dexter. *A History of the Monroe Doctrine.* Boston, MA: Little, Brown & Company, 1963. Explains the background and diplomacy that established the Monroe Doctrine.

Renehan, Edward. *The Monroe Doctrine: Cornerstone of American Foreign Policy.* New York: Chelsea House, 2007. Written for secondary school students, this work provides an outstanding overview and outline of the pro and con issues surrounding the use of the Monroe Doctrine.

Smith, Gaddis. *The Last Years of the Monroe Doctrine, 1945–1993.* New York: Hill and Wang, 1995. Provides a scholarly account of the Monroe Doctrine and how it has been used to justify unwarranted intervention in the affairs of Latin American countries.

Taft, William H. *The President and his Powers; and, the United States and Peace.* Athens, OH: Ohio University Press, 2003. Contains information about the history and enforcement of the Monroe Doctrine.

Whitaker, A. *The U.S. and the Independence of Latin America, 1800–1830.* New York: W. W. Norton & Company, 2000. Discusses the impetus for the establishment of the Monroe Doctrine with the creation of various Latin American republics during the nineteenth century.

Whitcomb, Roger S. *The American Approach to Foreign Affairs: An Uncertain Tradition.* Westport, CT: Praeger Publishers, 1998. Chapter 2 is devoted to a discussion of the sometimes contradictory isolationist and interventionist policies imbued in the Monroe Doctrine.

World Wide Web

"The Avalon Project at Yale Law School the Papers of James Monroe." http://www.yale.edu/lawweb/avalon/presiden/monroepa.htm. Includes two inaugural addresses, the full text of the Monroe Doctrine, and correspondence with Charles Bagot regarding U.S. Naval forces.

"James Monroe (1758–1831)." http://www.millercenter.virginia.edu/academic/americanpresident/monroe?PHPSESSID=8669f3d93e42c9780bc4826c16dfe457. Includes Monroe's speeches, addresses, and a bibliography along with basic facts about President James Monroe's life.

"Library of Congress—Letter, James Monroe to Thomas Jefferson Seeking Foreign Policy Advice, 17 October 1823. (Thomas Jefferson Papers)."

http://memory.loc.gov/cgi-bin/query/r?ammem/mcc:@field(DOCID +@lit(mcc/082)). Provides the full text of the letter.

"Library of Congress—The Monroe Doctrine in 1881." http://memory.loc .gov/cgi-bin/query/r?ammem/ncps:@field(DOCID+@lit(ABQ7578 -0133-44)). Contains the full text of an article published in the December 1881 issue of *North American Review,* which gives the historical background behind the creation of the Monroe Doctrine.

"The Monroe Doctrine." http://www.ushistory.org/documents/monroe.htm. Provides an overview of the Monroe Doctrine followed by the doctrine's text.

"U.S. Territorial Maps, 1775–1920." http://xroads.virginia.edu/~MAP/terr _hp.html. Contains useful maps of the U.S. Territory before and after the Monroe Doctrine was stated as a U.S. foreign policy.

"The White House—James Monroe." http://www.whitehouse.gov/history/ presidents/jm5.html. Contains a short biographical sketch of President James Monroe that includes mention of his legacy concerning the Monroe Doctrine.

Multimedia Sources

Between the Wars Volume 5—Recognition of Russia/Latin America: Intervention in Our Own Backyard. Great Neck, NY: Best Film & Video, 1987. 1 DVD. 60 minutes. Discusses how the Monroe Doctrine has been used to intervene in the internal affairs of various Latin American countries.

U.S. History From 1809–1865: America Divided. Chicago, IL: Questar, 2006. 1 DVD. 58 minutes. Disc 2 of this series spans the presidencies of James Madison to Abraham Lincoln. Part of it is devoted to a discussion of the Monroe Doctrine.

27. Presidential Election of 1824, "A Corrupt Bargain"

The presidential election of 1824 was a hard-fought favorite-son contest among John Quincy Adams, Henry Clay, Andrew Jackson, and William H. Crawford. Although all were members of the Democratic-Republican party, there were significant differences in their attitudes and policies. To win the presidency one of them had to win a majority of electoral votes, which were awarded by special electors chosen by the states. Andrew Jackson took the lead and won the popular vote along with 99 out of

261 electoral votes. Adams came in second with 84 votes, followed by Crawford with 41 and Clay with 37. Since no one had a majority, the election was thrown into the House of Representatives. Henry Clay became a major power broker when he gave his political support and Kentucky's electoral votes to Adams. He did so, however, in exchange for his appointment as Adam's secretary of state. Andrew Jackson and his supporters were outraged by the political deal between Adams and Clay and termed it "a corrupt bargain." They continued to focus on the issue for the remaining three years of Adams's presidency until Jackson easily won the presidency in 1828. The election of 1824 also set a record for firsts. It was the only time, since the passage of the Twelfth Amendment, that the House of Representatives elected a president and the only presidential election in which the candidate receiving the most electoral votes did not become president.

TERM PAPER SUGGESTIONS

1. The election of 1824 was one of personalities and popularity rather than accomplishments and vision for the country. Based on historical descriptions of each candidate, draw psychological profiles showing how each might or might not have appealed to voters.

2. Relate how Henry Clay brokered the election of 1824 by delivering Kentucky's and other Congressmen's electoral votes. Compare the political machinations to the 2004 election.

3. Clay and Adams were proponents of the American system that supported the national government taking a leading role in building roads, canals, and subsidizing manufacturing. Discuss the differences between Adams's and Jackson's views on the American system's goals.

4. Henry Clay was an ambitious man. He sought the presidency four times after his Cabinet appointment but was unsuccessful each time. Argue that he did make a corrupt bargain with Adams and deserved to be tainted with Jackson's charge of corruption.

5. Read John Quincy Adams's inaugural speech at http://yale.edu/lawweb/avalon/presiden/inaug/qadams.htm. Compare his hopes of overcoming the divisions created by the election of 1824 to what he actually achieved during his four years in office.

6. Research the personal disagreements that Clay and Jackson had over Jackson's capture of several Spanish forts during the Seminole Wars and his willingness to risk a greater war. When did their disagreements become personal?

ALTERNATIVE TERM PAPER SUGGESTIONS

1. Assume you are a political consultant for newly elected President John Quincy Adams. Present a series of PowerPoint recommendations for mending the political fences caused by the election of 1824.

2. The election of 1824 was the first in which all free White men without property could vote. Use an Excel document, if necessary, to graph and demonstrate why this change in voting rules may have been a significant factor in Andrew Jackson's winning the popular vote.

SUGGESTED SOURCES

Primary Sources

Adams, John Quincy. *Diary of John Quincy Adams.* Cambridge, MA: Harvard University Press, 1981. Contains entries regarding the year 1824 when Adams was seeking the presidency.

Clay, Henry. *An address of Henry Clay, to the public: Containing certain testimony, in refutation of the charges against him by Gen. Andrew Jackson, touching the last presidential election.* Washington, DC: P. Force, 1827. This forty-eight page text contains the speech Henry Clay gave refuting the charges leveled against him by Andrew Jackson.

Clay, Henry. *Papers of Henry Clay,* edited by James F. Hopkins et al., 11 vols. Lexington, KY: University of Kentucky Press, 1959–1992. Contains information about the election of 1824 and how Clay became secretary of state under John Quincy Adams.

Secondary Sources

Boller, Paul F. *Presidential Campaigns from George Washington to George W. Bush.* New York: Oxford University Press, 2004. Chapter 10 provides an excellent analysis of John Quincy Adams and "the corrupt bargain" charge.

Brookhiser, Richard. *America's First Dynasty: The Adamses, 1735–1918.* New York: Free Press, 2002. Describes and analyzes the four generations of Adamses including John Quincy Adams's election as president.

Carson, Jamie L., and Erik J. Engstrom. "Assessing the Electoral Connection: Evidence from the Early United States." *American Journal of Political Science* 49 (October 2005): 746–757. (Available in JSTOR.) Analyzes the aftermath of the election of 1824 in terms of the effects it had on electors who did not vote for Andrew Jackson.

Hargreaves, Mary W. M. *The Presidency of John Quincy Adams.* Lawrence, KS: University Press of Kansas, 1985. Provides an academic account of what Adams actually achieved during his four years in office.

Nagel, Paul C. "The Election of 1824: Reconsideration Based on Newspaper Opinion." *The Journal of Southern History* 26 (August 1960): 315–319. (Available in JSTOR.) Using newspaper articles from the time period, Nagel shows that personalities may not have driven the election so much as issues concerning, for example, the Missouri Compromise, the Denmark Vesey rebellion, and tariff questions.

Remini, Robert V. *Henry Clay: Statesman for the Union.* New York: Norton, 1991. Furnishes a solid overview of Henry Clay's life and his role in the election of 1824.

Remini, Robert Vincent. *John Quincy Adams.* New York: Times Books, 2002. Furnishes a short biography of John Quincy Adams that delves into the election of 1824 and how Adams came to the office with the help of Henry Clay.

Russell, Greg. *John Quincy Adams and the Public Virtues of Diplomacy.* Columbia, MO: University Press of Missouri, 1995. Furnishes an analysis of Adams's beliefs and philosophical foundation that guided his decision making.

Stevens, Harry R. "Henry Clay, the Bank, and the West in 1824." *The American Historical Review* 60 (July 1955): 843–848. (Available in JSTOR.) Henry Clay unsuccessfully sought the presidency four times. This article analyzes his connection as counsel to the Second Bank of the United States and the antagonism it caused in western states as a possible cause of his failure to achieve the presidency.

World Wide Web

"1824 Presidential Election Results." http://uselectionatlas.org/USPRESI DENT/GENERAL/pe1824.html. Furnishes a detailed statistical analysis of the 1824 election, including colored pie graphs and maps showing how each state and region voted.

"The Election Is in the House: 1824. The candidates and the Issues." http://edsitement.neh.gov/view_lesson_plan.asp?id=551. Contains biographical sketches, links to primary sources, lesson plans, and curriculum units that are all based on National History Curriculum Standards concerning the election of 1824.

"Election of 1824." http://www.u-s-history.com/pages/h262.html. Furnishes a useful, hyperlinked overview of the major candidates, issues, and election problems during 1824.

"Electoral College Box Scores 1789–1996." http://www.archives.gov/federal -register/electoral-college/scores.html#1824. This National Archives site provides the official Electoral College vote count for each candidate during the 1824 election.

"House Journal—Wednesday, February 9, 1825." http://memory.loc.gov/cgi-bin/query/r?ammem/hlaw:@field(DOCID+@lit(hj01849)). Provides specific pages from *Journal of the House of Representatives* concerning the Electoral College votes that each candidate received during the election of 1824.

"John Quincy Adams (1767–1848)." http://www.millercenter.virginia.edu/academic/americanpresident/jqadams. This site includes academic information presented by renowned scholars about John Quincy Adams in the form of links to manuscripts, speeches, papers, memoirs, and books.

"Memoirs of John Quincy Adams: Comprising Portions of His Diary from 1795–1848." http://books.google.com/books?vid=ISBN0836950216&id=KPQrq0LBvbYC&pg=PA501. Pages from Adams's diary are displayed in Google Books. In it, Adams discusses how the votes turned in favor of him for his eventual election in 1824.

"What Are They All Doing, Anyway? An Historical Analysis of the Electoral College." http://www.thegreenpapers.com/Hx/ElectoralCollege.html. Analyzes from a Constitutional standpoint the strengths and weaknesses of the Electoral College system for choosing a president and vice president.

Multimedia Sources

The Adams Chronicles. Chapter VIII, John Quincy Adams, Secretary of State (1817–1825). New York: Educational Broadcasting Corporation, 1976. 1 DVD. 58 minutes. Provides information about the role of John Quincy Adams in the 1824 election.

Jacksonian Democracy. Pleasantville, NY: Educational Audio Visual, 1976. 1 videocassette. 36 minutes. Discusses the legacy of the 1824 election and how it gave rise to the concept of Jacksonian democracy.

28. New Harmony, Indiana, Founded (1825)

New Harmony was a utopian community founded by Welshman Robert Owen in 1825 for the purposes of freedom of speech and action and equality of labor, property, and opportunity. In 1825, he purchased twenty thousand acres of land on the Wabash River in Indiana from George Rapp who began a similar community in 1814 called Harmony. Owen's utopian community, however, had a secular base, whereas Rapp's community had a religious foundation. Owen was assisted in his endeavor by William Maclure, a Scottish geologist, businessman, and philanthropist who was a proponent

of Johann Heinrich Pestalozzi's educational methods. Instruction pro-
ceeded from the familiar to the new, allowed for individual differences in
learning, incorporated the performing arts, and encouraged group participation. Together they agreed to recruit distinguished educators and finance
New Harmony's schools, scientific equipment, and library. By December
1825, New Harmony had a population of about one thousand people.
The community prospered for a time under Owen's guidance, but soon
fractured as differences arose over who was in charge, the lack of governance
procedures, and the absence of a major role for religion. On May 26, 1827,
Owen admitted that his experiment had failed and that he had lost
80 percent of his fortune in trying to establish it. The property was divided
among his eight children, one of whom stayed on to found a notable
pre–Civil War cultural center. New Harmony was restored in the late
1990s as a model nineteenth-century agricultural center and tourist site.

TERM PAPER SUGGESTIONS

1. England and America were undergoing significant economic and social
   changes during the Industrial Revolution. Discuss those changes as they relate
   to a motivation to create a utopian society such as New Harmony.

2. Josiah Warren was an individual anarchist and a member of the New Harmony community. He argued that New Harmony was doomed to fail because
   it did not allow for individual rights or private ownership of property. Refer to
   some of the research about New Harmony that supported his conclusion.

3. Most flourishing communities have a healthy balance between conformity
   and diversity. Use the New Harmony community as an example to discuss
   the need for diversity as a necessary component of a prosperous society.

4. Research the socialistic philosophy of Robert Owen and discuss his legacy,
   especially in regard to the Cooperative Movement.

5. Analyze how the absence of an official religion may have played a role in the
   failure of New Harmony.

6. One of Owen's reasons for creating New Harmony was to alleviate poverty.
   Discuss how creating this utopian community might have achieved his goal.

ALTERNATIVE TERM PAPER SUGGESTIONS

1. Research the architectural plans for New Harmony and design a new one that
   would allow for some communally and some privately owned property.
   Prepare a series of broadsides including pictures that could be used to recruit
   people to join New Harmony.

2. Incorporate and cite images from New Harmony and other American utopian communities such as Oneida, the Shakers, and Brooks Farm, and create an online virtual tour. Use *rollover* hyperlinks to identify and describe specific areas and buildings and their purpose.

SUGGESTED SOURCES

Primary Sources

Indiana Historical Commission. *New Harmony as Seen by Participants and Travelers*. Philadelphia, PA: Porcupine Press, 1975. Contains first-person accounts of Owenites and visitors to New Harmony in the 1820s.

Nordhoff, Charles. *American Utopias*. Reprint. Stockbridge, MA: Berkshire House Publishers, 1993. This 1875 reprint contains the observations of Charles Nordhoff's visits to the major utopian communities including the Shakers, Harmonists, the Wallington and Oneida Perfectionists, the Aurora and Bethel Communities, the Bishop Hill Colony, and others.

Owen, Robert. *A View of Society and Other Writings*. New York: Penguin, 1991. Contains Owen's socialist philosophy and writings about his belief that poverty can be obliterated with education and shared communal resources.

Secondary Sources

Blair, Don E. *The New Harmony Story*. New Harmony, IN: New Harmony Publications Committee, 1967. Provides the background and details of the creation of New Harmony.

Brown, Paul. *Twelve Months in New Harmony*. Philadelphia, PA: Porcupine Press, 1973. Describes twelve months in the daily life of the New Harmony community.

Donnachie, Ian. *Robert Owen: Owen of New Lanark and New Harmony*. East Linton, Scotland: Tuckwell Press, 2000. Provides information about the life of Robert Owen and his creation of the model factory town Lanark and community New Harmony.

Harris, W. T., and George Blackwood. *New Harmony Movement*. Whitefish, MT: Kessinger Publishing, 2003. Provides a context for New Harmony's place in the history of all utopian communities, and also includes Robert Owen's farewell address when he left the community and returned to Europe.

Holloway, Mark. *Utopian Communities in America, 1680–1880*. New York: Dover Publications, 1966. Along with fifteen illustrations, this work gives a useful account of several utopian American communities including New Harmony, the Shakers, and Ephrata.

Kanter Moss, Rosabeth. *Community and Commitment: Communes and Utopias in Sociological Perspective*. Cambridge, MA: Harvard University Press, 2005. Discusses the problems and limitations of living in a commune or utopian community in regard to the trade-offs between conformity and diversity.

Pitzer, Donald E. *America's Communal Utopias*. Chapel Hill, NC: University of North Carolina Press, 1997. One essay in this book is devoted solely to Robert Owens and his establishment of the utopian community New Harmony. The work also investigates other utopian movements founded before 1965 and how they either thrived or failed.

Sargant, William Lucas. *Robert Owen and His Socialist Philosophy*. Reprint. Boston, MA: Adamant Media Corporation, 2005. Excels as a source about Owen's childhood and his innovative factory system where he practiced his personal, socialistic philosophy.

Sutton, Robert P. *Communal Utopias and the American Experience: Secular Communities, 1824–2000*. Westport, CT: Praeger Publishers, 2004. Chapter 1 is devoted solely to New Harmony and other Owenite communities. The remainder of the book discusses similar American utopian communities and shows how establishing them has always served an essential role in America's history.

Taylor, Barbara. *Eve and the New Jerusalem: Socialism and Feminism in the Nineteenth Century*. Cambridge, MA: Harvard University Press, 1993. Gives a scholarly account of the concepts of nineteenth-century socialism and how it was practiced in communities such as New Harmony.

World Wide Web

"Equitable Commerce: A Document of Principles by Josiah Warren." http://tmh.floonet.net/pdf/jwarren.pdf. Provides the seventy-nine page full text document of Josiah Warren's reasons why the New Harmony utopian experiment failed.

"Historic New Harmony, Indiana." http://www.ulib.iupui.edu/kade/newharmony/home.html. Contains a brief history of the utopian community along with links to other aspects of it.

"Indiana Commission on Public Records—New Harmony, Indiana." http://www.in.gov/icpr/archives/databases/posey/posey6.html. Contains an excellent, accurate overview of the founding of New Harmony.

"New Harmony Scientists, Educators, Writers & Artists." http://faculty.evansville.edu/ck6/bstud/nh.html. Provides an extensive annotated bibliography of important books about New Harmony and hyperlinked biographical sketches concerning the professionals who tried to assist in making it function successfully.

"Robert Owen 1771–1858." http://robert-owen.midwales.com/rowen/index
.html. Provides a lengthy biographical sketch of Robert Owen with
excerpts from many recorded conversations and passages from his autobiography.

"Robert Owen (1771–1858) Social Reformer, Founder of New Harmony."
http://faculty.evansville.edu/ck6/bstud/robtowen.html. Contains an
image of an oil portrait of Robert Owen followed by a short biographical
portrait and the full text from his autobiography of a conversation that he
had with one of his sons concerning religion.

"West Street Log Cabins." http://www.ulib.iupui.edu/kade/newharmony/
cabins.html. Provides pictures of the original Harmony community and
New Harmony community log cabins and other structures, along with
explanations concerning their function.

"William Maclure (1763–1840) Geologist, Educational Reformer." http://
faculty.evansville.edu/ck6/bstud/maclure.html. Provides a short biography of William Maclure and the partnership he had with Robert Owen
and the idealistic founding of New Harmony.

Multimedia Sources

New Harmony an Example and a Beacon. Bloomington, IN: Indianan Instructional Support sources, 2000. 1 DVD. 29 minutes. Traces the history
and significance of New Harmony, Indiana, from its early start as a
utopian community to its evolution to an historical site.

29. Jacksonian Democracy and the Spoils System (1829–1837)

In 1828 after harassing John Quincy Adams for three years over his "corrupt bargain" with Henry Clay to gain the presidency, Andrew Jackson
took office. He ushered in a period that was basically a misnomer if one
were not a White American male. Known as Jacksonian democracy, it
fostered expanded voting rights for White men who did not own land,
expanded access to lands belonging to Indians, a strict interpretation of
the Constitution, replacement of all civil servants by ones belonging to
the winner's party, and a live and let live philosophy for the economy. This
philosophy, with many political adjustments, continued through the
administrations of five presidents until it finally collided with the
issues of slavery and basic human rights for all Americans. Jacksonian

democracy arose during an era of rapid transitions in sections of the country causing many Americans to believe that a class system was developing along the lines of the European one that either they or their ancestors had fled. These profound social and economic changes spawned an egalitarian movement that appealed to voters in every part of the country whether they were factory workers, settlers, slave owners, or farmers. Most truly believed that a growing elite class of chartered factory owners, land speculators, and large slave holders were depriving them of an equal opportunity to partake of the American dream, so they instituted a series of reforms that was basically a course correction for American history.

TERM PAPER SUGGESTIONS

1. Analyze how the term "Jacksonian democracy reforms" was basically a misnomer if one were a slave, a White woman, or an immigrant.

2. Discuss the major economic and social conditions that gave birth to the Jacksonian Democracy movement.

3. Explore the pros and cons of the "Spoils System."

4. One of Jackson's major policy thrusts was to dismantle credit-driven entities that placed people and the government at the mercy of nonelected bankers who could control the nation's economy. Investigate Jackson's war against the corrupt Second Bank of the United States.

5. Explain how Jackson's reforms to give land-hungry settlers access to cheap land came at the expense of vast numbers of Indians.

6. Jacksonian democrats espoused equal rights for all and limited government so that already privileged classes of people would not enrich themselves further by taking over public institutions. Investigate the paradox between their public avowal of equal rights and their belief that Sabbatarians, Nativists, temperance advocates, and abolitionists should not impose their views on others.

ALTERNATIVE TERM PAPER SUGGESTIONS

1. Assume you are the campaign manager for Martin Van Buren, President Jackson's intended successor. Create a Web site that taps into the disaffection that many citizens were feeling in these decades. How might one appeal to their fears, aspirations, and desires? What promises might you make to guarantee a vote for Van Buren?

2. Assume you are a member of the opposing party who believes that the expansionist position of Andrew Jackson comes at the expense of building up the current infrastructure of America's cities and towns. Create a Web site

complete with images that embody the essence of a green movement for America.

SUGGESTED SOURCES

Primary Sources

"Andrew Jackson (1767–1845)." http://www.millercenter.virginia.edu/aca demic/americanpresident/jackson. This site, from the University of Virginia, features a biographical sketch of Andrew Jackson, the full text of some speeches, an inaugural address, and a bibliography.

"White House Historical Association—The Rise for Jacksonian Democracy— Eyewitness Accounts." http://www.whitehousehistory.org/04/subs/ 1828_b.html. Contains the full text of a letter written by Margaret Bayard Smith to Jane Bayard Kirkpatrick regarding her witnessing of the inauguration and reception for Andrew Jackson in March 1829.

Wilentz, Sean. *Major Problems in the Early Republic, 1787–1848: Documents and Essays.* Furnishes primary sources concerning some of the major issues dealing with Jacksonian democracy and the spoils system.

Secondary Sources

Blau, J. L. *Social Theories of Jacksonian Democracy: Representative Writing of the Period 1825–1850.* Indianapolis, IN: Hackett Publishing Company, 2000. Discusses the egalitarian theories behind Jackson's policies of enlarging the franchise for people who were not landowners and appointing new people to all government positions.

Brands, H. W. *Andrew Jackson: His Life and Times.* New York: Random House, 2005. A noted historian discusses the events that helped form President Jackson's character and his strong dislike of the class system and belief in a more egalitarian form of government.

Doutrich, Paul E. *Shapers of the Great Debate on Jacksonian Democracy: A Biographical Dictionary.* Westport, CT: Greenwood Press, 2004. This outstanding biographical dictionary features chapters on all the presidents and other people who were associated with the concept of Jacksonian democracy, along with an analysis of the major events that affected their policies.

Feller, Daniel. *The Jacksonian Promise: America, 1815–1840.* Baltimore, MD: The Johns Hopkins University Press, 1995. Succeeds in bringing the Jacksonian period to life with vivid descriptions of early industrialization, canal constructions, and westward expansion.

Friedrich, Carl Joachim. "The Rise and Decline of the Spoils Tradition." *Annals of the American Academy of Political and Social Sciences* 189

(January 1937): 10–16. (Available in JSTOR.) Furnishes historical evidence that the spoils system was not only characteristic of the Jacksonian period but also other presidential administrations.

Lloyd Jones, Chester. "Spoils and the Party." *Annals of the Academy of Political and Social Science* 64 (March 1916): 66–76. (Available in JSTOR.) Argues that the spoils system has been endemic to each political party in America before and after President Jackson and that it is tolerated by the average voter and railed against by intellectuals.

Magliocca, Gerald N. *Andrew Jackson and the Constitution: The Rise and Fall of Generational Regimes.* Lawrence, KS: University Press of Kansas, 2007. Gives a scholarly analysis of the legal battles that President Jackson and his administration fought over western expansion, presidential authority, states' rights, and other issues.

Remini, Robert. *The Life of Andrew Jackson.* New York: Harper, 2001. This classic one-volume biography covers all of the major issues in the life and presidency of Andrew Jackson.

Schlesinger, Arthur Meir, Jr. *The Age of Jackson.* Boston, MA: Back Bay Books, 1988. The last three chapters of this useful work deal directly with Jacksonian democracy as it related to the law, industrialization, and religion.

Sellers, Charles. *The Market Revolution: Jacksonian America, 1815–1846.* New York: Oxford University Press, 1994. Deals with the issues of capitalism that contributed to the rise of Jacksonian democracy.

Watson, Harry L. *Liberty and Power: The Politics of Jacksonian America.* New York: Hill and Wang, 2006. Presents an understandable history of how the social, economic, and cultural forces in nineteenth-century America coalesced to produce Jacksonian democracy.

Wilentz, Sean. *Andrew Jackson.* New York: Henry Holt & Company, 2005. Written by a Princeton historian, this biography also discusses Jackson's policies toward Indians and his position on slavery as being somewhat in opposition to the ideals of Jacksonian democracy.

World Wide Web

"Andrew Jackson." http://www.historycentral.com/Bio/presidents/jackson.html. Provides a hyperlinked biographical sketch of President Andrew Jackson, including the full text of two inaugural addresses.

"Chapter 12—Jacksonian Democracy." http://ppl.nhmccd.edu/~craigl/12.html. Chapter 12 of this online textbook outline provides a table comparing the principles of Jacksonian democracy with the way it differed from the Republican Party of Thomas Jefferson.

"Eagleton Institute of Politics—Jacksonian Democracy." http://www.eagleton
.rutgers.edu/e-gov/e-politicalarchive-Jackson.htm. Includes an excellent
hyperlinked overview of the issues involved in Jacksonian democracy.

"Historyteacher.net—Andrew Jackson." www.historyteacher.net/AHAP/Power
Points/AndrewJackson.ppt. Furnishes an excellent slide presentation of
all the main events and issues concerning Andrew Jackson's presidency.

"Politics and Public Service: The Spoils System versus the Merit System: Public
Service as Reward." http://www.u-s-history.com/pages/h965.html.
Provides historical evidence that the "Spoils System" did not originate
with President Andrew Jackson's administration.

"The Social Studies Help Center—Should Andrew Jackson be Considered a
Champion of Democracy?" http://www.socialstudieshelp.com/
Lesson_27_Notes.htm. Contains numerous provocative questions about
the tenure of President Andrew Jackson that can serve as excellent topics
for term papers.

"Spoils System." http://www.answers.com/topic/spoils-system. Furnishes several
definitions of the "Spoils System" and an annotated list of all the U.S.
Presidents associated with it.

Multimedia Sources

Andrew Jackson: A Man for the People. New York: New Video Group, 1995.
1 DVD. 50 minutes. Provides expert commentary by noted historians
about the life and times of President Andrew Jackson, including his association with the political concept, Jacksonian democracy.

"Audio and Video Three Hours with Robert Remini, the Pre-Eminent Jacksonian
Scholar." http://www.isidore-of-seville.com/jackson/3.html. Includes
several hours of interviews taped with Remini on September 7, 2002,
about his book, *The Life of Andrew Jackson*. New York: Harper, 2001.

"History.com—Andrew Jackson." www.history.com. Type in the name "Andrew
Jackson" at this site to retrieve a biographical sketch of Jackson plus
an image and video gallery of famous battles that he waged and events
associated with his presidency.

30. Davy Crockett "Frontier Hero"

"Born on a mountaintop in Tennessee, killed him a 'bar' when he was only
three." These lyrics to a Davy Crockett ballad describe the quintessential
frontier folk hero, and separating fact from legend has been the task of
historians ever since. Davy Crockett, who went by the name "David,"

was born in Tennessee in 1786, but it was not on a mountaintop. He ran away from home after an altercation with a schoolmaster and developed a wanderlust that never left him despite two marriages and five children. He fought in two Indian Wars, was a justice of the peace, and served two terms in the Tennessee legislature. Crockett was elected to Congress in 1827 and 1829 as a Democrat, but he publicly disagreed with President Andrew Jackson's policies concerning the Second Bank of the United States and the Indian Removal Act. After his defeat in 1831, he returned to Congress in 1833 as a Whig. Defeated again in 1835, he was quoted as saying, "You can all go to Hell and I'm going to Texas." The lure of cheap land and the chance to start over politically were the main incentives for Crockett's decision to move to Texas. He swore an oath to the Provisional Government of Texas in exchange for 4,600 acres of land as payment. Crockett never collected on the promise because he died at the Battle of the Alamo on March 6, 1836. Prior to his heroic death defending the Alamo, Crockett was well on his way to becoming a legend in his own time. His tall stories, pseudo-biographies, and almanacs attracted the attention of journalists because the frontier lingo was so colorful and imaginative that they became a permanent part of American history and folklore.

TERM PAPER SUGGESTIONS

1. Examine how David Crockett personified the concept of Manifest Destiny.

2. Sift through some of the historical evidence surrounding the life of David Crockett and debunk several myths or legends about some aspect of his life.

3. Investigate Crockett's position on President Andrew Jackson's Indian Removal Act. Discuss how it differed from what many people thought were Crockett's beliefs concerning Native Americans' rights to their ancestral lands.

4. Research and analyze the controversy surrounding Crockett's death at the Alamo.

5. Read some portions of the Crockett-narrated almanacs and autobiography. Examine how Crockett contributed to the development of his own legend as a "Frontier Hero."

6. Crockett ran for Congress during a time characterized by more democracy for all. His speech, mannerisms, and exploits spoke of a homespun character who appealed to a less educated voter. Were these characteristics necessary for his election from Tennessee during those times? Discuss how Crockett embodied the concepts of Jacksonian democracy.

ALTERNATIVE TERM PAPER SUGGESTIONS

1. Create a hyperlinked chronology that traces Crockett's life from his birth to his death at the Alamo.

2. Design a biographical Web site complete with images of the places that Crockett wrote about or where he experienced some major life event.

SUGGESTED SOURCES

Primary Sources

Crockett, David. *Narrative of the Life of David Crockett of the State of Tennessee.* Reprint. Lincoln, NE: University of Nebraska Press, 1987. Of the five books attributed to Crockett, this is the only one that he is considered to have written. It gives an account of his life in a backwoodsman's style that helped create the Crockett folk legend.

Lofaro, Michael A. *Davy Crockett's Riproarious Shemales and Sentimental Sisters: Women's Tall Tales from the Crockett Almanacs, 1835–1856.* Harrisburg, PA: Stackpole Books, 2001. Almanacs in the nineteenth century were usually used for weather prediction, but these, narrated by Davy Crockett, were to amuse people. Excerpts from these almanacs feature the tales of backwoods women.

Secondary Sources

Abbott, John Stevens. *David Crockett: His Life and Adventures.* Reprint. Boston, MA: Adamant Media Corporation, 2000. Recounts the life of Davy Crockett from early childhood, his adventures after running away from home, his marriage and family responsibilities, and his life as a soldier.

Cobia, Manley F., Jr. *Journey into the Land of Trials.* Franklin, TN: Hillsboro Press, 2003. Relates the story of Davy Crockett's final journey to the Alamo.

Davis, William C. *Three Roads to the Alamo: The Lives and Fortunes of David Crockett, James Bowie, and William Barret Travis.* New York: Harper-Collins, 1998. Traces the three different paths that led each of these famous Americans to die at the Alamo.

Derr, Mark. *The Frontiersman: The Real Life and the Many Legends of Davy Crockett.* New York: William Morrow, 1993. Uses historical evidence to disentangle the legend and the truth about Davy Crockett's life.

Groneman, William. *David Crockett: Hero of the Common Man.* New York: Forge Books, 2005. Paints an altogether different portrait of Crockett from that of a country bumpkin and teller of tall tales to an able politician, father, soldier, and true American hero.

Groneman, Bill. *Death of a Legend: The Myth and Mystery Surrounding the Death of Davy Crockett*. Plano, TX: Republic of Texas, 1999. Provides information about Davy Crockett's death at the Alamo.

Harmon, Daniel E. *Davy Crockett*. Philadelphia, PA: Chelsea House, 2001. Written for secondary school students, this work gives an overview of the life and times of Davy Crockett.

Hauck, Richard Boyd. *Crockett: A Bio-Bibliography*. Westport, CT: Greenwood Publishing Company, 1982. Reviews the actual facts surrounding the legend of Davy Crockett and evaluates the literature that has been considered research on Crockett's life.

Jones, Randell. *In Footsteps of Davy Crockett*. Winston-Salem, NC: John F. Blair Publishers, 2006. Combines biographical information that contradicts many of the legends surrounding Crockett's life along with travel information about the places where he lived and died.

Levy, Buddy. *American Legend: The Real Life Adventures of Davy Crockett*. New York: Putnam, 2005. Gives a fairly laudatory account of Davy Crockett's life, including his failure as a politician, but also his surprising stand against President Jackson's Indian Removal Act.

Lindley, Thomas Ricks. *Alamo Traces: New Evidence and New Conclusions*. Plano, TX: Republic of Texas Press, 2003. Thoroughly analyzes the historical evidence to determine what really happened at the Alamo.

Lofaro, Michael A. *Davy Crockett: The Man, the Legend, the Legacy, 1786–1986*. Knoxville, TN: University of Tennessee Press, 1985. Traces the legends of Davy Crockett and documents his real contributions as a legislator and soldier.

Walker, Dale L. *Legends and Lies: Great Mysteries of the American West*. New York: Forge Books, 1998. Uses historical evidence to examine the deaths of famous frontiersmen including Davy Crockett, Billy the Kid, Sacajawea, and Meriwether Lewis.

World Wide Web

"Crockett, David." http://www.tsha.utexas.edu/handbook/online/articles/CC/fcr24.html. Contains a lengthy biographical sketch of Davy Crockett including excerpts from speeches, sayings attributed to him, and a bibliography.

"David Crockett." http://xroads.virginia.edu/~HYPER/HNS/Swhumor/acrocket.htm. Contains a short biography of Davy Crockett, including a full text excerpt from his autobiography concerning bear hunting in Tennessee.

"Digital History—David Crockett to Charles Schultz." http://www.digital history.uh.edu/documents/documents_p2.cfm?doc=67. David Crockett writes of his dissatisfaction with soon-to-be President Martin Van Buren and his intention to move to "the wilds of Texas."

"Digital History—David Crockett to John Drurey, 1834, by David Crockett." http://www.digitalhistory.uh.edu/documents/documents_p1.cfm. Contains the full text of a letter written by Davy Crockett concerning his opposition to President Andrew Jackson's decision to withdraw government funds from the Bank of the United States. Crockett blamed the Panic of 1819 on Jackson's action, which subsequently brought about Crockett's defeat in the 1835 election.

"Historynet.com—Frontier Hero Davy Crockett." http://www.historynet.com/ culture/wild_west/3030086.html. Provides a lengthy biographical sketch of Davy Crockett along with excerpts from some of his speeches and stated positions on Andrew Jackson's presidency.

"The Life, Legend of Davy Crockett." http://www.texnews.com/1998/2002/texas/ davy0302.html. Contains an FAQ from a new exhibit at Bob Bullock Texas State History Museum that attempts to debunk some of the more popular legends surrounding the life and times of Davy Crockett.

"Old Wild West.com—The Alamo." http://www.oldwildwest.com/history.html. Supplies numerous links of newspaper reports and other historical evidence of Davy Crockett's death at the Alamo.

Multimedia Sources

Alamo. New York: A&E Home Video, 2003. 1 DVD. 240 minutes. Provides interviews with historians and reenactments of the Battle of the Alamo.

The Alamo. North Reading, MA: Colonial Radio Theatre on the Air, 1999. 87 minutes. Dramatized by Jerry Robbins, this audio can be purchased through Amazon.com. It contains a well-researched audio tape reenactment of the battle of the Alamo where Davy Crockett, Jim Bowie, and sixteen-year-old David Cummings were killed in 1836.

Biography: David Crockett —American Frontier Legend. New York: A&E Network, 2005. 1 DVD. 60 minutes. Stresses the accomplishments of Davy Crockett by interviewing scholars, viewing artifacts, and summarizing his life.

31. Abolitionist Movement (1830s)

Although the first proposal to abolish slavery occurred in the United States as early as 1688, it was not until the 1830s that it coalesced into a moral and militant crusade that polarized Northern and Southern states. The origins of the Abolitionist Movement were religious, political, and economic. By the 1830s, Northern states had developed a more industrialized economy that did not require slave labor. Southern states, on the other hand, were still agrarian and needed slave labor to run large, cotton-producing plantations. America had also just undergone a "Second Awakening," which was a religious revival that stressed confessing one's sins, accepting Jesus, and improving society. Countenancing slavery was in total opposition to the religious tenets of the day. Politics also played a part as abolitionists called for an end to federal support of slavery and besieged Congress with requests for antislavery legislation. The movement had many notable leaders, including William Lloyd Garrison, Theodore D. Weld, Arthur and Lewis Tappan, and Elizur Wright Jr. Their vigorous battle waged in the press, in churches, and in speaking forums also spawned a backlash that included reactions ranging from violent mob responses to the passage in the House of Representatives of a "gag rule" that banned consideration of antislavery petitions. The movement fractured somewhat in the 1840s over issues of full or gradual emancipation and colonization efforts to Africa, but it succeeded in forcing the country to confront the issue of slavery and its position as a slave-holding nation in the eyes of the rest of the world.

TERM PAPER SUGGESTIONS

1. Abolitionists based their beliefs against slavery in the Declaration of Independence and the Bible as did anti-abolitionists. Use these two sources and show the pros and cons of each side's argument.

2. William Lloyd Garrison was the editor of *The Liberator,* an abolitionist newspaper. Although he called for an immediate end to slavery, he was directly opposed to any colonization movements such as the American Colonization Society proposed. Examine Garrison's reasons for his opposition.

3. David Walker was a free person of color who became an ardent abolitionist. He constantly spoke out against slavery and also published *An Appeal to Colored People of the World* that called for slave rebellions. Discuss his influence and the reactions of some states that tried to prevent distribution of his pamphlet and ban teaching slaves to read.

4. Investigate the positive roles of Wendell Phillips, Lydia Maria Child, Angelina Grimke Weld, Theodore Weld, and Sarah Grimke in the Abolitionist Movement.

5. Discuss the constitutionality of the passage of the "Gag Rule" by the House of Representatives.

6. Examine what led to divisions in the Abolitionist Movement in the 1840s. What areas led to their most significant disagreement?

ALTERNATIVE TERM PAPER SUGGESTIONS

1. Create an online sermon similar to one written by Theodore Weld that outlines the moral, ethical, and religious reasons against slavery.

2. Write an editorial in praise of Elijah Lovejoy, editor of an Illinois abolitionist newspaper who was murdered in 1837 for his antislavery views.

SUGGESTED SOURCES

Primary Sources

Walker, David. *David Walker's Appeal, in Four Articles, together with a Preamble to the Coloured Citizens of the World, but in Particular, and Very Expressly, to Those of the United States of America*. Rev. ed. New York: Hill and Wang, 1995. Provides abolitionist Walker's views on slavery including his opinion that slaves should rebel.

Weld, Theodore Dwight. *American Slavery as It Is*. Itasca, IL: F. E. Peacock Publishers, 1972. Contains Weld's religious, ethical, and moral reasons for opposing slavery.

Secondary Sources

Azbug, Robert. *Passionate Liberator: Theodore Dwight Weld and the Dilemma of Reform*. New York: Oxford University Press, 2004. Relates the life and times of abolitionist Theodore Weld and the doubts that sometimes beset him concerning the movement.

Bacon, Jacqueline. *The Humblest May Stand Forth: Rhetoric, Empowerment and Abolition*. Columbia, SC: University of South Carolina Press, 2002. Draws on primary sources in the form of letters, editorials, and proslavery and antislavery tracts to show how a group of abolitionists fashioned their arguments against slavery.

Blue, Frederick J. *No Taint of Compromise: Crusaders in Antislavery Politics*. Baton Rouge, LA: Louisiana State University Press, 2002. Provides the stories of eleven Congressmen, journalists, and educators and their battle against slavery in the 1830s.

Davis, David Brion. *Inhuman Bondage: The Rise and Fall of Slavery in the New World*. New York: Oxford University Press, 2006. Dwells on the politics of America slavery and slave rebellions.

Fanuzzi, Robert. *Abolition's Public Sphere*. Minneapolis, MN: University of Minnesota Press, 2003. Examines the writings of William Lloyd Garrison, the Grimke sisters, Frederick Douglass, Henry David Thoreau, and Thomas Paine and their campaign against slavery in the newspapers, with pamphlets, and in speaking forums.

Harrold, Stanley. *The American Abolitionists*. New York: Longman, 2007. Discusses the origin, nature, tactics, major leaders, and significance of the American Abolitionist Movement.

Harrold, Stanley. *The Rise of Aggressive Abolitionism: Addresses to the Slaves*. Lexington, KY: University Press of Kentucky, 2004. Discusses the type of speeches and sermons that were used to help convince slaves of their need for emancipation.

McKivigan, John R. *The War Against Proslavery Religion: Abolitionism and the Northern Churches, 1830–1865*. Ithaca, NY: Cornell University Press, 1984. Discusses the role of noted, Northern church leaders who used the pulpit to dispel proslavery arguments.

Mayer, Henry. *All on Fire: William Lloyd Garrison and the Abolition of Slavery*. Boston, MA: St. Martin's Press, 1998. Relates the life of William Lloyd Garrison, who crusaded for emancipation of slaves by running an abolitionist newspaper, *The Liberator,* for thirty-five years.

Salerno, Beth A. *Sister Societies: Women's Antislavery Organizations in Antebellum America*. DeKalb, IL: Northern Illinois University Press, 2005. Sheds light on the role that women played in the Abolitionist Movement.

Speicher, Anna M. *The Religious World of Antislavery Women: Spirituality in the Lives of Five Abolitionist Lecturers*. Syracuse, NY: Syracuse University Press, 2000. Interweaves the role that religion played in the lives of Angelina Grimke, Sarah Grimke, Lucretia Mott, Abby Kelley, and Sallie Holly in their battles over slavery in America.

World Wide Web

"The Abolitionist Movement." http://afgen.com/abmovement.html. Presents an easy-to-understand overview of the Abolitionist Movement from the *Reader's Companion to American History.*

"American Abolitionism." http://americanabolitionist.liberalarts.iupui.edu/docs.htm. Provides one of the best overall sources for biographical sketches of abolitionists, full texts of slave narratives, government documents concerning slavery, and nineteenth-century newspaper articles, pamphlets, and magazine articles.

"The Antislavery Literature Project." http://antislavery.eserver.org/. This invaluable project brings together all kinds of literature that was used in the fight against slavery. It ranges from children's literature to poetry, journalistic reportage, militant tracts, essays, editorials, speeches, and videos of antislavery choral music.

"Library of Congress—African-American Mosaic—Abolition." http://www.loc .gov/exhibits/african/afam005.html. Presents an overview of the abolition movement and primary sources that relate to it.

"Slavery in Massachusetts by Henry David Thoreau." http://thoreau.eserver.org/ slavery.html. Gives the full text of an antislavery address made by famous author and essayist Thoreau specifically in response to the conviction in Boston of fugitive slave Anthony Burns.

"Slave Trade and the Abolition of Slavery." http://www.blackhistory4 schools.com/slavetrade/. Furnishes a series of Web sites dealing with abolition and slavery that include teacher resources as well as lesson plans.

"Thirteenth Amendment." http://www.answers.com/topic/amendment-xiii -to-the-u-s-constitution. Provides the background and full text of the Thirteenth Amendment that finally abolished slavery in the United States.

Multimedia Sources

American Experience: Roots of Resistance: A Story of the Underground Railroad. Los Angeles, CA: PBS Home Video, 1990. 1 DVD. 56 minutes. Provides one historian's overview of the Underground Railroad and the role that the Abolitionist Movement played in it. Most of the DVD consists of interviews with the descendants of slaves and their oral histories.

32. Baltimore and Ohio Railroad (1830)

After the Erie Canal opened in 1825, New York City, Buffalo, and many other towns along it became hubs for western trade. Navigable rivers and lakes were still the cheapest transportation system at the time, and the profits were huge for merchants and manufacturers who brought food in from midwestern states in exchange for shipping manufactured goods back to them. Other towns and cities soon followed suit by either constructing their own canal projects or building toll roads and turnpikes. Despite having a natural harbor, the city of Baltimore, Maryland, was fast becoming a backwater when compared with the Erie Canal trade. In 1826, several Baltimore businessmen met to propose a railroad that linked the city with the Ohio Valley. They bypassed government funding and sold stock to citizens, the city, and the state until they had the requisite amount to commence construction. By the summer of 1828, they had enough track laid to declare Baltimore the terminus of the first long-distance railroad and commemorate it with the laying of a cornerstone by one of the last surviving signers of the Declaration of Independence, Charles Carroll. Two years later the Baltimore and Ohio opened a passenger line between Pratt Street and the Carrollton viaduct. Although the cars were pulled by a team of horses, the cars allowed for 120 passengers to ride. Construction, however, was still slow, and it would take another twenty years for the rail system to actually reach Ohio. Still, the Baltimore and Ohio Railroad (B & O) became a showcase for early railroading, and it revolutionized transportation in the United States.

TERM PAPER SUGGESTIONS

1. Discuss why the building of the B & O Railroad was the result of private initiative rather than government policy. What were the implications for future large construction projects?

2. Research maps from the mid 1830s and investigate the major construction hurdles that engineers and surveyors faced in trying to complete the B & O.

3. Philip Evan Thomas, Evan Thomas, Peter Cooper, and John Eager Howard played prominent roles in obtaining the funding and investigating the feasibility of the B & O. Discuss the significance of their roles.

4. Selling shares in the B & O before it was constructed was considered an ingenious plan as a means for creating the necessary funds to complete the project. Describe and analyze how private enterprise basically created a public utility.

5. Examine how the growth of railroads allowed the absorption of immigrants throughout the country rather than just where they initially arrived in the United States.

6. Investigate how the growth of railroads encouraged western expansion and the eventual displacement of American Indians from their ancestral lands.

ALTERNATIVE TERM PAPER SUGGESTIONS

1. Assume you are a surveyor recently hired by the B & O Railroad to ascertain the geographical and engineering problems of the first section from Baltimore west to Ellicott's Mills (currently known as Ellicott City). Prepare a surveyors'

report that analyzes the problems and the means you intend to use to solve them.

2. Prepare an initial price stock offering to the citizens of Baltimore and Maryland that will raise sufficient funds to begin construction of the B & O Railroad.

SUGGESTED SOURCES

Primary Sources

Hungerford, Edward. *The Story of the Baltimore and Ohio Railroad.* 2 volumes. New York: G. P. Putnam's Sons, 1928. Contains primary source documents about how the initial entrepreneurs began the B & O as well as the history of its construction.

Maynard, Peter. *Into the Battle—Peacefully: A 19th Century Quake Confronts the Dilemmas Posed by his Friends, his Work, and his Faith: Being the Special journal of Jonathan Knight, Railroad Engr.* Brunswick, MD: Brunswick Historical Press, 2001. Provides a first-person account of what it was like to work on the B & O Railroad during the nineteenth century.

Secondary Sources

Barry, Steve. *Railroads: A History in Photographs.* Sarasota, FL: Crestline, 2002. Uses photographs to show how railroads transformed America by connecting goods and people in sparsely and heavily populated areas of the country.

Douglas, George H. *All Aboard! The Railroad in American Life.* New York: Paragon House, 1992. Explores how the railroad affected the lives of Americans and their communities.

Faith, Nicholas. *The World the Railways Made.* New York: Carroll & Graf, 1991. Investigates the societal effect that railways had all over the world.

Fishlow, Albert. *American Railroads and the Transformation of the Antebellum Economy.* Cambridge, MA: Harvard University Press, 1965. Examines how the expansion of railroads affected the economy of the pre–Civil War America.

Goddard, Stephen. *Getting There: The Epic Struggle between Road and Rail in the American Century.* Chicago, IL: University of Chicago Press, 1996. Takes the growth and development of the railroads into the twenty-first century as railroad barons engaged in epic battles against the development of interstate highways, cheap fuel, and the American desire for more private means of travel.

Harwood, Herbert, Jr. *Impossible Challenge: The Baltimore and Ohio Railroad in Maryland*. Baltimore, MD: Barnard Roberts & Company, 1979. Explores the major engineering, surveying, and construction problems concerning the building of the B & O Railroad.

Hornung, Clarence. *Wheels Across America*. New York: A. S. Barnes, 1959. Replete with illustrations, this book shows how early railroads used teams of horses to move the cars across the rails.

McGuirk, Martin J. *Baltimore & Ohio Railroad in the Potomac Valley*. Waukesha, WI: Kalmbach Publishing Company, 2000. Contains maps and photographs that detail the B & O's move from steam to diesel and its operations throughout the eastern part of the United States.

Roberts, Charles. *Triumph VIII: Pittsburgh—Eye of Two Storms 1749–2006*. Baltimore, MD: Barnard-Roberts, 2006. Discusses how Pittsburgh, Pennsylvania, became the nexus for a battle between the B & O Railroad and the Potomac Patuxent Railroad for control of the business and passenger traffic in the upper Ohio Valley.

Ross, David. *The Willing Servant: A History of the Steam Engine*. Stroud, England: Tempus, 2004. Beginning with Richard Trevithick's invention of the steam engine to James Watts's perfection of it, this work traces the history of the steam engine's impact on society in the early nineteenth century.

Stover, John F. *American Railroads*. Chicago, IL: University of Chicago Press, 1961. Discusses the establishment of the B & O among other great railroad lines in America.

World Wide Web

"Baltimore and Ohio Railroad Museum." http://www.nps.gov/nr/. Includes pictures of locomotives, a short history of the B & O, and other information. The museum's five thousand volumes book collection must be used on site.

"The Baltimore and Ohio Railroad Network." http://www.geocities.com/scott_w_dunlap/BORRTIME.htm. Contains links to maps, photographs, museum exhibits, and construction information concerning the B & O Railroad.

"Baltimore and Ohio Railroad Timeline." http://www.geocities.com/scott_w_dunlap/BORRTIME.htm. Furnishes a timeline regarding the growth and development of the B & O Railroad.

"Early 'Doers' Phillip Evan Thomas." http://www.sandyspringmuseum.org/d231.html. Provides a brief biographical sketch of "The Father of American Railroads."

"History of the B & O Railroad." http://www.meyersdalepa.org/railroad/
    borailhistory.html. Provides a short, annotated timeline history of the
    B & O Railroad.

Moody, John. *The Railroad Builders, A Chronicle of the Welding of the States.*
    New Haven, CT: Yale University Press, 1919. http://cprr.org/Museum/
    Railroad_Builders/Railroad_Builders_05.html. Chapter 5, "Crossing
    the Appalachian Range," is devoted solely to a history of the B & O
    Railroad.

"World's Greatest Railroads." http://www.geocities.com/Yosemite/9954/
    photo2.html. Furnishes picture, images, maps, and narratives about the
    B & O Railroad.

Multimedia Sources

America's Railroads. Alexandria, VA: PBS Home Video, 2002. 3 DVDs. 420
    minutes. Provides a history of the railroads with information about travel
    on locomotives from earlier periods. Captures the life and times of the
    early railroads.

33. Indian Removal Act (1830)

On May 28, 1830, President Andrew Jackson signed a law that gave
American Indian tribes unsettled land in the western part of the United
States in exchange for their ancestral lands. The pressure to enact the law
came primarily from southern states, particularly Georgia. The discovery
of gold on Cherokee lands in Georgia and the prospect of purchasing land
at $1.25 per acre were just two economic incentives that had dire conse-
quences for more than one hundred thousand American Indians. Although
the act did not order the forcible removal of American Indian tribes, great
coercion was applied on various tribes to sign removal treaties; when they
did not comply, many were forcibly removed from their lands. The effect
on American Indians was devastating. During the 1830s, up to one hundred thousand American Indians were forced to move west under military
pressure in exchange for land that could neither be cultivated nor sustain
life without outside assistance. While the government was supposed to
pay for their passage, government contracts to the lowest bidder ensured
that the transported had little in the way of supplies and equipment with
which to rebuild their lives. After President Jackson's landslide reelection,
most Indian tribes complied with the Act. Some tribes, however, such as

the Cherokee, Creeks, Seminoles, and Sauks, fought valiantly either militarily or legally to stave off the loss of their lands and way of life. By 1842 most American Indians, with the exception of the Seminoles, had been pushed off their lands by a government that no longer respected their legal or political rights as American citizens.

TERM PAPER SUGGESTIONS

1. Although the majority of Americans agreed with President Jackson's removal act, there was some opposition by missionaries and legislators. Discuss the opposing viewpoints of missionary Jeremiah Evarts, New Jersey Senator Theodore Frelinghuysen, and Tennessee Congressman David (Davy) Crockett. Analyze the feasibility of the solutions that they proposed.

2. The discovery of gold in Georgia and availability of cheap land on Indian lands were just some economic incentives to taking Indian lands. Explore those motivations and others that encouraged President Jackson to enact such a law.

3. Although many Indian tribes went fairly peaceably westward, others decided to fight to retain their lands. Examine the lands that were occupied by the Creeks and Sauks before and after their wars with the United States. Were these tribes better or worse off for their decision?

4. Before President Jackson took office, he was known as a great Indian fighter. Examine his campaign promises and proposed policies regarding American Indians and explore whether his reelection hinged on promises to remove Indians from their lands.

5. Historians often say that "hindsight explains the injury that foresight would have prevented." Investigate the legal arguments that the Cherokees made to retain the rights to their ancestral lands. Use some of these arguments to fashion a U.S. government policy that may have worked as a compromise between the affected American Indian tribes and land hungry settlers.

6. Many of the treaties between Indian tribes and the government were not signed by their elected leaders. Examine the Treaty of Dancing Rabbit Creek and Treaty of New Echota for irregularities.

ALTERNATIVE TERM PAPER SUGGESTIONS

1. Assume you are a Choctaw chieftain who has decided that the members of your tribe should sign a removal treaty with the government. Prepare a podcast for your people stating the reasons why it is in their best interest to move westward.

2. Create an online, hyperlinked map showing the routes of various Indian tribes that decided to sign treaties, where their ancestral lands were, and where they ended up.

SUGGESTED SOURCES

Primary Sources

"Indian Affairs: Laws and Treaties." http://digital.library.okstate.edu/kappler/index.htm. Arranged in volumes by spans of years, these online books provide the full text of pages that relate to all U.S. treaties and laws with American Indians during the time of the Indian Removal Act.

"The Indian Removal Act of 1830." http://www.synaptic.bc.ca/ejournal/IndianRemovalAct.htm. Provides the full text of the act that legislated the removal of American Indians from their ancestral lands. A copy of Andrew Jackson's first inaugural address and nine annual addresses to Congress.

"Library of Congress—Indian Removal Act." http://www.loc.gov/rr/program/bib/ourdocs/Indian.html. Furnishes primary sources in the form of maps, images, speeches, laws, and legislative history concerning the Indian Removal Act of 1830.

"National Archives Administration—President Andrew Jackson's Message to Congress 'On Indian Removal' (1830)." http://www.ourdocuments.gov/doc.php?flash=true&doc=25. Furnishes the full text of President Jackson's message to Congress concerning the need for an Indian Removal policy.

Secondary Sources

Burstein, Andrew. *The Passions of Andrew Jackson*. New York: Knopf, 2003. This psychobiography of Andrew Jackson supports a thesis that his enmity toward the American Indian eclipsed that of the usual racism of the era.

Hoxie, Frederick E. *A Final Promise: The Campaign to Assimilate the Indians, 1880–1920*. Lincoln, NE: University of Nebraska Press, 2001. The beginning part of this book traces the history of treatment of the American Indian, particularly by President Jackson's administration.

O'Brien, Sean Michael. *In Bitterness and in Tears: Andrew Jackson's Destruction of the Creeks and Seminoles*. Guilford, CT: The Lyons Press, 2005. Describes Andrew Jackson's campaign to eradicate Creek and Seminole resistance to expansion in the southeastern part of the United States.

Remini, Robert V. *Andrew Jackson and His Indian Wars*. New York: Viking Press, 2001. Discusses the significant role that President Andrew Jackson played in America's relations with American Indians beginning with his childhood experiences, prejudices against them, and government policies that he personally espoused.

Satz, Ronald N. *American Indian Policy in the Jacksonian Era.* Reprint. Norman, OK: University of Oklahoma Press, 2002. Contradicts Burstein's book and depicts Jackson as a person who truly believed that it was best to separate American Indians from settlers who were intent on taking their lands.

Stewart, Mark, ed. *The Indian Removal Act: Forced Relocation.* Minneapolis, MN: Compass Point, 2007. Written for secondary school students, this work begins with the hardships of the Cherokees on the "Trail of Tears" and then traces the history of European-American encroachment on the five tribes affected by the Indian Removal Act.

Strouth, Theresa, ed. *To Marry an Indian: The Marriage of Harriett Gold and Elias Boudinot in Letters, 1823–1839.* Chapel Hill, NC: University of North Carolina Press, 2005. Relates the experiences of the marriage of American Harriett Gold to a Cherokee and their life in the Cherokee capitol, New Echota before the Trail of Tears.

Thornton, Russell. *American Indian Holocaust and Survival: A Population History Since 1492.* Norman, OK: University of Oklahoma Press, 1987. Discusses the impact of removal and relocation on various American tribes and its unfortunate legacy.

Vandervort, Bruce. *Indian Wars of Canada, Mexico and the United States: 1812–1900.* London: Routledge, 2006. Gives specific information about various Indian battles, including maps and illustrations. Chapter 5 is devoted solely to a discussion of the ones involving the Indian Removal Act.

Wallace, Anthony. *The Long, Bitter Trail: Andrew Jackson and the Indians.* New York: Hill and Wang, 1993. Presents a scholarly treatment of the Indian removal saga, including the effect relocation had on the Choctaw, Cherokee, and Seminole tribes. Wallace also demonstrates that the results of this plan linger today.

World Wide Web

"American History Timeline Clashes Between U.S. Soldiers and Native Americans in the Wild West." http://americanhistory.about.com/library/time lines/bltimelineusnative.htm. Furnishes an annotated chronology of conflicts that occurred between the U.S. government and American Indians from 1824 to 1890.

"Digital History—Indian Removal." http://www.digitalhistory.uh.edu/database/article_display.cfm?HHID=638. Contains an easy-to-understand overview of the Indian Removal Act.

"The Effects of Removal on American Indian Tribes." http://www.nhc.rtp.nc.us/
tserve/nattrans/ntecoindian/essays/indianremovalb.htm. Includes maps,
illustrations, and images of primary source documents that show the negative effects of relocating thousands of Americans west of the Mississippi
River including the Choctaw, Cherokee, Chickasaw, Creek, and Seminole
tribes.

"Indian Removal Act (1830)." http://www.historicaldocuments.com/
IndianRemovalAct.htm. Gives the full text of the Indian Removal Act
along with important additional primary source links to treaty and legal
battles that were unsuccessfully fought by American Indians in an
attempt to retain their ancestral lands.

"PBS—Indian Removal 1814–1858." http://www.pbs.org/wgbh/aia/part4/
4p2959.html. Provides a lengthy explanation of the events and issues
behind the Indian Removal Act.

"President Andrew Jackson's Case for the Removal Act: First Annual Message to
Congress, 8 December 1830." http://www.mtholyoke.edu/acad/intrel/an
drew.htm. Furnishes the full text of the reasons why President Andrew
Jackson desired to relocate all American Indians west of the Mississippi
River.

"U.S. Department of State—Indian Treaties and the Removal Act of 1830."
http://www.state.gov/r/pa/ho/time/dwe/16338.htm. This brief, government overview of the Indian Removal Act comes very close to an apolo-
gia regarding the U.S. government's treatment of American Indians
during the nineteenth century.

Multimedia Sources

"Jacksonian Democracy and the Indian Removal Act of 1830." http://www.osv
.org/school/lesson_plans/ShowLessons.php?LessonID=40&UnitID=6.
This fifty-six page presentation includes copies of primary sources, questions about the Indian Removal Act, and a multitude of lesson plans.

Tribal Nations: The Story of Federal Law. Fairbanks, AK: Tanana Chiefs Conference and Signature Media Productions, 2006. 1 DVD. 60 minutes.
Provides a history of how specific federal laws were developed to work
with various American Indian tribes.

34. Nat Turner's Slave Rebellion (1831)

Nothing scared slave-owning Southerners more than the idea of a slave
revolt. By the 1820s, for example, the slave population in many parts of

South Carolina outnumbered the Whites. Slave rebellions were not new to Southerners either. In 1739, slaves in a bloody uprising under the leadership of a slave named Jemmy killed twenty-five Whites. In 1800, Gabriel Prosser led a group of one thousand slaves in revolt in Richmond, Virginia, which failed when the word of his plans got out, and he was apprehended and hanged. Twenty-two years later, Denmark Vesey planned a huge rebellion that entailed the capture of Charleston, South Carolina. His plans, however, were also leaked, and he was executed. When the Abolitionist Movement grew and many well-known statesmen and clergy began to agitate for the emancipation of slaves, rumors flew that they might incite them to murder their masters. William Lloyd Garrison, author of the abolitionist newspaper *The Liberator,* thundered and railed against slavery to a degree that some historians have conjectured that he influenced Nat Turner to lead his revolt. In 1831 Turner, a literate slave from Southampton, Virginia, led a revolt with six fellow slaves. Turner was extremely religious, and among his fellow slaves he enjoyed a reputation as a preacher and prophet. His group killed his master and the rest of the family, and then went on to murder other Whites on neighboring farms. Turner and his band were eventually caught by over three thousand armed federal and local militias. While awaiting execution, he was interviewed by attorney Thomas Gray who was seeking to discover the reasons for the insurrection. His work, titled *The Confessions of Nat Turner,* is an excellent account of the entire episode.

TERM PAPER SUGGESTIONS

1. Nat Turner was referred to in the newspapers of 1831 as "General Nat." In his confessions, investigate what qualities and characteristics he displayed that make this an apt title.

2. Write an analysis about why Nat Turner showed no remorse for the murders he committed.

3. Compare and contrast the rebellions of Nat Turner and the Roman slave Spartacus. Were both men justified in their actions?

4. Rumors of Nat Turner's rebellion swept South Carolina and are thought to have been one of the underlying fears that caused South Carolina to take such an extreme position about states' rights during the Nullification Crisis. Discuss how this insurrection may have influenced South Carolinians to be apprehensive about future government laws.

5. Describe what might have happened in 1831 in Virginia if Nat Turner's revolt had not taken place. Discuss any movement for gradual emancipation. Were Virginians expressing abolitionist sentiments in the local newspapers or other public means of communication?

6. Compare the rebellions of Jemmy, Prosser, Vesey, and Turner for similarities and their reasons for failure.

ALTERNATIVE TERM PAPER SUGGESTIONS

1. Write several online editorials expressing the view that Nat Turner's rebellion was a moral success and that he should be considered one of the greatest social reformers of the day.

2. Imagine that you are Nat Turner and have decided to give a television interview to Thomas Gray, an attorney who is not even representing you. What issues would you want to cover to make sure that your voice was heard before you were executed?

SUGGESTED SOURCES

Primary Sources

Aptheker, Herbert. *Nat Turner's Slave Rebellion: Together with the Full Text of the So-Called: "Confessions" of Nat Turner Made in Prison in 1831.* Mineola, NY: Dover Publications, 2006. Noted African American historian Aptheker presents the complete set of primary source documents concerning the Nat Turner insurrection.

Baker, James T. *Nat Turner: Cry Freedom in America.* Fort Worth, TX: Harcourt Brace, 1998. Combines primary and secondary sources to shed light on the Turner insurrection.

Turner, Nat. *The Confessions of Nat Turner and other Related Documents.* New York: St. Martin's Press, 1996. Provides an excellent introduction giving the details of the insurrection and the full text of Nat Turner's interview with Thomas Gray.

Secondary Sources

Bisson, Terry, and John Davenport. *Nat Turner: Slave Revolt Leader.* Philadelphia, PA: Chelsea House, 2004. Written for secondary school students, this work gives an excellent overview together with excerpts from Turner's book.

DeLombard, Jeannine Marie. *Slavery on Trial: Law, Abolitionism, and Print Culture.* Chapel Hill, NC: University of North Carolina Press, 2007.

Discusses how slavery trials, including Nat Turner's, were treated in the press during a period of growing abolitionism.

Foner, Eric. *Nat Turner*. Englewood Cliffs, NJ: Prentice-Hall, 1971. Noted historian Foner considers the slave revolt of Nat Turner in light of the early Abolitionist Movement.

French, Scot. *The Rebellious Slave: Nat Turner in American Memory*. Boston, MA: Houghton Mifflin, 2004. Examines how Nat Turner's rebellion is viewed in terms of popular culture.

Greenberg, Kenneth. *Nat Turner: A Slave Rebellion in History and Memory*. New York: Oxford University Press, 2003. Successfully weaves all of the latest research and scholarship concerning the rebellion of Nat Turner.

Oates, Stephen B. *The Fires of Jubilee: Nat Turner's Fierce Rebellion*. New York: Harper, 1990. Provides a riveting narrative of the life and times of Nat Turner and the slave system that drove him to his rebellion.

Robertson, David M. *Denmark Vesey: The Buried Story of America's Largest Slave Rebellion and the Man Who Led It*. New York: Knopf, 2000. Relates the story of Denmark Vesey's life and his final act of defiance in leading a slave revolt in 1822.

Sidbury, James. *Ploughshares into Swords: Race, Rebellion, and Identity in Gabriel's Virginia, 1730–1810*. New York: Cambridge University Press, 1997. Presents the story of Gabriel Prosser's attempted slave rebellion in Richmond, Virginia.

Styron, William. *The Confessions of Nat Turner*. New York: Vintage, 1992. Although this book is considered fiction, it is based upon meticulous historical research by a major American author.

Tragle, Henry Irving. *The Southampton Slave Revolt of 1831: A Compilation of Source Material*. Amherst, MA: University of Massachusetts Press, 1971. Contains a list of all documents, articles, and books pertaining to the Nat Turner slave rebellion.

Walker, Lois A., and Susan R. Silverman. *A Documentary History of Gullah Jack Pritchard and the Denmark Vesey Slave Insurrection of 1822*. Lewiston, DE: Edwin Mellen Press, 2000. Based on primary sources, the authors relate the story of Denmark Vesey and Jack Pritchard's attempted slave insurrection in 1822.

World Wide Web

"The Confessions of Nat Turner by Nat Turner." http://www.gutenberg.org/etext/15333. Project Gutenberg contains the full online text of Nat Turner's confessions.

"Fear of Insurrection." http://www.pbs.org/wgbh/aia/part3/3h1519t.html. Contains an excerpt from Chapter 12, *Incidents in the Life of a Slave Girl Written by Herself* by Hariette Jacobs about the constant harassment and even murder of Blacks as a reaction to Nat Turner's slave rebellion.

"'The Insurrection' by William Lloyd Garrison, *The Liberator,* September 3, 1831." http://fair-use.org/the-liberator/1831/09/03/the-insurrection. Provides the full text of William Lloyd Garrison's story in his abolitionist newspaper, *The Liberator,* concerning Nat Turner's rebellion.

"Nat Turner's Rebellion." http://afroamhistory.about.com/od/natturner/a/turnerrebellion.htm. Presents a succinct overview of the facts concerning the rebellion, including some useful resource links.

"PBS—Africans in America. Nat Turner's Rebellion." http://www.pbs.org/wgbh/aia/part3/3p1518.html. Contains a short overview of the facts concerning Nat Turner's rebellion, including several excellent resource links.

"PBS—The Richmond *Enquirer* on Nat Turner's Rebellion." http://www.pbs.org/wgbh/aia/part3/3h499t.html. Provides the full text of the newspaper article from the Richmond *Enquirer* about Nat Turner's rebellion.

"The Southampton Slave Revolt." http://www.historybuff.com/library/refslave.html. Provides an overview of events followed by a full text letter, dated November 2, 1831, describing the revolt to the editor of *The American Beacon of Norfolk.*

Multimedia Sources

The Confessions of Nat Turner: America's Black Spartacus Remembered. New York: Masterbuy Audiobooks, 1999. 1 Audiocassette. 90 minutes. Narrated by Bernard Addison, Michael Collins, and Allen Gilmore, this audiobook relates the story of Nat Turner's rebellion and compares it with that of the Roman slave, Spartacus.

Nat Turner: A Troublesome Property. San Francisco CA: California Newsreel, 2003. 1 DVD. 60 minutes. Discusses the legacy of the Nat Turner slave revolt and the impact it had on the times.

35. Nullification Crisis (1832–1833)

The Nullification Crisis was no insignificant matter. Within its constitutional arguments and debate over states' rights versus those of the national government were sown the seeds for the future Civil War and discord that continues to arise today. It pitted President Andrew Jackson and South Carolina Senator John C. Calhoun against each other in a battle that almost resulted in South Carolina seceding from the Union as early as 1833. The two waged war in 1828 over the passage of tariffs that were designed to protect emerging northern manufacturing industries such as clothing, clockmaking, and iron processing by imposing an extra tax on any similar foreign product. The tariffs also let American manufacturers charge more for their products as long as the price was still below the cost of the foreign product. South Carolina was in economic decline from poor cotton production and population decreases, and South Carolina leaders believed that the tariff would impose an additional financial hardship on their citizens. Led by Senator Calhoun, South Carolina declared the Tariff Act of 1828 null and void, which precipitated a constitutional law debate of monumental proportions between Senator Daniel Webster of Massachusetts and Senator Robert Hayne of South Carolina and severely taxed the negotiating skills of three ex-Presidents and the "Great Compromiser": Senator Henry Clay of Kentucky. At the eleventh hour, a compromise tariff bill was enacted that barely prevented President Jackson from sending federal troops to Charleston to keep South Carolina from seceding and violating the passage of a federal law.

TERM PAPER SUGGESTIONS

1. Ostensibly the Nullification Crisis was a battle over states' rights, but it was also about the election of President Andrew Jackson. Investigate the role of Martin Van Buren in using the Tariff Act of 1828 to get Jackson elected president.

2. Early tariffs were supported by the entire country including South Carolina. Discuss how the changing economic situation of South Carolina may have caused the Nullification Crisis by researching the Panic of 1819, soil erosion and nutrient depletion from overplanting of cotton, population decreases, and competition from other cotton-growing areas such as Georgia and Alabama.

3. Read some of Senator Calhoun's position papers such as "Exposition and Protest," analyze the validity of the constitutional issues he addresses, and provide an opinion on their merit.

4. Lurking beneath the current of the tariff debate was the "peculiar institution of slavery." Examine why South Carolina believed that the imposition of burdensome tariffs by the federal government would open the door to a law against slavery in the state.

5. Explore one of the most exciting congressional debates in the nation's history between Senators Daniel Webster and Robert Hayne. Analyze their arguments from a forensic debate format.

6. President Jackson, without equivocation, chose to maintain the Union over South Carolina's nullification and secession threats. Discuss all of his efforts to prevent South Carolina from secession, including seeking the help of ex-presidents, the passage of the Force Bill, additional compromises, and behind-the-scenes strategies and ploys.

ALTERNATIVE TERM PAPER SUGGESTIONS

1. Both political parties owned various newspapers in the 1830s. Using cartoon software programs such as "Comic Life Software" (available at plasq.com) or drawing by hand, create eight political opposing viewpoints cartoons. Accompany each one with an historical explanation of the issues depicted in each cartoon.

2. Prepare an annotated, online timeline of events and issues beginning with the passage of the Alien and Sedition Laws of 1788–1789 that led up to the Nullification Crisis.

SUGGESTED SOURCES

Primary Sources

Sellers, Charles. *Andrew Jackson, Nullification and the State-Rights Tradition.* Chicago, IL: Rand McNally, 1963. Provides an anthology of primary sources concerning the Nullification Crisis of 1832–1833.

Webster, Daniel, Robert Hayne, and Herman Beltz. *The Webster-Hayne Debate on the Nature of the Union: Selected Documents.* Indianapolis, IN: Liberty Fund, 2000. Contains the full text of many nullification debates that took place between Hayne and Webster.

Secondary Sources

Brands, H. W. *Andrew Jackson: His Life and Times.* New York: Random House, 2005. This psychobiography of President Andrew Jackson examines some of the political motives and personal characteristics that may have contributed to his positions on various important decisions during his administration.

Ellis, Richard E. *The Union at Risk: Jacksonian Democracy, States' Rights, and Nullification Crisis.* New York: Oxford University Press, 1989. This is one of the standard, academic works about President Andrew Jackson's most critical presidential crisis and how he handled it.

Ericson, David F. *The Shaping of American Liberalism: The Debates over Ratification, Nullification, and Slavery.* Chicago, IL: University of Chicago

Press, 1993. Part two of this work analyzes the debates between John C. Calhoun and Daniel Webster concerning states' versus federal constitutional rights.

Frehling, William F. *Prelude to Civil War: The Nullification Controversy in South Carolina, 1816–1836.* Reprint. New York: Oxford University Press, 2005. Winner of several prestigious history prizes, this work brings the times during the Nullification Crisis alive and explains why it led to South Carolina's eventual secession prior to the Civil War.

Magliocca, Gerald N. *Andrew Jackson and the Constitution: The Rise and Fall of Generational Regimes.* Lawrence, KS: University Press of Kansas, 2007. Provides an academic examination of the legal battles that President Jackson and his administration waged including states' rights and the Nullification Crisis.

Peterson, Merrill D. *The Great Triumvirate, Webster, Clay, and Calhoun.* New York: Oxford University Press, 1989. Discusses the important roles that each cited senator played during the Nullification Crisis.

Powell, Edward Payson. *Nullification and Secession in the United States: A History of the Six Attempts during the First Century of the Republic.* New York: Lawbook Exchange Ltd., 2002. Places the Nullification Crisis of 1832–1833 in historical perspective with a discussion of previous proposals in both the North and the South.

Remini, Robert V. *Andrew Jackson: The Course of Democracy, 1833–1845.* Baltimore, MD: The Johns Hopkins University Press, 1998. Deals with President Jackson's handling of the Nullification Crisis.

Remini, Robert V. *Henry Clay: Statesman for the Union.* Reprint. New York: W. W. Norton & Company, 1993. This outstanding biography of Henry Clay details the role he played in solving the Nullification Crisis.

Sinha, Manisha. *The Counterrevolution of Slavery: Politics and Ideology in Antebellum South Carolina.* Chapel Hill, NC: University of North Carolina, 2000. Concludes that states' rights arguments and other positions on the need for states' autonomy was basically a subterfuge for legally maintaining the institution of slavery in South Carolina.

Wilentz, Sean. *Andrew Jackson.* New York: Henry Holt & Company, 2005. Princeton historian Wilentz analyzes Jackson's policies and positions on all events during his administration including the Nullification Crisis.

World Wide Web

"The American System Speeches on the Tariff Question and on Internal Improvements Principally Delivered in the House of Representatives of the United States by Andrew Stewart." http://quod.lib.umich.eda/cgi/text/pageviewer=idx?c=moa;cc=moa;q1=American%20system. Provides the full text of several speeches by Andrew Stewart concerning how the American system worked.

"Andrew Jackson 7th President of the United States." http://www.andrewjackson.org/. Contains an extensive online biography of President Andrew Jackson and discussion of the factors behind the Nullification Crisis.

"The Avalon Project at Yale Law School—President Jackson's Message to the Senate and House Regarding South Carolina's Nullification Ordinance; January 16, 1833." http://www.yale.edu/lawweb/avalon/presiden/messages/ajack001.htm. Provides the full text of the Force Bill that President Jackson sent to Congress in response to South Carolina's decision to declare the Tariff Act null and void.

"The Avalon Project at Yale Law School—South Carolina Ordinance of Nullification, November 24, 1832." http://www.yale.edu/lawweb/avalon/states/sc/ordnull.htm. Furnishes the full text of the resolution that the South Carolina legislature passed declaring the U.S. Tariff Act of 1828 null and void.

"A Critical Study of Nullification in South Carolina by David Franklin Houston." http://books.google.com/books?id=-XssAAAAIAAJ. Published by Googlebooks.com, this online 1896 text provides a complete history of the Nullification Crisis written from a nineteenth-century viewpoint.

"John C. Calhoun's Exposition and Protest." http://oll.libertyfund.org/?option=com_staticxt&staticfile=show.php%3Ftitle=683&chapter=107117&layout=html&Itemid=27. Contains the full text of the document that Senator John C. Calhoun prepared for the South Carolina legislature concerning its right to declare a federal act null and void.

"State of the Union Address: Andrew Jackson, 4 December 1832." http://www.thisnation.com/library/sotu/1832aj.html. Supplies the full text of President Jackson's state of the union address indicating that he was not totally behind the tariff law and viewed it as a temporary expedient.

Multimedia Sources

Biography—Andrew Jackson: A Man for the People. New York: A&E Home Video, 1995. 1 DVD. 50 minutes. Provides expert commentary and period art to tell the story of the life and times of Andrew Jackson and the crises he faced as America's seventh president.

36. *Democracy in America* (1835 and 1840) by Alexis de Tocqueville

In May 1831, Frenchmen Alexis de Tocqueville (1805–1859) and Gustave de Beaumont (1802–1865) were commissioned by the French government to study the American prison system. They toured the country for nine months visiting New England, New York, Philadelphia, Baltimore, Cincinnati, Tennessee, New Orleans, and Washington, D.C., observing the society, economy, and political system. Beaumont wrote a book about prisons and a novel about American race relations. Tocqueville published a two-volume work titled *Democracy in America* that earned him the appellation "Father of Sociology." Although often misquoted, Tocqueville's work proved amazingly prophetic about the future growth, changes, and development of American society. Bringing an outsider's sometimes prescient viewpoint, de Tocqueville was struck by the lack of a class system in the United States, which he saw as both a strength and a weakness. While he believed that equality gave every person greater opportunities to improve his or her lot in life, he also saw how the majority might be tempted by leaders who would stifle the opinion of a necessary minority. Tocqueville saw three balances to the potential "tyranny of the majority: freedom of the press, the rule of law, and the opportunity to worship as one pleased." Although he misjudged the potential for poverty in a capitalistic country, gender inequality, and the coming civil war over slavery, his work provides a monumental insight into nineteenth-century America, and it continues to be cited as a resource for many government twenty-first century problems.

TERM PAPER SUGGESTIONS

1. Access Chapter VI of *Democracy in America* at http://xroads.virginia.edu/~Hyper/DETOC/ch4_06.htm. Read *What Sort of Despotism Democratic Nations Have to Fear*. Write a paper that either agrees or disagrees with Tocqueville's opinion that the United States is susceptible to this type of despotism.

2. Read Chapter IX, *Education of Young Women in the United States,* at http://xroads.virginia.edu/~Hyper/DETOC/ch3_09.htm. In light of today's society, would you describe Tocqueville's views on women as conservative or liberal?

3. Tocqueville saw the country at a time of increasing industrialization. Explore some of the fears that he perceived that democracy would have as a result of this change.

4. Discuss Tocqueville's prescience concerning the potential enmity between Russia and the United States and his reasons for coming to that conclusion.

5. Tocqueville believed that the party system could be an instrument of constant agitation because there might be frequent elections that would disrupt the normal processes of government. Discuss the potential virtues and evils of a two party system and why Tocqueville might have missed its growth and political potential.

6. Describe what Tocqueville observed that made him correctly predict the abolishment of slavery but not the end of racism and discrimination.

ALTERNATIVE TERM PAPER SUGGESTIONS

1. Design a Web site tracing Tocqueville's route and investigate how he may have reached some of his conclusions about American society concerning the issues of individualism and equality.

2. Prepare a two-minute iMovie of Tocqueville's life that is similar to an A&E Biography showing why he might have been not only astonished by nineteenth-century American society but also repelled.

SUGGESTED SOURCES

Primary Sources

"Alexis de Tocqueville, *Democracy in America.*" http://xroads.virginia.edu/ ~HYPER/DETOC/toc_indx.html. Contains the full text of both volumes of Tocqueville's *Democracy in America.*

De Tocqueville, Alexis. *Democracy in America.* New York: Penguin, 2003. Contains two volumes of Tocqueville's observations and commentary concerning nineteenth-century American society, including his sojourn among the Iroquois in Michigan and his trip to Lake Oneida.

De Tocqueville, Alexis. *Writings on Empire and Slavery.* Baltimore, MD: The Johns Hopkins University Press, 2003. Contains the thoughts of Tocqueville on slavery and colonialism.

Secondary Sources

Brogan, Hugh. *Alexis de Tocqueville: A Life.* New Haven, CT: Yale University Press, 2007. Provides the definitive biography of de Tocqueville in English, including many excerpts with explanations from *Democracy in America.*

Cohen, David. *Chasing the Red, White, and Blue: A Journey in Tocqueville's Footsteps through Contemporary America.* New York: Picador, 2001. Using statistical data, Cohen argues that American is no longer the land of equality as Tocqueville once envisioned it, but is strongly divided by wealth and race.

Drolet, Michael. *Democracy and Social Reform.* New York: Palgrave Macmillan, 2004. Discusses Tocqueville's other writings about prisons, poverty, and orphaned children and shows how they enlightened his thinking about *Democracy in America.*

Epstein, Joseph. *Alexis de Tocqueville Democracy's Guide.* New York: Harper-Collins, 2007. This outstanding biography of the life and work of Tocqueville analyzes his influence and significance through two centuries of American history.

McGowan, John. *American Liberalism: An Interpretation for Our Time.* Chapel Hill, NC: University of North Carolina Press, 2007. Refers to Tocqueville's *Democracy in America* as it relates to the political definition of liberalism in the United States.

Mancini, Matthew. *Alexis de Tocqueville.* New York: Twayne Publishers, 1993. Analyzes Tocqueville's work from a literary point of view. The work is also part of the Twayne author series online that is available through Thomson Gale.

Mancini, Matthew. *Alexis de Tocqueville and American Intellectuals: From His Times to Ours.* Landham, MD: Rowman & Littlefield, 2003. Explores the reception of Tocqueville's work in America from 1831 to the present day.

Mitchell, Joshua. *The Fragility of Freedom: Tocqueville on Religion, Democracy, and the American Future.* Chicago, IL: University of Chicago Press, 1999. Explores the observations from Tocqueville's *Democracy in America* about the role of religion in politics.

Pierson, George. *Tocqueville in America.* Reprint. Baltimore, MD: The Johns Hopkins University Press, 1996. Describes the nine month travels of Tocqueville and Beaumont in 1831, including Beaumont's observations of the prison system.

Schleifer, James T. *The Making of Tocqueville's Democracy in America.* Indianapolis, IN: Liberty Funds, 2000. Provides information about how prophetic Tocqueville's observations on American society were and which ones have not been realized.

Welch, Cheryl B. *The Cambridge Companion to Tocqueville.* New York: Cambridge University Press, 2006. Provides excellent interpretative essays by noted scholars concerning Tocqueville's observations on democracy, religion, despotism, and liberty in America.

World Wide Web

"Alexis de Tocqueville (1805–59)." http://www.nagasaki-gaigo.ac.jp/ishikawa/amlit/t/tocqueville19ro.htm. Furnishes a short biography of Tocqueville along with links related to his book, *Democracy in America.*

"The Alexis de Tocqueville Tour Exploring Democracy in America May 9, 1997–February 20, 1998." http://www.tocqueville.org/. This Web site contains excellent links to C-SPAN's bus tour that recreated Tocqueville's tour of America in 1831. It features some of his journal entries, modern references to the places he visited, the full text of *Democracy in America,* a bibliography, and a set of useful lesson plans.

"All About Alexis de Tocqueville." http://www.tocqueville.org/chap1.htm. Furnishes a lengthy, annotated chronology of Tocqueville's life.

"Democracy in America." http://xroads.virginia.edu/~HYPER/DETOC/home.html. Use images from this outstanding multimedia site to create an iMovie. It contains maps, diary entries, letters, virtual itinerary tours, 1840 census data, and Beaumont's and Tocqueville's observations about slavery, women, and religion.

"Economics of the 1830s: An Overview." http://www.connerprairie.org/historyonline/economy.html. Provides a brief economic summary of the 1830s that places Tocqueville's work in perspective.

"Ordinary Living in 1830s America." http://www.geocities.com/old_lead/ordinarylife.htm. This outstanding site features diary entries and descriptions of life in 1830s America plus information about how many people lived on farms and in cities and towns. It provides a snapshot view of some of the life that Tocqueville probably observed on his tour.

"Resources on Alexis de Tocqueville." http://faculty.law.lsu.edu/ccorcos/resume/tocqueind.htm. Provides a well-maintained set of resource links about Tocqueville.

Multimedia Sources

Traveling Tocqueville's America. Washington, DC: C-SPAN.ORG Video, 1998. 1 videocassette. 96 minutes. Shows the nine month school bus C-SPAN tour that celebrated Tocqueville's writing of *Democracy in America* and explores how the book relates to democracy in the twentieth century.

37. Texas Revolution (1835–1836)

Euro-Americans began to colonize Texas as early as 1821 when Spanish officials granted Moses Austin a large tract of unpopulated land. The grant, however, had to be renegotiated by his son Stephen Fuller Austin when Mexico became an independent country. Within a decade some twenty to twenty-five thousand Americans had migrated to Texas, and they far outnumbered the resident Mexicans known as Tejanos. Mexican officials noticed that Texans were not assimilating. They were not learning Spanish, were not practicing Roman Catholicism, and continued to have slaves in defiance of Mexican laws that banned it. In 1830 Mexico passed the Colonization Law forbidding further immigration from the United States. Texans chafed under the new law and also under a government that interfered with trade and did little to dispense justice in criminal and civil matters. After several skirmishes between Texans and local Mexican troops, President and General Antonio López de Santa Anna with a force of four thousand soldiers massacred about 189 Texans at the Alamo in San Antonio, Texas. It made martyrs of Davy Crockett and Jim Bowie, and the phrase "Remember the Alamo" became a rallying cry for full scale rebellion against Mexico. General Santa Anna was eventually defeated at the Battle of San Jacinto River in 1836 and Texas became an independent republic. It was not until 1845, however, that Texas was annexed by the United States and became the twenty-eighth state.

TERM PAPER SUGGESTIONS

1. Discuss the roles that Moses and Stephen Fuller Austin played in creating the state of Texas.

2. Examine the feasibility of the plan by Mexican General Manuel de Mier y Terán (1789–1832) to limit U.S. influence in Texas.

3. Analyze the previous skirmishes between Mexican troops and Texans at Anahuac, Velasco, and Gonzales from a military perspective. Explain how they might have contributed to a false belief on the part of Texans that they could prevail at the Siege of the Alamo.

4. Investigate how Tejanos (native born Texans of Hispanic descent) were divided in their loyalties. Be sure to mention the role that the Tejano brothers Jose Antonio and Angel Navarro played on either side. Draw inferences to the same divided loyalties that conflicted similar families during the American Civil War.

5. Research the geographic boundaries of the Louisiana Purchase and use its parameters to argue a claim that Texas was included as part of the Louisiana Purchase.

6. U.S. Presidents Andrew Jackson, Martin Van Buren, and William Henry Harrison were each reluctant to annex Texas. Examine the reasons behind their resistance.

ALTERNATIVE TERM PAPER SUGGESTIONS

1. Assume you are Sam Houston, soon to be the first president of the Republic of Texas. Draft a Declaration of Independence from Mexico enumerating the grievances against Mexico and the reasons they warrant regional autonomy for Texas.

2. Prepare a series of maps within a PowerPoint presentation that shows the geographic and military importance of the State of Texas to the United States.

SUGGESTED SOURCES

Primary Sources

Gaddy, Jerry J., comp. *Texas in Revolt: Contemporary Newspaper Accounts of the Texas Revolution*. Ft. Collins, CO: Old Army Press, 1973. Contains newspaper accounts from 1835 to 1836 about the Texas Revolution.

Tierina, Andres. *Tejanos and Texas Under the Mexican Flag 1821–1836*. College Station, TX: Texas A&M University, 1994. This award-winning book provides extensive excerpts from Texan and Mexican archives concerning the relationship between Tejanos and Texans prior to and during the Texas Revolution.

Secondary Sources

Calvert, Robert, and Arnoldo De Leon. *The History of Texas*. 3rd ed. Wheeling, IL: Harlan Davidson, 2002. Several chapters of this contemporary history of Texas contain a good overview of the Texas revolution and annexation.

Cantrell, Gregg. *Stephen F. Austin: Empresario of Texas*. New Haven, CT: Yale University Press, 1999. Explores how Austin put aside his own commercial self-interest in land speculation to pursue a course of independence for the Republic of Texas.

Crisp. James E. *Sleuthing the Alamo: Davy Crockett's Last Stand and Other Mysteries of the Texas Revolution*. New York: Oxford University Press, 2005. Sheds light on how Davy Crockett died at the Alamo.

Davis, William C. *Lone Star Rising: The Revolutionary Birth of the Texas Republic*. College Station, TX: Texas A&M University, 2006. This almost encyclopedic history concerns the background of the Texas Revolution and the annexation of Texas in 1845.

Davis, William C. *Three Roads to the Alamo: The Lives and Fortunes of David Crockett, James Bowie, and William Barret Travis.* New York: HarperCollins, 1998. Discusses the lives of three disparate Americans and the circumstances that brought them to the Siege of the Alamo.

Dingus, Anne. *The Truth about Texas.* Houston, TX: Gulf Publishing Company, 1995. Furnishes an overview of Texas history that is useful for beginning one's research.

Fehrenbach, T. R. "The Clash of Cultures," "Revolution," and "Blood and Soil." In *Lone Star: A History of Texas and Texans.* New York: Wing Books, 1991. Relates the facts concerning nonconformists and confrontations between Euro-Americans and Mexicans in Texas that contributed to the Texas Revolution.

Gurasich, Marj. *Benito and the White Dove: A Story of Jose Antonio Navarro.* Austin, TX: Eakin Press, 1989. This fictionalized biography relates the story of Antonio Jose Navarro and the role he played in the Texas Revolution.

Hardin, Stephen L. *Texian Iliad.* Austin, TX: University of Texas Press, 1994. Provides a balanced history of the Texas Revolution as seen from the Mexican and Texan perspectives.

Lack, Paul D. *The Texas Revolutionary Experience: A Political and Social History, 1835–1836.* College Station, TX: Texas A&M Press, 1992. Provides an academic account of the various factions involved in the Texas Revolution and the effects it had on each of them.

Nofi, Albert A. *The Alamo and the Texas War of Independence, September 30, 1835 to April 21, 1836.* Conshohocken, PA: Combined Books, 1992. Furnishes information about all the combatants and their roles in the Texas Revolution plus detailed battle plans involving major confrontations.

Reichstein, Andreas. *Rise of the Lone Star: The Making of Texas.* College Station, TX: Texas A&M University, 1989. Contains an excellent military history of all the significant battles that took place between the Republic of Texas and Mexico during the Texas Revolution.

World Wide Web

"Evacuation of Texas: Translation of the Representation Addressed to the Supreme Government / by Vicente Filisola, in Defence of his Honor, and Explanation of his Operations as Commander-in-Chief of the Army against Texas." http://texashistory.unt.edu/data/UNT/Books/meta-pth -6110.tkl. This online book explains why the Mexican army withdrew from Texas after it lost at the Battle of San Jacinto.

"History of the Revolution in Texas, Particularly of the War of 1835 & 36; Together with the Latest Geographical, Topographical, and Statistical Accounts of the Country, from the Most Authentic Sources." http:// texashistory.unt.edu/data/UNT/Books/meta-pth-6109.tkl. Provides primary sources in English and Spanish about the Texas Revolution. Users can search by era, collection, and subject.

"Military Maps of the Texas Revolution." http://texashistory.unt.edu/data/ UNT/Maps/meta-pth-2489.tkl. Contains a series of maps about different battles that took place prior to and during the Texas War of Independence.

"Texas Revolution." http://www.tsha.utexas.edu/handbook/online/articles/TT/ qdt1.html. Presents an overview of the Texas Revolution beginning with the Battle of Gonzales.

"The Texas War of Independence 1836." http://www.answers.com/topic/texas -revolution-and-annexation. Includes an overview of the Texas Revolution and a history of the annexation of Texas that did not occur until 1845 for domestic and international reasons.

"War of Independence 1832–1836." http://www.tamu.edu/ccbn/dewitt/ independcon.htm. This superb site is filled with primary sources consisting of the papers of Texan and Mexican leaders and detailed accounts of various battles prior to and during the Texas Revolution.

"Westward Expansion—The Texas Revolution." http://www.digitalhistory .uh.edu/database/article_display.cfm?HHID=312. Gives an overview of the Texas Revolution together with short, biographical sketches of the major leaders on both sides.

Multimedia Sources

James Michener's Texas. Los Angeles, CA: Republic Entertainment Pictures, 2002. 1 DVD. 180 minutes. This DVD accompanies James Michener's book about Texas and includes narration about the founding of Texas by Moses and Stephen Austin and the war of independence from Mexico.

Remember the Alamo. Hollywood, CA: PBS Home video, 2004. 1 DVD. 137 minutes. Although this movie was produced for entertainment rather than educational purposes, it does not mythologize leaders such as Davy Crockett, James Bowie, William Travis, and General Santa Anna. It succeeds in creating multidimensional characters that provide a genuine history of the event.

38. Samuel Colt and the Revolver (1836)

Up until 1836, a skilled warrior with a bow and arrow could shoot about twenty arrows per minute, while a soldier equipped with a standard musket could load and fire two or three shots per minute. With the invention of Samuel Colt's repeating revolver, the balance on the frontier tipped in favor of the settler and helped seal the fate of many American Indians who were desperately fighting to retain their ancestral lands. Colt's invention also altered how wars were fought in many countries, including America during the Civil War. Samuel Colt (1814–1862) was a determined inventor, manufacturer, and entrepreneur. Sent to sea as a sailor, he was inspired to design his revolver by observing how ship captains used a lever to prevent their helms from rotating backwards, and while on board he carved his first prototype out of wood. Colt spent the next five years raising capital to promote his invention and was finally awarded a patent for a revolver that rotated the cylinder by cocking a hammer, locked the hammer in position after it was fully cocked, and partitioned the rear of the cylinder to prevent premature firing of the other chambers. He had his big marketing breakthrough with sales to the Texas Rangers for use in the 1846 Mexican War. Colt went on to open a large manufacturing plant in Hartford, Connecticut, that prospered during the Civil War. His name is forever associated with the phrase—"Colt, the gun that tamed the West."

TERM PAPER SUGGESTIONS

1. Research Samuel Colt's innovative revolver design and explain how it differed from that of a smoothbore musket. Examine the implications that Colt's invention had for frontier wars.

2. Samuel Colt pursued other inventions such as electrically fired underwater mines and waterproof cable. He was influenced by his friendship with Samuel Morse, inventor of the telegraph, and Robert Fulton's work regarding underwater mines. Research and discuss his innovative efforts in this area.

3. Promoting the invention of his revolver was an uphill battle for Samuel Colt that entailed obtaining a letter of recommendation from President Andrew Jackson, a patent, and a Congressional bill that would allow him to demonstrate it to the military. Trace the marketing history of Samuel Colt's path to commercial success.

4. Analyze how the California gold rush and western expansion were a boon to Colt's business.

5. Colt's armory in Connecticut was a model factory for its time. Research and describe aspects including employee hours, working conditions, worker qualifications, and opportunities for recreation. Contrast them against those of a nineteenth-century mill worker.

6. Colt experienced problems with his revolver when it was first used in the Seminole Wars and his company's trustee board refused to fund new machinery to make interchangeable parts. Investigate what Colt did to solve these problems.

ALTERNATIVE TERM PAPER SUGGESTIONS

1. Assume you have been hired by Samuel Colt to market his new revolver. Create a series of advertisements showing its unique properties for protection along the frontier and for traveling out West.

2. Design a Web-based assembly line with appropriate explanatory hyperlinks that shows how Colt's assembly line probably functioned in the 1830s.

SUGGESTED SOURCES

Primary Sources

Barnard, Henry. *Armsmear: The Home, the Arm, and the Armory of Samuel Colt.* New York: Alvord, 1866. Contains primary sources about Colt's Connecticut factory operations and his mansion, Armsmear.

Mowbray, Stuart C. *The Darling Pepperbox: The Story of Samuel Colt's Forgotten Competitors in Bellingham, Mass. and Woonsocket, R.I.* Lincoln, RI: Andrew Mowbray, 2003. Provides illustrations and other primary sources about a competitor's revolver that some historians believe was the real prototype for Colt's revolver rather than the wooden one he carved while on a ship.

Secondary Sources

Boorman, Dean K. *The History of Colt Firearms.* Guilford, CT: The Lyons Press, 2001. Replete with picture, illustrations, and diagrams of revolvers, this outstanding book discusses how Colt improved upon each model and set up assembly line manufacturing plants that were models for their time.

Grant, Ellsworth S. *The Colt Armory: A History of Colt's Manufacturing Company.* Lincoln, RI: Mowbray, 1995. Contains a history of Samuel Colt's factory and manufacturing process.

Haven, Charles T., and Frank T. Belden. *A History of the Colt Revolver*. New York: Bonanza Books, 1978. Includes many illustrations of various Colt revolvers and how they were improved in the manufacturing process.

Hosley, William N. *Colt: The Making of an American Legend*. Amherst, MA: University of Massachusetts Press, 1996. Provides a scholarly biography of the life and times of Samuel Colt.

Houze, Herbert G. *Samuel Colt: Arms, Art, and Invention*. New Haven, CT: Yale University Press, 2006. Contains illustrations of each of Colt's models, and gives a history of his invention and how he marketed each model.

Howard, Robert A. "Interchangeable Parts Reexamined: The Private Sector of the American Arms Industry on the Eve of the Civil War." *Technology and Culture* 19 (October, 1978): 633–649. (Available in JSTOR.) Disputes the claim of Colt and other weapons manufacturers concerning their ability to truly have interchangeable parts. Instead the author argues that they tried to produce high quality weapons in the most economical ways during the nineteenth century.

Keating, Bern. *The Flamboyant Mr. Colt and his Deadly Six-Shooter*. Garden City, NY: Doubleday, 1978. This nonacademic biography provides a great deal of information concerning Colt's life and family, including how he performed public exhibitions with nitrous oxide to obtain funds to continue marketing his revolver.

Kinard. Jeff. *Pistols: An Illustrated History of Their Impact*. Santa Barbara, CA: ABC-CLIO, 2003. Although this book provides an illustrated history of the growth and development of pistols, one chapter is devoted solely to the invention of the revolver.

Lundeberg, Philip K. *Samuel Colt's Submarine Battery: The Secret and the Enigma*. Washington, DC: Smithsonian Institute Press, 1974. Sheds light on one of Samuel Colt's other inventions that was used to develop underwater electric land mines.

Roland, Alex. *Underwater Warfare in the Age of Sail*. Bloomington, IN: Indiana University Press, 1978. Cites primary source documents that demonstrate Robert Fulton's and Samuel Colt's contributions to developing underwater electric land mines in the nineteenth century.

World Wide Web

"Colt History." http://www.colt.com/mil/history.asp. Provides information about Samuel Colt and the invention of the revolver.

"Colt: Legend and Legacy." http://www.simonpure.com/colt.htm. Contains the full text transcript of a 1997 broadcast program conducted with Herbert Halsey, author of *Colt: The Making of an American Legend,* and Karen

Blanchfield, Curator of the Wadsworth Athenaeum in Hartford, Connecticut, regarding Samuel Colt's life and legacy.

"Coltsville National Historic Landmark Nomination." http://www.coltsville study.org/. This National Park Service site contains maps, photographs, and biographical information about Samuel Colt and the factory he built to manufacture revolvers in Hartford, Connecticut.

"Historic American Buildings—Samuel Colt House." http://lcweb2.loc.gov/cgi -bin/query/S?pp/hh:@FIELD(ALTTITLE+@od1(+armsmear+)). Provides three black and white photographs of Samuel Colt's mansion, Armsmear.

"Samuel Colt." http://www.netstate.com/states/peop/people/ct_sc.htm. Gives an accurate and reliable biographical sketch of Samuel Colt.

"Samuel Colt (1814–1862)*." http://www.ctheritage.org/encyclopedia/topical surveys/colt.htm. Contains the full text of Chapter 1 of Ellsworth S. Grant's book, *The Colt Legacy: The Colt Armory in Hartford*.

"Who Made America?—Samuel Colt." http://www.pbs.org/wgbh/theymade america/whomade/colt_hi.html. This PBS site contains a biographical sketch of Samuel Colt and a short account of the invention that made him famous.

Multimedia Sources

Wild West Tech—Six-Shooter Tech. New York: A&E Home Video Entertainment, 2006. 1 DVD. 60 minutes. Narrates an interesting history of revolvers and what was missing from the Colt revolver that Smith and Wesson exploited to make a fortune.

39. Trail of Tears (1838)

One of the most shameful chapters in America's treatment of American Indians occurred in 1838 when President Martin Van Buren, continuing the work of his predecessor, Andrew Jackson, countenanced the removal of the Cherokees from Georgia. Known as one of the "five civilized tribes," the Cherokees had adapted totally to Euro-American culture. They had a constitution, a system of representational government, well-developed farmlands, and a written language. They lived in houses and constructed churches and schools. Their lands, however, were in an area that was perfect for cotton growing, and gold had also been discovered on them. Pressure mounted to get the Cherokees to sign treaties that would cede their ancestral lands to settlers and prospectors. The Cherokees, however, did not abandon their lands without a legal fight that not only challenged the removal laws but also attempted to establish an independent Cherokee nation within the United States. The case, known as *Cherokee Nation v. Georgia*, went to the Supreme Court, which denied the Cherokee's right to sovereignty. After the fraudulent signing of the Treaty of Echota (1835), troops rounded up fifteen thousand to seventeen thousand Cherokees and force marched them in the dead of winter through Tennessee and Kentucky, to what would eventually become Oklahoma. About four thousand died along the route from disease, starvation, and exposure. Their route became known as "The Trail of Tears."

TERM PAPER SUGGESTIONS

1. The Cherokees themselves were divided in their approach to encroachment onto their lands. A group known as "The Ridge Party" advocated negotiations with the U.S. government before settlers moved onto Cherokee lands, while principal Chief John Ross and the majority strongly opposed any compromise. Analyze the pros and cons of each approach.

2. The Treaty of Echota was the impetus that the government needed to relocate the Cherokees. Review the background of the treaty and explain how the Cherokees were manipulated into signing it with false promises and threats.

3. Trace the legal battle that the Cherokees waged to defend their ancestral lands by analyzing the cases *Cherokee Nation v. Georgia* and *Worcester v. State of Georgia*. Present a dissenting opinion with historical support for challenging the Supreme Court's disposition of the cases.

4. One of the safeguards that was supposedly in place for American Indians was the American government's support of those tribes that became "civilized." The Cherokees were considered a civilized tribe because they had adopted a Euro-American lifestyle. Describe this way of life. Why did it fail to protect the Cherokees from loss of their lands?

5. Refer to some of the works that contain Cherokee first-person accounts of what it was like to journey eight hundred miles without adequate food, shelter, or clothing. Describe the conditions on the Trail of Tears. Write a legal brief on behalf of a group of survivors that makes a strong case for legal reparations because of their suffering.

6. Trace the history and from a socioeconomic perspective discuss the various government decisions that led to passage of the Indian Removal Act.

ALTERNATIVE TERM PAPER SUGGESTIONS

1. The Cherokees were not removed en masse during the Trail of Tears. Instead, they traveled to a series of removal forts. Create a Web site showing the locations of the forts with hyperlinked materials, describing the living conditions at the forts and the traveling conditions for the Cherokees.

2. The Trail of Tears was a violation of human rights, and contemporary military and government officials would probably have been charged with war crimes. Prepare an indictment of military officers and government leaders who you believe were most responsible for the debacle known as the Trail of Tears. Use historical evidence from eyewitness testimony and demographic data to support the charges.

SUGGESTED SOURCES

Primary Sources

Norgren, Jill. *Cherokee Cases: Two Landmark Federal Decisions in the Fight for Sovereignty.* Norman, OK: University of Oklahoma Press, 2004. Provides extensive excerpts and legal analysis of two cases that the Cherokees took through the courts to establish their rights to ancestral lands: *Cherokee Nation v. Georgia* (1831) and *Worcester v. State of Georgia* (1832).

Rozema, Vicki. *Voices from the Trail of Tears.* Winston-Salem, NC: John F. Blair Publishers, 2003. Contains first-person accounts ranging from missionaries who opposed the relocation of the Cherokees to eyewitnesses who experienced and survived the Trail of Tears.

Strouth, Theresa, ed. *To Marry an Indian: The Marriage of Harriett Gold and Elias Boudinot in Letters, 1823–1839.* Chapel Hill, NC: University of North Carolina Press, 2005. Furnishes the letters of Harriett Gold to her parents in Connecticut after she married a Cherokee and went to live in New Echota prior to the Trail of Tears.

Secondary Sources

Boudinot, Elias. *Cherokee Editor: The Writings of Elias Boudinot.* Athens, GA: University of Georgia, 1996. These letters written by the Cherokee husband of Harriett Gold describe the attempts by the Cherokees under the leadership of John Ross to recoup their losses and reestablish a nation in what is now Oklahoma.

Conley, Robert J. *The Cherokee Nation: A History.* Albuquerque, NM: University of New Mexico Press, 2005. Furnishes a scholarly history of the Cherokee people covering the period known as the Trail of Tears.

Duthu, Bruce N. *American Indians and the Law.* New York: Viking, 2008. Analyzes the Supreme Court case *Worcester v. Georgia* that ended up being a pyrrhic victory for the Cherokee.

Ehle, John. *Trail of Tears: The Rise and Fall of the Cherokee Nation.* New York: Anchor Books, 1997. Relates the story of the Cherokees' fruitless attempts to legally battle the U.S. government to retain rights to their ancestral lands, establish a sovereign nation, and stave the inevitable relocation by adopting the ways of Euro-Americans.

Jahoda, Gloria. *Trail of Tears: The Story of the American Indian Removals 1813–1855.* Avenel, NJ: Wings, 1995. Presents many first-person accounts of the Trail of Tears along with an appendix of selected government documents that relate to the event.

King, Duane H. *Cherokee Indian Nation: A Troubled History.* Knoxville, TN: University of Tennessee, 1979. Presents a scholarly account of the Cherokees and their valiant attempts to retain their ancestral lands.

Perdue, Theda. *The Cherokees.* Philadelphia, PA: Chelsea House, 2004. Written for secondary school students, this work gives a history of the Cherokee people, including the issues and events that led to the Trail of Tears.

Perdue, Theda, and Michael Green. *The Cherokee Nation and the Trail of Tears.* New York: Viking Press, 2007. Written by award-winning historians, this excellent overview details the competing interests of Cherokees, settlers, and the U.S. government that resulted in the debacle known as the Trail of Tears.

Prucha, Francis Paul. *The Great Father: The United States Government and the American Indians.* Vol. I. Lincoln, NE: University of Nebraska Press, 1984. Classic text concerns the complexities of the federal government policies regarding the American Indians. Volume I covers the Trail of Tears.

Thornton, Russell. "Cherokee Population Losses during the Trail of Tears: A New Perspective and a New Estimate." *EthnoHistory* 31 (Autumn 1984): 289–300. (Available in JSTOR.) Using demographic data, this article proposes that the four thousand deaths on the Trail of Tears was grossly underestimated.

Underwood, Tom. *Cherokee Legends and the Trail of Tears.* Roanoke, VA: Book Publishing, 2002. This thirty-two page classic has undergone its twentieth reprinting. It contains the first-person account of a U.S. soldier who accompanied the Cherokees on the Trail of Tears along with several famous Cherokee legends.

Wilkins, Thurman. *Cherokee Tragedy: The Ridge Family and the Decimation of a People.* Norman, OK: University of Oklahoma Press, 1989. Recounts legal and assimilation attempts of the Cherokee to stave off relocation and the eventual Trail of Tears.

World Wide Web

"Cherokee Indian Removal Debate U.S. Senate, April 15–17, 1830." http://www.cviog.uga.edu/Projects/gainfo/chdebate.htm. Contains the full text of the senate debate concerning the passage of the Indian Removal Act and the opposing testimony of New Jersey Senator Theodore Frelinghuysen.

"Elias Boudinot's Editorials in the Cherokee Phoenix, 1829, 1831." http://www.cerritos.edu/soliver/Student%20Activites/Trail%20of%20Tears/web/boudinot.htm. Furnishes the full text of Elias Boudinot's position on what the Cherokees should do vis-à-vis the U.S. government. Boudinot was a member of the Ridge Party that began secret negotiations with the government in an effort to stop encroachment on Cherokee lands by settlers and prospectors.

"Indian Affairs: Laws and Treaties—Treaty with the Cherokee, 1835." http://digital.library.okstate.edu/kappler/Vol2/treaties/che0439.htm. Contains the full text of the Treaty of New Echota, 1835.

"Removal of the Indians, January 1830, by Lewis Cass." http://www.cerritos.edu/soliver/Student%20Activites/Trail%20of%20Tears/web/cass2.htm. Provides the testimony of Lewis Cass, Governor of the Michigan Territory, who was in favor of passage of the Indian Removal Act.

"The Trail of Tears." http://ngeorgia.com/history/nghisttt.html. Contains a lengthy hyperlinked overview of the events, issues, and laws involving the Trail of Tears plus a series of additional links featuring maps, the location of Cherokee removal forts, and statistics regarding the number of Cherokees departing and arriving at their new location.

"The Trail of Tears." http://www.pbs.org/wgbh/aia/part4/4h1567.html. Contains a short overview of the Trail of Tears and several links to full text primary source documents relating to it.

"Virginia Center for Digital History—Trail of Tears Letter from Cherokee Leaders in Washington." http://www.vcdh.virginia.edu/solguide/VUS06/vus06b01.html. Supplies an 1831 letter written by Cherokee delegates in Washington, D.C., to John Ross, principal Chief of the Cherokee, about the hypocrisy of the government in dealing with them and with news of atrocities committed against the Cherokees in Georgia.

Multimedia Sources

How the West Was Lost; Cherokee—the Trail of Tears. Bethesda, MD: Discovery Enterprises Group, 1993. 1 videocassette. 50 minutes. Shows how the Cherokee had a highly developed civilization and despite that were victims of rapacious settlers and speculators who wanted their rich farming and hunting lands.

The Trail of Tears: Cherokee Legacy. Dallas, TX: Rich-Heap Films, Inc., 2006.
    1 DVD. 115 minutes. This film about the forced march of the Cherokee,
    narrated by James Earl Jones, has been shown at the Smithsonian's
    National Museum of the American Indian in Washington, D.C. It also
    won Best Documentary at the 2006 American Indian Film Festival.

40. The *Amistad* Mutiny (1839)

By 1808 the slave trade was officially outlawed in the United States, Great
Britain, and her colonies but it did not stop smugglers from human trafficking in parts of the world where enforcement of the law was negligible.
The trade was still lucrative and was particularly successful between Cuba
and Africa because Cuban colonial officials received kickbacks to provide
paperwork declaring African slaves to be ladinos, or slaves who worked in
Cuba before 1820. Slaves with this designation could be legally sold. In
1839, a Portuguese slave ship sailed from West Africa to Havana, Cuba,
with approximately five hundred illegally purchased slaves. Jose Ruiz
bought forty-nine African men and Pedro Montes purchased three girls
and one boy, loaded them onto a schooner called the *Amistad* and set sail
for Puerto Principe, Cuba. Convinced that they were going to be eaten,
the Africans freed themselves, took control of the ship, and killed the
captain and the cook. The Africans commandeered the ship and ordered
the crew to sail them back to Africa. Unbeknownst to the Africans, the
crew sailed northeast instead of southeast, and the Amistad was boarded
by a U.S. Naval brig off the coast of Long Island. The thirty-nine surviving Africans were jailed while Ruiz and Montes filed suit for the return of
their property and Spain sued to try them for murder and piracy. The case
became a *cause celebre* for abolitionists and finally went to the Supreme
Court where ex-President John Quincy Adams argued on behalf of the
Africans. They were finally freed and returned to Sierra Leone, Africa, in
1841, accompanied by several American missionaries.

TERM PAPER SUGGESTIONS

1. Examine and discuss the trial testimony of Joseph Cinque (also known as
   Sengbe Pieh), the African slave leader who freed himself and led the mutiny,
   at http://www.law.umkc.edu/faculty/projects/ftrials/amistad/AMI_TRI
   .HTM for its veracity and credibility concerning his belief that the crew was
   about to engage in cannibalism.

2. Thomas R. Gedney, Lieutenant of the U.S. Naval brig *The Washington,* also sued because he believed that he was entitled to salvage rights. Research and discuss nineteenth-century maritime laws concerning his rights, and explain what they were in the case of the *Amistad.*

3. Investigate why President Martin Van Buren agreed with Spain and, after the first Court case, ordered the Africans to be returned to Cuba before any appeals could be filed.

4. Describe and explain the role of The *Amistad* Committee, comprised of famous abolitionists Simeon Jocelyn, Joshua Leavitt, and Lewis Tappan, in raising funds for the Africans' legal counsel and appeals.

5. Explain how abolitionists saw an opportunity to use the *Amistad* case to further their antislavery cause, raise pubic awareness concerning the plight of slaves, and test the law regarding people of color.

6. Outline all the legal issues involved in the *Amistad* case, including maritime salvage rights, criminal law, and international law.

ALTERNATIVE TERM PAPER SUGGESTIONS

1. Download and cite images from the movie *Amistad* or *The Voyage of La Amistad* and make a two-minute movie trailer that can be used to raise funds for the victims of the *Amistad* journey and make people aware of the issues surrounding slavery.

2. Assume you are an editor of an abolitionist newspaper. Design a plan for reporters about how you wish them to keep the *Amistad* case in the public eye.

SUGGESTED SOURCES

Primary Sources

The Amistad Case: The Most Celebrated Slave Mutiny of the Nineteenth Century. New York: Johnson Reprint, 1968. Provides correspondence between the U.S. and Spanish governments regarding the *Amistad* case and the text of ex-President John Quincy Adams's Supreme Court argument.

Barber, John Warner. *A History of the "Amistad" Captives.* New York: Arno Press, 1969. Contains an 1840 reprinted account of the *Amistad* case along with biographical sketches of the Africans on trial.

Tappan, Lewis. *African Captives: Trial of the Prisoners of the Amistad on the Writ of Habeas Corpus, before the Circuit Court of the United States, for the District of . . . Thompson and Judson, September term, 1839.* Ithaca, NY: Cornell University Press, 2007. This reprint contains the account of noted American abolitionist Lewis Tappan's work on the *Amistad* case.

Secondary Sources

Cable, Mary. *Black Odyssey: The Case of the Slave Ship "Amistad."* New York: Viking Press, 1972. Provides an outstanding overview of the entire *Amistad* case, including the arguments made before the Supreme Court and the repatriation of the Africans to Sierra Leone.

Jackson, Donald Dale. "Mutiny on the Amistad." *Smithsonian* 28 (December 1997): 114–118. Presents an easy-to-understand overview of the events, people, and places involved in the *Amistad* Mutiny.

Jones, Howard. *Mutiny on the Amistad: The Saga of a Slave Revolt and Its Impact on American Abolition, Law, and Diplomacy.* New York: Oxford University Press, 1987. Provides a well-researched scholarly analysis of the incidents involving the *Amistad* case as well as a legal analysis of the trial testimony and legal briefs filed on behalf of the Africans.

Jones, Howard, et al. "Cinque of the *Amistad* a Slave Trader? Perpetuating a Myth," *Journal of American History* 87 (December 2000): 923–939. (Available in JSTOR.) Thoroughly explores the research to try and put to rest the rumor that Cinque returned to Sierra Leone only to become a slave trader.

Kromer, Helen. *Amistad: The Slave Uprising Aboard the Spanish Schooner.* Philadelphia, PA: Pilgrim Press, 1997. This short work gives a complete overview of the *Amistad* Mutiny.

Martin, Christopher. *The Amistad Affair.* New York: Abelard-Schuman, 1970. Contains a short background history of the slave trade and an interesting epilogue that outlines the case's reappearance long after 1841.

Myers, Walter Dean. *Amistad.* New York: Puffin, 2001. Written for secondary school students, this work cites primary sources in the form of letters, speeches, and other testimony to relate the story of the mutiny on the *Amistad* along with a summation of its moral and legal outcomes.

Nagel, Paul C. *John Quincy Adams: A Public Life, a Private Life.* New York: Random House, 1997. Relies upon Adams's extensive diary to provide an account of his life and his role in arguing the *Amistad* case before the Supreme Court.

Osagie, Iyunolu Folayan. *The Amistad Revolt: Memory, Slavery, and the Politics of Identity in the United States and Sierra Leone.* Athens, GA: University of Georgia Press, 2000. Provides details about the *Amistad* survivors' return to Sierra Leone and present-day conditions in the country.

Owens, William A. *Black Mutiny: The Revolt on the Schooner "Amistad."* Philadelphia, PA: Pilgrim Press, 1968. Using primary source dialogue and other resources, this work successfully re-creates the unbelievably complex *Amistad* case.

Zeinert, Karen. *The Amistad Slave Revolt and American Abolition*. North Haven, CT: Linnet Books, 1997. Focuses on the *Amistad* Mutiny and how it related to the American Abolitionist Movement.

World Wide Web

"*Amistad* at Mystic Seaport." http://www.amistad.org/. This commercial site contains a link to *Amistad* America, Inc., which built a replica of the *Amistad* schooner. It resides at Mystic Seaport in Connecticut, which was also the setting for part of the film, *Amistad* (1997), directed by Steven Spielberg.

"The *Amistad* Case." http://www.npg.si.edu/col/amistad/index.htm. Furnishes a useful overview of the people, places, and events regarding the *Amistad* Mutiny including National Portrait Gallery images of John Quincy Adams, Joseph Cinque, John C. Calhoun, James A. Thome, Martin Van Buren, and Joseph Story.

"*Amistad* Research Center—The *Amistad* Case and Its Consequences in U.S. History by Clifton Johnson." http://www.tulane.edu/~amistad/amessays.htm. This outstanding megasite contains extensive essays, a timeline, research and resource links about the *Amistad* Mutiny.

"The *Amistad* Revolt." http://usinfo.state.gov/products/pubs/amistad/. Provides a lengthy overview replete with primary source quotations from lawyers and other participants of the *Amistad* case.

"*Amistad* Story Ties into Roots of United Methodist Church in Africa." http://gbgm-umc.org/umhistory/sierra-leone/amistad2.html. Gives a brief account of the missionaries and the role they played in returning the *Amistad* slaves to Sierra Leone.

"Famous American Trials—*Amistad* Trials 1839–1840." http://www.law.umkc.edu/faculty/projects/ftrials/amistad/AMISTD.HTM. Provides newspaper accounts, a chronology of events, biographical sketches of all of the participants, images, letters, and diaries, maps of voyages, court decisions, and more about the *Amistad* Mutiny.

"National Archives Administration—Teaching with Documents: The *Amistad* Case." http://www.archives.gov/education/lessons/amistad/. Contains the full text of many of the documents pertaining to the *Amistad* case including the Supreme Court decision handed down on March 9, 1841, that freed all the *Amistad* mutineers.

Multimedia Sources

Amistad. Universal City, CA: DreamWorks, 1997. 2 DVDs. 155 minutes. This is the entertainment version of the *Amistad* case directed by Steven

Spielberg. While it could be used for educational purposes, caveats should be issued prior to viewing about its historical accuracy.

The Voyage of La Amistad. Oak Forrest, IL: MPI Home Video, 1998. 1 DVD. 70 minutes. This documentary is a much better teaching vehicle for the *Amistad* case because it attempts to give a faithful account of all the events surrounding the *Amistad* Mutiny.

41. Immigration (1840s)

America has always been a nation of immigrants, which has added greatly to its productivity and culture. What began with the arrival of the English and Africans in the seventeenth and eighteenth centuries soon swelled to include Scotch-Irish and Germans plus a host of people from other countries and of other nationalities. This immigration pattern was dwarfed, however, by what succeeded it in the nineteenth century. From 1815 to the beginning of the Civil War, five million people moved to the United States, about 50 percent from England and 40 percent from Ireland. The 1840 census revealed that of a total population of 31,500,000 persons, 4,736,000 were foreign born. The census also showed that most immigrants had arrived from one of two countries: Ireland or Germany. During the 1840s, emigration continued to rise for these two countries, but it surged enormously in the late 1840s when the potato famine struck Ireland and Germany. Ireland was hit sooner and harder than Germany, and the accompanying plagues together with famine resulted in from 1 to 1.5 million Irish dead and 2 million forced to emigrate. Of the latter, 1.3 million Irish immigrants were recorded as reaching the United States. German emigration also ballooned during the 1840s with more than 500,000 immigrants reaching the United States. Between 1841 and 1850 more than 1.7 million immigrants arrived, most of them from northern and central Europe. They were absorbed by a country that was expanding westward, undergoing industrialization, and offering land at cheap prices. Equipped with manual, craft, and mental skills, as well as a strong work ethic, these immigrants made lasting contributions to America's economy, political system, and society.

TERM PAPER SUGGESTIONS

1. Describe how the European industrial revolution affected the economic situation for many Europeans, causing them to emigrate to the United States.

2. Explain the economic and biological factors that precipitated the Irish famine and the subsequent emigration to America during the late 1840s.

3. Discuss the economic conditions in the United States that favored either the Germans or Irish.

4. Investigate the patterns of commerce between Europe and the United States that made it possible to transport large numbers of immigrants.

5. One of the first groups to leave Germany during the 1840s were Jews fleeing Bavaria because of social and economic persecution. Investigate the conditions that drove them to emigrate to the United States.

6. The reception given to Irish and German immigrants was not always welcoming. Examine the positive role that New York Governor William H. Seward played in recognizing their contributions.

ALTERNATIVE TERM PAPER SUGGESTIONS

1. Assume you are a TV producer who has been asked to make a short iMovie on the economic and societal contributions that Irish and German immigrants made to America during the 1840s. Use clips from the film or images from various Internet sites to show their work on canals, railroads, and farms.

2. Assume you are part of an "immigrant chain" who writes letters to people back home extolling the virtues of America. Write a series of letters describing the working conditions, housing, food, and customs that you have experienced as an immigrant factory worker in New York City.

SUGGESTED SOURCES

Primary Sources

Brownstone, David M., and Irene M. Franck. *Facts about American Immigration*. New York: H. W. Wilson, 2001. Provides primary sources in the form of four hundred census data tables including the 1840s period.

Ciment, James, ed. *Encyclopedia of American Immigration*. 4 vols. Armonk, NY: M. E. Sharpe, Inc., 2001. Section 2 of Vol. 1 presents census data about Irish and German immigration during the 1840s.

Secondary Sources

Bailyn, Bernard. *From Protestant Peasants to Jewish Intellectuals: The Germans in the Peopling of America*. New York: Oxford University Press, 1988. Focuses on the immigration of different types of German social classes and the contributions they made to the American economy and society.

Bankston, Carl, III, and Danielle Antoinette Hidalgo, eds. *Immigration in U.S. History.* 2 vols. Pasadena, CA: Salem Press, 2002. Contains overview articles on all areas of American immigration history.

Diner, Hasia. *Erin's Daughters in America: Irish Immigrant Women in the Nineteenth Century.* Baltimore, MD: The Johns Hopkins University Press, 1983. Explores the lives of Irish women who came to America in greater numbers than did Irish men and their successes and failures in experiencing the "American Dream."

Franck, Irene M. *The German-American Heritage.* New York: Facts on File, 1988. Discusses the contributions that German immigrants made to America during the 1840s.

Greene, Victor R. *A Singing Ambivalence: American Immigrants between Old World and New, 1830–1930.* Kent, OH: Kent State University Press, 2004. Compares the immigrant experiences of various ethnic groups, including those from Ireland and Germany.

Hoerder, Dirk, and Jorg Nagler, eds. *People in Transit: German Migrations in Comparative Perspective, 1820–1930.* New York: Cambridge University Press, 1995. Discusses the waves of German immigrants who came to America for economic, political, and religious reasons.

Knobel, Dale T. *"America for the Americans": The Nativist Movement in the United States.* New York: Twayne, 1995. Examines the American Nativist Movement from 1820–1920, which was attempting to keep immigrants from arriving and establishing permanent residence in America.

Paulson, Timothy J. *Irish Immigrants.* New York: Facts on File, 2005. Traces the history of Irish immigration from the seventeenth to twentieth centuries.

Ripley, LaVern J. *The German-Americans.* Boston, MA: Twayne, 1976. Investigates the impact of German immigration on America during the nineteenth century and describes German American contributions to U.S. culture.

Scally, Robert J. *The End of Hidden Ireland: Rebellion, Famine and Emigration.* New York: Oxford University Press, 1995. This scholarly work examines the political and economic factors that drove millions of Irish to emigrate to the United States, Canada, and Australia.

Tolzmann, Don H. *The German American Experience: A History of German Immigration, Settlement, and Influences in the United States.* Atlantic Highlands, NJ: Humanities, 1998. Explores and discusses the pattern of German immigration, including during the nineteenth century, and the effect it had on German immigrants and American society.

World Wide Web

"Center for Immigration Studies." http://www.cis.org/topics/history.html #Publications. Provides a short history of U.S. immigration history and the full text of various papers on immigration history.

"History of Immigration." http://ocp.hul.harvard.edu/immigration/links.html #history. This useful webography connects users to museums, universities, and other institutions all over the world that contain immigration data and histories.

"Immigration to the United States, 1789–1930." http://ocp.hul.harvard. edu/immigration/. Provides selected items from Harvard University's library concerning the history of immigration including the full text of 1,800 books and pamphlets, 6,000 photographs, and 13,000 pages from manuscript collections that capture the immigrant experience.

"Library of Congress: "American Memory: The Learning Page—Immigration." http://lcweb2.loc.gov/ammem/ndlpedu/features/immig/intro duction.html. Furnishes historical articles on immigration and educational resources for teachers planning lessons on immigration.

"Library of Congress—Immigration: The Changing Face of America." http://lcweb2.loc.gov/ammem/ndlpedu/features/immig/immigration _set1.html. Provides primary sources in the form of oral histories, letters, diaries, photographs, and more about the topic of immigration to the United States.

"Peopling North America: Population Movements and Migrations." http:// www.ucalgary.ca/applied_history/tutor/migrations/Fhome.html. Supplies a historical overview of the major human migrations to North America.

"University of Minnesota—Immigration History Research Center." http:// www.ihrc.umn.edu/. Includes one hundred thousand pages of primary sources on immigration, including letters, diaries, and oral histories from North American immigrants during 1800–1950.

Multimedia Sources

Destination America: US Immigration. Hollywood, CA: PBS Home Video, 2005. 1 DVD. 240 minutes. This video captures the spirit of immigrating to America with re-creations of specific immigrant experiences, diaries letters, and interviews with historians. The Web site at http://www.pbs .org/destinationamerica/usim.html also includes a timeline of European emigration and explorations of five freedoms that drew immigrants to the United States.

Out of Ireland: The Story of Irish Emigration to America. Newton, NJ: Shanachie Entertainment Corp., 1997. 1 DVD. 95 minutes. This documentary weaves narration, film footage of immigration debarkation sites, and first-person accounts to tell the story of the waves of Irish immigration throughout U.S. history.

They Came for Good—A History of the Jews in the United States—Taking Root, 1820–1880. Newton, NJ: Shanachie Entertainment Corp., 2001. 1 DVD. 60 minutes. This documentary explores the immigration cycle of thousands of German and Central European Jews who emigrated to the United States during the nineteenth century.

42. Dorr's Rebellion (1842)

Universal suffrage did not occur overnight in the United States and in some states it was hard won. For many years states had a requirement that one could vote only if one were a White male who owned property. By the early nineteenth century every state had repealed property qualification rules with the exception of Rhode Island. The state still limited the right to vote to White men who owned $134 worth of property and to their eldest sons. In 1802, Thomas Dorr, an attorney, Seth Luther, a radical labor leader, and others founded the Rhode Island Suffrage Association to challenge the law and allow every White male the right to vote. Dorr and his colleagues formed a People's Party, drafted a People's Constitution that removed the property ownership requirement, and reapportioned legislative seats to make elections more equitable. Although the document was overwhelmingly approved by the People's Party, the reaction of the Rhode Island state legislature was anything but harmonious. Elections by the People's Party produced a second governor, Thomas Dorr, and created a crisis that necessitated the mediation of President John Tyler who threatened to send federal troops to retain the legally elected government. After a bloodless skirmish, Dorr was arrested and found guilty of treason against the state. He was eventually pardoned, and the Rhode Island legislature wrote a Bill of Rights and amended its suffrage requirements to include all native-born males who paid a poll tax of $1. They did, however, retain the $134 property requirement for foreign-born citizens.

TERM PAPER SUGGESTIONS

1. Although Rhode Island had been the center for religious and political tolerance, it lacked an established church that might have been a rallying place

for constitutional reform. Discuss how the lack of an established church limited people's ability to foment for necessary suffrage reforms.

2. Analyze how the ownership requirement for voting disenfranchised a growing population who worked in manufacturing industries.

3. Examine how the depression of 1837 and the presidential campaign slogans of William Henry Harrison in 1840 may have spurred Dorr's Rebellion.

4. Many of Dorr's supporters were arrested under the Algerine Law, which was passed by the Rhode Island government to impose severe penalties for participating in the new government. Discuss the pros and cons of such a law.

5. Discuss the positive consequences of Dorr's Rebellion for Americans and the concept of Jacksonian democracy.

6. Examine the significance of Dorr's Rebellion and how it may have been one small step on the road to suffrage for non-Whites and females.

ALTERNATIVE TERM PAPER SUGGESTIONS

1. Assume you are Thomas Dorr. Prepare a podcast that can be broadcast to Rhode Islanders seeking their support for election and suffrage reforms.

2. Assume you are Seth Luther, the radical labor leader, who saw how bifurcated Rhode Island society was becoming because increasing numbers of people who worked in the manufacturing industries could not vote. Design a series of pamphlets that can be distributed outside of the factories that will help raise people's awareness of these critical inequities.

SUGGESTED SOURCES

Primary Sources

Desimone, Russell J., and Daniel C. Schofield. *Broadsides of the Dorr Rebellion.* Providence, RI: Rhode Island Supreme Court Historical Society, 1992. Displays the broadsides that were distributed to gain support for Dorr's protest against the Rhode Island government concerning suffrage rights.

McDougall, Francis Harriet. *Might and Right by a Rhode Islander.* Providence, RI: A. H. Stillwell, 1844. Furnishes testimony about the failed rebellion that was given by Thomas Dorr.

Secondary Sources

Adams, Peter. *The Bowery Boys: Street Corner Radicals and the Politics of Rebellion.* Westport, CT: Praeger Publishers, 2005. Discusses the politics of discontent that were emerging in New York City in New England from a growing division between the working class and property and factory owners. Dorr's Rebellion is thought to be an outgrowth of this societal separation.

Botelho, Joyce M. *Right & Might: The Dorr Rebellion & the Struggle for Equal Rights.* Providence, RI: Rhode Island Historical Society, 1992. Focuses on the Dorr Rebellion as a necessary confrontation between a potential landed aristocracy and citizens who wished a much broader concept of democracy.

Coleman, Pete J. *The Transformation of Rhode Island 1790–1860.* Providence, RI: Brown University Press, 1963. Describes the political and social conditions in Rhode Island during the period of Dorr's Rebellion.

Conley, Patrick T. *The Dorr Rebellion: Rhode Island's Crisis in Constitutional Government.* Providence, RI: Rhode Island Bicentennial Fund, 1976. Discusses the legal complications of the Dorr Rebellion that were generated by the existence of two governors and governments.

Dennison, George. *The Dorr War: Republicanism on Trial 1831–1861.* Lexington, KY: University Press of Kentucky, 1976. Provides an account and excellent analysis of the events, leaders, and consequences of Dorr's Rebellion.

Eno, Paul F., and Glenn Laxton. *Rhode Island: A Genial History.* Woonsocket, RI: New River Press, 2005. This history of Rhode Island depicts it as a founding state characterized by religious and political toleration. It also presents a dispassionate view of Dorr's Rebellion.

Gettleman, Marvin. *The Dorr Rebellion: A Study in American Radicalism.* New York: Random House, 1973. This book is considered the definitive history to date about Dorr's Rebellion.

Mowry, Arthur May. *The Dorr War or the Constitutional Struggle in Rhode Island.* New York: Chelsea House, 1983. Views Dorr as a radical who created a constitutional crisis rather than using the normal legislative channels for disagreement and a means to address constitutional wrongs.

Williamson, Chilton. *American Suffrage: From Property to Democracy.* Princeton, NJ: Princeton University Press, 1960. Discusses the Dorr Rebellion as part of the widening definition of American democracy prior to the Civil War.

Victor, Orville, J. *History of American Conspiracies; a Record of Treason, Insurrection, Rebellion, & C., in the United States of America, from 1760 to 1860.* Ann Arbor, MI: Scholarly Publishing Office, University of Michigan Library, 2006. Chapter 12 is devoted to New England conspiracies including Dorr's Rebellion.

Zinn, Howard. *A People's History of the United States.* New York: Harper & Row, 1980. Analyzes the Dorr Rebellion as an example of working-class radicalism.

World Wide Web

"Dorr's Rebellion." http://www.answers.com/topic/dorr-rebellion. Provides a short history of the rebellion including a brief citation to the 1849 Supreme Court case, *Luther v. Borden,* that voted against the idea of popular sovereignty as a solution to an unjust state constitution.

"Dorr, Thomas Wilson." http://www.bartleby.com/65/do/Dorr-Tho.html. Furnishes a short biographical sketch of Thomas Dorr and his role in Rhode Island's crisis over suffrage rights.

"1833–1849: The Dorr Rebellion." http://libcom.org/history/1833-1849-the -dorr-rebellion. Casts Dorr's Rebellion in light of its times when there was a growing bifurcation between working class people and immigrants and land and factory owners.

"Rhode Island in the New Republic, 1790–1845." http://www.rilin.state.ri.us/ RhodeIslandHistory/chapt4.html. Chapter 4 of *Rhode Island History* gives a fact-filled summary of the economic conditions that may have been one of the causes of Dorr's Rebellion.

"Thomas Wilson Dorr." http://www.dorrrebellionmuseum.org/dorr.htm. Provides a useful hyperlinked biographical sketch of Thomas Dorr and the role he played in leading a rebellion for suffrage rights.

"USA History—Wars—Dorr's Rebellion." http://www.usahistory.com/wars/ dorr.htm. Furnishes a brief summary of Dorr's Rebellion and its significance to U.S. history.

"Voting Rights and the Dorr Rebellion." http://www.woonsocket.org/ dorrwar.html. Contains a short history of some of the weaknesses in the Rhode Island charter that were partially responsible for Dorr's Rebellion.

Multimedia Sources

Biographies. Providence, RI: National Educational Association, 2000. 1 videocassette. 58 minutes. Contains biographical sketches of famous and infamous Rhode Islanders, including Thomas Dorr.

43. Samuel F. B. Morse and the Telegraph (1844)

On May 24, 1844, Samuel Morse sat at his desk in Washington, D.C., and by a series of coded clicks transmitted the message "What hath God wrought?" to Alfred Vail in Baltimore, Maryland, forty miles away. Little did people realize that Morse's perfection of the telegraph was going to revolutionize long-distance communication and that his invention is the equivalent of today's Internet, cell phones, and text messaging. Although highly educated, Samuel F. B. Morse was a most unlikely candidate for scientific experiments. He was professionally trained and worked for years as an artist. After witnessing a prototype of the telegraph at work in Europe, he discussed it in depth on a return voyage with Charles Thomas Jackson. By 1836, with the assistance of other scientists, Morse had produced an electric circuit that utilized an electromagnet in the receiver to alternate between connecting and interrupting the circuit. These audible clicks arranged in what is now called Morse Code proved a fast and reliable means of signaling. Morse quickly sought financial aid from Congress and finally received $30,000 for construction of the forty mile line. It was not, however, until business realized the utility of the telegraph to communicate commercial transactions that the demand for his invention skyrocketed. By 1852, the system soon comprised more than fifty thousand miles of telegraph lines. In 1856, the Western Union Telegraph Company standardized and consolidated all the different systems, synchronized the transmitters, and improved construction of telegraph poles so that the telegraph could send sixty words per minute.

TERM PAPER SUGGESTIONS

1. So many other inventors worked on Morse's telegraph system that he faced tremendous obstacles in obtaining a patent. Explore some of the other people's contributions to Morse's invention and discuss why they may have considered themselves partial owners of his intellectual property.

2. On May 24, 1844, when Morse chose to transmit the results of the Whig National Convention via telegraph, he was promoting his invention to Congress as a means to get additional funding. Using other examples from historical research, discuss Morse's ability at self-promotion.

3. During a visit to Rome, Morse was knocked to the ground by a soldier for failure to kneel at a Catholic procession. The incident, together with his anti-Catholic upbringing, intensified his prejudice against Catholics, particularly Irish Catholic immigrants. Investigate Morse's authorship of articles under the pseudonym "Brutus" against Roman Catholic immigrants.

4. Morse was also known as "The Father of the Nativist Movement." Research the movement and what positions were regarding immigration to the United States.

5. The telegraph was used fairly quickly by the railroads. Describe how its use made this form of transportation of goods and passengers safer.

6. Morse was also a strong proponent of the institution of slavery, and he even authored a treatise on it titled "An Argument on the Ethical Position of Slavery." Analyze his use of religion to defend this "peculiar institution."

ALTERNATIVE TERM PAPER SUGGESTIONS

1. Assume that Samuel Morse has hired you to acquire a patent for his invention. Write an application replete with diagrams and other necessary illustrations of his invention that could be submitted to the U.S. Patent Office.

2. Assume you are the sales manager for a grain company in the Midwest. Your superiors have never heard or seen the telegraph. Prepare a PowerPoint presentation that shows and tells them how this invention will revolutionize future communications and will affect their business.

SUGGESTED SOURCES

Primary Sources

Morse, Samuel F. B. *Samuel F. B. Morse: His Letters and Journals,* edited by Edward Morse. Reprint. Boston, MA: Houghton Mifflin, 1972. Contains illustrations and diagrams of Morse's telegraph and also discusses the assistance that Morse received from others along the way.

"Samuel F. B. Morse Papers at the Library of Congress, 1793–1919." http://memory.loc.gov/ammem/sfbmhtml/. This primary source megasite consists of 6,500 items in the form of correspondence, scrapbooks, diary entries, maps, and fifty thousand images concerning Samuel F. B. Morse and his invention of the telegraph.

Secondary Sources

Beauchamp, Ken. *History of Telegraphy.* London: Institution of Electrical Engineers, 2001. Gives a detailed history of the first two hundred years of the telegraph.

Coe, Lewis. *The Telegraph: A History of Morse's Invention and Its Predecessors in the United States.* Jefferson, NC: McFarland, 1993. Written by a former telegraph operator, this work places Morse's invention within a chronology of other people who also worked on it and may have believed that they were cheated by Morse's invention claim.

Hearn, Chester G. *Circuits in the Sea: The Men, the Ships, and the Atlantic Cable.* Westport, CT: Praeger Publishers, 2004. Traces the history of the laying of telegraphic cable across the Atlantic in 1858.

Kieve, Jeffrey. *The Electric Telegraph: A Social and Economic History.* Newton Abbot, England: David & Charles, 1973. Provides information about the contribution of British inventors such as William Fothergill Cooke, Charles Wheatstone, and others to the invention of the telegraph.

Mabee, Carleton. *The American Leonardo: The Life of Samuel F. B. Morse.* New York: Octagon Books, 1969. This definitive biography of the polymath Samuel F. B. Morse also discusses the role that Alfred Vail, Leonard Gale, and others played in the development of the electric telegraph.

Moyer, Albert E. *Joseph Henry: The Rise of An American Scientist.* Washington, DC: Smithsonian Institution Press, 1997. Provides a biography of Joseph Henry, who worked on developing a telegraph system before Morse.

Saiti, Paul J. *Samuel F. B. Morse.* Cambridge, England: Cambridge University Press, 1990. This scholarly biography places Morse's life in perspective with his other talents including art and design. It also includes a great deal of information about Morse's involvement with the Nativist Movement and his position on slavery.

Silverman, Kenneth. *Lightning Man: The Accursed Life of Samuel F. B. Morse.* New York: Alfred A. Knopf, 2003. This well-researched psychobiography portrays Morse as a dreamer who, despite his invention of the telegraph, considered himself a failure.

Standage, Tom. *The Victorian Internet: The Remarkable Story of the Telegraph and the Nineteenth Century On-Line Pioneers.* New York: Walker, 1998. Compares the invention and growth and development of the telegraph to the Internet.

Thompson, Robert L. *Wiring a Continent: The History of the Telegraphy Industry in the United States, 1832–1866.* New York: Arno Press, 1972. Chapters 1 and 2 treat the beginnings of telegraphy from 1832 to 1845.

Zannos, Susan. *Samuel Morse and the Story of the Telegraph.* Hockessin, DE: Mitchell Lane Publishers, 2005. Written for secondary school students, this biography discusses Morse's life not only from his role as an inventor but also as an artist and designer.

World Wide Web

"A Brush with History Teacher Resource Guide—Samuel F. B. Morse." http://www.npg.si.edu/edu/brush/guide/unit2/morse.html. Features a useful lesson plan about Morse's invention that includes a resource link to a Morse Code translation site.

"Hall of Fame/Inventor Profile—Samuel F. B. Morse." http://www.invent
.org/hall_of_fame/106.html. Furnishes a biographical sketch of Samuel
F. B. Morse with an emphasis on the impact that his invention of the
telegraph had on society.

"History Now—Dashes and Dots: A Product of the 19th Century." http://www
.historynow.org/12_2006/print/lp4.html. Contains an online lesson
constructed around Samuel Morse's invention of the telegraph along
with related primary source documents in the form of papers, diagrams,
and illustrations.

"Immigration and Public Policy." http://www.crl.edu/focus/Spr06
ImmPublicPolicy.asp?issID=35. Provides an online bibliography of all
Samuel Morse's publications regarding his work as the Father of the
Nativist Movement.

"Samuel F. B. Morse." http://www.nyu.edu/greyart/information/Samuel_F
_B__Morse/body_samuel_f_b__morse.html. Furnishes an online biographical sketch that contains information about Morse's career as a
well-known artist.

"Samuel F. B. Morse." http://www2.hs-esslingen.de/telehistory/morse.html.
Refer to this site to download diagrams and illustrations with an excellent
explanation of exactly how Samuel Morse's telegraph worked.

"Samuel Morse and the Telegraph." http://teachingamericanhistorymd.net/
000001/000000/000127/html/t127.html. Sponsored by Teaching
American History in Maryland, this site delineates specific sites from
the Library of Congress's huge collection and supplies lesson plans and
questions that meet the National History Standards.

Multimedia Sources

Morse and the Telegraph. AOL Video. http://video.aol.com/video-search/sim/
1412358916/familyfilter/1/pageCount/24/viewType/detail. This site
provides four videos ranging from several seconds to 7 minutes and
9 seconds that discuss Morse's invention of the telegraph, its significance
to the communications revolution, and its initial use. The programs are
titled: 1. "Telegraph Taps Out RSS Feed on Morse Code" (30 seconds);
2. "History of the Telegraph" (2 minutes and 10 seconds); 3. "The Live
Science Show Includes a Lesson in Morse Code" (7 minutes and 9 seconds); and 4. "Demonstration: Landline Morse Code Using Sounder"
(1 minute and 51 seconds).

Morse Demonstrates Telegraph. http://www.history.com. This 1 minute and 3 second online video combines black and white photographs and illustrations with an explanatory voice-over to show how early telegraphy
worked.

Samuel Morse and the Telegraph. Princeton, NJ: Films for the Humanities, 2004. 1 DVD. 58 minutes. Provides expert analysis concerning the significance of Morse's invention to the American field of communications.

44. Henry David Thoreau and the Transcendentalists (1846)

Writer and naturalist Henry David Thoreau (1817–1862) refused to pay a poll tax to a government that condoned slavery and waged an unjust war for territorial expansion against Mexico in 1846. His Aunt Maria was so shocked to hear about her nephew in jail that she paid the poll tax herself, thus ending what might have become an American *cause celebre* for abolitionists and antiwar protestors. Thoreau was a member of the Transcendentalists who numbered such writers and reformers as Ralph Waldo Emerson, Margaret Fuller, Amos Bronson Alcott, George Ripley, and Nathaniel Hawthorne. The movement was neither a religion nor a philosophy. Instead it centered around a belief that truths go beyond or transcend truths that are felt intuitively rather than through logic or reason. Transcendentalists also believed that one needed to act upon these intuitions even when it went against a policy or action by one's government. Thus Transcendentalists were opposed to slavery because intuitively it felt morally and spiritually wrong. After refusing to pay the poll tax, Thoreau penned a manifesto titled *Resistance to Civil Government.* In it he laid out the three actions for when citizens are faced with unjust laws or government actions: 1. obey them; 2. obey them until they can be amended; and 3. transgress them at once. His famous essay, now renamed *Civil Disobedience,* has been used by people all over the world to justify their civil rights and independence movements against demagogues.

TERM PAPER SUGGESTIONS

1. Investigate and write a paper that describes the beliefs of the Transcendentalists and include practical examples of their function.

2. The Transcendentalists formed two utopian communities, Brook Farm and Fruitlands. Nathaniel Hawthorne was a short-time member of the former community. He satirized the movement in a novel called *The Blithedale Romance.* Investigate what Hawthorne did not like about Brook Farm.

3. Ralph Waldo Emerson also wrote an essay that has withstood the test of time and has come to embody the spirit of individualism in American life called *Self-Reliance.* Discuss the principles in this book and how it relates to nineteenth-century life.

4. Many Transcendentalists abhorred a growing materialism in American life. Emerson's essay *Nature,* published in 1836, was a response to a country that was embarked on increasing industrialization at the expense of its natural resources. Read Emerson's essay and respond to it as an early green movement.

5. Analyze Thoreau's life and measure it against the principles that he proposed in his essays and great book, *Walden,* published in 1854. Do you think that he lived a life in accordance with them?

6. The Transcendentalists relied upon the works of Thomas Carlyle, Samuel Taylor Coleridge, Victor Cousin, and Germaine de Stael. Discuss how some of their writings influenced the growth and development of Transcendentalism.

ALTERNATIVE TERM PAPER SUGGESTIONS

1. Refer to Thoreau's essay, *Civil Disobedience,* and design several broadsides that promote active and passive resistance to the Mexican-American War and/or slavery.

2. Observe films about the lives of Martin Luther King Jr. and Mohandas Ghandi, respectively, and select and cite several film clips showing how they applied the principles of Thoreau's *Civil Disobedience* to their reform movements.

SUGGESTED SOURCES

Primary Sources

Emerson, Ralph Waldo. *The Essential Writings of Ralph Waldo Emerson.* New York: Modern Library, 2000. Provides all the major essays and lectures given by Transcendentalist and philosopher Ralph Waldo Emerson, including his 1836 essay, *Nature.*

"Henry David Thoreau and 'Civil Disobedience.'" http://thoreau.eserver.org/wendy.html. Provides an introduction and analysis of Thoreau's essay, *Civil Disobedience,* plus the full text.

Secondary Sources

Baker, Carlos. *Emerson Among the Eccentrics: A Group Portrait.* New York: Viking Press, 1996. This essential resource gives an overview of the New England Transcendentalist community.

Buell, Lawrence. *The American Transcendentalists: Essential Writings*. New York: Modern Library, 2006. Gives the full text of major writings by Transcendentalists Henry David Thoreau, Ralph Waldo Emerson, Margaret Fuller, and others.

Emerson, Ralph Waldo. *Emerson: Collected Poems and Translations*. New York: Library of America, 1994. Contains slightly edited notes and poems written by Emerson including a chronology of his life.

Frothingham, Octavius B. *Transcendentalism in New England: A History*. Gloucester, MA: Pete Smith, 1965. This reprint contains an 1876 account of the people involved in the New England Transcendentalism Movement.

Grodzins, Dean. *American Heretic: Theodore Parker and Transcendentalism*. Chapel Hill, NC: University of North Carolina, 2002. Examines the early start of the Transcendentalist Movement in New England and the role of Theodore Parker in noting its difference from the tenets of the Unitarian Church.

Hutchinson, William R. *The Transcendentalist Minister: Church Reform in the New England Renaissance*. New Haven, CT: Yale University Press, 1959. Discusses the split from Unitarianism that the Transcendentalists had at the beginning of the movement.

Miller, James E., Jr., et al. "Background American Classics 1840–1870." In *The United States in Literature*. Glenview, IL: Scott Foresman, 1985. Analyzes how Transcendentalist thought influenced the literature of the mid-nineteenth century.

Miller, Perry, ed. *The Transcendentalists: An Anthology*. Cambridge, MA: Harvard University Press, 1950. Provides the writings of the more obscure Transcendentalists and discusses the religious origin of the movement.

Porte, Joel. *Consciousness and Culture: Emerson and Thoreau Reviewed*. New Haven, CT: Yale University Press, 2004. Contains a literary criticism of Thoreau's and Emerson's works and how they contributed to the pantheon of world literature.

Richardson, Robert D. *Henry Thoreau: A Life of the Mind*. Berkeley, CA: University of California Press, 1988. Presents a scholarly biography of Henry David Thoreau.

Whicher, Stephen E. *Freedom and Fate: An Inner Life of Ralph Waldo Emerson*. Philadelphia, PA: University of Pennsylvania Press, 1953. Provides a psychobiography of Emerson that attempts to analyze the psychological motivations for his thoughts and works.

World Wide Web

"The American Renaissance and Transcendentalism." http://www.pbs.org/wnet/ihas/icon/transcend.html. Provides a hyperlinked overview of

Transcendentalism and images and photographs of the New England area where it originated.

"American Transcendentalism." http://thoreau.eserver.org/amertran.html. Provides an overview of Transcendentalism from a religious and philosophical viewpoint.

"Transcendentalism." http://plato.stanford.edu/entries/transcendentalism/. This site from the Stanford *Encyclopedia of Philosophy* provides a definition of Transcendentalism and the primary works associated with it.

"The Transcendentalist." http://www.emersoncentral.com/transcendentalist.htm. Contains the full text of a January 1842 lecture read by Ralph Waldo Emerson on Transcendentalism.

"The Web of American Transcendentalism." http://www.vcu.edu/engweb/transcendentalism/. This megasite features the full text of the work of Transcendentalists, writers and the works they wrote that influenced American Transcendentalists, and lists of Transcendentalist literature and criticism.

"What Is Transcendentalism?" http://womenshistory.about.com/bltranscend .htm. Gives a general overview of the beliefs associated with the movement and the most famous people associated with it.

Multimedia Sources

The New England Transcendentalists. Princeton, NJ: Films for the Humanities, 1997. 1 DVD. 27 minutes. Features interviews with scholars from Harvard University concerning the Transcendentalist Movement and dramatic re-creations at Walden Pond of the major writers involved in the Transcendentalist Movement.

45. Mexican-American War (1846–1848)

This war marked the first time that the United States waged a war to gain more territory. Through the intervention of President James K. Polk (1795–1849), who believed that the expansion of the United States was a duty and an obligation placed upon it by God, or its "manifest destiny," the United States acquired 500,000 square miles of Mexican territory. This acquisition included the present-day states of California, Nevada, Utah, most of New Mexico and Arizona, parts of Wyoming and Colorado, as well as Texas. Although disputes over borders and rivers were constant between the United States and Mexico, the annexation of Texas was the spark that started the war. Led by soon-to-be president General Zachary Taylor, U.S. troops successfully fought battles in northern Mexico, occupied the city of Monterey, and defeated General Antonio López de Santa Anna at the Battle of Buena Vista in 1847. A second army led by Stephen W. Kearney occupied Santa Fe, New Mexico, and then united with General Winfield Scott's army to lay siege to the city of Vera Cruz and eventually occupy Mexico City in 1847. The war ended with the signing of the Treaty of Guadalupe Hidalgo in 1848, whereupon the United States agreed to pay Mexico $15 million and assume claims against Mexico by U.S. citizens for $3.25 million in exchange for all of the territory. Although there was fierce opposition to the war by Whigs and New Englanders who saw this territorial expansion as an opportunity to also extend slavery into new states, President Polk succeeded in enlisting sixty thousand volunteers and persuading Congress to approve sending supplies and troops without officially declaring war.

TERM PAPER SUGGESTIONS

1. Discuss the opinions and views of some of the following legislators, statesmen, and military men who were opposed to the Mexican-American War: Abraham Lincoln of Illinois, Ulysses S. Grant, ex-President John Quincy Adams, John C. Calhoun of South Carolina, and Robert Toombs of Georgia.

2. One of the most dangerous precedents was started in the Mexican-American War when President Polk was able to obtain troops and supplies without having to obtain a declaration of war from Congress. Explore the implications of the precedent and how it applies to wars in Vietnam and Iraq.

3. Discuss how participation in the Mexican-American War gave the opportunity for military men such as Jefferson Davis, P. T. Beauregard, George McClellan, James Longstreet, Winfield Scott, and Robert E. Lee to practice military operations for a future Civil War.

4. Many historians have argued that by positioning troops directly on the disputed Rio Grande River that President Polk was hoping to escalate the conflict so that he could declare war on Mexico. Research this view of the war and analyze it from a historical perspective.

5. Examine the efforts of emissary John Slidell to negotiate a settlement with Mexico prior to the outbreak of war.

6. Discuss the military maneuvers of General Zachary Taylor during the war. How and why did they meet with the disapproval of President Polk?

ALTERNATIVE TERM PAPER SUGGESTIONS

1. Period newspapers were full of cartoons depicting approval and opposition of the war. Either using Comic Life Software (available at plasq.com) or drawing freehand, produce eight pro and con cartoons, accompanied by explanations, of the war.

2. Assume you are a military commander overseeing the Mexican-American War. Using period maps, draw up a series of battle plans for cities and towns that you wish to occupy or attack. Present the plans in a PowerPoint presentation. Be sure to indicate Mexican cities and other places where you believe American troops are vulnerable to counterattack.

SUGGESTED SOURCES

Primary Sources

Eisenhower, John S. *So Far from God: The U.S. War with Mexico*. New York: Random House, 1989. Using primary sources in the form of letters and diary entries, this work contains a detailed history of the war.

"Letters of General Winfield Scott." http://www.familytales.org/results.php ?tla=wfs. Contains the full text of many letters written by General Winfield Scott to former and present U.S. presidents and other leaders during the Mexican-American War.

Winders, Richard Bruce. *Mr. Polk's Army: The American Military Experience in the Mexican War*. College Station, TX: Texas A&M University Press, 1997. Uses diaries, journals, and oral histories to recount the daily life of soldiers who fought in the Mexican-American war and contrasts the leadership styles of Generals Taylor and Winfield Scott.

Secondary Sources

Bauer, K. Jack. *The Mexican War, 1846–1848*. Lincoln, NE: University of Nebraska Press, 1992. Provides a complete overview of the politics, diplomacy, and battles of the Mexican War, including maps and photographs of several of the participants on both sides.

Bergeron, Paul H. *The Presidency of the Polk Administration*. Lawrence, KS: University Press of Kansas, 1987. This history discusses opinions that Polk was already set on waging war with Mexico even before he was elected to office.

Eisenhower, John S. *Agent of Destiny: The Life and Times of General Winfield Scott*. New York: Free Press, 1997. Furnishes a detailed account of Scott's military engagements in the Mexican War.

Francaviglia, Richard V., and Douglas Richmond, eds. *Dueling Eagles: Reinterpreting the U.S.-Mexican War, 1846–1848.* Fort Worth, TX: Christian University Press, 2000. Contains a series of essays that interpret the war from both a twentieth-century and a Mexican perspective.

Haecker, Charles M., and Jeffrey G. Mauck. *On the Prairie of Palo Alto: Historical Archaeology of the U.S.-Mexican War Battlefield.* College Station, TX: Texas A&M University, 1997. Gives a revision of the Battle of Palo Alto after studying it as an archaeological site.

Henderson, Timothy J. *A Glorious Defeat: Mexico and Its War with the United States.* New York: Hill and Wang, 2007. Relates the story of the war from its legacy in creating an image of the United States that is arrogant, aggressive, and imperialistic toward its southern neighbors.

Johannsen, Robert. *To the Halls of Montezuma: The Mexican War in the American Imagination.* New York: Oxford University Press, 1985. Analyzes how military historians viewed the Mexican War and why General Zachary Taylor became a hero and General Winfield Hancock Scott did not.

Langley, Lester D. *America and the Americas: The United States in the Western Hemisphere.* Athens, GA: University of Georgia Press, 1989. Discusses the legacy of the Mexican-American War and how it affects ongoing relations today. This work also discusses the British influence in Texas and the value of California to President Polk.

Santoni, Pedro. *Mexicans at Arms: Puro Federalists and the Politics of War, 1845–1848.* Fort Worth, TX: Christian University Press, 1996. Examines the political and military issues in Mexico during the war.

Scheina, Robert L. *Santa Anna: A Curse upon Mexico.* Washington, DC: Brassey's, 2002. Explores the life and times of General and President Antonio Santa Anna, and portrays him as both a political opportunist and a brave military leader.

Schroeder, John H. *Mr. Polk's War: American Opposition and Dissent, 1846–1848.* Madison, WI: University of Wisconsin Press, 1973. Gives a scholarly and well-supported historical defense of the theory that President Polk decided on war even before American troops were fired upon at the Rio Grande River.

World Wide Web

"Establishing Borders: The Expansion of the United States, 1846–1848." http://www.smithsonianeducation.org/educators/lesson_plans/borders/start.html. Provides a history lesson with teaching materials and lesson plans concerning the expansion of the United States during the Mexican-America War that meets current National History Standards.

"The Handbook of Texas Online—Mexican War (1846–1848)." http://www
.tsha.utexas.edu/handbook/online/articles/MM/qdm2.html. Provides an
overview of the Mexican-American War from a military standpoint.

"Library of Congress—Treaty of Guadelupe Hidalgo." http://www.loc.gov/rr/
program/bib/ourdocs/Guadalupe.html. Provides the full text of the
treaty that ended the 1846–1848 war between the United States and
Mexico.

"The Mexican-American War and the Media, 1845–1848." http://www
.history.vt.edu/MxAmWar/INDEX.HTM#. Some of the primary
sources at this site are only available to Virginia Tech students, but most
of it is open to the public. It includes a bibliography, timelines, maps,
congressional documents and debate, images, and period newspaper
articles about the Mexican-American War.

"The Mexican War." http://www.lnstar.com/mall/texasinfo/mexicow.htm.
Presents a lengthy overview of the U.S. war with Mexico from the vantage point of the United States.

"The Mexican War." http://www.sonofthesouth.net/mexican-war/war.htm. Provides a treasure trove of links to maps, timelines, and information about
various generals, battles, and western expansion. It also discusses the war
from a neutral point of view.

"U.S.-Mexican War 1846–1848." http://www.pbs.org/kera/usmexicanwar/
index_flash.html. Features a prelude to the war, biographies of various
participants, maps, resources for educators, and more.

Multimedia Sources

The U.S.-Mexican War 1846–1848. Alexandria, VA: PBS Home Video, 2000.
2 DVDs. 240 minutes. Tells the story of the Mexican-American War
from multiple perspectives using interviews with historians from the
United States and Mexico.

46. The Donner Party Ordeal (1846–1847)

Westward expansion carried with it great risks for emigrants who usually
spent almost all the money they had to purchase supplies, oxen, and
covered wagons, hire guides, and endure tremendous hardships traveling
over mountains, crossing rivers, and trekking through deserts. It was an
ordeal that many did not survive. In April 1846, a group of families led
by George Donner, his brother Jacob, and James F. Reed set out for California. After leaving Independence, Missouri, they joined up with a large

wagon train and followed the California Trail until they reached Little Sandy River in present-day Wyoming. While camping out with several other caravans of emigrants, they learned of a new route being touted by Lansford Hastings, a local guide. Known as the Hastings Cutoff, it entailed going around the south side of the Great Salt Lake in contemporary Utah. A group of eighty-seven emigrants elected to try the Hastings Cutoff under the leadership of George Donner. Immediately they encountered difficulties crossing the Wasatch Mountains and barely survived the trip through the Great Salt Lake Desert. The Cutoff actually lengthened their journey, and when they reached the Sierra Nevada Mountains, they discovered that snow had already blocked the pass. They camped out at what is now called Donner Lake until they ran out of food. Faced with starvation, seventeen emigrants tried to cross the Sierras on snowshoes while the others resorted to cannibalism to stay alive. In the end, only forty of eighty-seven emigrants survived the tragedy.

TERM PAPER SUGGESTIONS

1. Investigate the truth behind Lansford Hastings and the Hastings Cutoff, and discuss the responsibility that Hastings should have borne for misleading the Donner party.

2. Discuss the controversy involving the issue of cannibalism surrounding the tragic story of the Donner Party. Why were the soccer players who survived the October 13, 1972, crash in the Andes treated more humanely for their survival skills than members of the Donner party?

3. Explore the idea of the "American Dream" in terms of rich soil, hope of prosperity, health, and a new life that led so many Americans to emigrate to California and how it was personified by the Donner party.

4. Discuss the legacy of the Donner party ordeal in terms of relief teams for future emigrants and gold rush travelers.

5. The Donner party actually blazed a new trail that was used by the Mormons to reach Utah in the following year. Explore their route and how it became a main part of the Mormon Trail.

6. Analyze how the very human desire to save time and human nature conspired to seal the fate of so many members of the Donner party.

ALTERNATIVE TERM PAPER SUGGESTIONS

1. Download and cite images and movie clips from PBS's *American Experience: The Donner Party* to create a two-minute iMovie of the event.

2. Design a Web site with appropriate hyperlinks showing the route that the Donner party traveled from their start in Springfield, Illinois, to their final camp at Donner Lake.

SUGGESTED SOURCES

Primary Sources

Houghton, Eliza Poor Donner. *The Expedition of the Donner Party and Its Tragic Fate*. Lincoln, NE: University of Nebraska Press, 1998. Contains survivor Eliza P. Donner's version of the horrible ordeal in the Sierra Nevadas.

McGlashan, Charles Fayette. *History of the Donner Party, a Tragedy of the Sierra*. New York: Barnes and Noble, 2006. This reprint cites many primary sources in the form of letters, survivors' testimony, and period newspaper articles that not only tell the story of the Donner party but also the public reaction to reports of cannibalism.

Morgan, Dale. *Overland in 1846*. 2 vols. Lincoln, NE: University of Nebraska Press, 1993. Contains primary sources of the Donner party in the form of diaries, letters, testimony, and newspaper articles and also puts their ordeal in the perspective of many other emigrants who traveled the California and Oregon Trails.

Secondary Sources

Calabro, Marian. *The Perilous Journey of the Donner Party*. New York: Clarion Books, 1999. Written for secondary school students, this work tells the story of the Donner party through the eyes of survivor twelve-year-old Virginia Reed.

Johnson, Kristen. *Unfortunate Emigrants*. Logan, UT: Utah State University Press, 1996. Contains many primary sources that relate the story of the Donner party.

King, Joseph A. *Winter of Entrapment: A New Look at the Donner Party*. Lafayette, CA: K & K Publications, 1998. Attempts to dispute the work of Stewart's *Ordeal by Hunger*. It disputes many of Stewart's interpretation of events as King poses his own about the Donner party.

Lavender, David. *Snowbound: The Tragic Story of the Donner Party*. New York: Holiday House, 1996. Written for secondary school students, this work gives an overview of the events that led to the fateful decision of the Donner party to take the Hastings Cutoff.

Limburg, Peter R. *Deceived: The Story of the Donner Party*. Pacifica, CA: Ipswich Borough, 1998. Recounts the story of how the Donner party was lured into taking the Hastings Cutoff by Lansford Hastings, was warned against it by several mountain men, but chose to make the fateful trek in the interest of saving time.

McLaughlin, Mark. *The Donner Party: Weathering the Storm.* Carnelian Bay, CA: Mic Mac Publishing Company, 2007. Retells the story of the Donner party, including what the weather conditions were like.

Mullen, Frank. *The Donner Party Chronicles: A Day-by-Day Account of a Doomed Wagon Train, 1846–47.* Carson City, NV: Nevada Humanities Committee, 1997. Provides maps and photographs of the Emigrant Trail and the Hastings Cutoff that the Donner party decided to take.

Murphy, Virginia Reed. *Across the Plains in the Donner Party: 1846–1847.* Fairfield, WA: Ye Galleon Press, 1998. Gives a useful overview of the facts surrounding the ordeal of the Donner party.

Rarick, Ethan. *Desperate Passage: The Donner Party's Perilous Journey West.* New York: Oxford University Press, 2007. Takes an unflinching look at the ordeal of the Donner party and spares no details in its grim retelling of the event.

Stewart, George R. *Donner Pass and Those Who Crossed It: The Story of the Country Made Notable by the Stevens Party, the Donner Party, the Gold-Hunters, and the Railroad Builders.* San Francisco, CA: California Historical Society, 1964. Considered a foremost historian on the Donner party, Stewart places the event within the perspective of the immigration in this area as a part of the great western expansion of America.

Stewart, George R. *Ordeal by Hunger: The Story of the Donner Party.* Temecula, CA: Reprint Services Corporation, 1994. This is one of the most well known of the scholarly works written about the Donner party. It is also a dramatic retelling of the tragedy.

World Wide Web

"Donner Online." http://www.kn.att.com/wired/donner/index.html. Is replete with excellent term paper questions, maps, diaries, articles, books, and more concerning the Donner party.

"The Donner Party." http://www.spartacus.schoolnet.co.uk/WWdonnerP.htm. Includes a lengthy, multihyperlinked summary of the events surrounding the Donner party's ordeal.

"The Donner Party—American Experience." http://www.pbs.org/wgbh/amex/ donner/filmmore/fr.html. Contains a list of primary source resource links relating to the Donner party.

"The Fateful Journey of the Donner Party." http://www.vw.vccs.edu/vwhansd/ HIS121/Donner.html. Presents an overview of the Donner party's trek from Springfield, Illinois, to its fateful miring in the Sierra Nevada Mountains during winter.

"Hastings Cutoff." http://www.route40.net/history/hastings.shtml. Furnishes information about the dubious reputation of Lansford Hastings and the untried cutoff that he promoted to people on the road to California.

"Nevada Gold History/The Donner Party." http://www.ncgold.com/History/donner.html. Provides a short summary of the ordeal of the Donner party, including a picture of the statue erected at Donner Lake in their memory.

"New Light on the Donner Party." http://www.utahcrossroads.org/DonnerParty/index.html. Contains many primary sources in the form of letters, overland diaries, maps, and guidebooks not only of the Donner party but also of other emigrants.

Multimedia Sources

The Donner Party. Alexandria, VA: PBS Home Video, 2003. 1 DVD. 90 minutes. Through the use of diaries, letters, archival photographs, essays, maps, and interviews, this film tells of the terrible ordeal of the Donner party when they were trapped in the Sierra Nevadas during the winter of 1846–1847. A teacher's guide and bibliography is also included at the Web site: http://www.pbs.org/wgbh/amex/donner/filmmore/fd.html.

47. The Life and Times of Frederick Douglass (1818–1895)

Frederick Douglass (1818–1895), also known as "The Lion of Anacostia," is without peer when the roll call of great nineteenth-century Black American leaders and reformers is read. Born a slave in Talbot County, Maryland, Douglass learned to read and write from discarded textbooks and acquired his remarkable oratorical skills by imitating speeches from *The Columbian Orator.* He finally escaped to New York in 1838 after enduring beatings from his slave master, Edward Covey. Douglass quickly became active in the abolitionist movement, and his autobiography, *Narrative of the Life of Frederick Douglass* (1845), sold thousands of copies. As his fame as a speaker increased, so did his risk of capture as an escaped slave. Douglass traveled to Europe in 1845 where he lectured extensively on the sin of slavery. In 1847, his friends purchased his freedom and gave him sufficient funds to finance *The North Star,* an antislavery newspaper that dealt with issues including injustice, discrimination, inequality, segregation, and capital punishment. Douglass lived up to the ideals on the paper's masthead, which stated "Right Is of No Sex—Truth Is of No Color—God Is the Father of Us All, and All We Are Brethren." He became a supporter of women's rights, used his own house as an underground railroad stop, lobbied hard with President Abraham Lincoln for the Emancipation Proclamation, and went on to advise and serve several U.S. presidents during Reconstruction.

TERM PAPER SUGGESTIONS

1. At first Douglass was inspired by the speeches and publications of William Lloyd Garrison, editor of *The Liberator,* but they soon became enemies over Garrison's patronizing of him and his objection to Douglass's publishing of *The North Star.* Investigate and analyze the relationship that Garrison and Douglass had and the issues that drove them apart,

2. Although Douglass approved of the abolitionist philosophy of John Brown, he did not countenance his plan to lead an armed slave rebellion. Examine the historical evidence of their relationship and the reasons why Douglass fled to Canada after Brown was arrested.

3. Narratives by fugitive slaves prior to the Civil War constitute an important influential tradition in African American literature and culture. Discuss their emotional impact and political significance on readers during this time.

4. When Douglass was just twelve years old, he discovered a book entitled *The Columbian Orator,* which he claimed changed his life. Within it there is a play containing a dialogue between a slave and his master. Explore how this dialogue helped change Douglass's life.

5. Discuss the role Douglass played in getting Blacks to fight in the Civil War.

6. Read and cite passages from *Narrative of the Life of Frederick Douglass* and other slave narratives. Describe the working conditions and maltreatment of slaves during this time.

ALTERNATIVE TERM PAPER SUGGESTIONS

1. In his autobiography, Douglass comments on some of the religious songs that slaves composed. Called spirituals, they offer insight into life under slavery. Examine the lyrics of songs such as "Wade in the Water," "Steal Away," and "The Gospel Train." Analyze them for their significance during slavery and for use on the Underground Railroad. Play some of the songs for your classmates to accompany your analysis.

2. Refer to all three of Douglass's autobiographies, *Narrative of the Life of Frederick Douglass, an American Slave* (1845), *My Bondage and My Freedom* (1855),

and *The Life and Times of Frederick Douglass* (1881). Research further details of his escape from slavery. Design a Web site that shows how he escaped based on his retelling of the events, including appropriate maps and hyperlinked explanations.

SUGGESTED SOURCES

Primary Sources

Douglass, Frederick. *The Frederick Douglass Papers*. Edited by John W. Blassingame and John R. McKivigan. 5 vols. New Haven, CT: Yale University Press, 1979–1992. Contains a collection of Douglass's thoughts and opinions from various newspapers and other publications.

Gates Henry Louis, ed. *Frederick Douglass: Autobiographies: Narrative of the Life of Frederick Douglass, an American Slave/My Bondage and My Freedom/ Life and Times of Frederick Douglass*. New York: Library of America, 1994. Contains all three of Douglass's autobiographies.

Secondary Sources

Cheseborough, David B. *Frederick Douglass: Oratory from Slavery*. Westport, CT: Greenwood Press, 1998. Explores Douglass's great skills as an orator and includes speech excerpts and quotations from his writings.

The Columbian Orator, Containing a Variety of Original and Selected Pieces, Together with Rules, Calculated to Improve Youth and Others in the Ornamental and Useful Art of Eloquence. Washington, DC: Caring Publications, 1993. Provides the slave/master dialogue that inspired Douglass to seek his freedom.

Holford, David M. *Lincoln and the Emancipation Proclamation in American History*. Berkeley Heights, NJ: Enslow Publishers, 2002. Written for secondary school students, this book discusses the role that Douglass played in urging President Lincoln to pass the Emancipation Proclamation.

Huggins, Nathan I. *Slave and Citizen: The Life of Frederick Douglass*. Boston, MA: Little Brown, 1980. Considered one of the definitive biographies of Douglass, this book also analyzes his sometimes self-contradictory thoughts.

Lawson, Bill E., and Frank M. Kirkland. *Frederick Douglass: A Critical Reader*. Malden, MA: Blackwell, 1999. This book of essays by Douglass scholars places his work and writings in a contemporary perspective.

Martin, Waldo E. *The Mind of Frederick Douglass*. Chapel Hill, NC: University of North Carolina Press, 1984. Discusses Douglass's formative years as a slave and how he developed his views on injustice, inequality, and slavery.

Meltzer, Milton, ed. *Frederick Douglass, in His Own Words*. San Diego, CA: Harcourt Brace, 1995. Discusses other prominent abolitionists and people who associated with Douglass, and provides excerpts of his articles from the *North Star* and other publications.

Rogers, William B. *"We Are All Together Now": Frederick Douglass, William Lloyd Garrison, and the Prophetic Tradition*. New York: Garland Press, 1995. Compares the values, beliefs, and actions between Garrison and Douglass.

Russell, Shaman Apt, and Nathan I. Huggins. *Frederick Douglass, Abolitionist Editor*. New York: Chelsea House, 2004. Written for secondary school students, this work presents information about the editorial and reporting life of Frederick Douglass and his contribution to the Abolitionist Movement.

Voss, Frederick S. *Majestic in His Wrath: A Pictorial Life of Frederick Douglass*. Washington, DC: Smithsonian Institution Press, 1995. Contains a collection of rare photos and commentary to commemorate the life of Frederick Douglass.

Wu, Jin-Ping. *Frederick Douglass and the Black Liberation Movement: The North Star of American Blacks*. New York: Garland Press, 2000. Analyzes the impact of Douglass's life on modern African American leaders and his legacy to African American history.

World Wide Web

"Frederick Douglass." http://winningthevote.org/FDouglass.html. Contains a lengthy hyperlinked biography of Frederick Douglass and information about his participation at the Seneca Falls Women's Rights Convention in 1848.

"Frederick Douglass: Abolitionist/Editor." http://www.history.rochester.edu/class/douglass/home.html. Furnishes an online biography of Frederick Douglas, including information about his years after emancipation when he served as a consul to the Haitian government and other U.S. government appointments.

"Frederick Douglass (1817–1895)." http://www.mrlincolnswhitehouse.org/inside.asp?ID=38&subjectID=2. Presents the details of a meeting held in August 1863 with Frederick Douglass and President Lincoln to discuss equal pay for Black soldiers who were fighting for the North during the Civil War.

"The Life of Frederick Douglass." http://www.nps.gov/archive/frdo/fdlife.htm. Produced by the National Park Service, this site features a biographical sketch of Frederick Douglass together with images of family members and places where he grew up and loved.

"Library of Congress—The Frederick Douglass Papers." http://memory.loc.gov/ ammem/doughtml/doughome.html. Contains the papers of Frederick Douglass in the form of correspondence, speeches, and articles along with 38,000 images. The papers span from 1841 to 1864, but most of the material is concentrated within the period 1862–1895.

"Mr. Lincoln and Freedom." http://www.mrlincolnandfreedom.org/inside.asp ?ID=69&subjectID=4. Furnishes information about the discussions and correspondence that Frederick Douglass and President Lincoln had concerning the Emancipation Proclamation, recruiting Blacks to fight in the Civil War, and planning what to do during the Reconstruction period.

"Timeline of Frederick Douglass and Family." http://www.math.buffalo.edu/ ~sww/0history/hwny-douglass-family.html. Features an annotated chronology of the life and times of Frederick Douglass.

Multimedia Sources

Frederick Douglass. New York: A&E Network, 1999. 1 DVD. 50 minutes. Accompanied by rare archival footage and other materials such as excerpts from speeches and letters, historians present the life and times of Frederick Douglass.

Frederick Douglass, Abolitionist Editor. Wynnewood, PA: Schlessinger Video Publishing, 2002. 1 videocassette. 60 minutes. Relates the story of Douglass's role as the editor of *The North Star*. Actors read passages from his newspaper articles and other works.

Frederick Douglass: When the Lion Wrote History. Atlanta, GA: Turner Home Entertainment, 1994. 1 videocassette. 90 minutes. Relates the story of Douglass's escape from slavery to his unbelievable achievements as the major African American reformer of the nineteenth century.

Race to Freedom: The Underground Railroad. Santa Monica, CA: Xenon Pictures, 2001. 1 videocassette. 100 minutes. Presents a fictionalized account of the Underground Railroad and many of the major leaders, including Frederick Douglass.

48. Mormon Migration to Utah (1846–1847)

The Mormon Church, a religious organization known officially as "Church of Jesus Christ of Latter-Day Saints," was founded by Joseph Smith in 1831. The religion, which is still based upon a strong family life, work ethic, group projects, and abstinence from tobacco, harmful drugs, and alcoholic beverages, grew rapidly. Within a decade, twenty thousand Mormons were living in a utopian community in Nauvoo, Illinois. Wherever they moved, however, they aroused antagonism because they bloc voted and drilled their private militia in front of the local populace; also, some of their leaders practiced polygamy. In 1844, Joseph Smith was murdered by an angry mob after helping to destroy a non-Mormon newspaper that was established to oppose his candidacy for U.S. president. His successor, Brigham Young, led the Mormons to the Salt Lake Basin in Utah because it was both isolated and arable. The resulting Mormon migration was the largest and most organized in American history. About two thousand Mormons migrated the first year with the remaining group migrating at the rate of three thousand per year for the next four years. Through their missionary activities, the Mormons had also converted thirty thousand more people who joined them in Utah from the eastern United States, Great Britain, and Scandinavia. By 1860, there were forty thousand Latter Day Saints living in communities all over what is now the state of Utah. The communities thrived because of their meticulous planning, self-sufficient agrarian economy, and cooperative and productive ways of living.

TERM PAPER SUGGESTIONS

1. Research some of the nineteenth-century customs and practices of the Mormons that may have contributed to their persecution in Ohio, Missouri, and Illinois.

2. Investigate and describe the planning by Brigham Young and others that resulted in such a successful migration, including the Mormons' invention of a roadometer that was the forerunner of an odometer.

3. Young also consulted with a famous mountain man named Jim Bridger who advised against the journey and settling in the Great Salt Lake Basin. Research Bridger's life and expertise that would account for taking his reservations seriously.

4. Refer to some of the primary source accounts of Mormon migrants and discuss what seemed to be their greatest hardships while on the Mormon trail.

5. The Mormons needed to be entrepreneurial to support the journey for more pioneers who were to come after them. Examine their construction of a ferry for non-Mormon pioneers, irrigation canals, forts, and the like to earn funds to help others make the trek from Illinois to the Great Salt Lake Basin.

6. Once the Mormons were free from outside persecution, they prospered. In 1896, Utah was admitted to the Union as a state. Analyze why the Mormons were able to succeed in Utah but not in Ohio, Missouri, and Illinois.

ALTERNATIVE TERM PAPER SUGGESTIONS

1. Using period maps, design a Web site of the Mormon Trail beginning in Illinois and arriving at the Great Salt Lake Basin.

2. Assume you are Brigham Young and you must convince twenty thousand Mormons to sell their land along with most of their possessions and travel approximately one thousand miles to a place they have never seen to start all over again. Prepare a series of persuasive speeches based on the things you observed on your initial trip that you will deliver to the Nauvoo Mormon community urging them to have faith in your plan.

SUGGESTED SOURCES

Primary Sources

Barney, Ronald O., ed. *The Mormon Vanguard Brigade of 1847: Norton Jacobs Record*. Logan, UT: Utah State University Press, 2005. Contains the diary entries and accounts of Vanguard member Norton Jacob as he blazed the Mormon Trail for future pioneers.

Bashore, Melvin L. *Mormon Pioneer Companies Crossing the Plains, 1847–1868*. Salt Lake City, UT: Historical Department, Church of Jesus Christ of Latter-Day Saints, 1989. Provides diary entries of the Mormon pioneers, including some of the people who walked pushing wheelbarrows filled with their only belongings.

Knight, Hal, and Stanley B. Kimball. *111 Days to Zion*. Salt Lake City, UT: Deseret Press, 1979. Contains the day-by-day accounts that the Mormon leaders required designated people to keep not only to remember the event but also to assist future pioneers on the trail.

Secondary Sources

Bennett, Richard E. *We'll Find the Place: The Mormon Exodus 1846–1848*. Salt Lake City, UT: Deseret Book Company, 1997. Furnishes a useful overview of the reasons why the Mormons decided to leave Illinois and of their search for a place that was both isolated and productive.

Bringhurst, Newell G. "A New Frontier Sanctuary." In *Brigham Young and the Expanding American Frontier*, edited by Newell G. Bringhurst et al. Boston, MA: Little Brown, 1986. Provides an overview of the Mormon migration and the role that the trail played in colonizing the western part of the United States.

Bushman, Richard Lyman. *Joseph Smith: Rough Stone Rolling.* New York: Alfred Knopf, 2005. Portrays Smith in a positive light as the founder of the Mormon Church.

Hafen, Leroy R., and Ann W. Hafen. *Handcarts to Zion: The Story of a Unique Western Migration 1856–1860.* Lincoln, NE: University of Nebraska Press, 1992. Describes the journey of many Mormons who could not afford covered wagons and walked the thirteen hundred miles pushing their belongings in the equivalent of a wheelbarrow.

Hill, William. *The Mormon Trail: Yesterday and Today.* Logan, UT: Utah State University Press, 1996. Provides a history of the Mormon trail and accompanies it with many maps, illustrations, and photographs of the trail.

Kimball, Stanley B., and Violet T. Kimball. *Mormon Trail: Voyage of Discovery.* Las Vegas, NV: KC Publications, 1995. This outstanding book traces the Mormon pioneers on the trail, identifying prominent markers, forts, trail sites, and more.

Madsen, Carol Cornwall. *Journey to Zion: Voices from the Mormon Trail.* Salt Lake City, UT: Deseret Book Company, 1997. Contains first-person accounts of the hardships and joys of traveling the Mormon Trail.

Slaughter, William, and Michael Landon. *Trail of Hope: The Story of the Mormon Trail.* Salt Lake City, UT: Deseret Book Company, 1997. Provides an exciting overview of the history of the Mormon Trail.

Smith, Joseph Fielding. "The Settlement in the Rocky Mountains." In *Essentials in Church History.* Part 5, 22nd ed. Salt Lake City, UT: Deseret Company, 1967. Provides an annotated chronology of the reasons for departing Illinois, planning and preparations for the departure, rules for travel, dangers encountered, and the settling of the Great Salt Lake area.

Stegner, Wallace. *The Gathering of Zion: The Story of the Mormon Trail.* Reprint. Lincoln, NE: University of Nebraska Press, 1992. This well-written account of the history of the Mormon Trail is captivating.

Talbot, Dan. "The Mormon Battalion." In *A Historical Guide to the Mormon Battalion and Butterfield Trail.* Tucson, AZ: Westernlore Press, 1992. Furnishes maps and an account of more than two thousand Mormons who enlisted in the Mexican-American War and sent part of their salaries home to assist Mormon pioneers traveling to Utah.

World Wide Web

"Gathering the Dispersed Nauvoo Saints, 1847–1852." http://library.lds.org/nxt/gateway.dll/Magazines/Ensign/1997.htm/ensign%20july%201997.htm/

gathering%20the%20dispersed%20nauvoo%20saints%2018471852
.htm. Citing primary sources, trail historian William Hartley summarizes
the events leading up to and during the Mormon migration to the Great
Salt Lake Basin.

"The Mormon Pioneer National Historic Trail." http://www.nps.gov/mopi/.
This National Park site gives directions and an auto route guide about
the trail that the pioneers traveled by oxcart and foot in the nineteenth
century.

"The Mormon Pioneers." http://www.so-utah.com/feature/pioneer/
homepage.html. Contains a useful, hyperlinked site about the events
leading up to and including the Mormon migration.

"The Mormon Pioneer Trail." http://www.americanwest.com/trails/pages/
mormtrl.htm. Features a history of the Mormon Trail together with illustrations, maps, and resource links.

"The Pioneer Story." http://lds.org/gospellibrary/pioneer/pioneerstory.htm.
Contains first-person accounts about various places and events as they
occurred on the Mormon Trail.

"Pioneer Trail Map—Location Green River: Lombard Ferry." http://
www.lds.org/gospellibrary/pioneer/32_Green_River.html. Describes
the entrepreneurial aspect of the Mormon Trail and its use by non-
Mormons.

"Pioneer Trail Map—Location Platte River." http://www.lds.org/gospellibrary/
pioneer/15_Platte_River.html. Contains short, first-person accounts
of pioneer Mormons' decision to stay on the north side of the Platte
River so they avoided any confrontations with other emigrants going
west.

"Route of the Oregon/California/Mormon Trail in Central Wyoming a Virtual
Tour." http://www.independencerock.org/index.html. Gives a photo
virtual tour of these three great western expanding trails.

Multimedia Sources

Trail of Hope: The Story of the Mormon Trail. Salt Lake City, UT: Bonneville
Worldwide Entertainment, 1997. 1 videocassette. 117 minutes. Narrated
by Hal Holbrook, this documentary relates the tremendous challenge
that the Mormon Trail was by showing the great deserts and mountains
that needed to be crossed.

The West. Santa Monica, CA: PBS Home Video, 1996. 5 DVDs. 70 minutes
each. Disc 2, *Empire Upon the Trails,* includes information about the
Mormons journey to Utah. Click on http://www.pbs.org/weta/thewest/
program to obtain a multimedia-guided tour of each episode in the
series, along with selected documentary materials, archival images, and

commentary, as well as links to background information and other resources of the Web site.

49. Seneca Falls Convention (1848)

If there was a "shot heard round the world" regarding women's rights, it sounded on July 19, 1848, in Seneca Falls, New York, when a group of approximately two hundred women and (shockingly) forty men met to speak and declare themselves in need of the right to vote, the right to own property, the right for an equal opportunity for employment and education, and all the other rights and privileges that accompanied citizens of the United States. Its leaders were abolitionists Lucretia Mott and Elizabeth Cady Stanton, who, while banished to the balcony during their attendance at an antislavery meeting in London, drew appropriate references to the similar slavery of women and decided to focus America's attention on women's rights. Stanton drafted a *Declaration of Sentiments* similar to the Declaration of Independence that stated women's grievances and proclaimed that women were going to initiate a reform movement to address these wrongs. The convention, ironically chaired by Mott's husband, James, met for two days debating the twelve resolutions to the document. In the end, all of them passed and were duly signed by sixty-eight women and thirty-two men, one being the great abolitionist Frederick Douglass. The only resolution that was hotly debated was the one demanding women's right to vote. Although much of the reaction to the Seneca Falls Convention was unfavorable in the press, the meeting became known as the first public forum held to discuss, debate, and demand women's rights in the United States.

TERM PAPER SUGGESTIONS

1. Discuss the beliefs of women about the ninth resolution demanding a woman's right to vote and why it was so controversial. Why did it pass by only a narrow majority?

2. Examine how the Abolitionist Movement may have given Lucretia Mott and Elizabeth Cady Stanton the ideas and methods for raising the public's awareness abut the rights of women in the United States.

3. Investigate how the tenets as espoused in the Second Great Awakening contributed to the Seneca Falls Convention.

4. Pro and con advocates of women's rights based their need for reform or lack of reform on the Bible and the Constitution. Research passages from the Bible and the Constitution and show how both sides exploited this rhetoric for their own goals.

5. Elizabeth Cady Stanton was also in favor of birth control and women's right to divorce. Discuss how her position on these issues weakened her support in the women's movement.

6. Analyze how Sarah Grimke's letters revealed the qualities of women that demonstrated their equality. How did she succeed in raising awareness of women's rights with her publications?

ALTERNATIVE TERM PAPER SUGGESTIONS

1. Prepare a podcast for the Seneca Falls Convention that is based on the resolutions that Mott and Stanton wished conventioneers to pass. Make sure that you include a list of grievances that will make women realize how lacking they are in rights as citizens of the United States.

2. Assume you are a newspaper reporter for a local newspaper. Your editor has asked you to prepare an op-ed piece that basically tears apart the Seneca Falls Convention platform. Be sure to use some of the nineteenth-century arguments regarding politics and religion as a basis for your article.

SUGGESTED SOURCES

Primary Sources

Du Bois, Ellen Carol, ed. *Elizabeth Cady Stanton, Susan B. Anthony: Correspondence, Writings, Speeches.* New York: Schocken Books, 1981. Provides the original speeches of both women together with critical commentary by W. E. B. Du Bois.

Mott, Lucretia. *Selected Letters of Lucretia Coffin Mott.* Urbana, IL: University of Illinois Press, 2002. Contains the annotated letters of Lucretia Mott from 1813 to 1879.

Secondary Sources

Banner, Lois W. *Elizabeth Cady Stanton: A Radical for Woman's Rights.* Boston, MA: Little, Brown, 1980. Provides a highly informative account of Stanton's life and her role in the Seneca Falls Convention.

Cromwell, Otelia. *Lucretia Mott.* Cambridge, MA: Harvard University Press, 1958. Chapter 12 of this scholarly biography of Lucretia Mott is devoted solely to a discussion of her role in the Seneca Falls Convention.

Debatable Issues in U.S. History. 1833–1868. Vol. 3. Westport, CT: Greenwood Press, 2004. Chapter 5 of this work contains an overview of the Seneca Falls Convention.

Frost-Knappman, Elizabeth, and Kathyrn-Cullen Dupont. *Women's Suffrage in America.* New York: Facts on File, 2004. Filled with primary source excerpts, this encyclopedia of the history of women's voting rights covers the Seneca Falls Convention and its aftermath.

Griffin, Elizabeth. *In Her Own Right: The Life of Elizabeth Cady Stanton.* New York: Oxford University Press, 1984. Chapter 4 of this definitive biography of Stanton discusses her role in the Seneca Falls Convention.

Gurko, Miriam. *Ladies of Seneca Falls.* New York: Pantheon Books, 1987. Outlines the roles that Elizabeth Cady Stanton and Susan B. Anthony played in getting the Nineteenth Amendment passed, which gave women the right to vote.

Lerner, Gerda. *The Feminist Thought of Sarah Grimke.* New York: Oxford University Press, 1998. Contains the letters, speeches, and thoughts of Sarah Grimke concerning women's rights.

Miller, Bradford. *Returning to Seneca Falls: The First Women's Rights Convention and Its Meaning for Men Today: A Journey into the Historical Soul of America.* Hudson, NY: Lindisfarne Books, 1995. The author, who grew up in historic Seneca Falls, sees this groundbreaking convention as an opportunity for both genders to finally be totally equal in rights and privileges.

Rife, Douglas. *Seneca Falls Declaration of Sentiments and Resolutions.* Carthage, IL: Teaching & Learning Company, 2002. Written for secondary school students, this work examines the convention's resolutions and includes handouts and discussion questions.

Wellman, Judith. *The Road to Seneca Falls: Elizabeth Cady Stanton and the First Women's Rights Convention.* Urbana, IL: University of Illinois Press, 2004. Outlines the Seneca Falls Convention's events and how the issues of abolitionism, radical Quakerism, and a campaign for legal reform shaped the proceedings.

Women Suffrage and Women's Rights. New York: New York University Press, 1998. Contains a collection of essays that give an excellent overview of the women's suffrage movement and the role that Stanton and Mott played in it.

World Wide Web

"American Treasures of the Library of Congress—Seneca Falls Convention." http://www.loc.gov/exhibits/treasures/trr040.html. Provides a wealth of primary sources in the form of period newspaper articles about the convention, the Declaration of Sentiments, and more.

"Declaration of Sentiments." http://www.nps.gov/archive/wori/declaration.htm. Supplies the full text of this groundbreaking document in service of women's rights.

"Elizabeth Cady Stanton." http://www.nps.gov/archive/wori/ecs.htm. Furnishes a biographical sketch of Stanton, including a short speech concerning her feelings regarding women's rights.

"International Woman Suffrage Timeline." http://womenshistory.about.com/od/suffrage/a/intl_timeline.htm. Presents an annotated timeline concerning the earliest stirrings regarding a woman's right to vote through the year 2005.

"The Seneca Falls Convention: Teaching about the Rights of Women and the Heritage of the Declaration of Independence." http://www.sahomeschool.com/Articles/Seneca%20Falls%20Convention.asp. Contains a set of lesson plans complete with primary sources and other resource links about the Seneca Falls Convention.

"Women's History." http://www.eduref.org/Resources/Subjects/Social_Studies/Womens_Studies/Womens_History.html. Provides a webography of sites not only of the Seneca Falls Convention but also of women's rights.

"Women's Rights Convention, Seneca Falls, NY 1848." http://www.pbs.org/stantonanthony/resources/index.html. This outstanding site contains speeches, writings, critical essays, resource links, a bibliography, and a list of related organizations pertaining to the Seneca Falls Convention.

Multimedia Sources

One Woman, One Vote. Alexandria, VA: PBS Home video, 2005. 1 DVD. 120 minutes. Accompanied by pictures, documents, and interviews with historians, this film relates the story of the women's suffrage movement including the Seneca Falls Convention.

Seneca Reflections: 150 Years of Women's Rights. Boston, MA: Reunion Productions, 1998. 1 videocassette. 60 minutes. Created in honor of the 150th anniversary of the Seneca Falls Convention, this video features addresses by women, including Betty Friedan, Hillary Rodham Clinton, Donna Shalala, and others, as they place the Seneca Falls Convention of 1848 in a twentieth-century perspective.

50. California Gold Rush (1849)

"There's gold in them thar hills" was officially confirmed by President James K. Polk in his annual address to Congress on December 5, 1848.

His speech helped trigger a stampede that created a booming economy for California Territory, which quickly propelled it to statehood in 1850. Almost a year earlier in January gold was discovered at Sutter's Mill on the American River. John Sutter desperately wished to keep it secret so he could protect his vast tracts of land granted by the Mexican government, but it was to no avail. Prospectors poured in not only from other parts of California, but also from Europe, Latin America, and China. They came overland by a series of long and difficult trails or by sea around the tip of South America. For early arrivals, many of them were rewarded with $10 to $50 worth of gold per day. Others also made handsome profits by selling supplies or by running restaurants, hotels, and taverns. Many, however, perished from diseases such as cholera and typhoid or lost their savings, their claim, and their families in a mad hunt for El Dorado. The migration of seventy-five thousand people to California questing for gold had significant environmental, social, and economic effects. In some cases California rivers were diverted to bare the river bed for gold panning. American Indians were displaced from their lands, and ethnic groups, including the Chinese and Latin Americans, suffered racial segregation and discrimination. California's economy boomed so much, however, that it permanently became associated with the "California Dream"—a phenomenon that still attracts entrepreneurs and people wishing to start over today.

TERM PAPER SUGGESTIONS

1. Gold was not discovered just at Sutter's Mill; it was also found in present-day Siskiyou, Shasta, and Trinity Counties and in southern California. Research these discoveries and discuss how they may have made prospectors believe that the entire state was filled with gold.

2. Discuss how and why the discovery of gold sped up California's admission as the thirty-first state.

3. As gold became scarcer, Americans began to discriminate more against foreigners even to the extent of passing a foreign miners' tax. Examine the attempts by Americans to drive out foreign born prospectors, especially the Chinese.

4. Prospectors, shopkeepers, and others drove American Indians from their ancestral lands during the gold rush. Investigate and report the effect the gold rush had on various Indian tribes.

5. Analyze how the gold rush helped fulfill President's Polk's idea of Manifest Destiny.

6. California was not a state when the gold rush started, so people had to create their own rules regarding staking claims to gold-producing property and other mineral rights matters. Discuss these rules and trace how they evolved into formal laws that are still used today.

ALTERNATIVE TERM PAPER SUGGESTIONS

1. Assume you have just read the news about gold being discovered in California. You and a partner have decided to leave right away, but first you must decide which route to take. Describe each route and its attendant advantages and disadvantages.

2. Read through some of the letters describing gold mining at the site "California as I Saw It: First Person Narratives of California's Early Years" at http://memory.loc.gov/ammem/cbhtml/. Write a series of letters to someone you love describing your experiences as a gold miner in a typical California gold mine.

SUGGESTED SOURCES

Primary Sources

Gordon, Mary M., ed. *Overland to California with the Pioneer Line*. Urbana, IL: University of Illinois Press, 1984. Contains the memoirs of a variety of people who migrated to California during the gold rush.

Holliday, J. S. *The World Rushed In: The California Gold Rush Experience*. Norman, OK: University of Oklahoma Press, 2002. Explores the California gold rush through the extensive correspondence of one prospector and draws appropriate inferences for the gold rush syndrome.

Secondary Sources

Brands, H. W. *The Age of Gold: The California Gold Rush and the New American Dream*. New York: Doubleday, 2002. This outstanding work places the gold rush within a grand historical perspective that compares the rush to the Crusades.

Hill, Mary. *Gold: The California Story*. Berkeley, CA: University of California Press, 1999. Provides a useful overview of the gold rush in California.

Johnson, Susan Lee. *Roaring Camp: The Social World of the California Gold Rush*. New York: W. W. Norton, 2000. This text explores the clashes among cultures as a result of the gold rush.

Levy, Jo Ann. "Forgotten Forty-Niners." In *American History*. Vol.1. Guilford, CT: Dushkin, 1995. Describes the experiences of women, many of whom migrated to California during the gold rush.

Meldahl, Keith Heyer. *Hard Road West: History & Geography Along the Gold Rush Trail*. Chicago, IL: University of Chicago Press, 2007. Weaves the geological history of the North American continent into the historical narrative of the California Gold Rush years.

Paul, Rodman W. *California Gold: The Beginning of Mining in the Far West*. Cambridge, MA: Harvard University Press, 1947. Focuses on the economic and social aspects of the gold rush and its effect on California. It also provides information about mining technology, the regulation of mining gold, and vigilante committees.

Rawls, James J., and Richard J. Orsi, eds. *A Golden State: Mining and Economic Development in Gold Rush California*. Berkeley, CA: University of California Press, 1999. Freshly interprets the environmental, social, and cultural effects of the gold rush on non-Americans and American Indians as well as the environmental effects of gold mining.

Royce, Sarah. *A Frontier Lady: Recollections of the Gold Rush and Early California*. Lincoln, NE: University of Nebraska Press, 1977. This diary features the author's experiences as a wife who migrated to California during the gold rush.

Starr, Kevin. *Americans and the California Dream: 1850–1915*. New York: Oxford University Press, 1973. This classic history of California begins with the gold rush and how it became synonymous with the idea of getting rich quick, starting over, and what is known as the "California Dream."

Starr, Kevin, and Richard J. Orsi, eds. *California History: Rooted in Barbarous Soil: People, Culture, and Community in Gold Rush California*. Berkeley, CA: University of California, 2000. California historian Starr recounts the story of the gold rush and places it within a social context that conveys the idea of the "California Dream."

Tutorow, Norman E. *The Governor: The Life and Legacy of Leland Stanford, a California Colossus*. 2 vols. Spokane, WA: Arthur H. Clark, 2004. This definitive biography of early prospector Leland Stanford tells how he went on to build a commercial empire in businesses that supported mining.

World Wide Web

"California Gold Rush Chronology 1846–1849." http://www.sfmuseum.org/hist/chron1.html. Provides an excellent, annotated chronology that juxtaposes the events during the gold rush with what was going on in the rest of the United States and the world. It assists in placing the gold rush within a broader historical perspective.

"The Discovery of Gold in California by Gen. John A. Sutter." http://www
.sfmuseum.net/hist2/gold.html. Contains the full text of Sutter's account
of the discovery of gold on his property.

"The Gold Discovery by Theodore H. Hittell." http://www.sfmuseum.net/hist6/
impact.html. Provides an extensive account of the impact of the discovery of gold in California.

"Gold Fever!" http://www.museumca.org/goldrush/fever.html. This outstanding
site contains audios of Chinese miners' experiences in Cantonese during
the gold rush, in addition to maps, artifacts, first-person accounts,
and historical analysis of the impact of the gold rush on the American
Indian.

"The Gold Rush—The American Experience." http://www.pbs.org/wgbh/amex/
goldrush/. Features biographical sketches, a timeline, and a description of
major events, maps, and teachers' resources about the California gold
rush.

"Mining History and Geology of the Mother Lode." http://virtual.yosemite
.cc.ca.us/ghayes/goldrush.htm. Contains excellent geological information about the nature of gold, where it is usually found, how to mine
it, and what the environmental effects were on California.

"The Siskiyou Trail." http://www.museumsiskiyoutrail.org/In_the_Museum
.html. Siskiyou County, California, was another place where gold was
discovered. This site provides primary sources from American Indians
who were displaced and other people who experienced the gold rush.

Multimedia Sources

The Gold Rush. Alexandria, VA: PBS Home Video, 2006. 1 DVD. 120 minutes.
Recounts the story of the California gold rush and the social, economic,
and cultural impact it had on not only indigenous peoples but also
foreigners.

51. Compromise of 1850

Each time the issue of slavery arose during most of the nineteenth century,
Congress struck a devilish bargain with southern states in a futile attempt
to avert civil war. When California petitioned for statehood in 1850,
the 1820 Missouri Compromise that maintained an even Senate balance
of thirty slave state and thirty free state members was no longer operative. Southern senators such as John C. Calhoun (South Carolina) and
Jefferson Davis (Mississippi) either openly proposed or spoke of a

secessionist movement and the formation of two national governments. In its hour of need the Senate turned to "The Great Compromiser," Henry Clay of Kentucky, who introduced five resolutions that were altered by the Senate in later debate. Combined into a series of bills, they admitted California as a free state; abolished the slave trade in the District of Columbia; allowed the territories of New Mexico, present-day Arizona, and Utah to vote whether to allow slavery; removed land from Texas that it was claiming; and paid off its debt of $10 million. Finally, it required U.S. citizens to assist in returning runaway slaves and to be subject to imprisonment and a fine for aiding or abetting in their escape. The economy was strong during this period and most Americans were not that concerned about slavery, so the bills passed. Again, the United States postponed for almost a decade the inevitable conflict that was to come.

TERM PAPER SUGGESTIONS

1. On May 8, 1850, Senator Jefferson Davis of Mississippi gave a speech hinting at a possible secessionist movement in the years to come. Discuss the reasons for his displeasure with the Compromise of 1850 and its implications for the southern slave states in general.

2. President Zachary Taylor died during the debates concerning the Compromise of 1850. He was a strict unionist and had threatened to veto the bills. Examine his objections and analyze how events may have turned out if he had lived.

3. The Fugitive Slave Act was the one bill that infuriated abolitionists and helped fuel the fires for continued agitation against slavery. Read the bill and comment on why many northerners would oppose it.

4. Beginning with the Northwest Ordinance of 1787, trace and discuss the economic issues that were at stake in the North and South in terms of competition for cheap labor, sale of crops, and other commercial products.

5. During the Mexican-American War of 1846–1848, David Wilmot introduced an amendment to an appropriations bill called the Wilmot Proviso, which stated that any territory acquired from Mexico must exclude slavery in perpetuity. Discuss the political implications in terms of the balance of power between southern and northern states.

6. When Vice-President Millard Fillmore took over after President Taylor died in office, one of the remaining stumbling blocks was removed concerning passage of the bills. Examine and discuss President Fillmore's reasons for signing them.

ALTERNATIVE TERM PAPER SUGGESTIONS

1. In most cases the type of land dictated whether a state would become a slave state. If it was suitable for growing cotton, it had high potential of becoming a slave state. Assume you are a government surveyor for the area acquired during the Mexican-American War. Draw a series of topographical maps and include analysis of their potential for various agricultural and/or industrial products.

2. Assume you are a Senate aide to Stephen A. Douglas, who broke Senator Clay's resolutions into five parts and shepherded them through the Senate and House of Representatives until they passed. Write Douglas a series of memos describing where his main road blocks lie with regard to legislators opposing him both from the North and the South.

SUGGESTED SOURCES

Primary Sources

Rhodes, James Ford. *History of the United States from the Compromise of 1850*. Vol. 1. Chicago, IL: University of Chicago Press, 1967. Contains primary sources in the form of speeches, legislation, and letters of the legislators who were involved in fashioning the Compromise of 1850.

Rozwenc, Edwin C., ed. *The Compromise of 1850*. Boston, MA: D. C. Heath, 1968. Contains a selection of primary source documents concerning the legislation and other correspondence of the 1850 Compromise.

Secondary Sources

Collins, Bruce. *The Origins of America's Civil War*. New York: Holmes and Meier Publishers, 1981. Provides an excellent overview of the events, people, and ideas of the period before the war including the opposing sides' positions concerning slavery and other matters.

Foner, Eric, ed. *Politics and Ideology in the Age of the Civil War*. New York: Oxford University Press, 1980. This scholarly work gives a thorough analysis of the competing ideas and values during the antebellum period and traces the political battles leading up to and through the Civil War.

Hamilton, Holman. *Prologue to Conflict: The Crisis and Compromise of 1850*. New York: W. W. Norton, 1966. Definitively examines the events relating to the last legislative attempt to avoid a civil war.

Holt, Michael F. *The Fate of Their Country: Politicians, Slavery Extension, and the Coming of the Civil War*. New York: Hill and Wang, 2005. Provides a fascinating rationale for the Civil War that discounts economic causes and instead finds that politicians needing to get reelected in their respective regions of the country upped the rhetoric that helped drive the country to divide.

Morrison, Michael A. *Slavery and the American West: The Eclipse of Manifest Destiny and the Coming of the Civil War.* Chapel Hill, NC: University of North Carolina Press, 1997. Discusses how the issue of slavery was inextricably linked to western expansion as southern states saw their loss of political strength with the abolishment of slavery for newly admitted states.

Potter, David. *The Impending Crisis, 1848–1861.* New York: Harper & Row, 1976. Historian Potter analyzes the political, social, and economic issues that combined to make the Civil War a foregone conclusion.

Shankman, Kimberly Christner. *Compromise and the Constitution: The Political Thought of Henry Clay.* Landham, MD: Lexington Books, 1999. Senator Clay was a slave holder, but also a strict unionist. This work examines his political thoughts and his approach to compromise on which his fame rests.

Sinha, Manisha. *The Counterrevolution of Slavery: Politics and Ideology in Antebellum South Carolina.* Chapel Hill, NC: University of North Carolina, 2000. South Carolina was the fulcrum in the growing secessionist movement. This work contains a well-researched analysis of the ideology and subsequent propaganda that South Carolina legislators used to win people over to their cause.

Sizer, Lyde Cullen. *The Political Work of Northern Women Writers and the Civil War, 1850–1872.* Chapel Hill, NC: University of North Carolina Press, 2000. Even though women could not vote, their political writings helped explore the nature of the debate concerning slavery. This work features the political writings of Louisa May Alcott and others on the abolition of slavery.

Stegmaier, Mark J. *Texas, New Mexico, and the Compromise of 1850: Boundary Dispute & Sectional Crisis.* Kent, OH: Kent State University, 1996. Discusses the areas that were in political dispute concerning the issue of slavery and other matters during the Compromise of 1850.

Waugh, John C. *On the Brink of Civil War: The Compromise of 1850 and How It Changed the Course of American History.* Wilmington, DE: Scholarly Resources, 2003. Explores the political wrangling among the northern abolitionists, southern secessionists, and neutrals from both parties.

World Wide Web

"The Compromise of 1850." http://blueandgraytrail.com/event/Compromise_of_1850. Presents an annotated chronology of the events leading up to the Compromise.

"Compromise of 1850 (1850)." http://www.ourdocuments.gov/doc.php?flash
=true&doc=27. Provides the full text of the bills that constituted the
Compromise of 1850.

"Daniel Webster's Speech on the Compromise of 1850." http://www.senate.gov/
artandhistory/history/minute/Speech_Costs_Senator_His_Seat.htm.
Contains the full text of the Senate speech that Daniel Webster gave on
the compromise and that caused him to resign from the Senate.

"Fugitive Slave act of 1850." http://americanhistory.about.com/od/beforethe
war/a/fugitiveslave.htm?terms=fugitive+slave%20act. Contains the full
text of the most controversial section of the Compromise of 1850, The
Fugitive Slave Act.

"Lesson Plan: The Compromise of 1850." http://www.congresslink.org/
print_lp_compromise1850.htm. Provided by Congress, this lesson plan
meets the requirement for the National History Standards and contains
some additional resource links.

"Library of Congress—Compromise of 1850." http://www.loc.gov/rr/program/
bib/ourdocs/Compromise1850.html. Contains a host of primary sources
about the compromise in the form of speeches, documents, correspondence, and images.

"Treasures of Congress—Struggles Over Slavery: the Compromise of 1850."
http://www.archives.gov/exhibits/treasures_of_congress/page_11.html.
Presents the full text of documents related to the Compromise of 1850.

Multimedia Sources

Causes of the Civil War. Wynnewood, PA: Schlessinger Media, 2000. 1 DVD.
30 minutes. Part of the *United States History Collection,* this documentary
discusses all the possible causes of the Civil War, including the Compromise of 1850.

Slavery and the Making of America. New York: Ambrose Video Productions,
2005. 1 DVD. 60 minutes. DVD No. 3 of this series discusses all the
events that contributed to the Civil War, including the Compromise of
1850.

52. Underground Railroad (1850s–1860)

Although President George Washington complained in 1797 of a group
of Quakers who had assisted one of his slaves to freedom, it was not until
the 1850s that a network of secret routes by which slaves traveled their
way to freedom reached its peak. Its organizational structure was not

formalized, but railroad terminology was definitely used. "Conductors" were people who helped slaves along their route, taking them to the next safe place or "station" to stay, even if it was a hayloft in an abandoned barn. "Station keepers," many of them free people of color, provided food or clothing along the journey, and "lines" were fairly established escape routes that took slaves out of Kentucky and Virginia into Ohio and from there north to New England and sometimes on through to Canada. Slaves in the Deep South had the farthest to go and many times fled farther south to live in Mexico or with the Seminole, Cherokee, and other American Indian tribes. The secretive nature of the underground railroad did not lend itself to record keeping, but historians estimate that between sixty thousand to one hundred thousand slaves escaped from 1800 to 1865. Many escaped without the aid of anyone, but others did receive aid from churches such as the Quakers and African Methodist Episcopal Church for temporary housing, food, employment, and the like until they were settled. As the Abolitionist Movement grew in the North, the Underground Railroad became even more active in the 1840s, leading southern slave owners to claim enormous losses of slave property that resulted in the passage of the Fugitive Slave Act of 1850.

TERM PAPER SUGGESTIONS

1. One of the best documented Underground Railroad workers was known as the "Moses of her People." Describe the role that Harriet Tubman played in the Underground Railroad and refer to the extra risks she undertook by going into the South as a free person of color.

2. Levi Coffin was a white station keeper who is also documented as having assisted thousands of slaves to freedom. Research his background and the role he played in the Underground Railroad.

3. Research the role that the African Methodist Episcopal Church played in extending financial and other forms of aid to escaped slaves.

4. Analyze how the existence and even rumor of an Underground Railroad may have kept hope alive for so many slaves during the 1850s.

5. Many slaves were positively ingenious in their escape methods. Research how some slaves had themselves shipped north in railroad crates, disguised themselves, passed as whites, or cross-dressed to foil pursuers.

6. Research how and why Oberlin College, Ohio, became a center for Underground Railroad activities.

ALTERNATIVE TERM PAPER SUGGESTIONS

1. Thomas Garrett was a Quaker from Wilmington, Delaware, who was so active in the Underground Railroad that he eventually lost his property to court costs. Assume you are an attorney representing Garrett. Use Henry David Thoreau's essay *Civil Disobedience* to argue that Garrett should not lose his property and that he should be allowed to continue his work with the Underground Railroad.

2. Assume you are an escaped slave who has journeyed back to the south to meet with a small group of slaves who are planning to escape. Using a map of the Underground Railroad, outline their possible escape routes and the dangers that they face no matter what route they choose.

SUGGESTED SOURCES

Primary Sources

Coffin, Levi. *Reminiscences of Levi Coffin*. New York: Arno Press, 1968. Coffin's detailed memoir of his work on the Underground Railroad is one of the best set of primary sources about this necessarily secretive nineteenth-century movement.

Humez, Jean M. *Harriet Tubman: The Life and the Life Stories*. Madison, WI: University of Wisconsin Press, 2003. Contains a collection of diary entries, letters, and speeches by Harriet Tubman and a biographical sketch of her life.

Secondary Sources

Blight, David. *Passages to Freedom: The Underground Railroad in History and Memory*. New York: Harper Collins, 2006. This excellent work features 78 color photographs and 174 black and white photographs of people and events of the Underground Railroad. The bulk of the book is a series of essays about various aspects of the Underground Railroad and its significance to the Civil War by noted historians.

Bordewich, Fergus. *Bound for Canaan: The Underground Railroad and the War for the Soul of America*. New York: Amistad, 2005. Using excerpts from memoirs and other primary sources, this work describes "the national geography of freedom" of spies, conductors, and station keepers that made up the Underground Railroad.

Clinton, Catherine. *Harriet Tubman: The Road to Freedom*. Boston, MA: Little, Brown, 2004. This well-researched work provides a biography of Harriet Tubman's life and the work she did on the Underground Railroad and for the Abolitionist Movement.

Gara, Larry. *The Liberty Line: The Legend of the Underground Railroad*. Lexington, KY: University of Kentucky Press, 1961. Focuses on the role that free persons of color played in assisting those to freedom rather than white abolitionists.

Hendrick, George. *Fleeing for Freedom: Stories of the Underground Railroad as Told by Levi Coffin and William Still*. Chicago, IL: Ivan R. Dee, 2004. Condenses the huge tomes by Still and Coffin into a more comprehensible collection and includes the stories of fugitives escaping by cross-dressing and shipping themselves in railroad crates such as Henry "Box" Brown.

Larson, Kate Clifford. *Bound for the Promised Land: Harriet Tubman, Portrait of an American Hero*. New York: Ballantine Books, 2004. Features period newspaper accounts, court records, and other correspondence to tell the story of Harriet Tubman's life.

Loguen, Jermain Wesley. *A Stop on the Underground Railroad: Rev. J. W. Loguen & Syracuse*. Reprint. Neptune, NJ: Hofmann Press, 2001. This short work is adapted from a memoir by Rev. J. W. Loguen in which he describes his work on the Underground Railroad when a fugitive slave was arrested and then freed in Syracuse, New York, by an angry, abolitionist mob.

May, Samuel. *The Fugitive Slave Law and its Victims*. Ithaca, NY: Cornell University Press, 2007. Contains primary sources in the form of personal accounts and oral histories of people who were victimized by the loss of property and jail terms for assisting fugitive slaves. The works represent accounts that have been digitized from Cornell University's Samuel May Anti-Slavery Collection.

Michael, Peter H. *An American Family of the Underground Railroad: The Story of One Family's Experience as Safe-House Operators on the Nation's Underground Railroad, and...Important Institutions of Their Country*. Bloomington, IN: Authorhouse, 2005. Relates the account of one family who tells the story of how their present-day farm, Cooling Springs, was used as a station during the Underground Railroad.

Quarles, Benjamin. *Black Abolitionists*. New York: Oxford University Press, 1969. Describes and discusses the role free persons of color played in the Underground Railroad.

Siebert, Wilbur H. *The Underground Railroad from Slavery to Freedom*. Reprint. New York: Arno Press, 1968. Considered one of the first academic accounts of the Underground Railroad, this work cites personal memoirs and other primary sources to detail its history.

World Wide Web

"Anna L. Curtis's Stories from the Underground Railroad." http://www
.shookfamily.net/underground/title.html. Written by Anna L. Curtis in
1941, this fascinating series of primary resource links contains stories,
memoirs, and descriptions about the Underground Railroad.

"Canada and the Underground Railroad Tracks to Freedom." http://www
.canada.com/ottawacitizen/features/freedom/index.html. Represents a
journey taken by journalist Chris Lackner for *The Ottawa Citizen* in
which he hikes the routes taken by slaves who fled to Canada and details
some of their experiences using short excerpts.

"Friends of the Underground Railroad." http://www.fourr.org/. Provides an
Underground Railroad timeline, photos, and locations where hiding
places have been preserved of Underground Railroad "stations."

"Oberlin Heritage Center." http://www.oberlinheritage.org/. Presents information about the role that Oberlin College played in the Abolitionist
Movement and with the Underground Railroad.

"The Underground Railroad." http://www.nationalgeographic.com/railroad/
j1.html. Sponsored by the National Geographic Society, this excellent
site contains resource links, lesson plans, and information about the
journey, routes, and more.

"The Underground Railroad by William Still." http://www.gutenberg.org/etext/
15263. Project Gutenberg contains the full text of William Still's massive
collection of slave narratives and oral histories that stresses fugitives' tales.
It also features a section on station keepers and conductors who assisted
fugitives on their journey.

"Underground Railroads." http://www.africanaonline.com/slavery_under
ground_railroad.htm. Gives short synopses of various events involving
the Underground Railroad, including information abut Henry "Box"
Brown, the use of spirituals in designating escape routes, and more.

Multimedia Sources

Pathways to Freedom: Maryland & the Underground Railroad. http://pathways
.thinkport.org/flash_home.cfm. Features images, interactive maps, audio
from an 1869 biography of Harriet Tubman, photographs of safe houses
and farms, and outstanding background material about the Underground Railroad.

Race to Freedom: The Story of the Underground Railroad. Santa Monica, CA:
Xenon, Pictures, 2001. 1 DVD. 90 minutes. This 2001 release of a
1994 movie of the Underground Railroad is not a documentary, but does

capture the fear and risk taken by a group of slaves as they were escorted to freedom by Harriet Tubman.

The Underground Railroad. New York: A&E Home Video, 2006. 1 DVD. 150 minutes. This documentary presents an excellent overview of the events, people, and places surrounding the workings of the Underground Railroad.

53. Rise of P. T. Barnum, Burlesque, and Vaudeville (1850s–1880s)

By the 1850s, the development of rail and water transportation made possible traveling entertainment acts that featured the same performers that appeared in big cities such as New York and Boston. Entrepreneurs such as P. T. Barnum (1810–1891) established museums filled with artifacts and then offered entertainment to attract visitors. Theater managers introduced a variety of acts to lengthen the stay of their patrons and to attract a more diverse audience. While drama and opera still thrived, a parallel entertainment form called burlesque also took root. Burlesque developed shows that made fun of more serious entertainment and in many cases played side by side on the same street. Theatergoers could attend a performance of *The Merchant of Venice* by Shakespeare at one theater and the next night see a burlesque of it at another. Since the entire country was a market for mass entertainment, another form of entertainment, involving comedians, acrobats, singers, dancers, jugglers, and the like, called vaudeville also emerged. Vaudeville had a universal appeal because it drew on every branch of the theater—grand opera, pantomime, choreography, concert, symphony, farce, drama, and other stage entertainments. There was indeed something for everyone to see or listen to. Vaudeville also fostered the star system because once people heard of a wonderful act in New York City, they would brook no substitute for it in Des Moines. Both entertainment forms are credited with giving birth to the musical, a form of amusement that continues to provide delight to millions of Americans.

TERM PAPER SUGGESTIONS

1. P. T. Barnum, Edward Franklin Albee, and Benjamin Keith were masters of public relations during this period. Discuss some of the techniques they used to bring people to the theater and museums.

2. Discuss how burlesque allowed satire of the upper classes and their pretensions in a socially acceptable way.

3. Explain how the star system was fostered through vaudeville. Discuss the positive and negative aspects of it.

4. Prior to May 1849, most theater productions encouraged the mingling of all classes of people. Discuss the Astor Place Riots as one of the reasons why entertainment evolved a little more on class lines.

5. Read reviews from some of the shows, including *Ixion* or *Man at the Wheel*. Discuss how they were the forerunners for Ziegfield's *Follies*.

6. Vaudeville had strict moral codes for patrons that included no profanity, eating, or drinking during the performance. Examine why this self-censorship was part of a marketing campaign on the part of the owners.

ALTERNATIVE TERM PAPER SUGGESTIONS

1. Assume that you have been hired by P. T. Barnum to draw up a publicity campaign to attract people to enter "Barnum's American Museum" at Broadway and Ann Street in New York City. The campaign should include several posters plus a list of entertainments and some of the museum's most interesting artifacts.

2. Prepare a podcast of songs, music, and skits that theatergoers would have heard during this period and intersperse the podcast with accurate historical details.

SUGGESTED SOURCES

Primary Sources

Barnum, P. T. *Art of Getting Money, or Golden Rules for Making Money*. Originally published in 1880. Bedford, MA: Applewood, 1999. Contains all of P. T. Barnum's advice about how to succeed in the entertainment world.

Barnum, P. T. *The Life of P. T. Barnum: Written by Himself*. Originally published in 1855. Champaign, IL: University of Illinois, 2000. Barnum was constantly publishing his autobiography as a means of self-promotion. He did this so many times that he eventually did not bother to copyright it.

Secondary Sources

Adams, Bluford. *E Pluribus Barnum: The Great Showman and the Making of American Culture*. Minneapolis, MN: University of Minnesota Press, 1997. Provides an entertaining, but informative, biography of

P. T. Barnum and his contribution to the life and culture of the nineteenth century.

Allen, Robert C. *Horrible Prettiness: Burlesque and American Culture*. Chapel
Hill, NC: University of North Carolina Press, 1991. Furnishes a definitive account of the growth and development of burlesque and vaudeville.

Cook, James W. *The Arts of Deception: Playing with Fraud in the Age of Barnum*.
Cambridge, MA: Harvard University Press, 2001. Analyzes Barnum's
mastering of hype or "humbug" as he called it and how it made its way
into other forms of entertainment such as vaudeville's magic shows.

Cullen, Frank, et al. *Vaudeville, Old and New: An Encyclopedia of Variety Performers in America, 2 volumes*. New York: Routledge, 2006. Provides the most
significant research to date on all three forms of entertainment, going
back to the early 1820s until the early twentieth century.

Erdman, Andrew L. *Blue Vaudeville: Sex, Morals, and the Mass Marketing of
Amusement, 1895–1915*. Jefferson, NC: McFarland & Company, 2004.
Discusses how vaudeville imposed serious behavior rules on its patrons
as part of a marketing campaign.

Fields, Armond. *Women Vaudeville Stars: Eighty Biographical Profiles*. Jefferson,
NC: McFarland & Company, 2006. Provides eighty biographical
sketches of nineteenth- and twentieth-century vaudeville stars and how
they came to the stage.

Glenn, Susan A. *Female Spectacle: The Theatrical Roots of Modern Feminism*.
Cambridge, MA: Harvard University Press, 2000. Focuses on early,
self-dramatizing vaudeville shows and the stars and how they marked a
change in the popular conceptions of womanhood.

Levine, Lawrence. *Highbrow/Lowbrow: The Emergence of Cultural Hierarchy in
America*. Cambridge, MA: Harvard University Press, 1990. Discusses
how at the beginning of the nineteenth century there were few cultural
divisions among classes of people about entertainment, but that there
were more by the close of the nineteenth century.

Slide, Anthony. *New York City Vaudeville*. Charleston, SC: Arcadia Publishing,
2006. Contains a pictorial history of New York City vaudeville from
the 1800s through the 1930s.

Snyder, Robert W. *The Voice of the City: Vaudeville and Popular Culture in New
York*. Reprint. Chicago, IL: Ivan R. Dee, 2000. Provides information
about how vaudeville served as an entertainment respite and temporary
escape from poverty for the lower classes.

Wertheim, Arthur Frank. *Vaudeville Wars: How the Keith-Albee and Orpheum
Circuits Controlled the Big-Time and Its Performers*. New York: Macmillan, 2006. Discusses the pros and cons of the star system and how it
was controlled by two of the biggest vaudeville owners, Albee and Keith.

World Wide Web

"The Barnum Museum." http://www.barnum-museum.org/. Contains lengthy descriptions of Barnum's most famous exhibits, including "Jumbo the elephant," and other artifacts from his museums.

"J. Willis Sayre Photographs." http://content.lib.washington.edu/sayrepublic web/index.html. This massive collection consists of 9,856 images of vaudevillians who played in Seattle between the 1870s and 1955. It is searchable by actress, actor, dramatist, comedian, and show title.

"The Life of Phineas T. Barnum." http://www.gutenberg.org/etext/1576. Supplies an online biography by Joel Benton on the life and times of P. T. Barnum.

"The Lost Museum." http://www.lostmuseum.cuny.edu/home.html. Contains primary sources from Barnum's American Museum in the form of exhibits and artifacts.

"19th Century Actors Photographs." http://content.lib.washington.edu/19thcenturyactorsweb/index.html. Contains a treasure trove of photographs of actors, managers, and dramatists from the 1800s.

"The Prior and Norris Troupe Photographs." http://content.lib.washington.edu/norrisweb/index.html. Provides 236 images of this famous performing vaudeville troupe and photos of other troupes going back to the 1800s.

"Vaudeville & Burlesque History & Lingo." http://www.goodmagic.com/carny/vaud.htm. Furnishes an A–Z index for circus, burlesque, and vaudeville lingo.

Multimedia Sources

P. T. Barnum: America's Greatest Showman. Bethesda, MD: A&E Home Video, 1999. 1 videocassette. 90 minutes. Part of a Hallmark Hall of Fame miniseries, this film, starring Beau Bridges as P. T. Barnum, relates the story of his life as one of the biggest promoters and impresarios of the nineteenth century.

Vaudeville. Seattle, WA: Palmer Fenester, Inc., 1997. 1 videocassette. 112 minutes. Traces the origins of vaudeville back to the English Music Halls using a variety of film clips of various types of performers.

54. Know-Nothing Party (1854–1856)

The second wave of nineteenth-century immigration comprised mainly Irish Catholics escaping the Great Potato Famine. Their arrival in such numbers spurred a backlash that took the form of a Nativist Movement sponsored by inventors such as Samuel F. B. Morse and members of the collapsed Whig Party. The Know-Nothings received their appellation from the statement, "I know nothing about it," which they were ordered to give when questioned about their activities. While cartoonists made fun of them, their political message worked well enough to elect eight governors, more than a thousand members of Congress, thousands of local officials, and mayors of several cities including those of Chicago, Boston, and Philadelphia. Sincerely believing that the Pope had plans to take over the United States with a population bomb of Roman Catholic immigrants, the Know-Nothing Party platform proposed the following: that America place severe restriction on immigration from Catholic countries, restrict political office to indigenous Americans, enact a waiting period of twenty-one years before citizenship could be gained, allow only Protestants to become schoolteachers, order daily Protestant Bible readings in schools, and curtail the sale of alcohol. For a while, the Know-Nothings appeared as if they would become the main opposition party in the United States when they backed former President Millard Fillmore in 1856. Soon, however, southern and northern members began to squabble over the slavery issue, and by 1860 they were no longer a national force.

TERM PAPER SUGGESTIONS

1. Examine how the Know-Nothings represented a persistent ethnoreligious hostility in American life that politicians ignored at their peril. Research how this hostility has manifested itself in twenty-first century political life.

2. Later on the Democratic Party used the term "Know-Nothings" as a code term to gain Catholic votes. Explore how they manipulated what the Know-Nothings stood for to their party's advantage.

3. The Know-Nothing Party was an outgrowth of an 1849 secret society called the Order of the Star Spangled Banner and the Nativist Movement founded by Samuel F. B. Morse. Research and describe their growth and development.

4. Analyze how and why Millard Fillmore tried to distance himself from the Know-Nothing Party despite being endorsed by them.

5. Examine the reasons that northern members of the Know-Nothing Party bolted when it endorsed the Kansas-Nebraska Act of 1854.

6. Describe and discuss some of the possible outcomes if the Know-Nothing Party had swept the election of 1856 and their platform proposals became laws.

ALTERNATIVE TERM PAPER SUGGESTIONS

1. The Know-Nothings are used as fodder by cartoonists today whenever immigration issues arise. Draw four cartoons depicting their concerns à la nineteenth-century style and four cartoons that place their issues in a contemporary perspective. Accompany the cartoons with explanations.

2. Write a political skit to be performed at a comedy club that depicts the absurdity of the Know-Nothings platform and reveals their ignorance of the significant role that immigrants have played in the building of America.

SUGGESTED SOURCES

Primary Sources

Billington, Ray Allen. *The Protestant Crusade 1800–1860: A Study of the Origins of American Nativism*. Chicago, IL: Quadrangle Books, 1964. Using a variety of primary sources about secret nativist societies, this work discusses the anti-Catholic crusade that took place in America during the 1800s.

Dash, Mark. "New Light on the Dark Lantern: The Initiation Rites and Ceremonies of a Know-Nothing Lodge in Shippenburg, Pennsylvania." *Pennsylvania Magazine of History and Biography* 17 (2003): 89–100. (Available in JSTOR.) Contains primary sources about the membership rites of a Know-Nothing lodge.

Secondary Sources

Anbinder, Tyler G. *Nativism and Slavery: The Northern Know Nothings and the Politics of the 1850s*. New York: Oxford University Press, 1994. This definitive history discusses how the Know-Nothing Party was well on its way to becoming the second national party when it split over the issue of slavery.

Gleeson, David T. *The Irish in the South, 1815–1877*. Chapel Hill, NC: University of North Carolina Press, 2000. Provides a thorough history of the Irish in the South and how they maintained their ethnic culture, which may have given rise to discrimination against them.

Holt, Michael F. *Political Parties and the American Political Development: From the Age of Jackson to the Age of Lincoln*. Baton Rouge, LA: Louisiana State University Press, 1992. Traces the origin and development of various political parties from 1828 to 1860.

Holt, Michael F. *The Rise and Fall of the American Whig Party: Jacksonian Politics and the Onset of the Civil War*. New York: Oxford University Press, 2003. Discusses how the Whig Party collapsed and left a window of opportunity for the Know-Nothings to temporarily take the political stage.

Leonard, Ira M. *American Nativism, 1830–1860*. Melbourne, FL: Krieger Publishing Company, 1979. Explores the origin and growth and development of the Nativism Movement that contributed to the rise of the Know-Nothing Party.

Melton, Tracy. *Hanging Henry Gambrill: The Violent Career of Baltimore's Plug Uglies, 1854–1860*. Baltimore, MD: Maryland Historical Society, 2006. Relates with engrossing detail the story of the 1850s immigrant street gangs of Baltimore, Maryland.

Mulkern, John. *The Know-Nothing Party in Massachusetts: The Rise and Fall of a People's Party*. Boston, MA: Northeastern University Press, 1990. Massachusetts was the northern stronghold of the Know-Nothings. This work discusses how and why they gained such power in the state.

O'Connor, Thomas H. *The Boston Irish*. Boston, MA: Backbay Books, 1997. Chapter 3 of this history of the Irish in Boston discusses their interactions with the Know-Nothing Party and unionists.

Phillips, Kevin P. *The Cousins' Wars: Religion, Politics, and the Triumph of Anglo-America*. New York: Harper Collins, 2000. The author researches several eighteenth- and nineteenth-century American wars, including the Civil War, to illustrate how Anglo-American "cousins" have systematically discriminated against Roman Catholics and other non-Anglo immigrant groups.

Togman, Jeffrey M. *The Ramparts of Nations: Institutions and Immigration Policies in France and the United States*. Westport, CT: Praeger Publishers, 2001. Discusses the barriers to immigration that the United States and France erected in the twentieth century.

Voss-Hubbard, Mark. *Beyond Party: Cultures of Antipartisanship in Northern Politics before the Civil War*. Baltimore, MD: Johns Hopkins University Press, 2002. Contains a persuasive thesis for how the Know-Nothings rose and fell from power so quickly.

World Wide Web

"America's Worst Immigration War." http://www.americanheritage.com/ events/articles/web/20061104-know-nothing-nativism-american-party -immigration-catholicism.shtml. Provides a lengthy overview of the American Nativist Movement and its subsequent birth into the Know-Nothing Party, and relates it to contemporary times.

"The Great American Battle: or, The Contest Between Christianity and Political Romanism. By Anna Ella Carroll." http://books.google.com/books ?vid=OCLC02013425&id=UeaNRey_RrAC&dq=%22american+party

%22+fillmore&as_brr=1. Available in Google Books.com, this work, published in 1856, expresses the anti-Catholic sentiments and reasoning that was used to form the American Nativist Movement and the Know-Nothing Party.

"Immigration: Its Evil and Consequences by Samuel Clagett Busey." http:// books.google.com/books?vid=OCLC17693259&id=f2ngt1goYTIC &dq=%22know+nothing+almanac%22&as_brr=1. Available in Google Books.com, this work shows the rhetoric that was used against immigrants and how it helped form the Know-Nothings party platform.

"Knownothingism." http://www.newadvent.org/cathen/08677a.htm. Provides a comprehensible overview of the Know-Nothing Party.

"The Millard Fillmore Papers." http://books.google.com/books?vid=OCL C11209746&id=x1cOAAAAIAAJ&dq=%22american+party%22+fill more&as_brr=1. Available in Google Book.com, this site contains the full text of Millard Fillmore's papers, including references to his association with the Know-Nothing Party.

"The Sons of the Sires: A History of the Rise, Progress, and Destiny of the American Party by Frederick Rinehart Anspach." http://books.google .com/books?vid=OCLC00224701&id=v3WhaJjLeJ0C&dq=%22know +nothing%22&as_brr=1. Available in Google Books.com, this work, published in 1855, describes the history and development of the American Party, which the Know-Nothings renamed it in 1855.

"The Wide-Awake Gift: A Know-Nothing Token for 1855." http://books .google.com/books?vid=OCLC11815023&id=dB0fAAAAMAAJ&dq= %22know+nothing%22&as_brr=1. Available in Google Books.com, this site contains the full text of a book outlining all the reasons why there should be anti-immigration laws and other deterrents against Roman Catholics in America.

Multimedia Sources

Destination America: The People and Cultures that Created a Nation. Hollywood, CA: PBS Paramount, 2006. 1 DVD. 220 minutes. This award-winning documentary recounts the immigrant experience upon arrival to the United States through the eyes of different immigrant families.

55. Kansas-Nebraska Act (1854)

Unlike the Compromises of 1820 and 1850 that were designed to postpone a decision on slavery, the Kansas-Nebraska Act accelerated it by polarizing slave and free states and starting a civil war in Kansas. Realizing that a northern transcontinental railroad would be economically advantageous to his constituents if it ran through Illinois, Senator Stephen A. Douglas proposed a bill to bring the territories of Kansas and Nebraska into the United States so that they and the railroad would be under U.S. jurisdiction. His proposal immediately set off a firestorm of protest on both sides of the slavery issue. Southerners argued that the Missouri Compromise called for any future territories that lay north of the 36°30′ latitude to be admitted as free states. The admission of Kansas and Nebraska would upset the balance of power in the Senate and House between slave and antislave votes and probably would force a vote on slavery in the future. When Douglas suggested repealing the Missouri Compromise of 1820 and allowing Kansas and Nebraska citizens to vote independently on whether to allow slavery, Missouri proslavery advocates known as "border ruffians" flooded Kansas in an attempt to vote illegally and turn Kansas into a proslavery state. By the time the act passed Congress, southern states had already begun to secede from the union and the country was virtually divided politically into two sections.

TERM PAPER SUGGESTIONS

1. Describe exactly how Senator Douglas opened Pandora's box when he proposed the Kansas-Nebraska Act.
2. President Franklin Pierce (1804–1869) supported Senator Douglas and was attacked not only in newspapers for his action but also by a group of northern Democrats who signed, "The Appeal of the Independent Democrats." Discuss their appeal and its significance.
3. Senator Douglas was the director of the Illinois Central Railroad and a land speculator. Discuss what he personally had to gain economically from ensuring that the Transcontinental Railroad terminated in Chicago and the consequences of his actions.
4. The firestorm that erupted over the Kansas-Nebraska Act finished off the Democratic Party in the North and gave birth to the Republican Party. Analyze the political implication of this event.
5. Examine how the political chaos that ensued from the Kansas-Nebraska Act debate gave an opportunity for the Know-Nothing Party with its anti-immigrant and Roman Catholic platform a powerful place in politics.
6. Describe and explore the role that Missouri "border ruffians" played in bringing Kansas to a state of civil war.

ALTERNATIVE TERM PAPER SUGGESTIONS

1. Assume that your newspaper editor has asked you to write the lead article about President Pierce's decision to support Senator Douglas's Kansas-Nebraska Act and to denounce the provisional free-state government set up by antislavery settlers in Topeka, Kansas. Write an article that analyzes Pierce's economic and political reasons for his position on both issues.

2. Senator David Rice Atchison of Missouri was another hothead during the Kansas-Nebraska debate. At one point he threatened to send five thousand men into Kansas to "kill...every abolitionist in the Territory." Write a series of letters to Senator Atchison that might appeal to his love of country and desire to keep the union intact. Describe how devastating war would be for both sides of the country and what the economic and political consequences would be for Missouri.

SUGGESTED SOURCES

Primary Sources

Malin, James C. "The Motives of Stephen A. Douglas in the Organization of Nebraska Territory: A Letter Dated December 17, 1853." *Kansas Historical Quarterly* 19 (November 1951): 321–353. (Available in JSTOR.) Focuses on Douglas's commitment to the north-central route for the Pacific railroad as motivation for the Kansas-Nebraska bill. Cites first-person account from Douglas's contemporaries James W. Sheahan and James M. Cutts, and furnishes a reprint of the Douglas letter.

Seward, William Henry. *Freedom and Public Faith: Speeches of William H. Seward, on the Abrogation of the Missouri Compromise, in the Kansas and Nebraska Bills: Delivered in...United States, February 17 and May 26, 1854.* Ithaca, NY: Cornell University Press, 2006. Includes the full text of New York Senator Seward's objection to the proposed passage of the Kansas-Nebraska Act of 1854.

Secondary Sources

Gienapp, William E. *The Origins of the Republican Party, 1852–1856.* New York: Oxford University Press, 1987. Discusses the rivalry between the Know-Nothing Party and the Republicans, and examines the collapse of the Whig Party and Nativist Movement.

Holt, Michael F. *The Political Crisis of the 1850s.* New York: W. W. Norton, 1978. Explores the economic and cultural factors that contributed to the 1850s crisis and the breakdown of the two-party system that played a role in causing the Civil War.

Johannsen, Robert W. *Stephen A. Douglas.* New York: Oxford University Press, 1973. Provides the definitive biography of Douglas, the Senator who proposed the Kansas-Nebraska Act.

McArthur, Debra. *The Kansas-Nebraska Act and Bleeding Kansas in American History.* Berkeley Heights, NJ: Enslow Publishers, 2003. Written for secondary school students, this work provides an excellent overview of the issues and personalities involved with the Kansas-Nebraska Act.

McPherson, James W. *Battle Cry of Freedom: The Era of the Civil War.* New York: Oxford University Press, 1988. Relates in narrative style the political, economic, and cultural differences between the North and the South that were major causes of the Civil War.

Morrison, Michael. *Slavery and the American West: The Eclipse of Manifest Destiny and the Coming of the Civil War.* Chapel Hill, NC: University of North Carolina Press, 1999. Discusses the Kansas-Nebraska Act of 1854 within the context of how it was linked to the slavery issue, addressed territorial expansion, and inevitably constituted a major cause of the Civil War.

Nevins, Allen. *A House Dividing, 1852–1857.* New York: Charles Scribner's Sons, 1947. Provides one of the most important works in gaining an understanding of all the factors that came to play when the Kansas-Nebraska Act triggered the final fissure between the North and the South.

Nichols, Roy Franklin. "The Kansas-Nebraska Act: A Century of Historiography." *Mississippi Valley Historical Review* 43 (September 1956): 187–212. (Available in JSTOR.) Discusses the legislative history, debates, and consequences of the act.

Waugh, John C. *On the Brink of Civil War: The Compromise of 1850 and How It Changed the Course of American History.* Washington, DC: Scholarly Resources, 2003. Analyzes the Compromise of 1850 and how it sowed the seeds for future clashes over the decision of popular sovereignty concerning states that were to be admitted in the future.

Wolff, Gerald. *The Kansas-Nebraska Bill: Party, Section, and the Coming of the Civil War.* New York: Revisionist Press, 1977. Examines how the breakdown in the two-party system over the Kansas-Nebraska Act was a major cause of the Civil War.

World Wide Web

"Kansas; Its Interior and Exterior Life." http://www.kancoll.org/books/robinson/r_intro.htm. Written in 1856 by Sara L. Robinson, the wife of the first governor of the free state of Kansas, this online book provides a window on what life was actually like during the time of civil war in Kansas.

"Kansas-Nebraska Act 1854." http://www.ourdocuments.gov/doc.php?flash =true&doc=28. Provides the full text of the act along with background material.

"The Kansas-Nebraska Act and the Rise of the Republican Party, 1854–1865." http://lincoln.lib.niu.edu/biography6text.html. Furnishes an outstanding overview of how the Kansas-Nebraska Act caused the birth of the Republican Party.

"Library of Congress—Kansas-Nebraska Act." http://www.loc.gov/rr/program/ bib/ourdocs/kansas.html. Supplies a host of primary sources in the form of maps, images, speeches, letters, and more about the Kansas-Nebraska Act and its impact on the nation.

"Territorial Kansas—Online 1854–1861." http://www.territorialkansas online.org/cgiwrap/imlskto/index.php. Contains primary source documents, maps, lesson plans, resource links, a timeline, bibliography, and images of historic sites concerning the Kansas-Nebraska Act.

"Transcript of the Kansas-Nebraska Act 1854." http://www.ourdocuments.gov/ doc.php?flash=true&doc=28&page=transcript. Provides the full text of the Kansas-Nebraska Act.

"U. S. Congress, House of Representatives. Report of the Special Committee Appointed to Investigate the Troubles in Kansas; With the Views of the Minority of Said Committee. Report No. 200, 34th Congress, 1st Session, 1856." http://quod.lib.umich.edu/cgi/t/text/text-idx?sort=author; type=simple;ALLSELECTED=1;sid=9cee55f3513c400ac616174c0b4b 760f;xc=1;g=moagrp;xg=1;rgn=full%20text;q1=kansas%20territory; c=moa;c=moajrnl;view=toc;subview=detail;start=1;size=25;cc=moa; idno=AFK4445.0001.001. Presents the full text of a lengthy report that gives the majority and minority views and Congressional publications, including *The Globe,* that have information pertaining to the Kansas question during the 1850s.

Multimedia Sources

The Civil War: A Nation Divided. Silver Spring, MD: Discovery Channel, 2005. 1 DVD. 90 minutes. Provides a documentary on the Civil War and the events leading up to it, including the passage of the Kansas-Nebraska Act.

56. William Walker and Nicaragua (1856–1857)

Filibuster William Walker, at the age of thirty-six, was executed by a Honduran firing squad in 1860 at the behest of British authorities. Before that time he lived a life more suited to the movies. Graduating from the University of Nashville at the age of fourteen, he went on to finish medical and law schools and finally took up a career as a journalist. None of these professions, however, interested him as much as his career as a filibuster and soldier of fortune in Mexico and Central America. After capturing La Paz, the capital of Baja, California, with forty-five men, he pronounced himself president until he was forced to retreat back to California by Mexican authorities. Undaunted, Walker sailed with another group of men to Nicaragua where he defeated the Nicaraguan Army involved in a civil war and installed himself as president. Walker even received recognition by President Franklin Pierce as leader of the legitimate government of Nicaragua. Soon, however, Walker ran afoul not only of Cornelius Vanderbilt, who was bankrolling him, but also all of Central America when he revealed his intentions to establish a Central American empire that would attract Atlantic and Pacific shipping and to use slave labor to develop it. Vanderbilt quickly withdrew his political and economic support, and a coalition of Central American nations consisting of Nicaragua, Honduras, and Costa Rica rose up to defeat Walker. After surrendering to a U.S. Navy captain in 1857, Walker had a hero's welcome in New Orleans, but fatefully returned to Honduras three years later where he met his death.

TERM PAPER SUGGESTIONS

1. Although Walker's conquest of Nicaragua sounds absurd, he was living in a period of U.S. history that truly believed in its "Manifest Destiny." Discuss the origin of this term and how the U.S. government would have definitely considered acquiring Nicaragua as part of its "manifest destiny."

2. Cornelius Vanderbilt was the owner of the Accessory Transit Company that shipped goods and transported passengers from the Atlantic to Pacific Coasts via Nicaragua's two lakes. Analyze Vanderbilt's motives for bankrolling Walker's invading army.

3. Describe and examine the political, military, and economic conditions in Nicaragua that enabled such an easy first victory for Walker.

4. Walker went to great lengths to draw up a contract stating that his "invitation" to invade Nicaragua was for the purposes of colonization rather than military intervention. Discuss his reasons for this type of contract and the risks he ran with other foreign governments if he had openly indicated his intentions.

5. Analyze how Walker's invasion of Nicaragua resulted in a rise of nationalism throughout Central America.

6. Investigate the role of British authorities in the death of William Walker.

ALTERNATIVE TERM PAPER SUGGESTIONS

1. Assume that you are a mercenary sent to invade Nicaragua with an initial force of fifty-seven men. Using maps, draw up a series of battle plans for your conquest of the country. Be sure to include the use of Winchester Repeating Rifles, which the Nicaraguan forces lacked.

2. For a highly educated man, William Walker was a flawed human being. Assume you are a Central American psychiatrist who has been asked to formulate a psychological profile of William Walker for the purposes of overthrowing him. Analyze his strengths and weaknesses.

SUGGESTED SOURCES

Primary Sources

Rosengarten, Frederic, Jr. *Freebooters Must Die! The Life and Death of William Walker, the Most Notorious Filibuster of the Nineteenth Century.* Wayne, PA: Haverford House, 1976. Replete with primary source excerpts from period newspapers and the like, this work provides information about the life and times of William Walker.

Walker, William. *War in Nicaragua.* Tucson, AZ: University of Arizona Press, 1985. After returning to the United States, William Walker went on to write this account of his experiences there.

Secondary Sources

Belohlavek, John M., et al. *Manifest Destiny: American Antebellum Expansionism.* College Station, TX: Texas A&M University Press, 1996. Contains essays and analyses by a group of noted historians concerning America's vision of expanding control of the Northern Hemisphere.

Harrison, Brady. *Agent of Empire: William Walker and the Imperial Self in American Literature*. Athens, GA: University of Georgia Press, 2004. This scholarly work examines Walker and his myth in the context of American imperialism and the idea of "Manifest Destiny."

Hietala, Thomas R. *Manifest Design: Anxious Aggrandizement in Late Jacksonian America*. Ithaca, NY: Cornell University Press, 1990. Investigate how America's sometimes schizophrenic policies of expansionism manifested themselves during the nineteenth century, including William Walker's designs on Nicaragua.

Langley, Lester D., and Thomas D. Schoonover. *The Banana Men: Mercenaries and Entrepreneurs in Central America, 1880–1930*. Lexington, KY: University of Kentucky Press, 1996. Traces the history of nineteenth-century military and political intervention by the United States in the affairs of Latin America.

May, Robert. *Manifest Destiny's Underworld: Filibustering in Antebellum America*. Chapel Hill, NC: University of North Carolina Press, 2002. Contains abundant information about Walker's invasion of Nicaragua, in addition to a history of other private military expeditions in Latin America.

May, Robert E. *The Southern Dream of a Caribbean Empire, 1854–1861*. Gainesville, FL: University of Florida, 2002. Provides a fascinating account of the attempt on the part of southerners to establish slavery in Latin America and the Caribbean. It also includes a section on William Walker's abortive attempt to rule Nicaragua and establish slavery there.

Merck, Frederick. *Manifest Destiny and Mission in American History*. Cambridge, MA: Harvard University Press, 1995. Analyzes the concept of "Manifest Destiny" not as a national policy, but simply as a euphemism for the actions of a small group of politicians and businessmen.

Owsley, Frank L. *Filibusters and Expansionists: Jeffersonian Manifest Destiny, 1800–1821*. Tuscaloosa, AL: University of Alabama Press, 1997. Shows how filibustering and expansionism were part of the concept of "Manifest Destiny" long before William Walker's expedition to Nicaragua.

Scroggs, William O. *Filibusters and Financiers: The Story of William Walker and His Associates*. Reprint. New York: Russell & Russell, 1969. Considered the definitive biography of William Walker, this book places his actions within the times of "Manifest Destiny" in which he lived.

Stephanson, Anders. *Manifest Destiny: American Expansion and the Empire of Right*. New York: Hill and Wang, 1996. Traces the roots of the concept of "Manifest Destiny" from the eighteenth through twentieth centuries.

Walker, Thomas W. *Nicaragua*. Boulder, CO: Westview Press, 2003. This is the fourth edition of what is considered a seminal work of Nicaraguan history. It includes information about Walker's invasion.

World Wide Web

"Accessory Transit Company." http://www.answers.com/topic/accessory-transit
-company. Provides a description of the company that Cornelius Vanderbilt owned in Nicaragua to transport gold rush miners from the Atlantic
to Pacific coasts along with additional resource links.

"Commodore Cornelius Vanderbilt Fought War over Route through Central
America." http://www.vanderbilt.edu/News/register/Mar11_02/story8
.html. Furnishes an overview of the role that Vanderbilt played with
William Walker concerning the invasion of Nicaragua.

"Costa Rica in 1856: Defeating William Walker While Creating a National
Identity." http://jrscience.wcp.muohio.edu/FieldCourses00/Papers
CostaRicaArticles/CostaRicain1856.Defeating.html. Discusses how the
defeat of William Walker helped create a movement of nationalism in
not only Nicaragua but also in other Central American countries.

"Manifest Destiny, William Walker, and U.S. Filibustering to Central America
in the 1850s." http://www.ucr.ac.cr/documentos/Manifest_Destiny
_Robert_E._May.doc. Contains the full text of a thirty-nine page lecture
by Robert E. May regarding his book, *Manifest Destiny. . .,* delivered in
March 2006 at the University of Costa Rica.

"The Saga of William Walker." http://www.calnative.com/stories/n_walk.htm.
Supplies a short biographical sketch of William Walker.

"Walker's Expeditions." http://www.globalsecurity.org/military/ops/walker.htm.
Provides an excellent overview of Walker's expeditions in Mexico and Nicaragua, especially from the standpoint of the involved business interests.

"William Walker." http://www.sfmuseum.org/hist1/walker.html. Furnishes an
interesting overview of the life and times of William Walker that dwells
on his filibustering expeditions to Mexico and Nicaragua, respectively.

Multimedia Sources

The Complete DVD History of U.S. Wars 1700–2004. 2004. New York: Ambrose
Video Publishing, 2004. 4 DVDs. 156 minutes. This four part documentary of U.S. wars has a part devoted to all U.S. "Manifest Destiny"
wars.

57. *Dred Scott* Case (1857)

Of all the Supreme Court decisions in U.S. history regarding human
beings, this one is probably the most repugnant. Under the leadership of
Chief Justice Roger Taney, seven justices ruled that Congress could not

limit slavery in the territories, nullified the Missouri Compromise of 1820 and Compromise of 1850, and stated that African Americans could never be U.S. citizens. Two justices, John McLean and Benjamin Curtis, dissented. Justice Taney's opinion was particularly dastardly because he stated that African Americans were "beings of an inferior order" who "had no rights which the white man was bound to respect." The opinion of the court went right to the heart of the issue concerning equality and basically stated that there could be none because African Americans were nothing but property and as such could not even be considered as human beings. It was a legal odyssey for Dred Scott as his case wound its way through a series of courts. Initially he won his freedom in a Missouri lower court only to have it taken away by the Supreme Court. Scott was owned by John Emerson, an Army surgeon, who took him to various free states to work until he returned to the slave state of Missouri in 1838 where he died. After trying to purchase his freedom, Scott had to sue Emerson's widow for it. When the decision was rendered, southerners were so jubilant that they entertained the idea of opening slave markets again in the North. Opponents of slavery, however, went on the attack immediately with articles, promises of additional legal action, and legislative solutions. Scott's first owner's sons purchased his freedom and that of his family on May 26, 1857, but Scott tasted it only for a year. He died on September 17, 1858.

TERM PAPER SUGGESTIONS

1. President-elect James Buchanan was hoping that the Supreme Court would decide the *Dred Scott* case before he took office and settle the conflict once and for all concerning slavery. He wanted the decision to appear as neutral as possible, so he pressured Justice Robert Grier, a northerner, to join the southern majority opinion. Discuss his conduct from a legal standpoint. Did Buchanan violate any laws?

2. Analyze how Taney and members of the court used or misused the Constitution to formulate their decision.

3. Evaluate and discuss the legal analysis of the dissenting justices, John McLean and Benjamin Curtis.

4. Discuss the legacy of the *Dred Scott* decision concerning race relations in the United States.

5. Discuss the immediate effects of the *Dred Scott* case on the country and why it polarized it even more.

6. In 1851, the U.S. Supreme Court decided a similar case called *Strader v. Graham*. Examine how this case may have influenced the court's decision concerning Dred Scott.

ALTERNATIVE TERM PAPER SUGGESTIONS

1. Assume that you are the attorney representing Dred Scott before the U.S. Supreme Court. Prepare a legal brief that argues why Scott is entitled to his freedom under the laws and Constitution of the United States.

2. Despite this Supreme Court decision on Dred Scott, the great African American reformer Frederick Douglass never gave up hope that the "national conscience" would awaken. Research his reaction and comments to the case and prepare a podcast containing a message to African Americans everywhere to keep hope alive.

SUGGESTED SOURCES

Primary Sources

Allen, Austin. *Origins of the Dred Scott Case: Jacksonian Jurisprudence and the Supreme Court, 1837–1857*. Athens, GA: University of Georgia Press, 2006. Explores the background that contributed to the *Dred Scott* case, including excerpts from the *Strader v. Graham* Supreme Court decision.

Finkelman, Paul. *Dred Scott v. Sandford: A Brief History with Documents*. New York: St. Martin's Press, 1997. Provides a short account of the case along with the full text of various legal decisions.

Secondary Sources

Abraham, Henry J. *Freedom and the Court: Civil Rights and Liberties in the United States*. New York: Oxford University Press, 1967. Contains information about the civil rights and liberties of African Americans in the United States.

Bell, Derrick. *Race, Racism and American Law*. 2nd ed. Boston, MA: Little, Brown, 1980. Furnishes an analysis of U.S. law that demonstrates how racial bias is thoroughly integrated into the legislative and judicial branches of government.

Einhorn, Robin L. *American Taxation, American Slavery*. Chicago, IL: University of Chicago Press, 2006. Demonstrates how issues of taxation concerning property were always about the issue of the right to own slaves.

Fehrenbacher, Don E. *The Dred Scott Case: Its Significance in American Law and Politics*. New York: Oxford University Press, 1978. This outstanding academic work not only examines the legal ramifications of the case but also discusses the impact it had on the United States prior to the Civil War.

Fleischner, Jennifer. *The Dred Scott Case: Testing the Right to Live Free.* Brookfield, CT: Millbrook Press, 1997. Written for secondary school students, this work provides a useful overview to the case and places it within a human perspective.

Graber, Mark A. *Dred Scott and the Problem of Constitutional Evil.* New York: Cambridge University Press, 2006. This fascinating work argues that the Supreme Court made a decision to seek peace rather than justice and based on its other precedent setting cases made the correct, but evil, decision regarding the *Dred Scott* case.

Huebner, Timothy S. *The Taney Court: Justices, Rulings, and Legacy.* Santa Barbara, CA: ABC-Clio, 2003. Examines Taney's twenty-eight year tenure on the Supreme Court, including background information, short biographies of the various justices, and analyses of their major decisions and legacies.

Kaufman, Kenneth C. *Dred Scott's Advocate: A Biography of Roswell M. Field.* Columbia, MO: University of Missouri Press, 1996. Provides an excellent biography of Field, the St. Louis, Missouri, attorney who pled Scott's case before the U.S. Supreme Court.

Lewis, Thomas, and Richard L. Wilson, eds. *Encyclopedia of the U.S. Supreme Court.* 3 vols. Pasadena, CA: Salem Press, 2001. Provides a substantive overview of the *Dred Scott* case and its legal implications, a biographical sketch of Justice Roger Taney, and information about other related legal topics.

Maltz, Earl M. *Dred Scott and the Politics of Slavery.* Lawrence, KS: University Press of Kansas, 2007. Presents a balanced view of the *Dred Scott* case by showing the social climate of the times in both the North and the South.

Paul, Arnold, ed. *Black Americans and the Supreme Court since Emancipation: Betrayal or Protection?* New York: Holt, Rinehart and Winston, 1972. Investigates various landmark Supreme Court cases that reveal a consistent pattern by the court not to provide equal rights for African Americans.

World Wide Web

"About the Dred Scott Case." http://www.nps.gov/jeff/historyculture/dredscottsesquicentennial.htm. Although this site contains but a brief summary of the case, it does feature a portrait of Dred Scott that was commissioned by a "group of Negro Citizens" and presented to the Missouri Historical Society in St. Louis, Missouri, in 1882.

"Dred Scott Decision: The Lawsuit that Started the Civil War." http://www
.historynet.com/magazines/civil_war_times/3037746.html. Provides an
excellent analysis of the legal case that helped propel the United States
into a civil war, along with additional resource links.

Dred Scott Sesquicentennial." http://www.nps.gov/jeff/historyculture/
dredscottsesquicentennial.htm. The city of St. Louis, Missouri, presents
a site celebrating the life of Dred Scott that includes links to other sites,
the history and background of the case, contemporary commentary on
its significance and legacy, and more.

"Introduction Dred Scott Trial." http://www.nps.gov/jeff/forteachers/upload/
dred4.pdf. Contains a sixteen-page mock trial manuscript and other trial
information that can be used as a classroom resource to conduct a mock
trial of Dred Scott.

"James Buchanan." http://www.whitehouse.gov/history/presidents/jb15.html.
Contains a biographical sketch of James Buchanan with mention of the
role he played in the *Dred Scott* decision.

"Scott v. Sandford." http://www.oyez.org/cases/1851-1900/1856/1856_0/.
From the Oyez project, this site contains a summary of the case and the
facts and opinion of the Supreme Court decision. It also supplies a
chronological link to similar cases on slavery.

"60 U.S. 393 Scott v. Sandford." http://www.law.cornell.edu/supct/html/
historics/USSC_CR_0060_0393_ZS.html. Sponsored by Cornell University, this site provides the individual opinions of each justice, including the dissenters on the *Dred Scott* case.

Multimedia Sources

Dred Scott v. Sandford. http://www.audiocasefiles.com/featured/dredscott.
Presents a short summary of the case, the full text of the opinion, a series
of external Web resources, information about related cases, and an audio
edited opinion of the case.

The Supreme Court. New York: Ambrose Video Publishing, 2007. 4 DVDs.
240 minutes. The *Dred Scott* case is discussed in DVD No. 1. It
contains narration plus images of manuscripts and other period documents.

58. Lincoln-Douglas Debates (1858)

In 1858 a Washington, D.C., newspaper stated that "the battle for the
Union is to be fought in Illinois." In many ways it was correct because a

series of seven debates between Abraham Lincoln, Republican nominee for the U.S. Senate, and Stephen A. Douglas, Democratic candidate, brought the issue of slavery to the public's attention as never before. Each man traveled thousands of miles crisscrossing the state, speaking from the back platforms of railroad cars. Even though senators were elected by state legislators until 1913, thousands of people came from Illinois and other states to listen and ponder the issues as each candidate tried to define them. As the debates continued, it became clear that Lincoln believed slavery to be against the Declaration of Independence, which states "all men are created equal." Douglas, who was desperately trying to appease President Buchanan and the southern Democratic leadership for his opposition to Kansas being admitted as a slave state, believed that state sovereignty should prevail on the issue of slavery. By this he meant that people at the state level should be able to vote to allow slavery. Although Lincoln stumbled during the first debate and was less prepared, the remaining debates were conducted at a level that has become a model and hope for present and future public discourse. Both men won something through the debates. Douglas narrowly won reelection to the Senate. Lincoln won national recognition, and he published the debates as a book that he used to successfully seek and win the office of president in 1860.

TERM PAPER SUGGESTIONS

1. Abraham Lincoln had been just an obscure House of Representatives member from Illinois when he debated Stephen A. Douglas. Investigate how he used the debates to further his own political ambitions.

2. Discuss how President Buchanan opposed Douglas for defeating the Lecompton Constitution. How did he go about trying to defeat Douglas?

3. Explain the differences between Douglas and Lincoln on the issue of slavery.

4. Research the Freeport Doctrine that Douglas proposed and how it harmed his chances to win the presidency in 1860.

5. Research and evaluate Lincoln's responses to Douglas's charge that he was an abolitionist and compare it with Lincoln's decision to issue the Emancipation Proclamation years later.

6. Lincoln said that "public sentiment is everything." How did he use moral arguments about slavery in the debates to start to sway public opinion to accept the eventual emancipation of slaves?

ALTERNATIVE TERM PAPER SUGGESTIONS

1. Assume you are a reporter for a neutral newspaper. Write a description of Lincoln's performance at the first debate. Do you think he was prepared, well-organized, and logical, and did he make an emotional connection with the audience? Based on this performance, how do you predict he will do in the second debate?

2. Assume that you are a campaign manager for Stephen Douglas. Describe why it is necessary that he paint a portrait of Lincoln as an abolitionist in all the debates. Write a campaign plan for each debate on this issue.

SUGGESTED SOURCES

Primary Sources

Angle, Paul M., ed. *Created Equal? The Complete Lincoln-Douglas Debates of 1858.* Chicago, IL: University of Chicago Press, 1958. Contains the full text of the debates, but they were also edited by each candidate's favoring newspapers and Lincoln. While they are an excellent source, the unexpurgated ones are now considered to be the best historical record of the debates.

Holzer, Harold. *The Lincoln-Douglas Debates: The First Complete, Unexpurgated Text.* New York: Fordham University Press, 2004. Contains the unedited full texts of the debates.

Secondary Sources

Fehrenbacher, Don. *Prelude to Greatness: Lincoln in the 1850's.* Stanford, CA: Stanford University Press, 1962. Reissued in paperback, this classic work focuses on how the real issue of the Civil War was slavery and that Lincoln brought this to the forefront for the American public by eloquently debating Douglas.

Guelzo, Allen C. *Lincoln and Douglas: The Debates That Defined America.* New York: Simon & Schuster, 2008. Succeeds in bringing these crucial debates concerning people's basic right to freedom to life.

Jaffa, Harry V. *A New Birth of Freedom: Abraham Lincoln and the Coming of the Civil War.* Landham, MD: Rowman and Littlefield Publishers, 2004. Noted historian Jaffa cogently synthesizes the meaning and content of the Lincoln-Douglas debates.

Jaffa, Harry V. *Crisis of the House Divided.* New York: Doubleday, 1959. Provides the definitive work on the debates and places them within the climate of the times.

Johannsen, Robert W. *The Frontier, the Union and Stephen A. Douglas*. Urbana, IL: University of Illinois Press, 1989. Furnishes fifteen essays by the author that shed light on issues, including slavery, secession, and the nature of the antebellum union.

Johannsen, Robert W. *Stephen A. Douglas*. Urbana, IL: University of Illinois Press, 1997. Provides a biography of Douglas that devotes many pages to his debates with Lincoln.

Meyer, Daniel. *Stephen Douglas and the American Union*. Chicago, IL: University of Chicago Press, 1994. Provides a scholarly biography that emphasizes Douglas's involvement with slavery issues.

Morrison, Michael. *Slavery and the American West: The Eclipse of Manifest Destiny*. Chapel Hill, NC: University of North Carolina Press, 1997. Focuses on westward expansion into new territories and how a decision regarding the issue of slavery in each territory was a causative factor of the Civil War.

Nevins, Allan. *Ordeal of the Union: Fruits of Manifest Destiny: 1847–1852*. New York: Charles Scribner's Sons, 1975. Explains how, as America expanded, it created new territories seeking statehood that brought the issue of slavery to the forefront of American politics and threatened the union.

Wilson, Douglas L. *Honor's Voice: The Transformation of Abraham Lincoln*. New York: Random House, 1998. This biography concentrates on Lincoln's young adult years when he had just started practicing law, was a member of the House of Representatives, and was finding his way into politics.

Zaresky, David. *Lincoln, Douglas, and Slavery: In the Crucible of Public Debate*. Chicago, IL: University of Chicago Press, 1993. Discusses and analyzes each candidate's speeches as they relate to the issue of slavery.

World Wide Web

"James Buchanan." http://www.whitehouse.gov/history/presidents/jb15.html. Provides a biographical sketch of President James Buchanan, who was opposed to Douglas winning the 1858 election.

"The Lincoln-Douglas Debates." http://www.lincoln-douglas.org/. This outstanding site provides the text of the debates plus biographical sketches of Lincoln and Douglas, a description of the times and the campaigns, and more.

"The Lincoln-Douglas Debates." http://www.mrlincolnandfreedom.org/inside.asp?ID=21&subjectID=2. Presents a great deal of pre-Civil War background information in addition to the full text of the debates and other speeches made by Lincoln during this time frame. The site also features images and information about relevant personalities during the time of the debates.

"Lincoln-Douglas Debates of 1858." http://www.illinoiscivilwar.org/debates .html. Provides a brief overview of the debates with additional resource links and a map of the congressional districts in Illinois.

"The Lincoln-Douglas Debates of 1858." http://www.nps.gov/archive/liho/ debates.htm. Includes a map that is connected to the cities where each debate took place plus the full text of the debates.

"Political Debates between Abraham Lincoln and Stephen A. Douglas." http:// www.bartleby.com/251/. Furnishes the full text of the debates, including the replies that each man was allowed.

"Stephen A. Douglas Association." http://www.stephenadouglas.org/. Dedicated to the memory of Douglas, this site provides a biographical sketch, images of Douglas, and a set of related resource links.

Multimedia Sources

The Lincoln Douglas Debates of 1858. http://lincoln.lib.niu.edu/lincolndouglas/ index.html. This outstanding megasite contains the full text of the debates, a video, images of the relevant people, maps, period newspaper commentary, lesson plans, and more.

The Lincoln-Douglas Debates. Madison, WI: C-Span Video.org., 1994. 7 video-cassettes. 240 minutes. Presents reenactments performed in the summer and fall of 1994 that includes the debates, TV interviews with historians, and discussions held before and after the political exchanges.

19th Century Turning Points in U.S. History. New York: Ambrose Video, 2002. 4 DVDs. 184 minutes. DVD No. 4—1846–1860 contains documentary information concerning the Lincoln-Douglas debates.

59. Black Gold Discovered in Pennsylvania (1859)

On August 27, 1859, after months of fruitless digging, William A. Smith struck oil in a well that he had been drilling for Edwin Drake on Oil Creek near Titusville, Pennsylvania. His discovery was not serendipitous. For several years a group of investors had been examining the oil springs at Francis Brewer's lumber company and thought that there was a commercial potential for oil to be used as an illuminant, a lubricant, and a medicine. The timing was also propitious as whale oil used to light homes and factories was becoming increasingly scarce and expensive. Drake's investors also had the advantage of a free, premarket test. In 1847, Samuel M. Kier of Pittsburgh had begun bottling and selling petroleum from his salt wells. He also developed a distillation process that rendered oil into an illuminant, which he called carbon oil. People all over western Pennsylvania and New York City began using it. The product was so rare that the price rose steadily, thus creating a need to find more oil. With Smith's "eureka-like" discovery, Drake's investors quickly founded the first U.S. oil company called the Pennsylvania Rock Oil Company of Connecticut. Within six years, Pennsylvania was producing one-half million barrels of oil per year. Drake and Smith succeeded in ushering in a "black gold" boom in western Pennsylvania and establishing the foundation for a giant U.S. industry.

TERM PAPER SUGGESTIONS

1. Oil had been encountered as early as the sixteenth century when people saw oil slicks off the coast of California. Seneca Indians traded oil around present-day Niagara, New York, during the eighteenth century. Trace the history of the reports of oil in the United States and describe its use during those times.

2. Drake's investors were very cautious venture capitalists. Explore the role that Yale Professor Benjamin Silliman Jr. played in their decision-making process.

3. Samuel Downer Jr. patented "Kerosene" as a trademark in 1859 and licensed its usage. Discuss the significance of his product for the industry.

4. One of the people who learned of the Titusville discovery was John D. Rockefeller, whose genius lay in organizing companies that were vertically and horizontally integrated. Describe Rockefeller's initial foray into the oil industry with a partner in Cleveland in 1859.

5. Edwin Drake was a thirty-eight-year-old railroad conductor, yet he played a major role in developing the Pennsylvania oil field. Research his contribution to the establishment of a major U.S. industry.

6. As additional discoveries occurred near the Titusville oil field, numerous companies were formed to extract and market the oil. Discuss the role that John D. Rockefeller played in acquiring these companies.

ALTERNATIVE TERM PAPER SUGGESTIONS

1. Assume you are a nineteenth-century chemist who has been asked by a group of investors to prepare a report on the potential for digging an oil well near

Titusville, Pennsylvania. Provide your clients with information concerning the construction, expenses, quantity of oil to be extracted, potential product uses, and labor costs.

2. Assume you are an eighteenth-century civil engineer. Draw a series of diagrams accompanied by explanations for drilling tools, devices, and rigs to create the most efficient extraction methods.

SUGGESTED SOURCES

Primary Sources

Giddens, Paul H. *Early Days of Oil: A Pictorial History of the Beginnings of the Oil Industry in Pennsylvania.* Princeton, NJ: Princeton University Press, 1948. Contains photographs and illustrations of life in the western Pennsylvania oil fields.

Tarbell, Ida. *The History of the Standard Oil Company: Briefer Version.* Mineola, NY: Dover Publications, 2003. This classic muckraking book is filled with primary sources in the form of period newspaper articles that document how John D. Rockefeller came to dominate the U.S. oil industry as early as the nineteenth century.

Secondary Sources

Chernow, Ron. *Titan: The Life of John D. Rockefeller, Sr.* New York: Vintage, 2004. Furnishes a well-written biography of John D. Rockefeller and how he gained a monopoly over the oil industry beginning in the nineteenth century.

Clark, J. Stanley. *The Oil Century: From the Drake Well to the Conservation Era.* Norman, OK: University of Oklahoma Press, 1959. Focuses on the discovery of oil prior to 1865.

Economides, Michael, and Ronald Oligney. *The Color of Oil: The History, the Money, and the Politics of the World's Biggest Business.* Katey, TX: Round Oak, 2000. Gives an exciting account of the oil industry and the role that the discovery of Drake's well played in it.

Knowles, Ruth Sheldon. *The First Pictorial History of the America Oil and Gas Industry, 1859–1983.* Athens, OH: Ohio University Press, 1985. Furnishes a discussion and photographs of the Drake well and its ecological and industrial consequences for the general area.

Knowles, Ruth Sheldon. *The Greatest Gamblers: The Epic of American Oil Exploration.* Norman, OK: University of Oklahoma Press, 1980. Contains exciting tales about the lure of oil and the work that was done to extract it from the ground. It also furnishes information about the role that John D. Rockefeller played in standardizing the industry.

Margonelli, Lisa. *Oil on the Brain: Adventures from the Pump to the Pipeline.* New York: Doubleday, 2007. Discusses the eternal search for oil, including a chapter on how it is created and drilled.

Maugeri, Leonardo. *The Age of Oil: The Mythology, History, and Future of the World's Most Controversial Resource.* Westport, CT: Praeger Publishers, 2006. Furnishes a history of the discovery of oil plus information about its cycles of booms and busts.

Plazak, Dan. *A Hole in the Ground with a Liar at the Top: Fraud and Deceit in the Golden Age of American Mining.* Salt Lake City, UT: University of Utah Press, 2006. Yale professor Benjamin Silliman Jr. went on to provide extremely bad advice about ore reserves in Utah and New Mexico. This work discusses the role he played as an unreliable mine consultant.

Shah, Sonia. *Crude: The Story of Oil.* New York: Seven Stories Press, 2006. Provides a history of oil that ranges from discoveries in the United States to the Middle East.

Williamson, Harold F., and Arnold Daum. *The American Petroleum Industry: The Age of Illumination, 1859–1899.* Evanston, IL: Northwestern University Press, 1959. Supplies a well-documented history of the early oil industry and the drilling of the Drake well.

Yergin, Daniel. "Oil on the Brain: The Beginning." In *The Prize: The Epic Quest for Oil, Money & Power.* New York: Simon & Schuster, 1991. Pulitzer-prize winning author Yergin writes a thrilling description of the drilling of the Drake well and the subsequent oil boom in western Pennsylvania.

World Wide Web

"The History of the Oil Industry." http://www.sjgs.com/history.html. Click on the desired period link to retrieve a short synopsis of the history of oil. A link to the history of oil in Pennsylvania is also included.

"The History of the Standard Oil Company by Ida M. Tarbell." http://www.history.rochester.edu/fuels/tarbell/MAIN.HTM. Contains the full text of the classic muckraking book that traced John D. Rockefeller Sr.'s monopolization of the oil industry.

"Oil Region National Heritage Area." http://www.oilheritage.com/photo/photogallery.htm. Contains primary source photographs of the Drake well and other rigs in what was known as Oil City, Pennsylvania.

"Petroleum History Institute." http://www.petroleumhistory.org/. Furnishes an overview on the history of oil, including its discovery and marketing in the western Pennsylvania area.

"The Story of Oil in Pennsylvania." http://www.priweb.org/ed/pgws/history/pennsylvania/pennsylvania.html. Presents a short history with images of the discovery of oil in western Pennsylvania.

"What Is Petroleum and the History of Oil." http://lsa.colorado.edu/summary street/texts/petroleum.htm. Traces the history of oil from its use in biblical times to the present day.

"What's Oil Doing in Pennsylvania?" http://www.priweb.org/ed/pgws/backyard/pennsylvania/pennsylvania_oil.html. Shows diagrams and maps of how and where oil was formed and found in Pennsylvania.

Multimedia Sources

The Prize—The Epic Quest for Oil, Money & Power. Chatsworth, CA: Home Vision Entertainment, 2000. 4 VHS tapes. 480 minutes. Narrated by actor Donald Sutherland, this eight-part series relates the history of oil from the Pulitzer Prize winning book by Daniel Yergin.

60. John Brown and the Raid on Harper's Ferry (1859)

Two years after abolitionist John Brown's (1800–1859) hanging by the state of Virginia for treason, murder, and conspiracy, his prophecy that "the crimes of this guilty land will never be purged away; but with blood" came true. The Civil War began and northern troops marched into battle singing "John Brown's body lies a-mouldering in the grave, But his soul is marching on." Fanatic, assassin, martyr—Brown was called all of these names after he took the law into his own hands by capturing the arsenal at Harper's Ferry, Virginia (now West Virginia), with a complement of twenty-one men including three of his sons. Planned for months, the October 16, 1859, raid would have netted Brown and his men thousands of guns and rounds of ammunition to begin leading slave insurrections throughout the South, eventually leading to emancipation for all. No one, however, joined Brown. By the next day federal troops under the command of Colonel Robert E. Lee and Lieutenant J. E. B. Stuart, local farmers, and militia assaulted the arsenal, killing two of Brown's sons, wounding Brown, and killing ten defenders. Brown's men had killed four and wounded nine people. His subsequent trial became a *cause celebre* with poets and reformers such as Ralph Waldo Emerson, France's Victor Hugo, William Lloyd Garrison, John Greenleaf Whittier, Henry David Thoreau, and Frederick Douglass either writing on his behalf or expressing their beliefs that John Brown shed his blood in sacrifice for the sins of slavery.

TERM PAPER SUGGESTIONS

1. Historians are still debating whether John Brown was a fanatic, nineteenth-century terrorist, or martyr in the cause of emancipation. Research one of these viewpoints and provide your own defense of it.

2. John Brown was not new to insurrections. He was also known as "Osawatomie Brown" for leading an attack against proslavery Missouri "border ruffians" in Kansas in 1856 where he massacred five of them. Discuss his role in this event.

3. Even though John Brown did not avail himself of any religious support during his imprisonment, he was a deeply religious man who was raised as a Calvinist. Analyze how his religious beliefs may have affected his decision to lead armed insurrections.

4. John Brown was bankrolled by a group of dedicated reformers and abolitionists known as the Secret Six. Examine the role they played in the raid at Harper's Ferry and why they were not prosecuted as Brown's fellow conspirators.

5. Although this raid seems insignificant in light of the war that was to come, it struck fear in the hearts of southerners. Investigate their reaction to the raid and why they reconstituted the state militia system.

6. Abraham Lincoln characterized John Brown as a "delusional fanatic who was justly hanged." Discuss the political motivation behind Lincoln's statement.

ALTERNATIVE TERM PAPER SUGGESTIONS

1. Make a two-minute iMovie incorporating and citing video clips from films about John Brown that depict his raid on Harper's Ferry. You may also wish to narrate portions of it using research from print and Internet sources.

2. Attorneys George Hoyt and Hiram Griswold defended John Brown at his trial. Write a closing statement for them arguing that Brown could not be guilty of the crimes with which he is charged.

SUGGESTED SOURCES

Primary Sources

De Caro, Louis A. *John Brown—The Cost of Freedom: Selections from His Life and Letters.* New York: International Publications, 2007. Sheds light on some of the ways that historians have characterized Brown.

Quarles, Benjamin, comp. *Blacks on John Brown.* Urbana, IL: University of Illinois Press, 1972. Includes primary sources in the form of letters, poems, and reports written about John Brown from 1858 to 1972 by Langston Hughes, Frederick Douglass, W. E. B. Du Bois, and Countee Cullen.

Ruchames, Louis, ed. *A John Brown Reader: The Story of John Brown in His Own Words, in the Words of Those Who Knew Him and in the Poetry and Prose of the Literary Heritage.* New York: Abelard-Schuman, 1959. Contains the thoughts of John Brown pertaining to slavery and an account of his life in his own words.

Secondary Sources

Benet, Stephen Vincent. *John Brown's Body.* Chicago, IL: Elephant Paperbacks, 1990. This popular epic poem about John Brown captures some of the sentiments that went into creating his legend.

Boyer, Richard O. *The Legend of John Brown: A Biography and a History.* New York: Alfred A. Knopf, 1972. Documents the climate of the times, and places the events of John Brown's life within the period.

DeCaro, Louis A., and Louis A. DeCaro Jr. *Fire from the Midst of You: A Religious Life of John Brown.* New York: New York University Press, 2005. Discusses John Brown's religious upbringing and the influence it had on his work as an abolitionist and eventual insurrectionist.

Finkelman, Paul, ed. *His Soul Goes Marching on: Responses to John Brown and the Harper's Ferry Raid.* Charlottesville, VA: University of Virginia, 1995. Presents a series of essays about John Brown's raid and how it should be viewed from a twentieth-century standpoint.

Goodrich, Thomas. *War to the Knife: Bleeding Kansas, 1854–1861.* Lincoln, NE: Bison Books, 2004. Examines John Brown's role in the civil war in Kansas and his participation in the Osawatomie massacre.

Oates, Stephen B. *Our Fiery Trial: Abraham Lincoln, John Brown, and the Civil War Era.* Amherst: University of Massachusetts Press, 1979. Weaves the lives of Nat Turner, John Brown, and Abraham Lincoln together to show how they were interrelated in their battle against slavery.

Oates, Stephen B. *To Purge This Land with Blood: A Biography of John Brown.* 2nd ed. Amherst, MA: University of Massachusetts Press, 1984.

This scholarly biography of Brown also features maps, portraits of Brown, and pictures of various Harper's Ferry locales.

Peterson, Merrill D. *John Brown: The Legend Revisited*. Charlottesville, VA: University of Virginia, 2004. Reconstructs the life and times of John Brown and discusses the changes that his reputation has undergone in light of so many new historical events.

Renehan, Edward J. *The Secret Six: The True Tale of the Men Who Conspired with John Brown*. New York: Crown, 1995. Furnishes detailed accounts of the lives of six unlikely revolutionaries who financed John Brown's raid.

Reynolds, David S. *John Brown, Abolitionist: The Man Who Killed Slavery, Sparked the Civil War, and Seeded Civil Rights*. New York: Alfred A. Knopf, 2005. Depicts Brown as a religious, but avenging angel against the evils of slavery.

Stauffer, John. *The Black Hearts of Men: Radical Abolitionists and the Transformation of Race*. Cambridge, MA: Harvard University Press, 2002. Tells the story of how an interracial group of abolitionists, including James McCune Smith, Frederick Douglass, and Gerrit Smith disbanded in the wake of the armed insurrection led by John Brown.

World Wide Web

"The Father of American Terrorism." http://www.americanheritage.com/articles/magazine/ah/2000/1/2000_1_81.shtml. This article from *American Heritage Magazine* portrays John Brown as a terrorist.

"Images of Harper's Ferry." http://www.dickinson.edu/departments/hist/NEH workshops/NEH/resource/gallery3.htm. Provides a series of woodcut drawings and a map of the buildings and surrounding area of Harper's Ferry.

"John Brown and the Valley of the Shadow." http://www3.iath.virginia.edu/jbrown/master.html. Contains a biographical sketch of John Brown and his leadership during the Harper's Ferry raid.

"John Brown State Historic Site." http://www.kshs.org/places/johnbrown/index.htm. Click on the online exhibits to retrieve a set of excellent resource links about the life of John Brown when he was in Kansas.

"John Brown's Final Address to the Court November 2, 1859. http://members.aol.com/jfepperson/brown.html. Contains the full text of John Brown's speech to the court concerning his beliefs about slavery and his role in the Harper's Ferry raid.

"The Last Days of John Brown." http://www.sniggle.net/Experiment/index.php?entry=johnbrown#lastdays. Contains the full text of an article written about the final days of John Brown before his execution and the significance of his raid on Harper's Ferry as a blow against slavery by *Civil Disobedience* essayist Henry David Thoreau.

"What John Brown Did in Kansas: Andrew Johnson of Tennessee, United States House of Representatives, December 12 1859." http://www.adena.com/adena/usa/cw/cw234.htm. Provides soon-to-be President Andrew Johnson's testimony regarding John Brown's role in the Osawatomie massacre in Kansas prior to his raid on Harper's Ferry.

Multimedia Sources

John Brown's Holy War. Alexandria, VA: PBS Home Video, 1999. 1 DVD. 90 minutes. This documentary brings the life and times of John Brown alive with excerpts from letters, speeches, and interviews with noted historians.

61. Abraham Lincoln's Presidential Election and Secession (1860–1861)

Abraham Lincoln's election as President of the United States on November 6, 1860, is totally connected to the secession of the southern states from the union. Before Lincoln was inaugurated on March 4, 1861, seven states had seceded and formed their own government called the Confederate States of America. As compromises and court decisions failed to end the debate and fight over slavery, political parties splintered as well. The Constitutional Union Party, a party formed by former Whigs, nominated John Bell of Tennessee. He wished to preserve the union and was against the Kansas-Nebraska Act of 1854. Southern Democrats broke away from the northern Democrats and nominated John Cabell Breckenridge of Kentucky, a proslavery candidate. The other part of the Democratic Party nominated Stephen A. Douglas of Illinois, who did not support the expansion of slavery into new U.S. territories and states. These divisions guaranteed that Lincoln, the only candidate of the newly formed Republican Party, would win the election. Unlike the other candidates, Lincoln stayed in Illinois throughout the campaign period. His speeches carefully avoided the slavery issue and reinitiated his wish to save the union. Although Lincoln won only 40 percent of the popular vote, he did receive 180 electoral votes to his opponents' 123. Almost 70 percent of the voters opposed the expansion of slavery into

U.S. territories. Already under threat of assassination, Lincoln took the oath of office with seven states absent from the union and made a decision to provision Fort Sumter in Charleston, South Carolina, the following day, fearing a possible Confederate attack.

TERM PAPER SUGGESTIONS

1. The day after Lincoln was inaugurated, he decided to send provisions to Fort Sumter in Charleston Harbor, South Carolina. On April 12, 1861, Confederate troops fired on Fort Sumter, officially beginning the hostilities between the two sides. Examine the events leading up to the shots fired at Fort Sumter for opportunities for further negotiation and compromise. Did opportunities still exist for preventing war?

2. Prior to secession, Kentucky Senator John J. Crittenden proposed one more compromise to prevent the southern states from leaving the Union. Analyze the contents of the Crittenden Compromise and the reasons for its failure.

3. Secession by the southern states was justified under a "compact theory" of states' rights that provides for the sovereignty of each state. Discuss this theory and how it was used by southern states in the U.S. Civil War and during the Civil Rights Movement to countenance defiance of federal laws.

4. Lincoln carefully avoided the slavery issue during his campaign, stressing only that he wished to preserve the Union. Analyze his political motives for not taking a stand on the slavery issue prior to his election.

5. President James Buchanan was in office during the time the southern states were threatening to and eventually did secede from the Union. Examine why he did nothing to stop them.

6. Once Lincoln was elected president, southern states believed that it was only a matter of time until slavery was abolished and that the political balance of power would be tipped in favor of northern and newly created nonslave states. Explore the ramifications and consequences of this denouement for these southern states.

ALTERNATIVE TERM PAPER SUGGESTIONS

1. Assume that you have been asked to draft a constitution for the Confederate States of America. Although you intend to base it on the U.S. Constitution, draft provisions for the states' rights, southern agricultural interests, the continuance of slavery, and expenditure provisions.

2. Assume that you have been asked to design a Web site for the Confederacy that will help you gain recognition by foreign nations for purposes of

importing and exporting various goods and perhaps come to your aid militarily. Be sure to address the issue of southern agricultural products, including cotton and indigo, as well as the access to a supply of cheap labor.

SUGGESTED SOURCES

Primary Sources

Dumond, Dwight Lowell, ed. *Southern Editorials on Secession.* Gloucester, MA: Peter Smith, 1964. Furnishes hundreds of reprinted editorials about secession from a southern point of view.

Luthin, Reinhard H. *The First Lincoln Campaign.* Gloucester, MA: Peter Smith, 1964. Contains primary sources in the form of speeches and correspondence concerning Lincoln's first campaign that he conducted primarily from Springfield, Illinois.

Perkins, Howard Cecil, ed. *Northern Editorials on Secession.* 2 vols. New York: Appleton-Century, 1942. Contains hundreds of reprinted editorials about the impending secessions of the southern states from a northern point of view.

Proquest Civil War Era. www.il.proquest.com. This subscription online database provides access to two thousand period pamphlets and eight newspapers from 1840 to 1865 that explore the stories and events of the Civil War.

Secondary Sources

Arnold, James R., and Weiner Roberts. *Divided in Two: The Road to Civil War, 1861.* Minneapolis, MN: Lerner Publications, 2002. Written for secondary school students, this work provides an outstanding overview of the issues leading up to secession and the beginning of the U.S. Civil War.

Crofts, Daniel W. *Reluctant Confederates: Upper South Unionists in the Secession Crisis.* Chapel Hill, NC: University of North Carolina Press, 1989. Discusses how several upper southern states might not have joined the confederacy.

Davis, William C. *A Government of Our Own: The Making of the Confederacy.* New York: Free Press, 1994. Provides a comprehensive history of the process of secession and the creation of the Confederate States of America.

Davis, William C. *The Union that Shaped the Confederacy: Robert Toombs and Alexander H. Stephens.* Lawrence, KS: University Press of Kansas, 2001. Relates the story of the close alliance between Confederate Vice President Alexander Stephens and Robert Toombs, secretary of the Confederacy, and the roles they played in the secession of the southern states.

Donald, David Herbert. *Lincoln.* New York: Simon and Schuster, 1995. This insightful biography explains the political motivations behind all of Lincoln's most controversial decisions.

Foner, Eric. *Free Soil, Free Labor, Free Men: The Ideology of the Republican Party before the Civil War.* New York: Oxford University Press, 1995. Examines the factions inside the newly formed Republican Party and the political implications for Lincoln's nomination and subsequent election.

Gienapp, William E. *Abraham Lincoln and Civil War America: A Biography.* New York: Oxford University Press, 2002. Reveals Lincoln's ambivalence and second thoughts about the issue of slavery and southern secession.

McPherson, James M. *Abraham Lincoln and the Second American Revolution.* New York: Oxford University Press, 1990. This major work on Lincoln and the Civil War analyzes the war as a revolutionary event similar to the one that took place in 1776.

McPherson, James M. *Battle Cry of Freedom: The Civil War Era.* New York: Oxford University Press, 1988. This Pulitzer Prize winning work discusses and analyzes the Civil War from a variety of perspectives.

Mansch, Larry D. *Abraham Lincoln, President-Elect: The Four Critical Months from Election to Inauguration.* Jefferson, NC: McFarland, 2005. Describes and analyzes the emotional and political four month tug of war that Lincoln experienced as he attempted to preserve the Union.

Thomas, Emory M. *The Confederacy as a Revolutionary Experience.* Columbia, SC: University of South Carolina Press, 1991. Discusses the major events of the Confederacy and provides details about the formation of the government.

World Wide Web

"Abraham Lincoln's First Inaugural Address." http://en.wikisource.org/wiki/Abraham_Lincoln%27s_First_Inaugural_Address. Provides the full text of Lincoln's first inaugural address.

"Constitution of the Confederate States of America." http://en.wikisource.org/wiki/Constitution_of_the_Confederate_States_of_America. Furnishes the full text of the constitution of the Confederate States of America.

"Crittenden Compromise." http://en.wikisource.org/wiki/Crittenden_Compromise. Contains the full text of the Crittenden Compromise, a proposal by Kentucky Senator John Crittenden to resolve the secession crisis by prohibiting slavery north of the 36 degree parallel while preserving it below that line.

"1860 Presidential Election Percent of Popular Vote." http://www.multied.com/elections/1860Pop.html. Furnishes a colored map showing the percent of the 1860 popular vote among all of the voting states broken down by each of the four candidates' totals.

"The Election of 1860." http://www.tulane.edu/~latner/Background/ BackgroundElection.html. Provides an outstanding overview of all of the issues concerning Lincoln's election in 1860.

"Fort Sumter." http://blueandgraytrail.com/event/Fort_Sumter. Presents a detailed timeline and narrative of the Fort Sumter crisis and Lincoln's early role and decision to defend it.

"Presidential Election 1860–1912." http://elections.harpweek.com/1864/Over view-1864-1.htm. Furnishes an overview of the issues and results of the 1864 presidential election.

Multimedia Sources

The Civil War. Alexandria, VA: PBS Home Video, 2004. 5 DVDs. 690 minutes. 1993. Narrated by Ken Burns, this outstanding epic contains primary sources in the form of music, photographs, letters, speeches, and interviews with noted American Civil War historians. The first DVD provides information about Lincoln's election, the secession of the southern states, and the firing on Fort Sumter.

62. Battles of Bull Run (1861 and 1862)

The first battle of Bull Run (July 21, 1861) during the Civil War was a clash of amateur armies driven by newspapers and Congressmen clamoring for action to face off before they were armed and trained. People rode out from Washington, D.C., in buggies, in carriages, and on horseback to watch the battle and picnic. Once it was over, both sides soberly realized that a great deal of blood was going to be shed and that the conflict would not be over simply after a few shots were fired at each other. With the Confederate decision to make their capital in Richmond, Virginia, only ninety miles from Washington, D.C., President Abraham Lincoln placed an untrained army of volunteers under the command of Brigadier General Irwin McDowell to engage similarly green, volunteer rebel soldiers under the command of General P. G. T. Beauregard and General Joseph Eggleston Johnson. They finally clashed at a meandering creek called Bull Run in Manassas, Virginia, where Northern troops were routed losing 460, while the South lost 387 men. The second battle (August 28, 1862), fought in the same area, brought seasoned troops under the Northern command of General John Pope and Southern commanders Robert E. Lee, James

Longstreet, and Stonewall Jackson. This time federal troops were truly outmaneuvered in a fierce battle that cost General Pope his command and the lives of 1,747 Federalists. The South lost 1,553 rebel soldiers and headed next to the Battle of Antietam in Maryland.

TERM PAPER SUGGESTIONS

1. Discuss how the South was more predisposed for war by having men who had been members of state militias, were good horsemen, were more accustomed to using arms, and were more committed to the cause.
2. The U.S. Army largely comprised Southerners who, once war was declared, defected to the Southern side and went on to lead armies. Explore how many left the U.S. Army and what role they played in battles for the Confederacy. Explore the advantages that their leadership gave the South.
3. Investigate the pressure from newspapers and Congressmen that President Lincoln was under to battle with the enemy. Should he have taken General Winfield Scott's advice and continued to wait until he had more and better trained troops?
4. Describe the roles that General Thomas Jonathan Jackson, aka "Stonewall Jackson," played at the first and second Battles of Bull Run.
5. Analyze General Pope's mistakes from a military point of view in the second Battle of Bull Run and why he was cashiered from the army.
6. Northern General Winfield Scott had developed an "Anaconda Plan" for winning the war. Describe the military strategies and tactics that he intended to use.

ALTERNATIVE TERM PAPER SUGGESTIONS

1. Use an Excel sheet with research data to show the advantages and disadvantages that each side had during the Civil War. Be sure to include information such as the number of states that were on each side, number of troops, factories, railroads, and the like.
2. Assume you are a southern newspaper editor. Write several opinion pieces stating why the first Battle of Bull Run should not be celebrated as a victory by your readers.

SUGGESTED SOURCES

Primary Sources

"The Battle of Bull Run (First Manassas) (July 21, 1861)." http://www.sonofthe south.net/leefoundation/civil-war/1861/august/battle-bull-run.htm.

Provides primary sources in the form of accounts written by many of the generals who were at the first Battle of Bull Run.

"The Battle of Second Manassas August 28–30, 1862." http://www.civilwar home.com/2manassa.htm. Provides the full text of military orders, letters, diary entries, and battle plans for the second Battle of Bull Run.

"Proquest Civil War Era." http://il.proquest.com. This online subscription database provides the full text of eight period newspapers and two thousand pamphlets from 1840 to 1865 that report the issues of slavery and anti-slavery, plus the battles of the Civil War.

Secondary Sources

Davis, Donald A. *Stonewall Jackson*. New York: Palgrave Macmillan, 2007. Provides an exciting biography of Stonewall Jackson with insightful military analyses of his strategic role at the first Battle of Bull Run.

Davis, William C. *Battle at Bull Run*. Garden City, NY: Doubleday, 1977. Provides one of the most detailed accounts of the First Battle of Bull Run.

Davis, William C. *First Blood: Fort Sumter to Bull Run*. Alexandria, VA: Time Life Books, 1983. Complete with pictures, battle plans, and illustrations, this work is also filled with personal accounts of the Bull Run battles.

Detzer, David. *Dissonance between Fort Sumter and Bull Run in the First Turbulent Days of the Civil War*. Orlando, FL: Harcourt, 2007. Using primary sources in the form of letters, dairy entries, and newspaper accounts, the author discusses and analyzes the events one hundred days prior to the first Battle of Bull Run and the pressure on Lincoln to begin the war.

Detzer, David. *Donnybrook: The Battle of Bull Run, 1861*. Orlando, FL: Harcourt, 2004. Provides one of the most comprehensive narratives of the first battle of Bull Run.

Hennessy, John J. *Return to Bull Run: The Campaign and Battle of Second Manassas*. Norman, OK: University of Oklahoma Press, 1999. This scholarly work discusses how General Robert E. Lee was able to outmaneuver General Pope and defeat Northern troops at the second Battle of Bull Run despite overwhelming odds.

Langellier, John. *Second Manassas 1862: Robert E. Lee's Greatest Victory*. Westport, CT: Praeger Publishers, 2004. Contains an outstanding narrative history of Robert E. Lee's victory over General Pope at the second Battle of Bull Run.

McDonald, JoAnna H. *We Shall Meet Again: The First Battle of Manassas (Bull Run, July 18–21, 1861)*. New York: Oxford University Press, 2000. This scholarly work contains a thorough analysis of the first Battle of Bull Run.

Peskin, Allan. *Winfield Scott and the Profession of Arms*. Kent, OH: Kent State University Press, 2003. Although Scott was seventy-five years old when he was asked to take command of the U.S. Army, this biography shows that he was indeed a military visionary with his "Anaconda Plan" for subduing the South.

Robertson, James. *Stonewall Jackson: The Man, the Soldier, the Legend.* New York: Macmillan, 1997. Provides information about the character of Stonewall Jackson and what may have motivated him to take such daring and successful risks with the men under his command.

Williams, Harry T. *P. G. T. Beauregard: Napoleon in Gray.* Baton Rouge, LA: Louisiana State University Press, 1955. Remains the definitive biography of Beauregard.

World Wide Web

"The Battle of Bull Run." http://www.sonofthesouth.net/leefoundation/civil -war/1861/august/battle-bull-run.htm. Provides the full text of an 1861 article from *Harper's Weekly* describing the first Battle of Bull Run. This site also has numerous resource links to other Civil War information.

"The Battle of Second Manassas." http://www.army.mil/cmh-pg/books/Staff -Rides/2Manassas/2mns-fm.htm. This outstanding site provides a self-guided tour of the second battle replete with maps, photographs, and descriptions of the combatants.

"Bull Run." http://www.historyanimated.com/BullRunh.html. Provides an animated history of the first Battle of Bull Run that includes photographs of all the major generals from both sides of the conflict.

"Civil War Battles." http://www.sonofthesouth.net/leefoundation/second-battle -bull-run.htm. Provides information about both Battles of Bull Run.

"First Bullrun.com." http://www.firstbullrun.com/RESOURCE/osprey.html. Contains an outstanding bibliography of additional resources concerning the first Battle of Bull Run.

"Manassas National Battlefield Park." http://www.nps.gov/mana. Furnishes a description of both battles with pictures and illustrations of each armies' positions.

"Second Bull Run (Manassas) Order of Battle." http://www.brettschulte.net/ OOBs/SecondBullRun/SecondBullRun.html. This Master's thesis analyzes the military maneuvers by both sides during the second Battle of Bull Run.

Multimedia Sources

Civil War Combat. New York: A&E Home Entertainment, 1999. 4 DVDs. 400 minutes. Narrated by Roger Mudd, this digital video set tells the stories of the most famous Civil War battles including that of Bull Run.

Stonewall Jackson. New York: A&E Home Entertainment, 1996. 1 DVD. 50 minutes. Relates the story of Stonewall Jackson's life and his career as a great military commander during the Civil War.

63. Emancipation Proclamation (1862)

Until September 22, 1862, Abraham Lincoln was tortured by his political ambitions and the practical considerations of trying to preserve the Union, which he fervently believed to be worth any human cost. Assailed by abolitionists, reporters, and members of his party with their own plans and agendas concerning slavery, Lincoln was in a tug-of-war with forces that were sometimes contradictory to his goals. He wished to abolish slavery only if it would bring about peace and unite the country again. Lincoln was deeply concerned that issuing such an emancipation proclamation might risk the secession of the slave states Delaware, Kentucky, Maryland, and Missouri that were still loyal to the Union. He was also worried about the future of four million freed slaves and kept discussing a plan with his cabinet that entailed compensating slave owners for their loss of property and voluntary colonization to Africa to ease racial adjustments. The war was also not going well. The North had lost the Battle of Bull Run, Wilson's Creek in Missouri, and the Battle of Ball's Bluff in Virginia. Lincoln desperately needed a military victory so that his proclamation would not seem like a desperate act of a defeated side. After the Union won the Battle of Antietam, Lincoln announced that he was emancipating all slaves who lived in states in rebellion against the Union. By limiting the proclamation to states in rebellion, Lincoln hoped to persuade Congress to decide issues of compensation and voluntary colonization with regard to slaves and their owners in areas that were still loyal to the Union.

TERM PAPER SUGGESTIONS

1. Describe the reaction of doctrinaire abolitionists and leaders to President Lincoln's proclamation.

2. Discuss why the issuance of the Emancipation Proclamation actually strengthened the resolve of Southerners to continue the Civil War.

3. Analyze the legal powers that Lincoln had to issue the Emancipation Proclamation. How was he legally able to free the slaves only in Southern states

but needed to have Congress address the question of universal emancipation?

4. Despite the lack of universal emancipation, reformers and abolitionists such as Frederick Douglass and William Lloyd Garrison heralded Lincoln's decision. Examine and explain their reasons for doing so.

5. The South was already making diplomatic overtures to France and Great Britain for recognition of the Confederate States of America. Discuss the impact that the Emancipation Proclamation had on this process.

6. Once the Civil War also involved a fight to end slavery, many Northerners not only withdrew their support but also stopped volunteering to fight in it. Discuss the impact that the proclamation had on the Northern war effort. What were some of the economic concerns of Northerners concerning the freeing of four million slaves? Discuss the Conscription Act of 1863, which authorized the President to draft citizens between the ages of 18 and 35 for three-year terms of military service.

ALTERNATIVE TERM PAPER SUGGESTIONS

1. In August 1864, Lincoln showed great presidential courage when his campaign managers told him that in order to win the 1864 election, he needed to renounce the Emancipation Proclamation. Assume you are a campaign manager who believes he can win without renouncing the proclamation. Prepare a podcast using some of his most effective speeches and letters to date that will rally the voters to his cause.

2. One of the important effects of the Emancipation Proclamation was that it encouraged African Americans to join the battle to end slavery. Design seven Army recruitment posters that might entice freed slaves to fight for the Union and accompany the drawings with appropriate explanations.

SUGGESTED SOURCES

Primary Sources

"The Collected Works of Abraham Lincoln." http://quod.lib.umich.edu/l/lincoln/. Contains eight volumes of primary sources about the life of Abraham Lincoln, including speeches, letters, proclamations, and orders that are keyword searchable.

Lincoln, Abraham. *Lincoln on Democracy*, edited by Mario M. Cuomo and Harold Holzer. New York: Harper Collins, 1990. Contains a collection of primary sources in the form of speeches, letters, and diary entries on the subjects of freedom and equality.

Secondary Sources

Beschloss, Michael. *Presidential Courage: Brave Leaders and How They Changed America 1789–1989.* New York: Simon and Schuster, 2007. Discusses selected presidential decisions and how they changed America, including President Lincoln's Emancipation Proclamation.

Donald, David Herbert. *Lincoln.* New York: Simon and Schuster, 1995. Portrays Lincoln as a man who was often afflicted with self-doubts concerning his decisions about such matters as the Emancipation Proclamation and the conduct of the war.

Ewan, Christopher. "The Emancipation Proclamation and British Public Opinion," *The Historian* 67 (March 22, 2005): 1–19. Also available at http://www.encyclopedia.com/doc/1G1-135466323.html. Describes and analyzes the British reaction to the Emancipation Proclamation and how it affected its tentative diplomatic ties with the South.

Franklin, John Hope. *The Emancipation Proclamation.* Garden City, NY: Doubleday, 1963. Discusses Lincoln's position on slavery within the context of the times in which he lived.

Gienapp, William E. *Abraham Lincoln and Civil War America: A Biography.* New York: Oxford University Press, 2002. Looks at the part of Lincoln's life that involved the Civil War.

Guelzo, Allen C. *Lincoln's Emancipation Proclamation: The End of Slavery in America.* New York: Simon and Schuster, 2004. Explores the reasons why Lincoln issued the proclamation and how well he understood the reaction it would receive and its impact on continuing the war effort.

Holford, David M. *Lincoln and the Emancipation Proclamation.* Berkeley Heights, NJ: Enslow Publications, 2002. Written for secondary school students, this work provides an excellent overview of the issues surrounding Lincoln's decision to issue the Emancipation Proclamation.

Holzer, Harold, et al. *The Emancipation Proclamation: Three Views.* Baton Rouge, LA: Louisiana State University Press, 2006. Presents three differing viewpoints from noted historians about the reaction and impact of the Emancipation Proclamation on both sides of the Civil War.

McPherson, James M. *Abraham Lincoln and the Second American Revolution.* New York: Oxford University Press, 1990. Provides a series of essays about how the Civil War affected America in ways that were similar to the American Revolution.

McPherson, James M. *The Struggle for Equality: Abolitionists and the Negro in the Civil War and Reconstruction.* Princeton, NJ: Princeton University Press, 1964. Furnishes information about the pressure that Lincoln was under to issue the Emancipation Proclamation from abolitionist groups and other social reformers.

Neely, Mark E., Jr. *The Last Best Hope of Earth: Abraham Lincoln and the Promise of America*. Cambridge, MA: Harvard University Press, 1993. This scholarly work examines how Lincoln developed as a national leader and what his role was in preserving the union.

Roberts, Russell. *Lincoln and the Abolition of Slavery*. San Diego, CA: Greenhaven Press, 2000. Presents an excellent overview of the role that Lincoln played in freeing the slaves not only with the Emancipation Proclamation but also with his speeches and decision to continue the war.

Silvana, R. Siddali. *From Property to Person: Slavery and the Confiscation Acts, 1961–1862*. Baton Rouge, LA: Louisiana State University Press, 2005. Discusses the reaction by Northerners who wanted confiscated southern property to also consist of slaves and how the Confiscation Acts after the Emancipation Proclamation were finally configured to address those concerns.

World Wide Web

"Emancipation Proclamation, 1863." http://www.archives.gov/exhibits/american_originals_iv/sections/emancipation_proclamation.html. Contains primary sources in the form of letters reacting to the proclamation, the full text of it, images of it, and more.

"I Will Be Heard: Abolitionism in America." http://rmc.library.cornell.edu/abolitionism/index.htm. Provides the full text of letters, newspaper articles, and diary entries concerning the Emancipation Proclamation, plus an overview and full text of the document.

"Library of Congress—Emancipation Proclamation." http://www.loc.gov/rr/program/bib/ourdocs/EmanProc.html. Contains a treasure trove of primary sources pertaining to the Emancipation Proclamation, including the full text of the document, images, biographical information about Lincoln, and more.

"Mr. Lincoln and Freedom." http://www.mrlincolnandfreedom.org/home.html. Supplies resource links, biographical sketches, and overviews of the issues surrounding the Emancipation Proclamation, along with a set of resource links and student lesson plans.

"Slave Trade and Abolition of Slavery." http://www.blackhistory4schools.com/slavetrade/. Furnishes an excellent series of resource links concerning the Abolitionist Movement and the Emancipation Proclamation.

"Toward Racial Equality *Harper's Weekly* Reports on Black America, 1857–1874." http://blackhistory.harpweek.com/. Contains the full text of period *Harper's Weekly* articles concerning slavery, the Civil War, society, and culture. The site also includes a simulation game.

"Virtual Exhibit: The Emancipation Proclamation." http://www.nysl.nysed.gov/library/features/ep/index.html. Presents the full text and images of the preliminary proclamation and overviews of its significance.

Multimedia Sources

The Fight for Freedom. New York: Ambrose Video/Centre Communications, 2005. 1 DVD. 27 minutes. Program 3 of *A History of Black Achievement in America* series contains information about Abraham Lincoln's issuance of the Emancipation Proclamation and its contribution toward the freedom and equality for all Americans.

64. The Battles of Gettysburg, Vicksburg, and Chattanooga (1863)

Even though the North had superior numbers in terms of men of combat age, workers, miles of railroad, bank deposits, and factories, they continued to lose battles to the South. The North was also unable to take the South's capital in Richmond, Virginia, only ninety miles away from Washington, D.C. The losses at Fredericksburg on December 13, 1863, and Chancellorsville on May 2, 1863, both in Virginia, were proof of their failure. The numerical advantage began to weigh in the North's favor, however, after the battles of Gettysburg, Pennsylvania, Vicksburg, Mississippi, and Chattanooga, Tennessee. Flush with the Chancellorsville victory, Rebel General Robert E. Lee decided to invade the North with 72,000 men to gain needed food and supplies. Federal General George G. Meade with 94,000 men collided with Lee's army at Gettysburg where they battled from July 1 to 3, 1863. Lee sustained 23,231 casualties and Meade suffered 23,055 casualties. Lee's army retreated, never to return to invade the North. In Vicksburg, Union Commander Ulysses S. Grant laid successful siege to the city with 70,000 soldiers and accepted its surrender on July 4, 1863. Grant swiftly moved to Chattanooga, a railroad center and one of the strongholds in the Confederacy, and captured it on November 25, 1863. These three battles effectively destroyed the South's offensive capabilities. Although there would be many battles to come, the South was also now engaged in a battle of attrition as the overwhelming numbers in terms of food, supplies, fighting men, government funds to wage war, and munitions factories began to take an inexorable toll.

TERM PAPER SUGGESTIONS

1. The North had twenty-three states in the Union compared with the South's eleven. The balance was also uneven with regard to the numbers of men of combat age, miles of railroad track, government war funds, munitions factories, and the like. Despite these losing odds, the South won many battles and came close to invading the North at Gettysburg. Discuss the reasons for the South's success and the implications for civil wars in general.

2. General James Longstreet argued vociferously with General Robert E. Lee over his decision to invade the North and fight a battle at Gettysburg. Discuss and explain Longstreet's reservations and why he was correct in his judgment.

3. The Battle of Vicksburg took its toll on civilians as well as soldiers. During the siege, many of the residents lived in caves along the bluffs to avoid the bombardments. Soldiers were reduced to eating mules and shoe leather, and many died from dysentery and other diseases. Read first-person civilian and soldier accounts of the Siege of Vicksburg, and describe its effects on the population.

4. Rebel Lieutenant General John C. Pemberton held Vicksburg from May 18 through July 4, 1863, because he knew that it was of strategic importance to the South. Analyze his assumption and discuss whether he should have surrendered sooner to relieve the human suffering.

5. Discuss why the Battle of Chattanooga was critical to placing the western part of the country firmly in the hands of the Union.

6. Union Commander George H. Thomas provided Grant with his victory at Chattanooga by making a feint up Missionary Ridge. Describe and analyze this part of the battle and why it clinched a victory for Grant.

ALTERNATIVE TERM PAPER SUGGESTIONS

1. Create a series of online maps that show how these three battles marked a turning point in the South's inability to wage war in the North. Be sure to indicate railroad lines and major routes by road and water that were used to transport troops and supplies.

2. Assume you are either a Union or a Confederate soldier who has survived the three day Battle of Gettysburg. Write a series of letters to your mother describing the battle in full detail, including its horrible carnage.

SUGGESTED SOURCES

Primary Sources

Busey, John W. *Regimental Strengths and Losses at Gettysburg.* 4th ed. Highstown, NJ: Longstreet House, 2005. Presents tables and charts of the actual regiments and their losses at the Battle of Gettysburg.

"Proquest Civil War Era." http://il.proquest.com. This online subscription database provides the full text of eight period newspapers and two thousand pamphlets from 1840 to 1865 that report the issues of slavery and anti-slavery, plus the battles of the Civil War.

Pryor, Elizabeth Brown. *Reading the Man: A Portrait of Robert E. Lee through His Private Letters*. New York: Viking Press, 2007. Draws on a cache of previously undiscovered letters found in 2002 that reveal the multifaceted personality of Lee and that his decision to fight for the South was not easily made.

"West Point Atlas of American Wars." http://www.dean.usma.edu/history/web03/atlases/american_civil_war/index.htm. This amazing resource contains the maps detailing retreats, lines of attack, and advances for all battles in the Civil War, including those of Gettysburg, Vicksburg, and Chattanooga.

Secondary Sources

Carter, Samuel, III. *The Final Fortress*. New York: St. Martin's Press, 1980. Provides an excellent analysis of the Vicksburg siege and battle.

Cozzens, Peter. *The Shipwreck of Their Hopes: The Battle for Chattanooga*. Urbana, IL: University of Illinois Press, 1994. Examines both Confederate and Union mistakes and analyzes Grant's success at capturing the city.

Foote, Shelby. *Stars in Their Courses: The Gettysburg Campaign, June–July 1863*. New York: Modern Library, 1994. Historian Foote captures the true horror of the largest battle ever to be fought in the Western Hemisphere right down to groans of the wounded and cries of the dying.

Gottfried, Bradley M. *The Maps of Gettysburg: An Atlas of the Gettysburg Campaign, June 3–July 13, 1863*. New York: Casemate Publications, 2007. Provides 144 black and white maps of the Gettysburg battle, each with a single page commentary.

Jones, Archer. *Civil War Command and Strategy*. New York: Free Press, 1992. Provides an overview of the general strategies and tactics planned by Union generals, particularly Ulysses S. Grant.

Korda, Michael. *Ulysses S. Grant: The Unlikely Hero*. New York: Harper Collins, 2004. Provides a brief biography that hits all the highlights of Grant's career as a military officer and later president of the United States.

McFeely, William S. *Grant*. New York: W. W. Norton, 1981. Discusses Grant's motivation and tactics during the Vicksburg and Chattanooga campaigns.

McPherson, James M. *Hallowed Ground: A Walk at Gettysburg*. New York: Crown Books, 2003. Princeton historian McPherson walks the reader through each part of the Gettysburg battle revealing commanders' mistakes or praising them. He succeeds in bringing this awful battle to life.

Neillands, Robin. *Grant: The Man Who Won the Civil War.* Cold Spring Harbor, NY: Cold Spring Harbor Press, 2004. Provides a study of Grant's military career, including military details of all of the Civil War battles in which he was engaged.

Thomas, Emory. *Robert E. Lee: A Biography.* New York: W. W. Norton, 1995. Gives one of the definitive biographies of Lee, focusing on him as a person with human failings and inner conflicts.

Winschel, Terrence. *Triumph and Defeat: The Vicksburg Campaign.* New York: Savas Beatie, 2004. Shows the mistakes made by both Southern and Northern generals in the siege of Vicksburg.

World Wide Web

"Animated History of the Siege of Vicksburg." http://www.historyanimated .com/Vicksburg.html. Presents an interactive narrative of the battle for Vicksburg, including biographical sketches of the major Northern and Southern generals.

"Camp Letterman General Hospital." http://www.nps.gov/archive/gett/getttour/ sidebar/letterman.htm. Supplies photographs and a lengthy description of the hospital conditions, which was set up to treat 22,000 wounded at the Battle of Gettysburg.

"The Chattanooga Campaign." http://www.civilwarhome.com/chattanooga .htm. Filled with primary sources in the form of Confederate and Union battle reports, summaries of events, maps, and more, this site is useful for any type of military research concerning Chattanooga.

"The Generals of Gettysburg: The Leaders of America's Greatest Battle." http:// www.rocemabra.com/~roger/tagg/generals/. Presents biographical, alphabetically organized sketches of all the Confederate and Union generals involved in the Battle of Gettysburg.

"Interactive Battle of Gettysburg with Narratives." http://www.army.mil/gettys burg/flash.html. Contains first-person accounts, biographical sketches of the main generals, statistics, information about weapons, an epilogue, plus a list of resource links.

"The Siege of Vicksburg." http://www.us-civilwar.com/vicksburg.htm. Provides a lengthy overview of the siege of Vicksburg replete with illustrations and maps.

"Wars and Battles—The Chattanooga Campaign." http://www.u-s-history.com/ pages/h109.html. Presents a discussion group, a speech analyzing the campaign, and a brief overview.

Multimedia Sources

The Civil War. Alexandria, VA: PBS Paramount, 2004. 5 DVDs. 660 minutes. Narrated and produced by Ken Burns, this classic retelling of the Civil War contains photographs, illustrations, maps, music, letters, and more accounts of the people who lived and died during this period. All three battles are discussed in the series.

The Complete Battle of Gettysburg. Alexandria, VA: PBS Home Video, 2002. 4 VHS Tapes. 240 minutes. This documentary is accompanied by battle scenes, photographs, and illustrations, and it provides great detail covering every aspect of this momentous battle.

Gettysburg: The Boys in Blue and Gray. Alexandria, VA: PBS Home Video, 2002. 1 DVD. 70 minutes. Contains the vivid account of Union Lieutenant Frank A. Haskell from a series of letters that he wrote to his brother about the Battle of Gettysburg.

65. End of the Civil War and the Assassination of President Abraham Lincoln (1865)

General Winfield Scott's "Anaconda Plan" of squeezing the Confederacy until it no longer had enough men, arms, food, and supplies to fight finally worked. The rise of Union Generals Ulysses S. Grant and William Sherman and their willingness to wage total war by burning crops, leveling buildings, and leaving nothing but scorched earth hastened the Confederacy's end. After the Battle of Appomattox, General Robert E. Lee surrendered to General Ulysses S. Grant on April 9, 1865. The terms of the surrender were generous—allowing each soldier to keep his horses, mules, and side arms and simply return home. The war had been devastating to the country in human and economic terms. A total of 360,000 Union soldiers and 260,000 Confederate soldiers had died. The war cost the Union $6 million and the Confederate states approximately half that much. Just five days later, however, the exultation of a country finally at peace turned to grief as Abraham Lincoln, who had begun preaching reconciliation, was assassinated by actor John Wilkes Booth as he watched a play at Ford's Theatre in Washington, D.C. It was a true conspiracy as attacks were carried out on Secretary of State William Seward and his sons, who suffered knife wounds, and a failed attempt was made on the life of Vice President Andrew Johnson. Lincoln's body was taken on a 1,700-mile route that retraced the 1861 journey he made to Washington, D.C., for his first inauguration. Walt Whitman's poetic lament, "O Captain! My Captain! Our fearful trip is done. The ship has weather'd every rack, the prize sought is won," captured the grief of a reunited country that went into mourning over the loss of a truly great American president.

TERM PAPER SUGGESTIONS

1. On February 3, 1865, Lincoln and Jefferson Davis, president of the Confederacy, met for a peace conference. Discuss why the Confederacy was not willing to surrender.

2. Investigate the cost of the Civil War in human and economic terms. Explore the reasons that it took the South so long to recover economically.

3. In the days after the surrender, Lincoln gave several speeches concerning his views about Reconstruction. Explore how these views were strongly opposed by Radical Republicans who wished to punish the South for starting the war.

4. Lincoln's assassination netted two conspirators who were probably innocent: Samuel Mudd, the physician who set John Wilkes Booth's broken leg, and Mary E. Surratt, the owner of a boarding house where the conspirators met. Investigate their trials and subsequent punishment in light of the conspiracy climate in Washington, D.C., during that time.

5. Unlike Robert E. Lee, who led many of the battles for the South, Jefferson Davis, president of the Confederacy, did not travel home once the war was over. Instead, he was captured and held for two years without a trial and eventually released. Investigate the reasons for this treatment.

6. Assassins are fascinating figures in history, but many of their motives remain a mystery to historians. Research the life and times of John Wilkes Booth and the motivation that led him to kill a U.S. president.

ALTERNATIVE TERM PAPER SUGGESTIONS

1. Ulysses S. Grant conducted himself admirably at the surrender at Appomattox when he met with General Lee. Using movie clips from Ken Burn's series, *The Civil War*, or images from Web sites depicting the surrender, create a two-minute iMovie of this historic event.

2. The Battle of Appomattox that ended the war was not easily won. Create a series of annotated online maps of the final battles showing why Lee finally had no choice but to surrender or face annihilation of his remaining troops.

SUGGESTED SOURCES

Primary Sources

"Biography of Mary Surratt." http://www.law.umkc.edu/faculty/projects/ftrials/lincolnconspiracy/surrattm.html. Provides an online biography of Mary Surratt, the innkeeper who rented a room to the conspirators involved with Lincoln's assassination, including excerpts from her trial and defense.

"Library of Congress—Abraham Lincoln Papers." http://lcweb2.loc.gov/ammem/alhtml/malhome.html. Contains the full text of speeches, letters, and other writings by Abraham Lincoln, including those that pertain to the Civil War together with 61,000 images.

"Personal Memoirs of General Ulysses S. Grant—Complete by Ulysses S. Grant." http://www.gutenberg.org/etext/4367. Furnishes the full text of Grant's memoirs regarding his service during the war and his acceptance of Lee's surrender at Appomattox.

"Proquest Civil War Era." http://il.proquest.com. This online subscription database provides the full text of eight period newspapers and two thousand pamphlets from 1840 to 1865 that report the issues of slavery and antislavery, plus the battles of the Civil War.

Secondary Sources

Bishop, Jim. *The Day Lincoln Was Shot*. New York: Harper & Row, 1955. This classic work remains in print because it is considered one of the most fascinating hour-by-hour accounts of the last day of Lincoln's life.

Bonekemper, Edward H., III. *A Victor, Not a Butcher: Ulysses S. Grant's Overlooked Military Genius*. Washington, DC: Regnery Publishing, 2004. Describes Grant's skillful use of military tactics and the training that he received at West Point as the reasons for his victories on the battlefield.

Donald, David Herbert. *Lincoln*. New York: Simon & Schuster, 1995. This psychobiography examines Lincoln's emotional and psychological state during the war, and it investigates his political motivations for many of his actions regarding emancipation and his intended reconstruction of the South.

Giblin, James Cross. *Good Brother, Bad Brother: The Story of Edwin Booth and John Wilkes Booth*. New York: Clarion Books, 2005. Written for secondary school students, this work relates the story of the Booth family and how John Wilkes decided to kill President Lincoln.

Gienapp, William E. *Abraham Lincoln and Civil War America: A Biography*. New York: Oxford University Press, 2002. This biography focuses upon

Lincoln's years in the White House and how he dealt with all of the issues concerning the Civil War.

Glatthaar, Joseph T. *General Lee's Army: From Victory to Collapse.* New York: Free Press, 2008. Traces the battle campaigns of Lee's army from June 1862 until his surrender at Appomattox.

Kauffman, Michael W. *American Brutus: John Wilkes Booth and the Lincoln Conspiracies.* New York: Random House, 2005. Gives an exhaustive account of John Wilkes Booth's motivation behind the decision to either kidnap or kill President Lincoln.

McPherson, James M. *Battle Cry of Freedom.* New York: Oxford University Press, 1988. Princeton historian McPherson places the U.S. Civil War within a nineteenth-century perspective.

Marvel, William. *Lee's Last Retreat: The Flight to Appomattox.* Chapel Hill, NC: University of North Carolina Press, 2003. This academic work presents an analysis of the last battle campaigns of Robert E. Lee and the reasons why he had to surrender to Grant at Appomattox.

Moore, Guy. *The Case of Mrs. Surratt.* Norman, OK: University of Oklahoma Press, 1954. Discusses the role that Surratt, one of the "supposed conspirators" who rented rooms to the Lincoln conspirators, played in the assassination plot.

Reck, Emerson W. A. *Lincoln: His Last Twenty-Four Hours.* Columbia, SC: University of South Carolina Press, 1994. Provides an additional account of Lincoln's last day.

Simpson, Brooks D. *The Reconstruction Presidents.* Lawrence, KS: University Press of Kansas, 1998. Compares four presidents who were involved in Reconstruction: Abraham Lincoln, Andrew Jackson, Ulysses S. Grant, and Rutherford B. Hayes.

World Wide Web

"An Overview of John Wilkes Booth's Assassination of President Lincoln." http://home.att.net/~rjnorton/Lincoln75.html. Supplies a hyperlinked summary of the events surrounding the assassination of President Lincoln.

"Appomattox Court House, Virginia, The Surrender, April 9, 1865." http://www.nps.gov/archive/apco/surrend.htm. Gives the full text of the surrender terms, agreement to surrender, and list of officers present.

"Assassination of President Abraham Lincoln." http://lcweb2.loc.gov/ammem/alhtml/alrintr.html. Provides an excellent overview of the major events and people involved in the assassination of President Lincoln.

"Freeman, Douglass S.: R. E. Lee, A Biography (4 volumes), Scribner's, 1934." http://penelope.uchicago.edu/Thayer/E/Gazetteer/People/ Robert_E_Lee/FREREL/home.html. Contains the full text of a four-volume work about Robert E. Lee, including the role he played in the surrender at Appomattox.

"A History of John Wilkes Booth." http://www.jwbooth.com/history.shtml. Presents an overview of John Wilkes Booth's life and the acting family that he came from plus a list of his appearances at Ford's Theatre where he shot Abraham Lincoln.

"Lincoln Assassination Theories: A Simple or A Grand Conspiracy?" http:// home.att.net/~rjnorton/Lincoln74.html. Provides six plausible theories that Lincoln may not have just been the victim of a simple conspiracy, but was one involving members of his own cabinet or a group of Radical Republicans.

"Surrender at Appomattox, 1865." http://www.eyewitnesstohistory.com/ appomatx.htm. Furnishes the correspondence between Generals Robert E. Lee and Ulysses S. Grant as they arranged for Lee's surrender of his army at the Appomattox Courthouse in 1865.

Multimedia Sources

The Civil War. Alexandria, VA: PBS Paramount, 2004. 5 DVDs. 690 minutes. Narrated by Ken Burns, this award-winning series contains photographs, illustrations, maps, letters, and other primary sources, plus interviews with noted U.S. Civil War historians. The last DVD in the series contains information about the surrender at Appomattox and the assassination of Abraham Lincoln.

The Last Days of the Civil War. Alexandria, VA: PBS Home Video, 2003. 2 DVDs. 405 minutes. This excellent documentary presents information about the final days of the Civil War including the surrender of Robert E. Lee's army at the Appomattox Court House.

66. Reconstruction Amendments (1865–1870)

For more than two hundred years, African American slaves were considered property, not humans. Their freedom was still an issue in 1865 despite the Emancipation Proclamation and passage of the Civil Rights Act of 1866. Southern legislators quickly enacted Black Codes, which regulated African Americans' actions and behavior so that many were

262   RECONSTRUCTION AMENDMENTS

re-enslaved. Laws were passed that restricted their assembly in unsupervised groups, prevented them from carrying weapons, forced them into permanent employment contracts, restricted their children only to apprenticeships, and denied their right to vote. Radical Republicans looking for a way to strengthen their party and aid African Americans decided to pass three Amendments to the Constitution as a way to protect their rights and guarantee their equality. Known as the Reconstruction Amendments, the Thirteenth Amendment, ratified by December 6, 1865, officially banned any form of slavery in the United States and any place subject to its jurisdiction. The Fourteenth Amendment, ratified on July 9, 1868, provided that all persons born or naturalized in the United States were citizens and as such protected by the Bill of Rights. It abolished the three-fifths compromise of the Constitution, apportioned Congressional representation based on population size, and gave everyone the right to due process and equal protection by the laws of the United States. The Fifteenth Amendment, ratified on March 30, 1870, guaranteed the right to vote to all male citizens.

TERM PAPER SUGGESTIONS

1. Discuss why Congress needed to pass these Amendments to the Constitution rather than pass a series of Civil Rights Acts. Examine the dangers Congress faced from a conservative Supreme Court and presidential veto.

2. The Black Codes were enacted by a variety of southern states as a means to keep power in the hands of White people. Research specific provisions of these codes from different southern states and describe how they were meant to keep African Americans enslaved.

3. For years battles to abolish slavery and give women the right to vote were coordinated and mutually supported by abolitionists and women's suffrage groups until Congress began deliberating passage of the Fourteenth Amendment. Research the reasoning behind the separation of these two important issues.

4. The women's movement splintered over compromising between issues of universal suffrage and equality under the law. Research and analyze the controversy between Elizabeth Cady Stanton and Susan B. Anthony, who favored moving forward with equal rights and suffrage for women, and the faction led by Lucy Stone and Julia Ward Howe, who were more conservative and wanted to wait longer.

5. Assess how the Fourteenth Amendment's due process and equal protection clause has been used by the Supreme Court to expand the number and

breadth of rights protecting individuals by referring to two Supreme Court cases such as *Plessy v. Ferguson* (1896) and *Brown v. Board of Education Case* (1954).

6. On March 3, 1865, Congress created the Freedmen's Bureau to assist African Americans in adjusting to freedom. Examine the role they played in protecting the civil rights of former slaves, most of whom could neither read nor write.

ALTERNATIVE TERM PAPER SUGGESTIONS

1. Assume you are a Supreme Court reporter for National Public Radio. The Fourteenth Amendment has just been ratified. Prepare a podcast that will explain its implications for the American suffrage movement in a way that listeners will understand.

2. Assume you are the senatorial aide to Pennsylvania Senator Thaddeus Stevens. He is a Radical Republican and a strong supporter of equal rights. Stevens even advocates that former southern slave owners should be forced to give their farms to freedmen. Prepare a PowerPoint presentation for a Congressional bill that he wishes to pass dealing with reparations and other ideas that might right some grievous wrongs done during the time of slavery.

SUGGESTED SOURCES

Primary Sources

Owen, Robert Dale. *The Wrong of Slavery, the Right of Emancipation, and the Future of the African Race in the United States*. Philadelphia, PA: J. B. Lippincott, 1864. Contains the writings of Owen, an abolitionist, who had the most sway over Lincoln to obtain issuance of the Emancipation Proclamation and the Thirteenth Amendment, on the issue of slavery.

Sherr, Lynn. *Failure Is Impossible: Susan B. Anthony in Her Own Words*. New York: Times Books, 1995. Contains primary sources in the form of speech excerpts and letters written by Susan B. Anthony concerning women's rights and suffrage, including writings about the passage of the Fourteenth Amendment.

Secondary Sources

Baker, Jean H., ed. *Votes for Women: The Struggle for Suffrage Revisited*. New York: Oxford University Press, 2002. Researches the history of the women's suffrage movement including the split surrounding the passage of the Fourteenth Amendment.

Blackwell, Alice Stone. *Lucy Stone: Pioneer of Woman's Rights*. 2nd ed. Charlottesville, VA: University of Virginia Press, 2001. Written by Lucy Stone's daughter, this work summarizes Lucy Stone's life and the work she did with the women's suffrage movement.

Epps, Garrett. *Democracy Reborn: The Fourteenth Amendment and the Fight for Equal Rights in Post-Civil War America*. New York: Holt, 2007. This outstanding work contains everything concerning the history of the ratification of the Fourteenth Amendment including the issue and battle concerning women's suffrage.

Franklin, John Hope, and Alfred A. Moss Jr. *From Slavery to Freedom: A History of African Americans*. 8th ed. Boston, MA: McGraw-Hill, 2000. Focuses on the changes that African Americans underwent from the time of abolition to the time they received their citizenship under the Reconstruction Amendments.

Hensley, Thomas R., et al. *The Changing Supreme Court: Constitutional Rights and Liberties*. St. Paul, MN: West Publishing, 1997. Provides a study of the Supreme Court's evolving protections of citizens' rights under the Fourteenth Amendment.

Lehmann, Nicholas. *Redemption: The Last Battle of the Civil War*. New York: Farrar, Straus, and Giroux, 2006. This excellent work paints a grim picture of the enactment of Black Codes in post-Civil War Mississippi during Reconstruction.

Lewis, Thomas T., and Richard L. Wilson. *Encyclopedia of the U.S. Supreme Court*. 3 vols. Pasadena, CA: Salem Press, 2001. Contains background material and discussions on passage of the Constitutional Amendments.

Magdol, Edward. *A Right to Land: Essays on the Freedmen's Community*. Westport, CT: Greenwood Press, 1977. Analyzes the problems that African Americans confronted as freed men, women, and children during Reconstruction, including their struggles to acquire land.

Perry, Michael J. *We the People: The Fourteenth Amendment and the Supreme Court*. New York: Oxford University Press, 2002. Focuses on Supreme Court controversies surrounding the Fourteenth Amendment.

Stauffer, John. *The Black Hearts of Men: Radical Abolitionists and the Transformation of Race*. Cambridge, MA: Harvard University Press, 2002. Discusses the interracial alliance among John Brown, Frederick Douglass, James McCune Smith, and Gerrit Smith to obtain passage of the Emancipation Proclamation and eventually the Thirteenth Amendment.

Westwood, Howard C. "Getting Justice for the Freedmen." In *The Freedmen's Bureau and Black Freedom*, edited by Donald G. Nieman. New York: Garland, 1994. Focuses on how the Freedmen's Bureau concerned itself with the civil and legal rights of African Americans during the Reconstruction era.

World Wide Web

"Constitution of the United States Amendments 11–27." http://www.archives
.gov/national-archives-experience/charters/constitution_amendments
_11-27.html#14. Provides the full text of the Thirteenth, Fourteenth,
and Fifteenth Amendments.

"A Dummies Guide to Understanding the Fourteenth Amendment." http://
www.citizensforaconstitutionalrepublic.com/madison11-28-06.html.
Provides an easy-to-understand guide to the background and interpretation of the Fourteenth Amendment.

"Library of Congress—13th Amendment to the U.S. constitution." http://
www.loc.gov/rr/program/bib/ourdocs/13thamendment.html. Includes
primary sources in the form of speeches, letters, images, and correspondence concerning the drafting and eventual ratification of the Thirteenth
Amendment.

"Library of Congress—14th Amendment to the U.S. Constitution." http://
www.loc.gov/rr/program/bib/ourdocs/14thamendment.html. Provides a
wealth of primary sources including letters, speeches, biographical
sketches, images, and more regarding the Fourteenth Amendment.

"Library of Congress—15th Amendment to the U.S. Constitution." http://
www.loc.gov/rr/program/bib/ourdocs/15thamendment.html. Contains
a treasure trove of primary material including speeches, letters, images,
and correspondence pertaining to the ratification of the Fifteenth
Amendment.

"Mr. Lincoln and the Thirteenth Amendment." http://www.mrlincolnand
freedom.org/inside.asp?ID=56&subjectID=3. Gives the political and
moral background for Lincoln's decision to seek an amendment to the
constitution concerning the abolition of slavery throughout the United
States.

"U.S. Constitution: Fifteenth Amendment." http://caselaw.lp.findlaw.com/data/
constitution/amendment15/. Presents the full text of the amendment
along with legal opinions concerning literacy tests and congressional
enforcement of the Fifteenth Amendment.

Multimedia Sources

A DVD History of the U.S. Constitution, 1619–2005. New York: Ambrose Video
Publishing, 2005. 4 DVDs. 210 minutes. This excellent documentary
provides instruction about the U.S. Constitution and how it has

protected Americans against tyranny and injustice. Parts of it address the Reconstruction Amendments.

67. Formation of the Ku Klux Klan (1866)

The Civil War still left many Southerners feeling that they had been deprived of their natural rights to own another human being. With the creation of the Freedmen's Bureau and passage of the Civil Rights Act of 1866, four million former slaves, living mainly in the South, were given the right to enter into and enforce contracts; inherit, lease, sell, hold, and convey property; give evidence in courts; run for elected office; and benefit equally from all U.S. laws and ordinances. Southerners were also still rebelling against Radical Republicans who were voicing a need to further address African Americans' grievances with the ratification of proposed Reconstruction Amendments. The reaction to these swift changes was the formation of several anti–African American and Republican Party paramilitary organizations such as the Knights of the White Camellia, the White League, the Invisible Circle, the Pale Faces, and the Ku Klux Klan (KKK). The latter terrorist organization would eventually spread and thrive during various decades throughout the United States. The KKK originated in Pulaski, Tennessee, where members expressed their opposition to radical Reconstructionism and the need for Whites to retain the reins of power. It established the wearing of white robes and pointed hoods that covered members' faces to terrify and intimidate their victims. The hoods also protected them from prosecution by any local authorities who were courageous enough to arrest them. Their violence was brought to a temporary end in 1871 when Congress passed the Ku Klux Klan, or Force, Acts and federal troops and courts arrested and tried many of them.

TERM PAPER SUGGESTIONS

1. Investigate the reaction to African Americans gaining political and economic power as one reason for the birth of the Ku Klux Klan.
2. The KKK did meet with some resistance in certain areas in the South. Describe countervigilante efforts by White Union Army veterans in Blount County, Alabama, and African Americans in Bennettsville, South Carolina, at repressing KKK activities.

3. Even though President Ulysses S. Grant enforced the Ku Klux Klan Acts, a terrible massacre took place in 1873 in Colfax, Louisiana, that resulted in the deaths of more than two hundred African Americans. Report on the causes and events of the Colfax Massacre.

4. Many of KKK's atrocities were perpetrated on Radical Republican politicians. Investigate the Klan's power of assassinating legislators, including Governor William Holden of North Carolina, and removing other politicians from office.

5. The Klan thrived right after the Civil War because so many local people sympathized with it. Examine the economic and employment situation that many southern states experienced after the Civil War as possible reasons for their tolerance of the KKK.

6. Investigate the role of George Gordon, a former Confederate Brigadier General, and General Nathan Bedford Forrest of Tennessee in starting the KKK. Discuss how they organized it hierarchically to suit their original purpose.

ALTERNATIVE TERM PAPER SUGGESTIONS

1. The KKK seemed to proliferate in areas and states where the two political parties or races were evenly balanced. Use the Historical Census Browser at http://fisher.lib.virginia.edu/collections/stats/histcensus and research this hypothesis.

2. Assume you are an African American living in a rural area of South Carolina in 1867. Your family is urging you to open a small store. Present the dangers from the KKK posed to you and other family members if you decide to open the store.

SUGGESTED SOURCES

Primary Sources

"Organization and Principles of the Ku Klux Klan, 1868." http://www.albany.edu/faculty/gz580/his101/kkk.html. Presents the beliefs and tenets that members of the Klan were supposed to uphold.

Tourgee, Albion W. *The Invisible Empire: A Fool's Errand and a Concise History of Events*. New York: Fords, Howard & Hulbert, 1880. Provides an autobiographical account of the author's time in the South during the Reconstruction Era and his encounters with the KKK.

Secondary Sources

Budiansky, Stephen. *The Bloody Shirt: Terror after Appomattox*. New York: Viking, 2008. Describes the concerted Southern opposition to the

Reconstruction Amendments and the role that the Ku Klux Klan played in curtailing Black civil rights.

Chalmers, David Mark. *Hooded Americanism: The History of the Ku Klux Klan.* 3rd ed. Durham, NC: Duke University Press, 1987. Provides the definitive work about the rise and history of the KKK.

Ezekiel, Raphael. *The Racist Mind: Portraits of American Neo-Nazis and Klansmen.* New York: Viking Press, 1995. Focuses on the economic and employment conditions that may help create a racist who would be prone to participating in an organization such as the KKK.

MacLean, Nancy. *Behind the Mask of Chivalry: The Making of the Second Ku Klux Klan.* New York: Oxford University Press, 1995. Provides a scholarly treatment of the growth and development of the KKK during the twentieth century.

Newton, Michael. *The Ku Klux Klan: History, Organization, Language, Influence and Activities of America's Most Notorious Secret Society.* Jefferson, NC: McFarland & Company, 2006. Provides a comprehensive history of the KKK that includes several primary sources, including a compilation of victims and some KKK documents.

O'Donnell, Patrick, and David Jacobs. *Ku Klux Klan: America's First Terrorists Exposed.* Seattle, WA: Booksurge Publishing, 2006. Part I of this work contains a history of the rise and growth of the KKK during the Reconstruction Era plus a history of the Ku Klux Klan Acts of 1871 that attempted to stop the Klan's violence and prosecute the offenders.

Quarles, Chester L. *The Ku Klux Klan and Related American Racialist and Anti-Semitic Organizations: A History and Analysis.* Jefferson, NC: McFarland & Company, 1999. Gives a history about the birth and rise of the KKK within the context of other White supremacists organizations.

Randel, William. *The Ku Klux Klan: A Century of Infamy.* Philadelphia, PA: Chilton Books, 1965. Discusses the growth and development of the KKK from a moral perspective.

Stanton, Bill. *Klanwatch: Bringing the Ku Klux Klan to Justice.* New York: Weidenfeld, 1991. Written by a former Klanwatch director, this work provides a series of initiatives for how to dismantle the Klan.

Trelease, Allen W. *White Terror: The Ku Klux Klan Conspiracy and the Southern Reconstruction.* Baton Rouge, LA: Louisiana State University Press, 1995. Furnishes an academic study of the reign of the terror that the KKK unleashed on African Americans during the Reconstruction Era.

Wade, Wyn Craig. *The Fiery Cross: The Ku Klux Klan in America.* New York: Simon & Schuster, 1987. Provides an account of the KKK's history and documents various episodes of violence.

World Wide Web

"Black Legislators during Reconstruction." http://www.georgiaencyclopedia.org/
nge/Article.jsp?id=h-635. Furnishes a history, replete with short biographical sketches, of African Americans who were elected to office right
after the Civil War.

"An Extended Interview with Stanley F. Horn, author of *The Invisible Empire:
The Story of the Ku Klux Klan, 1866–1871* published in 1939." http://
www.foresthistory.org/Research/Biltmore_Project/OHIs/HornOHI.pdf.
Scroll down to page 53 of this oral history to access the part dealing with
his motivation for writing this groundbreaking book.

"History of the Ku Klux Klan." http://www.africanamericans.com/
KuKluxKlan.htm. Contains a short history of the Klan together with its
titles hierarchy and full text of its creed.

"The Ku Klux Klan, A Brief Biography!" http://www.aaregistry.com/african
_american_history/2207/The_Ku_Klux_Klan_a_brief_biography. Contains an excellent overview of the rise and growth of the Klan from
1866 to present day, including its power and effect on African Americans.

"The Ku Klux Klan Act of 1871." http://education.harpweek.com/KKKHear
ings/AppendixA.htm. Provides the full text of the act that Congress
passed in an attempt to stop the violent acts of the KKK.

"Ku Klux Klan history." http://www.spartacus.schoolnet.co.uk/USAkkk.htm.
Furnishes a brief, hyperlinked history of the KKK.

"The Ku Klux Klan in the Reconstruction Era." http://www.georgiaencyclo
pedia.org/nge/Article.jsp?id=h-694. Presents a hyperlinked overview of
the birth and growth of the KKK right after the Civil War.

Multimedia Sources

The Ku Klux Klan—A Secret History. New York: A&E Home Entertainment
Video, 1998. 1 DVD. 100 minutes. Relying on Klan historians David
Chalmers and Wyn Craig Wade, this documentary traces the rise of the
Klan from 1866 to present day.

68. Purchase of Alaska (1867)

Called "Seward's Folly," "Johnson's Polar Bear Garden," and "Walrussia"
by newspaper reporters who thought it a total waste of taxpayers' funds,
the purchase of Alaska on March 30, 1867, for $7.2 million was an

absolute prize in natural resources. U.S. Secretary of State William H. Seward was a true believer in Manifest Destiny and wished to expand the United States at any opportunity. Prior to the Civil War, discussions were initiated between Russia and the United States, but nothing came of them. In 1867, Seward requested fishing rights in Russian-American territorial waters and was refused. He then asked whether Russia would be willing to sell Alaska. Russia needed the funds and was also afraid that Great Britain might simply seize the area and make it part of Canada. Czar Alexander II appointed Baron Edouard de Stoeckl, Russian Minister to the United States, and Foreign Minister Aleksandr Gorchakov to commence negotiations at once. Seward's initial bid for 586,000 square miles of territory was $5 million, but Stoeckl held out for $7.2 million because he realized Seward's ardent desire to acquire it. Negotiations went smoothly compared with the protracted one-year delay that it took Congress to finally agree to pay for it. With the help of Senator Charles Sumner who shepherded the treaty through the House of Representatives and Senate, the United States finally paid for its purchase a year after acquiring it. Within thirty-one years the vast mineral wealth of Alaska was realized when gold was discovered and the Klondike rushes began.

TERM PAPER SUGGESTIONS

1. Russia sold Alaska because of the Crimean War, which had convinced the Russian government that the area could not be defended in case of another war with Britain. Research this reason as a motivation for the sale of Alaska.

2. As part of the sale, Russia wanted the United States to take over the failing Russian-American Company. Investigate why the company was failing and what monetary solution Seward applied to solve the problem.

3. Analyze why the purchase of Alaska was of strategic import to the United States.

4. Reference newspaper excerpts that describe the reaction of specific news reporters, including Horace Greeley, to the purchase of Alaska.

5. In an effort to combat the negative publicity concerning the Alaska purchase, Seward employed the services of Senator Robert J. Walker as a lobbyist. Investigate the role he played in creating a positive reception of the arrangement.

6. Discuss why native Alaskans fared better under Russian rule than they did under initial U.S. governance.

ALTERNATIVE TERM PAPER SUGGESTIONS

1. Assume that Secretary of State Seward has employed you to create a Web site of the Alaska territory that will convince Congress and the public that it is indeed a worthy purchase. Create a site based on nineteenth-century knowledge of the area.

2. Assume you are a newspaper reporter for a local Alaskan newspaper. Write a series of articles describing the gold strikes in the Klondike (1898) and Nome (1899).

SUGGESTED SOURCES

Primary Sources

Dickerson, Donna Lee. *The Reconstruction Era: Primary Documents on Events from 1865 to 1877*. Westport, CT: Greenwood Press, 2003. Contains a collection of primary source documents relating to the purchase of Alaska.

Shiels, Archie W. *The Purchase of Alaska*. Seattle, WA: University of Washington Press, 1967. Furnishes many primary source documents concerning the purchase of Alaska.

Secondary Sources

Bolkhovitinov, Nikolai N. *Russian-American Relations and the Sale of Alaska, 1834–1867,* edited and translated by Richard A. Pierce. Kingston, ON: Limestone Press, 1996. Explores the positive and friendly relations that existed between the United States and Russia during the nineteenth century.

Bolkhovitinov, Nikolai N. "The Sale of Alaska in Context of Russo-American Relations in the Nineteenth Century." In *Imperial Russian Foreign Policy,* edited by Hugh Ragsdale. New York: Cambridge University Press, 1993. Focuses on Russia's decision to sell Alaska to the United States because it was not only a gesture of friendship but also of indefensible strategic importance.

Chevigny, Hector. *Russian America: The Great Alaskan Venture, 1741–1867.* Reprint. Portland, OR: Binford & Mort, 1979. Presents a comprehensive history of the Russian period of Alaskan history.

Elliott, Henry W. "Alaska: Ten Years' Acquaintance With, 1867–1877." *Harper's New Monthly Magazine* 55 (1887). Available through the Library of Congress's Primary Documents in American History Web site. Provides an excellent overview of the ten-year period after the United States purchased Alaska.

Farrar, Victor J. *The Annexation of Russian America to the United States.* New York: Russell & Russell, 1966. This brief work gives the basic facts about the purchase of Alaska.

Ford, Corey. *Where the Sea Breaks Its Back: The Epic Story of Early Naturalist Georg Stellar and the Russian Exploration of Alaska.* Anchorage, AK: Alaska Northwest Books, 2003. Describes the 1741–1742 voyage of Georg Stellar and Vitus Bering and their discoveries in Alaska.

Jensen, Ronald J. *The Alaska Purchase and Russian-American Relations.* Seattle, WA: University of Washington Press, 1975. Places the purchase of Alaska within the greater context of Russian-American relations.

Miller, David Hunter. *The Alaska Treaty.* Kingston, Ontario: Limestone Press, 1981. Supplies a comprehensive analysis of the treaty.

Sherwood, Morgan B., ed. *Alaska and Its History.* Seattle, WA: University of Washington Press, 1967. Provides several important articles that discuss the purchase of Alaska.

Sumner, Charles. "The Cession of Russian America to the United States." Washington, DC: Congressional Globe Office, 1867. http://memory.loc.gov/cgi-bin/query/r?ammem/ncpm:@field(DOCID+@lit(ULA17058776)) Features Sumner's speech to Congress on the occasion of the Alaska purchase.

Van Deusen, Glyndon G. *William Henry Seward.* New York: Oxford University Press, 1967. Provides a well-written and documented biography of Seward, who made the purchase of Alaska on behalf of the United States.

World Wide Web

"Alaska and the Western Canada Collection." http://content.lib.washington.edu/alaskawcanadaweb/index.html. This multimedia site contains period photographs, maps, and descriptions of the Klondike gold rush areas.

"Federal Government Seward's Folly, the Purchase of Alaska." http://www.u-s-history.com/pages/h230.html. Provides a summary of the purchase, along with an additional set of resource links.

"Library of Congress—Meeting of Frontiers." http://international.loc.gov/intldl/mtfhtml/mfsplash.html. This outstanding bilingual Russian/English site explores the relationship between the two countries from the 1700s through the purchase of Alaska in 1867.

"Library of congress—Seward's Folly." http://memory.loc.gov/ammem/today/mar30.html. Presents an accurate and reliable webography of the events, people, places, and dates concerning the purchase of Alaska.

"Library of Congress—Treaty with Russia for the Purchase of Alaska." http://www.loc.gov/rr/program/bib/ourdocs/Alaska.html. Contains primary sources in the form of speeches, images, and the full text of the treaty between the United States and Russia.

"National Archives—Purchase of Alaska." http://www.archives.gov/education/lessons/alaska/cancelled-check.html. Shows the full text of the check and other primary source documents pertaining to the purchase of Alaska.

"Purchase of Alaska, March 30, 1867." http://www.americaslibrary.gov/cgi-bin/page.cgi/jb/recon/alaska_1. Contains a four-screen, short summary of the purchase along with questions that are suitable for term papers.

Multimedia Sources

Klondike: The Quest for Gold. Jersey City, NJ: Monarch Films, Inc., 2004. 4 DVDs. 240 minutes. This documentary uses reenactments to trace the discovery of gold and to explore the hardships and challenges that miners faced traveling to the areas and extracting it.

The Story of America's Last Frontier. Chicago, IL: Questar Video, 1993. 1 video-cassette. 60 minutes. Relates the story of the purchase of Alaska while showing its natural beauties and resources.

69. The Impeachment of President Andrew Johnson (1868)

Vice President Andrew Johnson became the seventeenth President of the United States upon Abraham Lincoln's assassination in 1965. Johnson's views did not coincide with prevailing Radical Republicans, many of whom wished to punish the South for starting the Civil War. Johnson was the only senator from a slave-holding state to remain loyal to the Union, and Lincoln rewarded him by selecting him as his vice-presidential running mate in 1864. Johnson, however, did not share Lincoln's views concerning African Americans. He was a former slave owner, and he did not believe that African Americans and Whites should be provided with equal opportunities. As Radical Republicans brought Reconstruction legislation to him in the form of the creation of the Freedmen's Bureau, the Civil Rights Act of 1866, and the Fourteenth Amendment, Johnson vetoed them all. Congress attempted to curtail his restoration of former southern politicians to state and national government by passing the Tenure of Office Act of 1867. It prevented Johnson from appointing anyone in his cabinet without the approval of Congress. In defiance of the law, Johnson fired Secretary of War Edwin M. Stanton and replaced him with General Ulysses S. Grant.

The House of Representatives in turn voted to impeach Johnson, but he survived impeachment in the Senate by one vote. Johnson remained the only president to be impeached until 1998 when President Bill Clinton was impeached for lying to Congress about his personal affairs.

TERM PAPER SUGGESTIONS

1. Analyze why the Radical Republican party wished to limit Johnson's powers as president.
2. Explain how restricting President Johnson's right to replace members of his Cabinet was beyond the power and scope of Congress.
3. President Johnson was also a target for assassination on the night Lincoln was shot, but the assassin never arrived. Many Republicans, however, believed that he was part of a "Grand Conspiracy" to kill Lincoln. Discuss how this theory may have contributed to his dislike by the Radical Republicans.
4. Analyze and discuss the effects that President Johnson had on Reconstruction.
5. Congress actually made two attempts to impeach President Johnson. The first occurred in the fall of 1866, and it failed in the House of Representatives. Examine the first set of impeachment articles and compare them to the second set for their legal and political significance.
6. Many historians insinuate that President Johnson was not a likeable man and that his personal dealings with legislators and his statements to the public definitely contributed to his impeachment. Research aspects of Johnson's life that might shed light on this conclusion.

ALTERNATIVE TERM PAPER SUGGESTIONS

1. Assume you are a lawyer for President Andrew Johnson. Write opening and closing statements for him declaring why the articles of impeachment should not be considered valid ones.
2. Based on all the Reconstruction legislation that President Johnson vetoed and his successful installation of many former Confederate politicians to office in southern states, prepare a contemporary document that charges him with racism and deliberate undermining of Congressional attempts to provide African Americans with desperately needed civil rights.

SUGGESTED SOURCES

Primary Sources

Haskins, Ralph W., et al. *The Papers of Andrew Johnson.* 16 volumes. Nashville, TN: University of Tennessee Press, 1967–2000. Provides primary sources in the form of all letters and speeches given by Johnson and also correspondence directed to him.

Simpson, Brooks D. *Advice after Appomattox: Letters to Andrew Johnson, 1865–1866.* Nashville, TN: University of Tennessee Press, 1988. Contains a series of letters written by prominent Republicans and other leaders about how to reconstruct the South after the Civil War.

Secondary Sources

Beale, Howard K. *The Critical Year: A Study of Andrew Johnson and Reconstruction.* New York: Frederick Ungar, 1958. Explicates clearly the positions that the legislative and executive branches took regarding the impeachment crisis.

Benedict, Michael Les. *The Impeachment and Trial of Andrew Johnson.* New York: W. W. Norton, 1973. Provides a thorough analysis of Johnson's impeachment and concludes that it was not only justified but also warranted a conviction.

Foster, Allen G. *Impeached: The President Who Almost Lost His Job.* New York: Criterion Books, 1974. Contains illustrations and photographs that secondary school students will find useful for research on Johnson's impeachment.

Hearn, Chester G. *The Impeachment of Andrew Johnson.* Jefferson, NC: McFarland & Company, 2000. Focuses on the climate and events of the times that helped precipitate Johnson's impeachment.

McKitrick, Eric L. *Andrew Johnson and Reconstruction.* New York: Oxford University Press, 1988. Discusses the impact that Andrew Johnson had on reconstruction of the South by vetoing all of the Radical Republicans' legislation.

McPherson, James M. *Ordeal by Fire: The Civil War and Reconstruction.* 2nd ed. New York: McGraw-Hill, 1992. Studies and examines the political intrigue that flourished after Lincoln's assassination and how Johnson was implicated.

Means, Howard. *The Avenger Takes His Place: Andrew Johnson and the 45 Days That Changed the Nation.* Orlando, FL: Harcourt, 2006. Succeeds in painting a more neutral portrait of Andrew Johnson.

Rehnquist, William H. *Grand Inquests: The Historic Impeachments of Justice Samuel Chase and President Andrew Johnson.* New York: Harper, 1999. Former Chief Justice of the Supreme Court and his son provide a legal analysis of Johnson's impeachment trials.

Schroeder-Lein, Glenna R., and Richard Zuczek. *Andrew Johnson: A Biographical Companion.* Santa Barbara, CA: ABC-Clio, 2001. Using an A–Z organizational format, readers can quickly research every aspect of Johnson's life. This work also includes many primary source documents.

Simpson, Brooks D. *The Reconstruction Presidents.* Lawrence, KS: University Press of Kansas, 1998. Compares the policies of Andrew Johnson, Abraham Lincoln, Ulysses S. Grant, and Rutherford B. Hayes as they applied to Reconstruction of the South after the Civil War.

Trefousse, Hans Louis. *Impeachment of a President: Andrew Johnson, the Blacks and Reconstruction.* New York: Fordham University Press, 1999. Focuses on why Congress failed to impeach Johnson and the subsequent consequences for the failure of Reconstruction.

World Wide Web

"Andrew Johnson (1808–1875)." http://www.millercenter.virginia.edu/index.php/academic/americanpresident/johnson. Provides an extensive biographical sketch of President Andrew Johnson.

"Andrew Johnson (1808–1875)." http://www.mlwh.org/inside.asp?ID=91&subjectID=2. Features an online biographical sketch of Johnson that contains quotes by those who met and knew him, revealing much of his character.

"Andrew Johnson Cleveland Speech (September 3, 1866)." http://www.usa-presidents.info/speeches/cleveland-speech.html. Contains the full text of a rather inopportune speech that Johnson made concerning his thoughts about legislation being proposed by Radical Republicans and the need for a new political party.

"Articles of Impeachment." http://www.law.umkc.edu/faculty/projects/ftrials/impeach/articles.html. Presents the full text of the articles of impeachment against President Andrew Johnson.

"Finding Precedent: The Impeachment of Andrew Johnson." http://www.impeach-andrewjohnson.com/. Contains impeachment-related primary sources in the form of letters, speeches, correspondence, period newspaper articles and editorials, cartoons, and legal briefs. It also features a set of lesson plans and questions concerning the impeachment.

Johnson, Andrew, 1808–1875." http://www.gutenberg.org/browse/authors/j#a1650. Contains the full text of Andrew Johnson's State of the Union address after the death of Lincoln.

"Library of Congress—Johnson's Inaugural Address." http://memory.loc.gov/cgi-bin/ampage?collId=llcg&fileName=069/llcg069.db&recNum=629. Features the full text of Johnson's inaugural address given on March 3, 1865.

Multimedia Sources

The Presidents: The Lives and Legacies of 43 Leaders of the U.S. 2005. New York: A&E Home Entertainment Video, 2005. 3 DVDs. 258 minutes. This set devotes approximately six minutes to each president. DVD 2 contains information about President Andrew Johnson and can be purchased separately.

70. Construction of the Transcontinental Railroad (1869)

By 1869 railroads were becoming big business in the United States. Few establishments had the ability to employ so many men with skills ranging from engineer to ditch digger from one end of the country to the other. The operations were also intricate, involving carving tunnels through solid rock, laying track up steep grades, and crossing large rivers. Railroad building also entailed convoluted financial arrangements since the government only partially supported their construction. Americans understood their vital importance for linking various parts of the country, however, and invested heavily in them. The total investment in American railroads grew from $300 million in 1850 to $2.5 billion in 1870. The largest project during this time was the construction of the Transcontinental Railroad, which joined the Union Pacific Railroad in the East to the Central Pacific Railroad in the West. Each raced the other to the finish with Union Pacific laying 1,087 miles of track primarily through the Great Plains and the Central Pacific laying 690 miles of track mainly through the Sierra Nevada Mountains. When the golden spike was driven on May 10, 1869, at Promontory Point, Utah, to celebrate the completion of this engineering feat, passengers and freight were able to travel from Omaha, Nebraska, to Sacramento, California. Overnight, wagon trains, the Pony Express, and stagecoaches became extinct as other railroads were built to provide the necessary links to other parts of the country. A journey of similar distance that used to take six months now took only seven days.

TERM PAPER SUGGESTIONS

1. Discuss the role that Irish immigrants and Civil War veterans played in the construction of the Union Pacific's branch.

2. Chinese workers were such outstanding employees that the Central Pacific Railroad Company traveled to China to recruit more of them. Explore their treatment, working conditions, and the risks they assumed to build this branch of the railroad. Discuss the reasons why they went on strike.

3. As the "Iron Horse" crept further across the country leaving a permanent route for thousands of others to follow, American Indians realized that their lands were being invaded and occupied. Research which tribes were most affected and discuss the implications for their way of life.

4. The Chinese workforce suffered extensive losses through the use of unstable nitroglycerin explosives to blast holes through solid rock to create train tunnels. Explore the dangers they faced, their mortality rate, and how their work with the chemical evolved as work progressed.

5. Once the Transcontinental Railroad had been built, the railroad companies had a vested interest in ensuring that these areas of the country became populated so that they had a constant flow of passenger traffic and freight. Examine the sometimes nefarious role they had in settling this area of the country by misrepresenting the yearly amount of rainfall the area received, living conditions, and the like to attract homesteaders.

6. One of the most important contributions to construction of the Central Pacific Railroad was the surveying work performed by Theodore Dehone Judah (1826–1863). Using maps and other geographical information, analyze his contribution to the western branch of the Transcontinental Railroad.

ALTERNATIVE TERM PAPER SUGGESTIONS

1. As the railroad was being built, it created small mobile towns that moved along as different parts of the railroad were under construction. Assume that you have been elected temporary mayor of one of these mobile towns. A group of laborers would like to remain behind and have asked that you work on a plan to make the town permanent. Describe what you need in terms of infrastructure to make the town a viable entity.

2. Both companies have asked you to prepare a Web site of the Transcontinental Railroad that will attract passenger traffic. Create a hyperlinked Web site showing some of the more scenic parts of the trip from a nineteenth-century perspective, including the prevalence of great herds of bison, swaths of prairie grass and flowers, the presence of various American Indian tribes, and the like.

SUGGESTED SOURCES

Primary Sources

"Library of Congress—Pacific Railway Act." http://www.loc.gov/rr/program/ bib/ourdocs/PacificRail.html. Contains primary sources in the form of the full text of the act, Lincoln's support of the idea, maps of the route, exhibits showing some of the scenery, period articles from magazines, and more.

"Library of Congress—The Chinese in California." http://memory.loc.gov/ ammem/award99/cubhtml/cichome.html. Provides primary sources in the form of letters, diaries, period newspaper accounts, and thousands of images of how the Chinese were treated and the work they did to build California, especially on the Transcontinental Railroad.

Secondary Sources

Ambrose, Stephen. *Nothing Like It in the World: The Men Who Built the Transcontinental Railroad 1863–1869.* New York: Simon & Schuster, 2000. This exciting history contains a great deal of information about the surveyors, engineers, and financiers who made it possible.

Bain, David Haward. *Empire Express: Building the First Transcontinental Railroad.* New York: Penguin, 2000. Considered one of the most evocative works for recreating the times, people, and events surrounding the building of the Transcontinental Railroad, this book contains a great deal of information concerning both the Irish and Chinese contributions.

Douglas, George H. *All Aboard! The Railroad in American Life.* New York: Paragon House, 1992. Provides a social history of the railroads in the United States and what it was like to travel on them as a passenger in the nineteenth century.

Griswold, Wesley S. *A Work of Giants: Building the First Transcontinental Railroad.* New York: McGraw-Hill, 1962. Replete with colorful details and stories, this history depicts the Transcontinental Railroad as a magnificent feat of engineering and human toil.

McCague, James. *Moguls and Iron Men: The Story of the First Transcontinental Railroad.* New York: Harper & Row, 1964. Presents a history of the financing and construction plans for the Transcontinental Railroad.

Mayer, Lynn Rhodes, and Ken Vose. *Makin' Tracks: The Saga of the Transcontinental Railroad.* New York: Barnes & Noble Books, 1995. Filled with excerpts from diaries, period newspapers, handbills, illustrations, and reports, this work gives an exciting overview of this huge project.

Ogburn, Charlton. *Railroaders: The Great American Adventure.* Washington, DC: National Geographic Society, 1977. Places the Transcontinental

Railroad within the context of other American railroads and the people who built them, financed them, and made their fortunes owning them.

Perl, Lila. *To the Golden Mountain: The Story of the Chinese Who Built the Transcontinental Railroad*. New York: Benchmark Books, 2002. Written for secondary school students, this work provides a portrait of the hazards and working conditions faced by the Chinese laborers on the Transcontinental Railroad.

Robertson, Donald B. *Encyclopedia of Western Railroad History*. Caldwell, ID: Caxton Books, 1986. Traces the history of the rise and decline of railroads throughout the western part of the country.

Strom, Claire. *Profiting from the Plains: The Great Northern Railway and Corporate Development of the American West*. Seattle, WA: University of Washington Press, 2003. Presents an academic analysis of the business leaders who were behind creating a market for passenger and freight railroad traffic so that they could make their fortunes.

Williams, John H. *A Great and Shining Road: The Epic Story of the Transcontinental Railroad*. New York: Times Books, 1988. Provides a dramatic history of the places that this great railroad impacted.

World Wide Web

"Central Pacific Railroad Photographic History Museum." http://cprr.org/. Replete with black and white photographs and illustrations of different sites along the Central Pacific Railroad route, this outstanding source also contains short biographical sketches and a list of resource links and information about the Union Pacific part of the route.

"Chinese-American Contribution to the Transcontinental Railroad." http://cprr.org/Museum/Chinese.html. Presents an outstanding amount of information in the form of exhibits, pictures, and other primary sources concerning the Chinese sacrifices to building the Central Pacific part of the railroad.

"Driving the Last Spike." http://www.sfmuseum.org/hist1/rail.html. Accompanied by a picture of this famous event, this site also features a biography of surveyor Theodore Judah, information about the "Big Four" financial backers of the Central Pacific part of the track, and Judah's plans for the route.

"Guidebook of the Western United States." http://www.nps.gov/history/history/online_books/geology/publications/bul/612/index.htm. Provides the full text of a 1916 guidebook by Willis T. Lee and others who were commissioned by the U.S. Geological Survey to map all the important landmarks along the Transcontinental Railroad route including information about indigenous flora and fauna.

"The Transcontinental Railroad: Different Faces Behind the Work of the Age." http://bushong.net/dawn/about/college/ids100/. Gives an overview of the people who planned and financed the railroad and a portrait of the immigrant Irish and Chinese who physically built it.

"Treasures of Congress—Congress and the American West—The Transcontinental Railroad." http://www.archives.gov/exhibits/treasures_of _congress/page_15.html#. Provides a full text exhibit, plus an overview of the major Congressional document authorizing the construction of the Transcontinental Railroad, and a summary of the intentions of Congress during that time.

"Union Pacific History and Photos." http://www.uprr.com/aboutup/history/ index.shtml. Contains a similar set of links as the Central Pacific Railroad Photographic History Museum, but also includes maps, information about the equipment that was used to build the railroad, passenger trains, and a timeline.

Multimedia Sources

American Experience: Transcontinental Railroad. Alexandria, VA: PBS Home Video, 2002. 1 DVD. 120 minutes. This documentary film contains primary sources in the form of narrated excerpts from diaries, letters, and first-person accounts plus interviews with noted historians concerning the building of the Transcontinental Railroad. It also features an outstanding Web site at http://www.pbs.org/wgbh/amex/tcrr/ that is filled with lesson plans, resource links, and additional railroad-related information.

71. Rise of the Robber Barons (1870–1880s)

The accumulation of money in a capitalist society has never been a sin, but several entrepreneurs and venture capitalists took it to such extremes in the late nineteenth century that their wealth still surpasses twenty-first century billionaires such as Bill Gates and Warren Buffet. They were known as the Robber Barons. Although there were more than four, John D. Rockefeller, Cornelius Vanderbilt, Andrew Carnegie, and John Pierpont Morgan stand out because each was associated with total dominance of an industry or business. Rockefeller, the founder of Standard Oil, purchased oil wells and refineries until he gained almost complete control of all oil production in America. Carnegie did the same with steel by purchasing the mines that produced iron ore, the factories that produced the steel, and even the steamships used to ship it. Vanderbilt established a steamship empire during the California gold rush and then at the age of seventy switched to owning most of the railroads in the eastern part of the United States. Morgan owned a huge bank that brokered and financed many of the mergers and acquisitions that occurred among these companies. Although none of these men used a gun to obtain their wealth, they mercilessly exploited immigrant labor by paying low wages, forced out their competitors with cutthroat competition and coerced many politicians into ensuring that their monopolies persisted. At the end of their lives, all became great philanthropists, endowing colleges, museums, libraries, and hospitals, many of which still bear their names.

TERM PAPER SUGGESTIONS

1. Many of the "Robber Barons" used a business practice called vertical integration. Explain the pros and cons of vertical integration from a business and societal perspective.

2. Using John D. Rockefeller as an example, explain how he established a monopoly in the oil business. Discuss the pros and cons of this monopoly.

3. Discuss how the labor practices and employment conditions of the Robber Barons give birth to labor unions.

4. John D. Rockefeller believed in targeted philanthropy. By the end of his life he had given away approximately $550 million. Research some of Rockefeller's gifts to colleges, medical institutions, and the like, and explain how his practice may have enabled them to continue to thrive into the twenty-first century.

5. Discuss the dangers inherent in a few people controlling basic commodities such as oil, the main means of transportation, and a basic building material such as steel. Be sure to mention their ability to determine prices, wages, and conditions of employment.

6. In the time of the Robber Barons there were laws that prohibited one corporation or company from owning factories or plants in other states. Investigate how Samuel C. T. Dodd, a lawyer for John D. Rockefeller, circumvented those laws by the invention of the "trust."

ALTERNATIVE TERM PAPER SUGGESTIONS

1. Andrew Carnegie's Homestead Steel Plant in Pennsylvania has been struck because his manager, Henry Clay Frick, cut wages and demanded an end to

the union. Assume you are Frick's assistant. Draw up a plan for how you are going to break the strike.

2. Assume that you are a union organizer at the Homestead Plant. Design a blog that describes the low wages, long hours, and working conditions at the plant that will persuade your fellow workers to strike the plant.

SUGGESTED SOURCES

Primary Sources

Carnegie, Andrew. *Autobiography of Andrew Carnegie and the Gospel of Wealth.* New York: Signet Classics, 2006. Contains the memoirs of Carnegie and the full text of his gospel about the great responsibilities that go with wealth.

Dear Father—Dear Son: The Correspondence of John D. Rockefeller and John D. Rockefeller, Jr. New York: Fordham University Press, 1994. Presents letters between John D. Rockefeller Sr. and his son concerning the bequeathment of the father's fortune and the economic and social responsibilities that are also conveyed with the estate, plus the son's implicit understanding.

Secondary Sources

Beatty, Jack. *Age of Betrayal: The Triumph of Money in America.* New York: Alfred A. Knopf, 2007. Characterizes the Robber Baron age as one of gross economic inequalities among classes because the government betrayed its public trust. Beatty compares it with the twenty-first century Republican administration.

Buenker, John D., and Joseph Buenker, eds. *The Encyclopedia of the Gilded Age and Progessive Era.* Armonk, NY: Sharpe Reference, 2005. Furnishes outstanding overviews of the people, events, and business practices associated with the Gilded Age.

Chernow, Ron. *The House of Morgan: An American Banking Dynasty and the Rise of Modern Finance.* New York: Grove Press, 2001. Journalist Chernow makes this period come alive with his engaging history of Morgan's life and rise to dominance in the banking industry.

Chernow, Ron. *Titan: The Life of John D. Rockefeller, Sr.* New York: Vintage, 2004. Provides a readable biography of the life and times of Rockefeller, including information about the philanthropic stage of his life.

Edwards, Rebecca. *New Spirits: Americans in the Gilded Age, 1865–1905.* New York: Oxford University Press, 2005. Succeeds in striking a balance between the excesses and achievements of the Gilded Age.

Livesay, Harold C. *Andrew Carnegie and the Rise of Big Business.* 3rd ed. New York: Longman, 2006. Provides an outstanding account of the life and times of Andrew Carnegie.

Morris, Charles R. *The Tycoons: How Andrew Carnegie, John D. Rockefeller, Jay Gould, and J. P. Morgan Invented the American Supereconomy.* New York: Holt & Company, 2006. Chronicles the lives of four Robber Barons and how they were able to establish such hegemonies in their respective business ventures.

Porter, Glen, et al. *The Rise of Big Business, 1860–1920.* Wheeling, IL: Harlan Davidson, 2006. Furnishes a useful overview of the economic and political conditions that gave rise to the Gilded Age and the emergence of the Robber Barons.

Standiford, Les. *Meet You in Hell: Andrew Carnegie, Henry Clay Frick, and the Bitter Partnership that Transformed America.* New York: Crown, 2005. Relates the role that Frick and Carnegie played together in the Homestead strike and their eventual lifetime enmity.

Strouse, Jane. *Morgan: American Financier.* New York: Random House, 2000. Winner of the Bancroft Prize for history, Strouse's biography of J. P. Morgan places it within a twentieth-century perspective.

Whitelaw, Nancy. *The Homestead Strike of 1892.* Greensboro, NC: Morgan Reynolds Publishing, 2006. Written for secondary school students, this work gives a complete overview of the working conditions in the steel plant that precipitated the strike and a history of the event.

World Wide Web

"A Classification of American Wealth—the Gilded Age." http://www.raken.com/american_wealth/Gilded_age_index7.asp. Contains a hyperlinked overview of all the major Robber Barons within the context of the Gilded Age.

"Cornelius Vanderbilt." http://www.stfrancis.edu/ba/ghkickul/stuwebs/bbios/biograph/vanderbi.htm. Furnishes an overview of the life and times of Cornelius Vanderbilt together with a bibliography of additional biographical works.

"Gilded Age 1878–1889." http://www.americaslibrary.gov/cgi-bin/page.cgi/jb/gilded. Outlines and describes the economic conditions that characterized the Gilded Age, a term coined by the great humorist, Mark Twain.

"The Homestead Strike." http://www.bgsu.edu/departments/acs/1890s/carnegie/strike.html. Gives an overview of the strike together with a chronology of events and resource links.

"John D. Rockefeller." http://johndrockefeller.org/. Provides an online bio-graphical sketch of John D. Rockefeller, the founder of the Standard Oil Company.

"John D. Rockefeller & the Standard Oil Company." http://www.micheloud .com/FXM/SO/index.htm. This rich, hyperlinked site shows how Rock-efeller came to dominate the oil industry.

"John Pierpont Morgan and the American Corporation." http://claver.gprep .org/fac/sjochs//jpmorgan-1.htm. Furnishes an overview of how J. P. Morgan exercised his banking and financial dominance during the Gilded Age.

Multimedia Sources

American Experience: The Richest Man in the World: Andrew Carnegie. Alexandria, VA: PBS Home Video, 1997. 1 DVD. 58 minutes. This site at http:// www.pbs.org/wgbh/amex/carnegie/filmmore/index.html accompanies the documentary. It features a timeline, gallery of photographs of various Robber Barons mansions, and a teacher's guide complete with lesson plans and questions concerning the Gilded Age.

Empires of Industry—Andrew Carnegie and the Age of Steel. New York: A&E Home Entertainment Video, 2005. 1 DVD. 50 minutes. This History Channel presentation relates the story of how Carnegie created his steel empire.

The Rockefellers. Alexandria, VA: PBS Home Video, 2000. 1 DVD. 210 minutes. Replete with illustrations and photographs, this documentary narrates the extraordinary impact that four generations of Rockefellers have had on America.

72. Final Solution for the American Indian (1871–1879)

Every treaty that had been signed between various American Indian tribes and the U.S. government had been abrogated in the name of the California and Colorado gold rushes, Manifest Destiny, the Mexican War, and other reasons that Euro-Americans had for taking Indian lands. What was left of three hundred thousand American Indians remained concentrated on the Great Plains. Their tribes, consisting mainly of the Sioux and the Cheyenne, were caught in a classic vise as settlers, cattlemen, farmers, and railroad workers arriving from both coasts sought to remove them as a last obstacle to progress. The passage of the Indian Appropriations Act in 1871 was the first step toward that goal. It stated that American Indians did not belong to their own sovereign nations and that the United States no longer needed to make treaties with them. Overnight, Indians became "wards" of the U.S. government subject to placement on designated reservations.

The second act targeted the buffalo, their sole source of food, clothing, shelter, and tools, for extinction. Generals William Tecumseh Sherman and Philip H. Sheridan recommended that the government fully support the buffalo slaughter to "settle the Indian question." The government obliged by supplying hunters with free ammunition to exterminate the buffalo, thus starving the remaining tribes and forcing them onto reservations. Immense herds of buffalo were eradicated from the plains area within four years. Although official records were not kept, historians place the number at more than six million.

TERM PAPER SUGGESTIONS

1. The Plains Indian tribes were nomadic, following their main source of food, clothing, shelter, and tools, the buffalo, from place to place. Analyze the implications of the Indian Appropriations Act of 1871 for sustaining the Indian way of life.

2. In 1874, Generals Sherman and Sheridan urged President Ullysses S. Grant to veto a federal bill to protect the dwindling buffalo herds. Examine their reasons and military tactics for doing so.

3. Buffalo hunter "Wild Bill" Cody recognized that the buffalo were being exterminated. Research his congressional testimony and the arguments that he made to save them.

4. Data on the buffalo slaughter were not kept, but estimates from an 1872 western Kansas report indicate that approximately two thousand hunters killed fifteen buffalo per day. Research and describe the massacre of the buffalo, including killing them from trains and "jumping" them from cliffs.

5. Investigate the changes in the American Indian population before and after passage of the Indian Appropriations Act of 1871.

6. Two tribes that valiantly strove to retain their lands were the Santee, Sioux of western Minnesota, and the Teton, Sioux of the Great Plains. The former tribe tried to adopt White ways while the latter fought as long as they could to keep their lands and way of life. Research how each tribe fared with their decision.

ALTERNATIVE TERM PAPER SUGGESTIONS

1. Assume that you are a cultural anthropologist who has been asked to make an online presentation about how the slaughter of the buffalo hastened the demise of the remaining plains tribes. Design a Web site with images of how the tribes were totally dependent upon the buffalo, including period images showing the extent of the buffalo slaughter.

2. Assume you are chief of the Teton Sioux who needs to persuade his people to fight against the encroachment of settlers and soldiers and not give up any more land. Prepare a podcast that will convince them to fight and not go to a reservation.

SUGGESTED SOURCES

Primary Sources

Bill, Buffalo. *The Life of Hon. William F. Cody/Buffalo Bill: An Autobiography.* Lincoln, NE: University of Nebraska Press, 1978. Provides primary sources in the form of first-person accounts, including Cody's views on the possible extinction of the buffalo.

Foster, John, ed. *Buffalo.* Edmonton, Canada: University of Alberta Press, 1992. Consists of a small set of papers analyzing the symbiotic relationship between the Plains Indians and the American bison.

Secondary Sources

Barker, Joanne. *Sovereignty Matters: Locations of Contestation and Possibility in Indigenous Struggles for Self-Determination.* Lincoln, NE: University of Nebraska Press, 2005. Discusses how the consideration of tribal sovereignty has affected Indian relations with other tribes and their history in dealing with governments.

Carter, Robert. *Buffalo Bill Cody: The Man Behind the Legend.* New York: John Wiley & Sons, 2000. Provides an exciting, readable biography of the life and times of Cody.

Churchill, Ward. *A Little Matter of Genocide: Holocaust and Denial in the Americas, 1492 to the Present.* San Francisco, CA: City Light Books, 1998. Noted Native American scholar Churchill presents a history of the broken treaties and maltreatment that constitutes a genocide of the American Indian from 1492 through the twentieth century.

Harvard Project on American Indian Economic Development. *The State of the Native Nations: Conditions under U.S. Policies of Self-Determination.* New York: Oxford University Press, 2007. Examines the political, economic, social, and cultural implications of the treaties that have been made with the American Indian within a contemporary context.

Isenberg, Andrew C. *The Destruction of the Bison: An Environmental History, 1750–1920.* New York: Cambridge University Press, 2000. Analyzes the human and environmental causes of the near extinction of the buffalo, which scientists believe may have numbered more than thirty million animals.

Jones, Dorothy V. *License for Empire: Colonialism by Treaty in Early America.* Chicago, IL: University of Chicago Press, 1982. Investigates and examines the abuses of the treaties by the U.S. government and how American Indians were unable to understand them.

Kvasnicka, Robert M. "United States Indian Treaties and Agreements." In *History of Indian-White Relations,* edited by Wilcomb E. Washburn. Vol. 4, *Handbook of North American Indians.* Washington, DC: Smithsonian Institution Press, 1988. Provides a discussion of the congressional debate concerning the Indian Appropriations Act of 1871 and how the process of treaty making ceased.

Matthews, Anne. *Where the Buffalo Roam.* New York: Grove Weidenfeld, 1992. Provides information about a plan to restore the Great Plains to their natural condition replete with indigenous prairie grasses and animals, including the buffalo.

Prucha, Francis Paul. *American Indian Treaties: The History of a Political Anomaly.* Berkeley, CA: University of California Press, 1994. Furnishes a history of treaty making between the U.S. government and American Indian including the historical background behind the passage of the Indian Appropriations Act of 1871.

Wetmore, Helen Cody, and Zane Grey. *Buffalo Bill: Last of the Great Scouts.* Lincoln, NE: University of Nebraska Press, 2003. This is a new edition of the 1899 book that was co-written by Helen Cody, sister of Buffalo Bill Cody, along with noted novelist Zane Grey. Laudatory of Buffalo Bill Cody's way of life, it also contains first-person accounts of the period.

Wilson, Waziyatawin Angela. *For Indigenous Eyes Only: A Decolonization Handbook.* Santa Fe, NM: School of American Research Press, 2005. Provides arguments for how Native Americans can escape the colonization mentality that has gripped them as a result of being relegated to reservations.

World Wide Web

"Buffalo Slaughter." http://history.cbc.ca/history/?MIval=EpisContent.html &lang=E&series_id=1&episode_id=10&chapter_id=2&page_id=2. This short overview of the eradication of the American bison also contains a set of resource links and teacher lesson plans. The initial overview mentions the role that Generals Sheridan and Sherman played in advocating the slaughter.

"A Chronological History of the United States Indian Policy and the Indian Response from 1789 to the Present." http://www.humboldt.edu/~go1/kellogg/Chrono.html. Furnishes an outstanding, annotated timeline of each American Indian treaty and the Indians' response to it.

"The Extermination of the American Bison by William Temple Hornaday." http://www.gutenberg.org/etext/17748. Contains the full text of a documentary book concerning the systematic slaughter of the American buffalo during the mid-nineteenth century.

"Indian Appropriations Act." http://www.murdoch.edu.au/elaw/issues/v2n1/ryser21.txt. Provides a legal and historical analysis of the relations between the U.S. government and American Indian tribes, including information about the effect of the Indian Appropriations Act of 1871.

"The National Bison Association." http://www.bisoncentral.com/. Click on the history category for a short overview of the history of the bison, plus some statistics and data.

"New Perspectives on the West." http://www.pbs.org/weta/thewest/people/a_c/buffalobill.htm. Scroll down the left-hand side of this site and click on individual names to retrieve biographical sketches of influential people who were involved in the West during the time of the Indian Appropriations Act of 1871 and the buffalo slaughter.

"Works by Buffalo Bill." http://www.gutenberg.org/browse/authors/c#a4524. Project Gutenberg contains the full text of three autobiographical works by William Frederick Cody, also known as Buffalo Bill and Wild Bill Cody.

Multimedia Sources

The West. Santa Monica, CA: PBS Home Video, 1996. 5 DVDs. 707 minutes. Discs 3 and 4 are best for showing how the American Indian way of life was intimately connected to the survival of the buffalo and how both were almost extinguished during a U.S. government-sponsored campaign to remove them from the West.

73. Boss Tweed's Ring (1871–1872)

Under the corrupt leadership of William Marcy Tweed (1823–1878), who at various times was a Democratic alderman, U.S. Congressman, State Senator, and grand Sachem of Tammany Hall, New York City was plundered of millions of dollars of taxpayers' funds. Beginning in 1870 Tweed's theft of monies accelerated when he pushed a charter through the New York legislature, giving the city authority to audit all city accounts in offices where he and his cronies had control. Within two years, New York City's debts increased from $36 million to about $136 million with no accounting to show how it had occurred. Tweed's modus operandi involved constructing large government buildings, such as the New York County Courthouse, taking kickbacks from all the work that was done and charging the city an enormous cost in overruns. The courthouse that was supposed to cost $500,000 eventually cost taxpayers $8,000,000. Tweed courted labor unions and Roman Catholics. Both groups were being persecuted and needed his civic support. While no accountant was ever able to determine the precise extent of his personal theft, estimates are that Tweed stole between $75 million to $200 million dollars. As public indignation mounted, Tweed was finally brought down in 1871 by the combined efforts of Samuel Jones Tilden and his Committee of Seventy, Thomas Nast, a muckraking cartoonist for *Harper's Weekly,* and the *New York Times,* which published a story containing proof of Tweed's crimes. Tweed died in jail in 1878.

TERM PAPER SUGGESTIONS

1. William Marcy Tweed was the epitome of a political system known as "boss-ism." The system still has its supporters and detractors. Examine the concept and discuss how Tweed symbolized its excesses and benefits.

2. Discuss how New York City politics are still thought to suffer from the legacy of the Tweed Ring.

3. Tammany Hall is an old politically based club that has been instrumental in electing many politicians, including U.S. presidents. Research the history of this club and describe how it was and still is able to have such a powerful influence on city and national politics.

4. Tweed feared Thomas Nast, the cartoonist for *Harper's Weekly,* because, although many of the constituents who voted for Tweed could not read, they could understand the message in Nast's cartoons. Analyze the power of Nast's cartoons and the role they played in dethroning Tweed and his ring of thieves.

5. A crony who had not received a sufficient bribe turned over evidence of Tweed's misdeeds to the *New York Times.* The paper was offered $5 million dollars not to publish the article. Examine the role that the *New York Times* played in convicting Tweed.

6. Many people still think that Tweed did some good things for the city by distributing welfare to the poor in the form of employment on huge public works projects. Discuss Tweed's building of public hospitals and orphanages and obtaining the land for the Metropolitan Museum of Art and other city works.

ALTERNATIVE TERM PAPER SUGGESTIONS

1. Using cartoon software such as "Comic Life" available at http://www.plasq .com, design a "graphic biography" of the life and times of Boss Tweed, and cite and incorporate some of Nast's cartoons about him.

2. Assume you have been charged with prosecuting the case against Tweed. Explain to the jurors step by step how Tweed built his empire of corruption and why they personally have been financially and morally harmed by it.

SUGGESTED SOURCES

Primary Sources

Riordan, William L., and Pete Quinn. *Plunkitt of Tammany Hall: A Series of Very Plain Talks on Very Practical Politics.* Reprint. New York: Signet Classics, 1995. George Washington Plunkitt was one of Tweed's cronies. This work explains exactly how a corrupt political machine works by the exchange of kickbacks, endorsements, and bribes for access, permits, and the like.

"Thomas Nast Gallery 1870–January 1871." http://greatcaricatures.com/ articles_galleries/nast/html/02_nast.html. Contains images of the cartoons created by Thomas Nast that depict the corruption of Boss Tweed and his political cronies.

Secondary Sources

Ackerman, Kenneth D. *Boss Tweed: The Rise and Fall of the Corrupt Pol Who Conceived the Soul of Modern New York.* New York: Carroll & Graf, 2005. Succeeds in showing both the corrupting side of the Tweed Ring and some of the things that they did to help the poor.

Allen, Oliver E. *The Tiger: The Rise and Fall of Tammany Hall.* Reading, MA: Addison-Wesley, 1993. Traces the history of the growth and development of Tammany Hall from 1786 to 1961, including the period when it was dominated by Tweed.

Burrows, Edwin G., and Mike Wallace. *Gotham: A History of New York City to 1898.* New York: Oxford University Press, 2000. This massive history brings the life and times of Tweed's New York City alive and places the events surrounding his ring within a nineteenth-century perspective.

Ellis, Edward Robb. *The Epic of New York City: A Narrative History*. New York: Carrol & Graf, 2004. Provides a well-written and massively researched work on the history of New York City, including information about daily operations of the Tweed Ring.

Gordon, Michael. *The Orange Riots: Irish Political Violence in New York City, 1870 and 1871*. Ithaca, NY: Cornell University Press, 1993. Describes the riots by the Irish in New York City during Tweed's time and includes a history of the discrimination they suffered and their reasons for supporting politicians like Tweed.

Jackson, Kenneth T., and David S. Dunbar. *Empire City: New York Through the Centuries*. New York: Columbia University Press, 2005. Gives a broad history of New York up to September 11, 2001, that includes information about the Tweed Ring.

Lynch, Dennis. *"Boss" Tweed: The Story of a Grim Generation*. New Brunswick, NJ: Transaction Publishers, 2002. Relates the story of the economic and political circumstances that created Boss Tweed and enabled him to thrive.

Mandelbaum, Seymour J. *Boss Tweed's New York*. Chicago, IL: Ivan R. Dee, 1990. Depicts Tweed as someone who actually helped democratize New York society by acknowledging the rights of immigrants and the poor to city services.

Mushabac, Jane, and Angela Wigan. *A Short and Remarkable History of New York City*. New York: Fordham University Press, 1999. Use this short work to get an overview of the before and after history concerning the Tweed Ring.

Mushkat, Jerome. *Tammany; The Evolution of a Political Machine, 1789–1865*. Syracuse, NY: Syracuse University Press, 1993. Gives the history of how Tammany Hall became a major political club that could deliver votes and win elections for various politicians.

Royko, Mike. *Boss: Richard J. Daley of Chicago*. New York: Plume, 1988. In more recent times, Mayor Richard J. Daley of Chicago was a legacy of the Boss Tweed School of city machine politics.

World Wide Web

"Bossism and the City." http://www.swarthmore.edu/SocSci/rbannis1/Progs/Bibs/Bossism.html. Furnishes a bibliography of books and periodical articles regarding the development of bossism in New York City and other major American cities.

"Boss Tweed and the Tammany Hall Machine." http://www.albany.edu/~dkw42/tweed.html. Shows both sides of the concept of bossism as typified by Tweed's Ring.

"Boss Tweed, July 4, 2005." http://www.gothamgazette.com/article/feature
-commentary/20050704/202/1467. Contains a lengthy edited transcript
of an interview with Ken Ackerman concerning his book, *Boss Tweed:
The Rise and Fall of the Corrupt Pol Who Conceived of the Soul of Modern
New York*.

"Tammany Hall Links: New York City's Legendary Political Machine." http://
www.davidpietrusza.com/tammany-hall-links.html. Contains hundreds
of biographical sketches relating to past mayors a well as many links to
Boss Tweed and the scandals involving his time as an elected official.

"The Tweed Ring: William Marcy Tweed (1823–1878)." http://www.u-s
-history.com/pages/h703.html. Provides a short biographical sketch of
Tweed together with hyperlinked sketches to Thomas Nast cartoon sites
and other people involved in Tweed's arrest and trial.

"Tweed, William Marcy, (1823–1878)." http://bioguide.congress.gov/scripts/
biodisplay.pl?index=T000440. Presents a short biographical sketch of
Boss Tweed.

"Urban Politics: Machines and Reformers." http://www1.cuny.edu/portal_ur/
content/voting_curriculum/7_8th_pdfs/8th%20Lesson%204_Voting
%20(38-52).pdf. This superb curriculum unit is replete with term
paper questions that can be used for the Tweed Ring, bossism, and
other urban political topics.

Multimedia Sources

*You Are There—American Grows Up/The Great Comstock Silver Strike/The Over-
throw of the Tweed Ring*. Chatsworth, CA: Woodhaven Entertainment,
2004. 1 DVD. 50 minutes. Narrated by former newscaster Walter
Cronkite, this DVD provides a brief history of how and why William
Marcy Tweed created a powerful urban political machine that almost
succeeded in bankrupting New York City.

74. Great Chicago Fire (1871)

Carl Sandburg's poem entitled, "Chicago," beginning with the lines "Hog
butcher for the world, tool maker, stacker of wheat, player with railroads
and the nation's freight handler," does justice to a thriving, bustling city
before October 8, 1871. It was filled with immigrants, factories, grain
silos, ten railroad lines, stockyards, and lumberyards. It was also constructed almost entirely of wood with fifty-seven miles of wood-paved
streets to combat roads and sidewalks that were usually packed with

mud. Since it was a city more in the making than it was established, many buildings and houses were substandard. Raising the requirements for fire protection would have incurred a tax increase, and no politician dared risk losing reelection. Chicago's nickname is also the "Windy City." Combine this natural state with a summer of drought and the conditions were perfect for an historic conflagration. The fire began in the west division of the city and, fanned by the wind, quickly spread to the south division, igniting the gasworks. It spread to the northern division, consumed the waterworks, and collapsed the roof housing the pumps needed to extinguish the fire. Although firemen from as far away as Pennsylvania came to Chicago's aid, it was too late. After burning for two and a half days, the fire took three hundred lives, destroyed the homes of ninety thousand residents, eighteen thousand buildings, and caused $200 million in damages. Historically it is compared with the Great Fire of London in 1666 and the damage that Napoleon's army did during the Siege of Moscow in 1812.

TERM PAPER SUGGESTIONS

1. Many times a series of contributing factors coalesces at a propitious time to help create natural disasters. Analyze the contributing factors of the Chicago fire and discuss which ones could have been controlled, possibly preventing the fire.

2. The alleged tipping of a lantern by Mrs. O'Leary's cow has been part of the folk legend concerning the fire's origin. Mrs. O'Leary, however, was finally cleared of any responsibility for starting the fire in 1997. Read accounts of the fire and its origins, and discuss their possibilities.

3. After such an event, many people look for a scapegoat to personalize their losses. Mrs. O'Leary was a woman, an immigrant, and Irish Catholic. Reporter Michael Ahern falsely described her connection to the fire in *The Chicago Tribune's* first postfire issue. He did not retract it until 1893. Analyze why people need a scapegoat for natural disasters and what Ahern's motives were for choosing Mrs. O'Leary as Chicago's.

4. Read accounts by people who survived the fire and describe their reaction to it. Determine if there are differences between the poor and rich concerning their optimism about starting over, loss of their possessions, and the like.

5. Chief Fire Marshal Robert A. Williams was on record as having urged city officials to pass and enforce more fire resistant building codes. Investigate why his warnings were ignored by other city officials.

6. Research and describe how fires were fought in the nineteenth century, including the use of explosives.

ALTERNATIVE TERM PAPER SUGGESTIONS

1. Assume you are an urban planner who has been assigned to plan a more fire-resistant section of the city that will contain some public buildings and residential areas. Draw a series of plans that are feasible given nineteenth-century construction materials.

2. Using before and after fire photographs of the city, research how long it took various areas of the city to recover.

SUGGESTED SOURCES

Primary Sources

Lowe, David, ed. *The Great Chicago Fire: Eyewitness Accounts and Seventy Contemporary Photographs and Illustrations.* Mineola, NY: Dover, 1979. Contains a collection of first-person accounts of the Great Chicago Fire.

Murphy, Jim. *The Great Fire.* New York: Scholastic, 2006. Written for secondary school students, this work weaves primary sources into a riveting account of the Great Chicago Fire.

Secondary Sources

Bales, Richard F. *The Great Chicago Fire and the Myth of Mrs. O'Leary's Cow.* Jefferson, NC: McFarland, 2002. Presents a scientific analysis of the origin and spread of the fire and debunks the myth that Mrs. O'Leary's cow ignited it by tipping over a kerosene lantern.

Cowan, Davis. *Great Chicago Fires: Historic Blazes That Shaped a City.* Chicago, IL: Lake Claremont Press, 2001. Focuses on other damaging fires during the development of Chicago and describes the evolution of fire fighters from a typical bucket brigade to a modern urban department.

Cromie, Robert. *The Great Chicago Fire.* Nashville, TN: Rutledge Hill Press, 1994. Gives a detailed narrative of the events during the fire, together with period photographs and illustrations.

The Great Chicago Fire of 1871: Three Illustrated Accounts from Harper's Weekly. Ashland, OR: Lewis Osborne, 1969. Provides three primary source accounts of the great fire that were published in an 1871 issue of *Harper's Weekly.*

Little, Kenneth. *History of Chicago Fire Houses of the 19th Century.* Chicago, IL: Ken Little and John McNalis, 1996. Although this book is self-published, it does contain interesting information about how nineteenth-century fire fighting was accomplished.

Lowe, David. *The Great Chicago Fire.* New York: Dover, 1979. Provides a narrative account that is filled with eyewitness accounts, including seventy original before and after photographs of the fire.

Miller, Donald L. *City of the Century: The Epic of Chicago and the Making of America.* New York: Simon & Schuster, 1997. Provides an exciting history of the birth and growth of Chicago, including information about the great fire of 1871.

Miller, Ross. *The Great Chicago Fire.* Chicago, IL: University of Illinois Press, 2000. Discusses the aftermath of the fire and how it affected Chicago during the next century.

Sawislak, Karen. *Smoldering City: Chicagoans and the Great Fire, 1871–1874.* Chicago, IL: University of Chicago Press, 1995. This outstanding book looks at the years immediately following the fire and the tremendous rebuilding efforts of the city.

Smith, Carl. *Urban Disorder and the Shape of Belief: The Great Chicago Fire, the Haymarket Bomb, and the Model Town of Pullman.* Chicago, IL: University of Chicago Press, 1996. Focuses on these three events as being inevitable in the birth and rise of a great American city.

Weskin, Mel. *Mrs. O'Leary's Comet: Cosmic Causes of the Great Chicago Fire.* Chicago, IL: Academy Chicago Publishers, 1985. Presents information regarding the meteor shower theory of the origin of the fire.

World Wide Web

"Chicago City of the Century." http://www.pbs.org/wgbh/amex/chicago/index.html. Accompanies the film referred to in the subsequent Multimedia Sources section. It features a map of various spots where the fire broke out and spread, a timeline, first-person accounts, teacher resources and lesson plans, and biographical sketches of famous Chicagoans.

"Did the Cow Do It?" http://www.thechicagofire.com/. Examines the cause of the Great Chicago Fire and provides a transcript of Mrs. O'Leary's testimony.

"1871: The Great Chicago Fire." http://www.chipublib.org/004chicago/disasters/great_fire.html. Gives a panoramic view of the aftermath of the fire in many of the city's divisions plus a timeline of events involving the fire and an excerpt from a police commissioner's report implicating Mrs. O'Leary and her cow.

"The Great Chicago Fire and the Web of Memory." http://www.chicagohs.org/fire/index.html. This superb site presents primary sources in the form of eyewitness accounts, period magazine articles, illustrations, images of artifacts that survived the fire, and a library of relevant texts and Web sites.

"Old Town Triangle District." http://www.cityofchicago.org/Landmarks/O/OldTown.html. Supplies maps and photographs of prefire areas of Chicago and some of the buildings.

"The O'Leary Legend." http://www.chicagohistory.org/fire/oleary/essay-2.html. Provides a brief history of the man who started the story about Mrs. O'Leary's cow starting the fire.

"Site of the Origin of the Chicago Fire of 1871." http://www.cityofchicago.org/Landmarks/S/SiteChicagoFire.html. Contains photographs and maps showing the exact spot where the fire originated.

Multimedia Sources

Chicago—City of the Century. Santa Monica, CA: PBS Paramount, 2004. 3 DVDs. 270 minutes. Provides information about the birth, growth, and development of Chicago as one of America's premier cities. It also includes information about the Chicago Fire of 1871.

The Great Chicago Fire. Silver Spring, MD: Discovery Communications, 2003. 1 DVD. 50 minutes. Experts re-create the events in Mrs. O'Leary's barn the day of the Chicago Fire and remake the fire to show what it would have been like to have experienced it

75. Creation of Yellowstone National Park (1872)

For years mountain men such as Jim Bridger and John Colter had been laughed at for their tales of a strange land in present-day Wyoming, Montana, and Idaho that contained magical blue pools of boiling hot water, geysers that erupted regularly and shot hundreds of feet in the air, mud pots that bubbled spontaneously at the surface of the ground, and other geological phenomena. Finally, in 1870 Nathaniel P. Langford and Henry D. Washburn formed an expedition to explore the area and set the record straight. Joining them was Lieutenant Gustavus Doane of Fort Ellis and several infantrymen. In the Yellowstone region, they confirmed the existence of the scenery and geological wonders that so many trappers and mountain men had wondrously described. At their last camp, they proposed that Congress set aside approximately 3,472 square miles or 2.2 million acres of canyons, lakes, rivers, and mountain ranges as a national park for future generations to camp in, sightsee, and enjoy. After several more expeditions designed to capture the beauty of the area in photographs and paintings so that Congress would pass the necessary legislation, the group convinced President Ulysses S. Grant to sign the Act of Dedication in 1872. Yellowstone became the first national park in the United States, thus initiating future parks and efforts toward conserving some of America's most beautiful natural possessions.

TERM PAPER SUGGESTIONS

1. Describe the visit of John Colter to Yellowstone in 1810 and his encounter with the Blackfoot and Crow tribes in 1809. Why did so many people think that he was lying about the geological phenomena that he observed?

2. Colter was followed by the Folsom expedition that did spur further investigation into Yellowstone. Describe their journey into the Gallatin Valley and what they would have seen.

3. The most enterprising expedition consisted of the Washburn-Langford-Doane party. Describe their educational backgrounds, how they planned their trip, and why their findings were accepted without question by the government.

4. Langford was so taken with the idea of a national park that he traveled east to speak to the news media, gave speeches and interviews, and did anything he could to make certain that Congress created Yellowstone National Park. Discuss his legacy as one of America's first conservationists.

5. Discuss and analyze how the artist Thomas Moran helped publicize the scenic beauty of Yellowstone.

6. Although Congress created Yellowstone National Park in 1872, they provided no funding for it to be preserved or maintained. Investigate the problems that early superintendents had managing a 2.2 million acre area park with no funds.

ALTERNATIVE TERM PAPER SUGGESTIONS

1. Assume you have been hired by Langford to travel east and present information about the natural beauty of Yellowstone. Create a Web site of images from all areas of the park that will captivate doubting members of Congress. Accompany the images with geological phenomena explanations of what is occurring so that you can answer legislators' questions.

2. Using images and montages from films of Yellowstone, create a two-minute iMovie that dwells primarily on nineteenth-century aspects of its history.

SUGGESTED SOURCES

Primary Sources

"The Discovery of Yellowstone Park by Nathaniel Pitt Langford." http://www
.gutenberg.org/etext/11145. Contains the full text of the expedition
notes that Langford took as he discovered the wonders of soon-to-be
Yellowstone National Park.

Murphy, Thomas D. *Three Wonderlands of the American West.* Boston, MA: Page,
1919. Features primary sources in the form of maps and photographs
of Ferdinand Hayden's expedition and Thomas Moran's paintings of
Yellowstone.

Vinton, Stallo. *John Colter, Discoverer of Yellowstone Park: An Account of his Explo-
ration in 1807 and of his Further Adventures as Hunter; Trapper; Indian
Fighter; Pathfinder…Member of the Lewis and Clark Expedition.*
New York: E. Eberstadt, 1926. This five-page monograph contains John
Colter's account of his experience in the Yellowstone area.

Secondary Sources

Fishbein, Seymour L. *Yellowstone Country: The Enduring Wonder.* Washington,
DC: National Geographic Society, 1989. Contains beautiful photographs suitable for scanning of many of the natural wonders of Yellowstone.

Frantz, Joe B. *Aspects of the American West.* College Station, TX: Texas A&M
University Press, 1976. Focuses on the philosophical aspect of conserving
wilderness areas for future generations and the problems that can be
encountered when obtaining funding.

Haines, Aubrey L. *Yellowstone National Park: Its Exploration and Establishment.*
Washington, DC: Government Printing Office, 1974. Provides a com-
plete history of the early expeditions that were instrumental in creating
Yellowstone National Park.

Janetski, Joel C. *The Indians of Yellowstone Park.* Salt Lake City, UT: University of
Utah Press, 1987. Describes various Indian tribes that lived in what is
now Yellowstone National Park.

Keller, Robert H., and Michael F. Turek. *American Indians & National Parks.*
Tucson, AZ: University of Arizona Press, 1999. Provides a scholarly
history of the relationship between various Indian tribes and the national
parks.

Kirk, Ruth. *Exploring Yellowstone.* Seattle, WA: University of Washington Press,
1972. Examines the issues involved with trying to maintain and conserve
a national park with no government funds, and with giving the public
access.

Nabokov, Peter, and Lawrence Loendorf. *Restoring a Presence: American Indians and Yellowstone National Park*. Norman, OK: University of Oklahoma Press, 2004. Focuses on the ownership of park lands by American Indian tribes and the consequences of those claims to the conservation and preservation of Yellowstone National Park.

Peterson, David. *Yellowstone: Like No Place on Earth*. Helena, MT: Farcountry Press. Contains contemporary landscape photographs of Yellowstone along with excerpts from the expedition book by Nathaniel Pitt Langford entitled *The Discovery of Yellowstone Park*.

Saunders, Richard L., ed. *A Yellowstone Reader: The National Park in Popular Fiction, Folklore, and Verse*. Salt Lake City, UT: University of Utah Press, 2003. Supplies a colorful collection of stories about Yellowstone National Park.

Smith, Robert B., and Lee J. Siegel. *Windows into the Earth: The Geologic Story of Yellowstone and Grand Teton National Parks*. New York: Oxford University Press, 2000. Contains the complete geological history of two great western national parks.

Spence, Mark David. *Dispossessing the Wilderness: Indian Removal and the National Parks*. New York: Oxford University Press, 2000. Documents the removal of various Indian tribes from national parks such as Yellowstone to create a pristine wilderness area for tourists.

World Wide Web

"The Exploring Era (1851–63)." http://www.nps.gov/history/history/online _books/haines1/iee1c.htm. Contains many primary sources in the form of first-person accounts of fur trappers and mountain men such as Jim Bridger, who describe the geological wonders of Yellowstone.

"The Folsom Party (1869)." http://www.nps.gov/history/history/online_books/ haines1/iee2b.htm. Refers to first-person accounts of the Folsom expedition to describe the natural wonders of the Yellowstone area.

"Geothermal Features and How They Work." http://www.nps.gov/yell/nature science/geothermal.htm. Gives an easy-to-understand account of how the geological wonders of Yellowstone actually function.

"The Greater Yellowstone Ecosystem." http://www.greateryellowstone.org/ ecosystem/. Provides an overview with maps and illustrations of the entire Yellowstone National Park.

"The Lewis and Clark Era (1805–1814)." http://www.nps.gov/history/history/ online_books/haines1/iee1a.htm. Presents an overview of the expedition's accounts of what is now part of Yellowstone National Park, including mention of Colter's experiences and sightings in the area.

"Yellowstone National Park." http://www.nps.gov/yell/. Contains the official National Parks Service site about Yellowstone, including links about its history, culture, and more.

"Yellowstone National Park: Its Exploration and Establishment: Biographical Appendix." http://www.nps.gov/history/history/online_books/haines1/iee4a.htm. Provides a series of biographical sketches of all the people who were instrumental in exploring and leading the battle to create the first national park at Yellowstone.

"Yellowstone National Park's First 130 Years." http://windowsintowonderland.org/history/army&nps/page3.htm. Contains a history replete with illustrations and photographs of the important people and events involved with the creation of the first national park.

Multimedia Sources

The Living Edens: Yellowstone: America's Sacred Wilderness. Alexandria, VA: PBS Home Video, 2001. 1 DVD. 60 minutes. Consists of a photographic display of the natural beauties and wonders of Yellowstone National Park.

Yellowstone—The World's First National Park. Chicago, IL: Questar, 2001. 1 DVD. 135 minutes. Presents significant information about the history of Yellowstone National Park.

76. Trial of Susan B. Anthony and the Rights of Women (1873)

Imagine if one were a woman on trial facing a jury totally composed of men? Imagine writing a check to the Internal Revenue Service every year, but being unable to vote in elections that decide the distribution of those collected taxes? While these rights seem self-evident now, they were not during the lifetime of suffragist Susan B. Anthony (1820–1902). In 1872, in violation of the law, she voted in the presidential election hoping that her eventual arrest could be used as a test case to put the issue of women's voting rights before the Supreme Court. Her case was somewhat bungled by her pro–women's rights attorney, Henry R. Selden. The minute he paid her bail, Anthony forfeited the right of using the writ of habeas corpus as a vehicle to having the Supreme Court hear her case. Anthony made a famous speech in court about the denial of her rights, was found guilty, and continued to speak on behalf of women's suffrage in other forums. In 1876, she and a group of six other women from the National Woman Suffrage Association marched into the Philadelphia Centennial Exposition and personally delivered a Declaration of the Rights of Women to visibly shocked U.S. Vice President Thomas W. Ferry. While cries of "Order! Order!" were shouted, the women quickly distributed written copies to the crowd while Anthony read it aloud. The manifesto attacked the Declaration of Independence for its neglect of women's rights to vote and to have a trial by a jury of one's peers while being subject to taxation without representation. Although Susan B. Anthony waged a tireless campaign for women's suffrage, she died twelve years before passage of the Nineteenth Amendment, giving women the right to vote, in 1920.

TERM PAPER SUGGESTIONS

1. There were legal errors on both sides of *United States v. Susan B. Anthony.* Selden, for example, paid Anthony's fine that subsequently removed Anthony's ability to use the writ of habeas corpus to have her case heard before the Supreme Court. On the other hand, Judge Ward Hunt had written his opinion and read it even before the trial began. Analyze these legal anomalies and discuss which ones most egregiously affected Anthony's case.

2. Anthony was ordered to be silent several times during the trial, but she persisted in making her views known before a jury of men. Research and discuss the validity of her remarks made during the trial.

3. Prior to the trial, Anthony had made so many speeches in Monroe County, where the case was scheduled to be heard, that the judge ordered a change of venue to Ontario County. Undeterred, Anthony continued to speak in Ontario County. Should Anthony have been allowed to try and prejudice a future jury? Discuss the venue option open to Judge Hunt, who was trying to avoid having the case go before the Supreme Court prior to or following her trial.

4. Examine the Declaration of the Rights of Women. Discuss the rights that have been achieved and the ones that are still issues for women today.

5. Many women were split over the best way to gain suffrage. Some women, such as suffragist Lucy Stone, wanted to attack the problem on a state-by-state basis and not attempt to get a Constitutional amendment. Anthony and Lucretia Mott were for an amendment, and Victoria Hull argued that the Constitution just needed to be reinterpreted to permit women's suffrage. Discuss these three diverging viewpoints and conclude which approach may have been best for the times.

6. Victoria Woodhull was an absolute firebrand compared with Anthony. Woodhull believed in free love, became the first female stockbroker, and was nominated to run for president in 1872 by the Equal Rights Party. Research her life and the role she played in the women's rights movement.

ALTERNATIVE TERM PAPER SUGGESTIONS

1. Assume you are a speech writer for Susan B. Anthony. Read through some of her past speeches and write two new ones that encapsulate her thoughts and beliefs concerning a woman's right to vote.

2. Assume that you have just joined the National Woman Suffrage Association and are having tea with a friend who is thinking of becoming a member too. Prepare an annotated list of reasons why your friend should become a member.

SUGGESTED SOURCES

Primary Sources

Sherr, Lynn. *Failure Is Impossible: Susan B. Anthony in Her Own Words*. New York: Times Books, 1995. Contains primary sources in the form of excerpts from Anthony's letters and speeches about her work in the women's suffrage movement.

Sherr, Lynn. *The Trial of Susan B. Anthony*. Amherst, NY: Humanity Books, 2003. Provides the transcript from the trial, plus commentary.

Stanton, Elizabeth Cady, Susan B. Anthony, and Matilda Joslyn Gage, eds. *History of Woman's Suffrage*. Vol. 2. Reprint. New York: Arno Press, 1969. This volume is part of an eleven-volume set that features primary sources amassed by the women who worked for the women's suffrage movement, including Anthony and Stanton.

Secondary Sources

Baker, Jean H., ed. *Votes for Women: The Struggle for Suffrage Revisited*. New York: Oxford University Press, 2002. This scholarly work focuses upon the entire history of the women's suffrage movement.

Barry, Kathleen. *Susan B. Anthony: A Biography of a Singular Feminist*. New York: Ballantine Books, 1988. Refutes charges that Anthony's ambitions and crusades were self-serving and shows how she was also involved in the abolition movement.

Clinton, Catherine. *The Other Civil War: American Women in the Nineteenth Century*. New York: Hill and Wang, 1984. Provides information about the Philadelphia Centennial Exposition and the split between Anthony and Stanton over building a women's pavilion.

Flexner, Eleanor. *Century of Struggle: The Woman's Rights Movement in the United States.* Cambridge, MA: Harvard University Press, 1959. Considered a definitive work on the women's rights movement, this book places events within a nineteenth-century context.

Griffith, Elisabeth. *In Her Own Right: The Life of Elizabeth Cady Stanton.* New York: Oxford University Press, 1984. Furnishes excerpts from Stanton's personal correspondence and diary that shed light on the "Declaration of the Rights of Women."

Lehman, Godfrey D. "Susan B. Anthony Casts Her Ballot for Ulysses S. Grant." *American Heritage* 37 (December 1985): 25–31. Sheds light on what happened to the voting inspectors and the reaction of the public to Anthony's voting.

Lerner, Gerda. *The Elizabeth Cady Stanton–Susan B. Anthony Reader: Correspondence, Writings, Speeches.* Boston, MA: Northeastern University Press, 1992. Features letters, speeches, and other correspondence between the two founders of the National Woman Suffrage Association.

McFadden, Margaret, ed. *Women's Issues.* 3 vols. Pasadena, CA: Salem Press, 1997. This comprehensive set provides many overview articles about Susan B. Anthony and other women active in the women's suffrage movement during the nineteenth century.

Palmer, Beverly Wilson, et al., eds. *Selected Letters of Lucretia Coffin Mott.* Urbana, IL: University of Illinois Press, 2002. Contains important letters about the suffrage movement that Mott wrote between 1813 and 1879.

Stanton, Elizabeth Cady. *Solitude of Self.* Ashfield, MA: Paris Press, 2001. Supplies the full text of one of the most important speeches that Stanton ever gave concerning gender equality.

Ward, Geoffrey C., and Ken Burns. *Not For Ourselves Alone: The Story of Elizabeth Cady Stanton and Susan B. Anthony.* New York: Knopf, 2001. This dual biography gives Stanton and Anthony double billing for their role in gaining women's suffrage.

World Wide Web

"Argument for the Defense Concerning Legal Issues in the case of United States vs. Susan B. Anthony." http://www.law.umkc.edu/faculty/projects/ftrials/anthony/defargument.html. Features the full text of Henry R. Selden's defense of Anthony during her trial.

"1876 Declaration of Rights." http://www.pinn.net/~sunshine/gage/features/1876.html. Contains the full text of the "Declaration of the Rights of

Women" as presented at the Philadelphia Centennial Exposition by Susan B. Anthony.

"The Elizabeth Cady Stanton and Susan B. Anthony Papers Project." http://ecssba.rutgers.edu/resources/resources.html. This megasite is replete with primary sources in the form of full text speeches, letters, and other writings by both women, biographical sketches of various women reformers, and a list of women who voted in the United States between 1868 and 1875.

"The Life and Work of Susan B. Anthony (Volume 1 of 2) Including Public Addresses, Her Own Letters and Many From Her Contemporaries During Fifty Years by Ida Husted Harper." http://www.gutenberg.org/etext/15220. Provides a scholarly online biography of the life and times of Susan B. Anthony.

"Susan B. Anthony: A Biography." http://www.law.umkc.edu/faculty/projects/ftrials/anthony/sbabiog.html. Furnishes a scholarly biographical sketch of Anthony that includes excerpts from some of her speeches.

"Susan B. Anthony by Alma Lutz." http://www.gutenberg.org/etext/20439. Presents a full text biography of Susan B. Anthony.

"The Trial of Susan B. Anthony." http://www.fjc.gov/history/anthony.nsf/auto frame?openForm&header=/history/anthony.nsf/page/header&nav=" &content=/history/anthony.nsf/page/home. This superb site consists of legal arguments made during the trial, a trial narrative, biographies of all participants, a bibliography, media and press coverage, and legal questions.

Multimedia Sources

Not for Ourselves Alone: The Story of Stanton & Anthony. Santa Monica, CA: PBS Paramount, 1999. 1 DVD. 180 minutes. Narrated by Ken Burns, this documentary contains excerpts from speeches, letters, and other writings by Stanton and Anthony, and makes them equal partners as pioneers of the women's rights movement in the nineteenth century.

77. Red River War and Sioux Wars (1875–1877)

These two wars waged against the American Indians marked the end of significant military opposition to the U.S. Army by the Indians and to occupation of their lands by settlers, gold miners, and railroads. In

1874, several hundred Cheyenne and Comanche warriors attacked some buffalo hunters at a Texas trading post known as Adobe Walls. A month later, the Kiowa attacked a group of Texas Rangers, Cheyenne warriors sniped along Kansas travel routes, and the Comanche threatened Texas ranches. For the first time, the army was given permission to pursue Indians on their reservations. Lieutenant General Philip Sheridan was ordered to annihilate the Indians at any opportunity. Five independent army columns converged on American Indian camps in the Texas panhandle defeating the tribes in Palo Duro Canyon by the Red River. The discovery of gold in the Black Hills of the Sioux's Dakota Territory and the construction of the Bozeman Trail through Lakota lands that brought thousands of settlers and miners into Nebraska and Montana triggered the Sioux Wars. As the tribes rose up in rebellion and attacked settlers and miners, another army force was dispatched to subdue them. One temporary victory ensued for the Sioux, however, when Chiefs Sitting Bull and Crazy Horse defeated Lieutenant Colonel George Armstrong Custer at the Battle of Little Bighorn in 1876. The Sioux's victory was extremely short-lived. The army relentlessly pursued them throughout the winter until the remaining Indians were driven back onto reservations. Although confrontations would continue up until the Battle of Wounded Knee in 1890, these two wars were the death knell for the American Indians' freedom and way of life.

TERM PAPER SUGGESTIONS

1. Research how inadequate food, employment, shelter, loss of freedom, and hunting prospects, because of the loss of the buffalo, contributed to the Red River War.

2. Lieutenant General Philip Sheridan was under the command of General William Tecumseh Sherman who advocated the concept of total war not only in the Civil War but also with the Kiowa, Comanche, and Cheyenne tribes. Describe the military tactics of Sheridan and evaluate them ethically.

3. Research the role that Kiowa Chief Lone Wolf, Cheyenne Chief Gray Beard, and Comanche Chief Quanah Parker played in leading their warriors in one last stand against loss of their freedom and lands.

4. Examine how the discovery of gold in the Black Hills of Dakota territory and construction of the Bozeman Trail triggered the Sioux Wars.

5. Investigate the role that Chiefs Sitting Bull and Crazy Horse played in leading the Sioux to war.

6. Just before the Battle of the Little Bighorn, the Sioux celebrated a victory over the army at the Rosebud River. Discuss the lessons that the army should have learned from the Indians' victory and how it may have prevented their loss at the Battle of the Little Bighorn.

ALTERNATIVE TERM PAPER SUGGESTIONS

1. There are several theories about how Lieutenant Colonel Custer met his death at the Battle of the Little Big Horn. Some forensic historians have postulated that he and his soldiers fought bravely against incredible odds and killed many Indians. Others have suggested the soldiers were simply outnumbered by a superior force and had little time to defend themselves. Discuss and analyze the different battle theories.

2. Assume you live on a present-day Sioux reservation and have been asked to represent tribal members at a Bureau of Indian Affairs meeting to discuss reservation fishing rights. Describe the advice that you might receive from elder members of the tribe who have survived either the Sioux Wars or the Red River War.

SUGGESTED SOURCES

Primary Sources

Carroll, John M., ed. *General Custer and the Battle of the Little Bighorn: The Federal View.* Mattituck, NJ: J. M. Carroll, 1986. Contains a collection of public documents relating to the battle.

Haley, James L. *The Buffalo War: The History of the Red River Indian Uprising of 1874.* Garden City, NY: Doubleday, 1976. Contains primary sources in the form of maps, illustrations, and military analysis of the Red River War.

Vestal, Stanley. *Warpath: The True Story of the Fighting Sioux Told in a Biography of Chief White Bull.* Lincoln, NE: University of Nebraska, 1984. Provides the autobiography of Joseph White Bull, Chief of the Lakota during the Sioux Wars.

Secondary Sources

Ambrose, Stephen E. *Crazy Horse and Custer: The Parallel Lives of Two American Warriors.* New York: Anchor, 1996. Focuses upon the similarities between Crazy Horse and Custer.

Chalfont, William Y. *Cheyennes at Dark Water Creek: The Last Fight of the Red River War.* Norman, OK: University of Oklahoma Press, 1997. Describes the massacre of the Cheyenne at Dark Water Creek during the Red River War.

Hatch, Thom. *The Custer Companion: A Comprehensive Guide to the Life of George Armstrong Custer and the Plains Indian Wars.* Mechanicsburg, PA: Stackpole Books, 2002. This complete guide to Custer's life and career contains a great deal of information about the controversies surrounding his defeat at the Battle of the Little Bighorn.

Hutton, Paul Andrew. *Phil Sheridan and His Army.* Lincoln, NE: University of Nebraska Press, 1985. Includes information about Sheridan's role as chief architect of the Red River War and proponent of waging total war against the American Indian.

Jauken, Arlene Feldmann. *The Moccasin Speaks: Living as Captives of the Dog Soldier Warriors, Red River War, 1874–1875.* Lincoln, NE: Dagforde, 1998. Provides a first-person account of a German family who was taken hostage by the Cheyenne during the Red River War.

Marshall, Joseph M., III. *The Journey of Crazy Horse: A Lakota History.* New York: Viking, 2004. Supplies a riveting biography of Crazy Horse, written by a member of the Lakota tribe.

Robinson, Charles M., III. *Bad Hand: A Biography of General Ranald Slidell Mackenzie.* Austin, TX: State House Press, 1993. Describes General Mackenzie's critical role in winning the Battle at Palo Duro Canyon by the Red River.

Robinson, Charles M., III. *Plains Wars, 1775–1900.* New York: Routledge, 2000. The Red River War and Sioux Wars are given extensive coverage in this encyclopedic work.

Sajna, Mike. *Crazy Horse: The Life Behind the Legend.* New York: John Wiley & Sons, 2000. Contains an authoritative biography of Crazy Horse and his role at the Battle of Little Bighorn, including his eventual surrender and murder.

Utley, Robert M. *The Indian Frontier of the American West 1846–1890.* Albuquerque, NM: University of New Mexico Press, 1984. This definitive work devotes much discussion to the causes and effects of the Red River and Sioux Wars.

Utley, Robert M. *The Lance and the Shield: The Life and Times of Sitting Bull.* New York: Henry Holt, 1993. Discusses the life of Chief Sitting Bull and his role at the Battle of the Little Bighorn.

World Wide Web

"Atlas of the Sioux Wars." http://cgsc.leavenworth.army.mil/carl/resources/csi/sioux/sioux.asp. Contains links to individuals who led the wars on both sides, maps, narratives, battle plans, and more.

"The Battle of Little Bighorn, 1876." http://www.eyewitnesstohistory.com/
    custer.htm. Provides first-person accounts of the battle from Indian and
    White survivors.

"The Battle of the Little Bighorn: An Eyewitness Account by the Lakota Chief
    Red Horse Recorded in Pictographs and Text at the Cheyenne River Res-
    ervation, 1881." http://www.pbs.org/weta/thewest/resources/archives/
    six/bighorn.htm. Provides a personal account of the battle by a Lakota
    survivor.

"Last Stand of the Indians." http://www.nps.gov/history/history/online_books/
    berkeley/brand1/brand1n.htm. Supplies an annotated timeline of the
    various Indian tribes involved in fighting off Euro-Americans trying to
    hunt and claim their ancestral lands in the Scotts Bluff, Nebraska, area
    from 1840 to 1876.

"Old Mobeetie Texas Association Red River War." http://www.mobeetie.com/
    pages/rrwar.htm. Gives an overview of the war and many eyewitness
    accounts of soldiers and buffalo hunters from the Red River area.

"The Red River War of 1874." http://www.texasbeyondhistory.net/redriver/
    index.html. Presents an extensive overview of the causes and events sur-
    rounding the Red River War, including maps, photographs, and images
    of artifacts.

"Take a Stand." http://custer.over-blog.com/. Claims one hundred pages devoted
    to the Battle of the Little Bighorn, including narratives, first-person
    accounts, lists of the dead, photographs, resource links, maps, and more.

Multimedia Sources

The West. Santa Monica, CA: PBS Home Video, 1996. 5 DVDs. 707 minutes.
    Narrated by Ken Burns, Disc 4 of this outstanding documentary series
    covers the last of the Plains Indian Wars, including the Battle of the Little
    Bighorn.

78. Alexander Graham Bell and the Invention of the Telephone (1876)

Alexander Graham Bell's (1847–1922) invention of the telephone came
about circuitously while he was working as a teacher of the deaf. His
mother was deaf and Bell was always attempting to create a device that
would transmit speech through sound wave vibrations to improve her
ability to communicate. In 1874, his father-in-law patented an invention

of Bell's called a harmonic telegraph that sent two or more messages simultaneously over the same wire. It was a sufficient incentive for Bell to keep experimenting until he could vary the electricity current in intensity to transmit speech telegraphically. On March 10, he spoke the famous words "Mr. Watson, come here; I want you" to his assistant on another floor of his laboratory with a receiving device, he was heard and understood, and thus the telephone was invented. Bell debuted the telephone at the 1876 Philadelphia Centennial Exposition in an attempt to solicit funding for further research and development, but most investors including Western Union thought it a one-time curiosity. In 1879, Bell adopted Thomas Alva Edison's patents for the carbon microphone from Western Union, which made his device work over long distances. Over the years he successfully defended his patent against six hundred lawsuits, including one filed by the U.S. government for fraud and misrepresentation. Within ten years of his invention, 150,000 people in the United States owned a Bell telephone. His contribution was so valued in his lifetime that people throughout North America refrained from using it during his funeral as a silent tribute.

TERM PAPER SUGGESTIONS

1. Discuss how Bell's invention revolutionized communication throughout the world.

2. Bell was a true polymath. In addition to the telephone, he invented a metal detector that was used unsuccessfully to locate the bullet lodged in President James Garfield's body, a hydrofoil that set the world's marine speed record of seventy miles per hour, and a metal jacket that was used by polio victims to assist in breathing. Research five of Bell's later inventions and comment on the contribution they made to further science and better society.

3. Bell had a lifelong friendship with Helen Keller who was both deaf and blind. He advised her parents to educate her and inspired her to live a normal life. Explore and discuss their friendship.

4. After inventing the telephone, Bell became a mentor to other scientists, founding and financing the journal *Science* and the National Geographic Society. Explore his contributions to these activities.

5. Bell's father-in-law was significantly instrumental in helping him obtain and retain his patent for the telephone. Describe their relationship and partnership in the Bell Telephone Company.

6. Bell's work with the telephone was influenced by the theories of Hermann von Helmholtz, a German physicist. Analyze how Bell's invention was able to bridge the gap between the knowledge that Helmholtz had about transmitting sound and his own creation.

ALTERNATIVE TERM PAPER SUGGESTIONS

1. Starting with the human ear that Bell obtained from a medical school to experiment with for a future telephone, draw a series of detailed diagrams showing Bell's creative process until he reached his final successful design.

2. Design a Web-based annotated chronology of Bell's inventions and other scientific interests.

SUGGESTED SOURCES

Primary Sources

MacKenzie, Catherine. *Alexander Graham Bell: The Man Who Contracted Space.* Boston, MA: Houghton Mifflin, 1928. Contains Bell's own recollections of his scientific struggle to invent the telephone.

Watson, Thomas A. *Exploring Life.* New York: D. Appleton, 1926. Contains the autobiography of Bell's laboratory assistant who was able to create the designs for Bell's visions.

Secondary Sources

Baker, Burton H. *The Gray Matter: The Forgotten Story of the Telephone.* St. Joseph, MI: Telepress, 2001. Recounts the intellectual and inventive race between Elisha Gray and Alexander Graham Bell for entitlement to receive the patent for the telephone.

Bruce, Robert B. *Bell: Alexander Graham Bell and the Conquest of Solitude.* Boston, MA: Little, Brown, 1973. Considered the definitive biography of Bell, this work includes a description of the scientific challenges of inventing the telephone.

Du Moncel, Theodore. *The Telephone, the Microphone, and the Phonograph.* 1879. Reprint. New York: Arno Press, 1974. Contains excellent nineteenth-century descriptions of how Bell invented the telephone and his knowledge of applied physics.

Evenson, A. Edward. *The Telephone Patent Conspiracy of 1876: The Elisha Gray-Alexander Bell Controversy and Its Many Players.* Jefferson, NC: McFarland & Company, 2001. Discusses one of the many patent challenges that Bell had to battle to defend his telephone invention.

Fischer, Claude S. *America Calling: A Social History of the Telephone to 1940.* Berkeley, CA: University of California Press, 1992. Includes a history of the telephone with a focus on how it changed the social fabric of America.

Giberti, Bruno. *Designing the Centennial: A History of the 1876 International Exhibition in Philadelphia.* Lexington, KY: University Press of Kentucky, 2002. Describes construction of the International Exhibition at which Bell debuted his telephone.

Gray, Charlotte. *Reluctant Genius: Alexander Graham Bell and the Passion for Invention.* New York: Arcade Publishing, 2006. Stresses the steadying influence of Bell's wife, Mabel, on his creative work, making this almost a dual biography.

Grosvenor, Edwin S., and Morgan Wesson. *Alexander Graham Bell: The Life and Times of the Man Who Invented the Telephone.* New York: N. Harry Abrams, 1997. Provides a photobiography of the life and inventions of Bell.

Mackay, James. *Alexander Graham Bell: A Life.* New York: John Wiley & Sons, 1997. Portrays Bell as a brilliant polymath and describes his other interests and inventions.

Ronell, Avital. *The Telephone Book: Technology, Schizophrenia, Electric Speech.* Lincoln, NE: University of Nebraska Press, 1989. Provides a history of the significance of the telephone from a philosophical, historical, literary, and psychological perspective.

Shulman, Seth. *The Telephone Gambit: Chasing Alexander Graham Bell's Secret.* New York: Norton, 2008. This title may result in a historical reassessment because the research attributes the invention of the telephone to Elisha Gray rather than Alexander Graham Bell.

World Wide Web

"Alexander Bell Family Collection." http://bell.uccb.ns.ca/index.asp. Contains an extensive image gallery of all of Bell's inventions, including the telephone, a documents section of primary sources that feature Bell's notes and sketches, and a section for students to plan experiments.

"Alexander Graham Bell." http://virtualology.com/AlexanderGrahambell.org/. Provides a biographical sketch, plus linkage to the Library of Congress site about Bell and his work.

"Alexander Graham Bell Association for the Deaf and Hard of Hearing." http://www.agbell.org/DesktopDefault.aspx. Click on the link "About AGB" to retrieve information about Bell's lifetime of work with the deaf.

"Alexander Graham Bell's Path to the Telephone." http://www3.iath.virginia.edu/albell/homepage.html. Contains biographical information, sketches from

Bell's notebooks, information about the stages of Bell's creative process regarding the telephone, his other inventions, and more.

"Antique Telephone History Web Site." http://atcaonline.com/phone/. Provides a significant amount of information about early stages of the telephone, diagrams of how they worked, and information about Alexander Graham Bell.

"Bell, Alexander Graham." http://www.biographi.ca/EN/ShowBio.asp ?BioId=42027. Provides a lengthy biographical portrait of Bell, including the significance of his contributions to science.

"Library of Congress—The Alexander Graham Bell Family Papers." http://memory.loc.gov/ammem/bellhtml/bellhome.html. This superb site is replete with primary sources including the full text of the scientific notebooks of Bell, his correspondence during his lifetime, sketches of various designs at different development stages, and more.

Multimedia Sources

Alexander Graham Bell. New York: A&E Home Entertainment Video, 2005. 1 DVD. 50 minutes. Replete with illustrations and photographs, this film thoroughly explores the creative genius of the inventor of not only the telephone but also many other useful creations.

The Telephone. Alexandria, VA: PBS Home Video, 1997. 1 DVD. 60 minutes. This documentary about Bell's invention of the telephone also has additional resources in the way of a timeline, related Web sites, a bibliography, and lesson plans at http://www.pbs.org/wgbh/amex/telephone/index.html.

79. Great Railroad Strike (1877)

In 1877, railroads were the largest industrial employer in the United States and their owners were some of the wealthiest Americans of the age. Railroad owners such as Cornelius Vanderbilt (New York Central Railroad) and Thomas Scott (Pennsylvania Railroad) wielded enormous political power and had connections that ran all the way to the White House. Railroad workers, on the other hand, labored twelve hours a day in conditions so dangerous that many locomotive engineers could not get life insurance policies. Wages for these positions were no better. An experienced fireman on the Baltimore & Ohio Railroad earned approximately $6 per week, which would be the equivalent of $100 a week in today's economy. In July workers at the B & O Railroad in Martinsburg, West Virginia, received a second pay cut in their wages and the workers refused to let the trains move until it was restored. When the local militia was called in to reestablish the train service, they refused to use force against the strikers. Meanwhile, the strike spread to Baltimore where ten people were killed battling the Maryland militia. The next hot spot was Pittsburgh where twenty thousand people fought troops, set fire to the railroad building, and destroyed two thousand railroad cars. Gaining momentum, the strike flared up like a wildfire in Chicago and St. Louis and then spread to San Francisco. President Rutherford B. Hayes, at the instigation of Thomas Scott, sent federal troops to quell the violence, and after forty-five days it was over.

TERM PAPER SUGGESTIONS

1. The Panic of 1873 was one of the economic factors that precipitated the Great Strike of 1877. It was triggered by the collapse of the banking firm, Jay Cooke and Company, that was overinvested in railroads. Discuss how this company lost its money and its connection during the Panic of 1873.

2. The Panic of 1873 triggered a depression that affected wages and employment. Businesses went bankrupt, credit was almost impossible to obtain, and unemployment reached 14 percent. Discuss these conditions as causative agents in the Great Railroad Strike of 1877.

3. The election of 1876 between Samuel J. Tilden and Rutherford B. Hayes had to be decided by a fifteen-member Electoral Commission. Investigate the role of Thomas Scott in getting Rutherford B. Hayes elected president and the implications for future dealings between the two.

4. Discuss how the strike sounded an alarm throughout the country about the great disparity between workers and their owners. Analyze the aftermath of the strike and how it presaged the formation of powerful labor unions.

5. Since the railroads were the largest industrial employer, they could dictate the terms and conditions for employment. Research and read first-person accounts that describe the life of different types of railroad workers, the dangers they faced from unsafe working conditions, and their typical salaries.

6. There was strong antiworker sentiment not only from owners but also from government officials and even famous clergymen such as Henry Beecher Stowe. Many were afraid that the strike had been instigated by Communists, immigrant agitators, and union leaders. Read articles from period newspapers that expressed negative views of the strike and evaluate their validity.

ALTERNATIVE TERM PAPER SUGGESTIONS

1. Assume you are a reporter for a newspaper that sympathized with the strikers. Write a front-page story with pictures depicting them in a positive light that will educate your readers about the arduous life of a railroad worker.

2. Assume that you are a personnel adviser to Thomas Scott. He desperately wants to get his trains running again and stop the strike. Draw up a plan for Mr. Scott involving concessions that will enable him to restore train service and prevent other strikes in the future.

SUGGESTED SOURCES

Primary Sources

"The Great Railroad Strike of 1877." http://www.library.pitt.edu/labor_legacy/rrstrike1877.html. The city of Pittsburgh had the worst strike in terms of numbers of people killed and railroad property damage. This outstanding site contains the forty-two photographs of the battle that took place between Federal troops and the strikers.

"The Great Strike *Harper's Weekly* August 11, 1877." http://www.catskillarchive.com/rrextra/sk7711.Html. Contains the full text of a pro-management article about the Great Railroad Strike. Scroll to the bottom of the article to view a series of illustrations showing the extent of the violence that took place in Baltimore and Pittsburgh.

Secondary Sources

Bruce, Robert V. *1877: Year of Violence*. Chicago, IL: Ivan R. Dee, 1989. This outstanding, readable account of the Great Railroad Strike of 1877 gives overview information about the causes and the aftermath.

Burbank, David T. *Reign of the Rabble: The St. Louis General Strike of 1877*. New York: A. M. Kelley, 1966. Describes the anarchy, chaos, and destruction wreaked by the striking railroad workers and their sympathizers during the St. Louis strike.

Dacus, Joseph A. *Annals of the Great Strike in the United States; a Reliable History and Graphic Description of the Causes and Thrilling Events of the Labor Strikes and Riots of 1877*. New York: B. F. Franklin, 1969. Presents an account of the Great Railroad Strike from a worker's perspective.

Fink, Leon. *Major Problems in the Gilded Age and the Progressive Era: Documents and Essays*. Boston, MA: Houghton Mifflin, 2000. Documents and analyzes the disparities between working class people and the wealthy during the late 1800s.

Foner, Philip Sheldon. *The Great Labor Uprising of 1877.* New York: Anchor Foundation, 1977. Describes the causes, events, and aftermath of the Great Railroad Strike.

McGerr, Michael. *A Fierce Discontent: The Rise and Fall of the Progressive Movement in America, 1870–1920.* New York: Oxford University Press, 2005. Shows how the development of a monopolistic business society created the poor social and economic conditions for workers that in turn helped foster the Progressive Movement in America.

McMath, Robert C. *American Populism: A Social History 1877–1898.* New York: Hill and Wang, 1990. Discusses how the American Populist Movement also had its origins in workers' protests against monopolies such as the railroads.

Morris, Roy, Jr. *Fraud of the Century: Rutherford B. Hayes, Samuel Tilden, and the Stolen Election of 1876.* New York: Simon & Schuster, 2003. Chapter 6 discusses the role of the fifteen-member Electoral Commission and the part that Thomas Scott played in it.

Robinson, Lloyd. *The Stolen Election: Hayes Versus Tilden—1876.* New York: Forge Books, 2001. Chapter 9 investigates the power that the fifteen-member Electoral Commission had to get Rutherford B. Hayes elected president.

Stowell, David O. *The Great Strikes of 1877.* Urbana, IL: University of Illinois, 2008. Analyzes the social, political, regional, and ethnic factors that came into play that helped cause the Great Strike of 1877.

Stowell, David O. *Streets, Railroads, and the Great Strike of 1877.* Chicago, IL: University of Chicago, 1999. Relates the events of the Great Railroad Strike, but spends much more time analyzing the economic and social causes of the strike.

Trachtenberg, Alan. *The Incorporation of America: Culture and Society in the Gilded Age.* New York: Hill and Wang, 2007. Chapter 3 discusses the intermix of capital and labor and how big business interests developed monopolies and trusts, which, in turn, caused the eventual labor unrest resulting in strikes such as the one in 1877.

World Wide Web

"The Baltimore Railroad Strike and Riot of 1977." http://www.stfrancis.edu/ba/ ghkickul/stuwebs/btopics/works/railroadstrike.htm. This excellent curriculum unit contains a set of documents in the form of first-person accounts of the strike, plus a set of classroom exercises and assignments.

"The Great Strike, Harper's Weekly—April 1, 1878." http://www.catskillarchive .com/rrextra/sk881.Html. Contains a period article describing and analyzing the resolution of the strike.

"The Great Strike, Harper's Weekly—August 11, 1877." http://www.catskill archive.com/rrextra/sk7711.Html. Provides a period magazine article about the great railroad strike.

"Pages from Labor History: The Great Railroad Strike of 1877." http://www .socialistappeal.org/uslaborhistory/great_railroad_strike_of_1877.htm. Presents an easy-to-understand overview of the event along with a brief discussion of the economic and social factors that probably contributed to the strike.

"Panic of 1873." http://www.u-s-history.com/pages/h213.html. Gives a brief overview of the social and economic issues that triggered the Panic of 1873 and helped contribute to the Great Railroad Strike of 1877.

"Strike of 1877." http://college.hmco.com/history/us/resources/students/ primary/strike1877.htm. Prepared by the publisher Houghton Mifflin, this site supplies a brief overview of the strike together with a series of term paper questions to consider. Each question is accompanied by a relevant and appropriate full text of primary sources.

"The Strike of 1877." http://teachingamericanhistorymd.net/000001/000000/ 000070/html/t70.html. This superb Maryland State Archives site weaves primary sources into a National History Standards lesson replete with term paper topic questions. The focus is totally on the Baltimore aspect of the strike.

Multimedia Sources

1877, The Grand Army of Starvation. Wycoff, NJ: American Social History Pro-
ductions, Inc., 1984. 1 videocassette. 30 minutes. This documentary uses period photographs to tell the story of the Great Strike and the effect that it had on the workers. It also draws appropriate inferences to future labor conflicts and the formation of labor unions.

80. Inventions of Thomas Edison (1877–1879)

Christened "The Wizard of Menlo Park" by newspaper reporters who marveled at his talent and creativity, Thomas Alva Edison (1847–1931) was without a doubt America's foremost inventor, holding 1,093 U.S. patents and numerous ones in Europe. Alone he was responsible for inventing or improving on the stock ticker, storage battery, dictaphone, ore separator, electric dynamo, compressing dies, and the forerunner of the motion picture projector. Edison's first breakthrough came when he invented an automated telegraph machine that allowed Western Union to send four messages simultaneously. The proceeds from its sale to Western Union allowed Edison to create his own laboratory in Menlo Park, New Jersey, and along with a group of talented engineers, scientists, and craftsman, begin inventing in earnest. His next notable invention was a cylinder phonograph that was capable of recording and playing back sound. It created a sensation when it was demonstrated, and, even though it was not commercially viable until 1890, it enabled Edison to attract investors for other projects. The banker J. P. Morgan and some other venture capitalists had funded Edison's previous work with electricity, but had been disappointed with the results. On October 21, 1879, however, they were shocked to learn that Edison had invented an economical, durable, practical light bulb. With one click of a switch, Edison ushered out the steam age and replaced it with the electric age.

TERM PAPER SUGGESTIONS

1. Examine how Thomas Edison created a research and development laboratory that was a bridge between the housebound solitary inventor and that of contemporary university and corporate research laboratories.

2. Edison waged a long-standing battle with George Westinghouse over the merits of direct current (DC) versus alternating current (AC). It led Edison to electrocute various animals, including an elephant, to prove his point. Research the history of their debate and how it resulted in states designing an electrocution chair for death penalty offenders.

3. Edison's genius also lay in being able to see the practical applications for his inventions. Explore his childhood and economic background and how it may have contributed to this aspect of his work.

4. For every new invention, others can become extinct. Describe some of the inventions, businesses, and industries that were negatively impacted by Edison's invention of the light bulb.

5. Edison stood on the shoulders of several giants who also had done groundbreaking work with electricity. Discuss the experiments of Alessandro Volta, Sir Humphry Davy, and Michael Faraday and how they helped Edison with his invention.

6. Edison was also responsible for designing a distribution system for electricity so that cities and towns could be lighted. Describe the new endeavors that were now possible in the 1870s as a result of generally distributed electricity.

ALTERNATIVE TERM PAPER SUGGESTIONS

1. Assume you are a nineteenth-century inventor in search of venture capital for a new invention. Prepare a description of some invention accompanied by sketches, and the means for mass producing it at a low cost.

2. Assume you are a nineteenth-century venture capitalist who has just witnessed one of Edison's latest inventions. It requires a great deal of capital to perfect, mass produce, and distribute it. Prepare a PowerPoint presentation that contains pictures, diagrams, or illustrations of the invention and a breakdown of all the problems and solutions associated with bringing it to the market. Propose a small company that will develop stock shares to finance it.

SUGGESTED SOURCES

Primary Sources

Baldwin, Neil. *Edison: Inventing the Century.* New York: Hyperion, 1995. Contains interviews with hundreds of Edison's associates and descendants about his life and times.

Edison, Thomas A. *Menlo Park: The Early Years, April 1876–December 1877.* Vol. 3. In *The Papers of Thomas A. Edison,* edited by Robert A. Rosenberg et al. Baltimore, MD: Johns Hopkins University Press, 1994. Includes Edison's notes on developing an electric lighting system.

Secondary Sources

Bazerman, Charles. *The Languages of Edison's Light.* New York: Cambridge University Press, 1999. Explores how Edison and his laboratory assistants created an entire language of symbols and communication to match the invention of electrical lighting.

Clark, Ronald W. *Edison: The Man Who Made the Future.* New York: G. P. Putnam's Sons, 1977. Filled with interesting anecdotes and obscure facts about Edison, this work also devotes an entire chapter to his invention of the light bulb.

Dillon, Maureen. *Artificial Sunshine: A Social History of Domestic Lighting.* London: National Trust, 2002. Provides an excellent cultural history of the impact that electricity had on society.

Essig, Mark. *Edison and the Electric Chair: A Story of Light and Death.* New York: Walker & Company, 2004. Focuses on the relationship between George Westinghouse, proponent of alternating current (AC), and Edison, whose experiments electrocuting animals inadvertently led to the development of the electric chair for capital punishment cases.

Friedel, Robert D. *Edison's Electric Light: Biography of an Invention*. New Brunswick, NJ: Rutgers University Press, 1986. Furnishes a complete history of the invention of the light bulb, including the inspiration that Edison received from examining William Wallace's dynamo to generate power.

Israel, Paul. *A Life of Invention*. New York: John Wiley & Sons, 1998. The author uses Edison's notebooks to show how Edison's inventive process worked and how tireless he was at pursuing new projects.

Jonnes, Jill. *Empires of Light: Edison, Tesla, Westinghouse, and the Race to Electrify the World*. New York: Random House, 2003. Presents information about the contribution that each of these men made to the business of providing safe, reliable electrical power.

McCormick, Blaine. *At Work With Thomas Edison*. Irvine, CA: Entrepreneur Press, 2001. Discusses Edison's research and development methods and how they were always geared to producing a durable, affordable product.

Moran, Richard. *Executioner's Current: Thomas Edison, George Westinghouse, and the Invention of the Electric Chair*. New York: Knopf, 2002. Presents information about the current debate between Edison and George Westinghouse and how it led to Edison's involvement in the development of the electric chair for executions.

Pretzer, William S. *Working at Inventing: Thomas A. Edison and the Menlo Park Experience*. Baltimore, MD: Johns Hopkins University Press, 2002. Describes the research and development methods that Edison and his colleagues used to continue inventing and innovating.

Wachhorst, Wyn. *Thomas Alva Edison: An American Myth*. Cambridge, MA: MIT Press, 1981. Provides a scholarly biography of the life and times of Edison and devotes several pages to his invention of the light bulb.

World Wide Web

"Edison Birthplace Museum." http://www.tomedison.org/. Excels for obtaining information about the economic circumstances that may have influenced Edison to become such an indefatigable inventor.

"Edison, His Life and Inventions." http://www.worldwideschool.org/library/books/hst/biography/Edison/toc.html. Contains significant information about each one of Edison's inventions, plus biographical information about him.

"The Edison Papers." http://edison.rutgers.edu/. Provides more than five million pages of primary source documents concerning Edison's life and inventions.

"Edison's Miracle of Light." http://www.pbs.org/wgbh/amex/edison/. Features a timeline, picture gallery, biographical information, teacher resources, and lesson plans concerning the life, times, and inventions of Edison.

"Thomas A. Edison and the Menlo Park Laboratory." http://www.hfmgv.org/ exhibits/edison/. Contains photographs and a narrative concerning the work done in Edison's laboratory.

"Thomas Edison Patent List." http://inventors.about.com/library/inventors/ bledisonpatents.htm. Provides a complete list of all of Edison's inventions and the date each was patented.

"Thomas Edison's Homepage." http://www.thomasedison.com/. Features a biographical sketch of Edison along with photographs from different periods of his life, a series of quotations attributed to Edison, and information about his invention of the light bulb.

Multimedia Sources

"Around the World on the Phonograph by Thomas A. Edison." http://www .gutenberg.org/etext/10311. Contains a free audio e-book available through Project Gutenberg that can be downloaded onto an MP3 player. It features a book written by Thomas Edison about his phonograph invention.

Edison's Miracle of Light. Alexandria, VA: PBS Home Video, 1999. 1 videocassette. 60 minutes. Supplies a documentary of Edison's life that also focuses on his invention of the light bulb.

Great Projects—The Building of America—Electric Nation. Alexandria, VA: PBS Home Video, 2002. 1 videocassette. 60 minutes. This documentary begins with Edison's invention and goes on to discuss other important people who helped bring electricity to the entire nation.

"Mary Had a Little Lamb by Thomas A. Edison." http://www.gutenberg.org/ etext/10137. Features a free audio e-book available through Project Gutenberg of Edison recording "Mary had a little lamb" for the first time on the cylinder phonograph that he invented.

81. Yellow Journalism (1880s–1890s)

Once publishers had the ability to print thousands of newspapers overnight, the competition to retain a loyal readership began an era known as yellow journalism. Two New York City newspapers in particular went head to head in a competition to outdo one another in reporting lurid human interest stories with little or no regard for their veracity. Their headlines were filled with colorful language, the articles contained gross exaggerations, and both papers featured significant numbers of cartoons. Joseph Pulitzer's paper, the *New York World,* carried a daily cartoon characterized with special yellow ink entitled, "The Yellow Kid." When William Randolph Hearst lured the cartoonist to his rival paper, the *New York Journal American,* both papers continued producing issues of the cartoon, hence the term "yellow journalism." Although Hearst and Pulitzer were not the only newspaper publishers to engage in tabloid journalism, they are most readily associated with it. As the competition increased between the two papers for market share, the price declined accordingly until readers were able to buy Pulitzer's twelve-page paper for two cents and Hearst's paper for one cent. The circulation of both papers compared to more staid newspapers such as *The New York Times, New York Herald Tribune,* and *New York Evening Post* skyrocketed. As pressure mounted in the late 1890s for America to wage war with Spain over Cuba and the Philippines, Hearst and Pulitzer fanned the flames for war with their biased articles of unsubstantiated atrocities committed by Spain against hapless Cubans. Historians cite both papers as major instigators of the Spanish-American War.

TERM PAPER SUGGESTIONS

1. Read about Gresham's Law, which states the bad drives out the good. Examine the circulation rates for the five newspapers cited in the summary above and determine how Gresham's Law applies. Discuss the implications for the future of journalism in the twenty-first century.

2. Joseph Pulitzer believed that newspapers were also attorneys for the poor and that they had a duty to report, for example, the deplorable living conditions in the slums of New York City or unscrupulous business practices that took advantage of immigrants who spoke little English. Read some period articles on these subjects from his paper and analyze why they appealed to his readership.

3. Although both papers were strongly linked as instigators of the Spanish-American War of 1898, William Randolph Hearst is so connected to sensationalistic articles urging President McKinley and Congress to go to war that the event was often referred to as Hearst's war. Read and discuss the role of Hearst and his newspaper in starting the war.

4. Hearst and Pulitzer knew that the market for their papers consisted primarily of women, laborers, Democrats, the poor, and immigrants. Read some of their articles and analyze why these groups might find the articles in yellow journalism newspapers so interesting and appealing.

5. Inaccurate and biased reporting sometimes cost people their jobs or reputations. Provide incidences where yellow journalism did and discuss the damaging effects it can have on individuals, businesses, and the like.

6. Explore the legacy of yellow journalism that still can be detected in current corporate media efforts that are now termed infotainment and supermarket tabloid journalism.

ALTERNATIVE TERM PAPER SUGGESTIONS

1. Assume you are a newspaper reporter who has been recently hired by Hearst's *New York Journal American*. Write two articles, including the headline, about a nineteenth-century crime or event. One should be based on the facts as they were known at the time. The other article should be in the style of yellow journalism.

2. Hearst may have been hoisted on his own petard when his paper's columnist Ambrose Bierce and editor Arthur Brisbane called for President McKinley's assassination. Write several op-ed pieces accusing and implicating Hearst in the assassination attempt that followed. Demand that the presidential aspirations of Hearst should be over.

SUGGESTED SOURCES

Primary Sources

Campbell, W. Joseph. *The Spanish-American War: American Wars and the Media in Primary Documents.* Westport, CT: Greenwood Press, 2005. Discusses the role that yellow journalism played in the Spanish-American War using examples from various yellow journalism newspapers.

Paley, Valerie. *The New-York Journal of American History.* New York: New York Historical Society, 2003. Contains primary source articles from Hearst's paper, written during the time of yellow journalism.

Secondary Sources

Brain, Denis. *Pulitzer: A Life.* New York: John Wiley & Sons, 2001. Recounts the life of Joseph Pulitzer, including his rivalry with William Randolph Hearst, involvement with yellow journalism, and eventual reform to a more accurate, unbiased form of reportage.

Campbell, W. Joseph. *Yellow Journalism: Puncturing the Myths, Defining the Legacies.* Westport, CT: Praeger Publishers, 2003. Provides the pros and cons of yellow journalism, discussing articles that helped people by exposing slum conditions, for example, and biased reporting of events that cost people their employment and reputations. It also discusses the legacy of yellow journalism within a contemporary context.

Emery, Edwin, and Michael Emery. *The Press and America*. 4th ed. Englewood Cliffs, NY: Prentice-Hall, 1984. Provides an outstanding history of the press, including the era known as yellow journalism.

Littlefield, Roy Everett. *William Randolph Hearst: His Role in American Progressivism*. Lanham, MD: Rowman & Littlefield, 1980. Explores Hearst's role in the Progressive Movement and political ambition to be president of the United States.

Milton, Joyce. *The Yellow Kids: Foreign Correspondents in the Heyday of Yellow Journalism*. New York: Harper & Row, 1989. Discusses the role of yellow journalism and the sensational war stories reporters wrote while based in Cuba.

Nasaw, David. *The Chief: The Life of William Randolph Hearst*. Boston, MA: Houghton Mifflin, 2000. Covers Hearst's life as a newspaper owner, movie producer, and politician.

Painter, Nell Irvin. *Standing at Armageddon: The United States 1877–1919*. New York: W. W. Norton, 1989. Provides an excellent cultural history of what America was like during the 1880s that is useful in analyzing the market that Pulitzer and Hearst targeted with their newspapers.

Procter, Ben. *William Randolph Hearst: The Early Years, 1863–1910*. New York: Oxford University Press, 1998. Examines the early years of Hearst when he was involved in the publishing business and the rivalry with Pulitzer. Large parts of the book are devoted to the role Hearst played in yellow journalism and in inflaming public opinion regarding the Spanish-American War.

Smythe, Ted Curtis. *The Gilded Age Press, 1865–1900*. Westport, CT: Praeger Publishers, 2003. Discusses how the press changed dramatically after the Civil War as owners began to target markets rather than to attempt reporting the news without bias.

Welter, Mark M. "The 1895–1898 Cuban Crisis in Minnesota Newspapers: Testing the Yellow Journalism Theory." *Journalism Quarterly* 47 (Winter 1970): 719–724. (Available in JSTOR.) Attempts to determine whether incendiary articles in the papers such as the *New York Journal American* and *New York World* actually helped start a war with Spain.

Whitelaw, Nancy. *Joseph Pulitzer and the New York World*. Greensboro, NC: Morgan Reynolds Publishing, 2001. Written for secondary school students, this work presents a realistic portrait of Pulitzer and the negative role he played in the growth and development of yellow journalism.

World Wide Web

"Crucible of Empire—Yellow Journalism." http://www.pbs.org/crucible/frames/_journalism.html. Supplies hyperlinked overviews about Hearst, Pulitzer, the Spanish-American War, and yellow journalism.

"Defining Yellow Journalism, Competition with Hearst." http://www.online
concepts.com/pulitzer/yellow.htm. Provides an overview of Pulitzer's
rivalry with Hearst and the role both men played in creating a sensational
form of reportage. This site also contains a series of resource links about
the life and times of Joseph Pulitzer.

"Not Likely Sent: The Hearst-Remington Telegrams." http://academic2
.american.edu/~wjc/wjc3/notlikely.html. Contains a lengthy analysis
of the tale that Hearst said his photographer, Frederick Remington,
would "furnish the pictures" and that Hearst himself would "furnish
the war."

"R. F. Outcault: The Father of the Sunday Comics, and the Truth about the
Yellow Kid." http://www.neponset.com/yellowkid/history.htm.
Contains the history of the creation of the *Yellow Kid* comic and the
association that the comic strip character has with the term "yellow journalism."

"The Sensational Beginnings of Yellow Journalism." http://alt.tnt.tv/movies/
tntoriginals/roughriders/jour.home.html. Describes how yellow journalism began and how Hearst and Pulitzer used their respective papers to
exert an influence.

"Yellow Journalism." http://library.thinkquest.org/C0111500/spanamer/
yellow.htm. Furnishes a lengthy, hyperlinked overview of yellow journalism and its origins that are linked to the cartoon, the "Yellow Kid."

"Yellow Journalism: Puncturing the Myths, Refining the Legacies." http://
www.yellowjournalism.net/. Presents lengthy articles from Joseph
W. Campbell's book that are sited in the secondary Sources sections
and illustrations from both Hearst's and Pulitzer's rival papers.

Multimedia Sources

The Battle over Citizen Kane. Alexandria, VA: PBS Home Video, 2000. 1 DVD.
120 minutes. The film relates the story of how the movie *Citizen Kane,*
1941, starring Orson Wells, was a thinly disguised documentary of the
life and times of William Randolph Hearst. It was almost never produced
because Hearst fought extremely hard to stop it.

Biography—Pulitzers. New York: A&E Home Entertainment Video, 2000. 1 videocassette. 60 minutes. Presents the life and times of Joseph Pulitzer,
including information about his fostering of sensationalistic reportage
called yellow journalism.

Crucible of Empire: Spanish American War. Alexandria, VA: PBS Home Video,
1999. 1 videocassette. 60 minutes. This documentary devotes part of
the program to a discussion of the role that yellow journalism played in
fanning the flames for war between the United States and Spain.

82. Assassination of President James A. Garfield (1881)

The twentieth President of the United States had little more than six months in office before he was assassinated at the Baltimore and Potomac Railway station in Washington, D.C., on July 2, 1861. James A. Garfield (1831–1881) had been planning to leave to speak at his alma mater, Williams College, and several members of his cabinet had traveled with him to wish him bon voyage. As he was conversing with Secretary of State James G. Blaine, two shots were heard and Garfield collapsed. Within minutes the shooter, thirty-nine-year-old Charles J. Guiteau, with little resistance on his part, was arrested. President Garfield was given first aid by physician Smith Townsend who ordered the President moved to an upstairs room with a mattress. The President's friend, D. W. Bliss, another physician, was summoned, and it was he who determined that Garfield had sustained a grazing wound to the arm and one bullet that entered his back near his spine. Later Garfield was moved to his bed in the White House. Mobs quickly formed threatening the life of Guiteau, and federal troops were sent to prevent a riot. Although Garfield's doctors gave him only a few hours to live, he lingered on for several weeks, finally succumbing to an aortic aneurysm in September 1881. Guiteau was judged a religious fanatic and, even though his lawyer pleaded insanity, he was found guilty of killing the president. He was executed by hanging on June 30, 1882. President Garfield was buried with great pomp and ceremony by a shocked nation, and a James A. Garfield Monument was dedicated to him in Washington, D.C., in 1887.

TERM PAPER SUGGESTIONS

1. Moments after he shot President Garfield, assassin Charles Guiteau was heard to cry, "I am a Stalwart of the Stalwarts! I did it and I want to be arrested! Arthur is President now." These alleged statements led to rumors of a conspiracy to assassinate Garfield, rather than a lone gunman. Investigate who the Stalwarts were and why Stalwart Chester A. Arthur was Garfield's vice president.

2. In March 1881, Guiteau managed to see Garfield and ask to be appointed either ambassador to Austria or consul to Paris. After being courteously

refused, he started pestering former President Ulysses S. Grant, Secretary of State Blaine, and Vice President Chester A. Arthur until he was barred from the White House. In May Guiteau wrote a threatening letter to Garfield, which was not answered. Examine the events of Guiteau's life up until the shooting and discuss Guiteau's state of mind.

3. Guiteau's trial was a Washington, D.C., spectacle. Guiteau was defended by his brother-in-law George Scoville who pled insanity for Guiteau, but to no avail. The jury deliberated only an hour before finding Guiteau guilty. Investigate trial documents and testimony and conclude whether Guiteau, under the circumstances, received a fair trial.

4. Many historians believe that President Garfield died of medical neglience on the part of his attending physicians. Research the treatment that Garfield received for his wounds and determine whether his care was up to late nineteenth-century medical practices.

5. Garfield's short presidency was somewhat tarnished by a patronage struggle with Senator Roscoe Conkling, a fanatical member of the Stalwart group. Research and discuss how Garfield handled this faction.

6. Garfield's assassination led to reforms in the hiring policies of the federal government and to passage of the nation's first civil service law. Research and discuss the Pendleton Act of January 16, 1883, and its contribution to civil service reform.

ALTERNATIVE TERM PAPER SUGGESTIONS

1. Compare the defense arguments during the trial of Charles J. Guiteau to that of John Hinckley, who attempted to assassinate President Ronald Reagan on March 30, 1981. Both assailants' lawyers used an insanity defense. Evaluate their effectiveness.

2. Garfield was the second President of the United States to be assassinated. In 1901, Leon Czolgosz would kill President William McKinley as he was giving a speech. The U.S. Secret Service was formed in 1865. Design a Web site using images from the assassinations of Presidents Abraham Lincoln, James A. Garfield, and William McKinley that will persuade Congress to provide protection for future presidents by the U.S. Secret Service.

SUGGESTED SOURCES

Primary Sources

Brown, Henry James, and Frederick D. Williams, eds. *The Diary of James A. Garfield. Vol. 4, 1878–1881.* East Lansing, MI: Michigan State University

Press, 1981. Contains diary entries by President Garfield up to the day before he was assassinated.

Clarke, Theodore Smith. *The Life and Letters of James Abram Garfield*. Hamden, CT: Archon Books, 1964. Features primary sources in the form of letters written by President James Garfield.

Conwell, Russell Herman. *The Life, Speeches, and Public Services of James A. Garfield*. Boston, MA: B. B. Russell, 1881. Contains the full text of many Garfield speeches that reflect his position on various governmental policies.

Secondary Sources

Ackerman, Kenneth D. *The Dark Horse: The Surprise Election and Political Murder of President James A. Garfield*. New York: Carroll & Graf, 2003. Discusses the close election between President Garfield and General Winfield Scott Hancock, the problem with the Stalwart faction and Garfield's assassination.

Doenecke, Justus D. *The Presidencies of James A. Garfield and Chester A. Arthur*. Lawrence, KS: University Press of Kansas, 1981. Presents the respective contributions and legacies of Presidents Garfield and Arthur.

Geary, Rick. *The Fatal Bullet: The True Account of the Assassination, Lingering Pain, Death, and Burial of James A. Garfield, Twentieth President of the United States...of Victorian Murder*. New York: Nantier Beall Minoust-chine Publishing, 1999. Written for secondary school students, this accurate, nonfiction graphic book depicts the assassination of President Garfield and the inept medical treatment that he received.

Gould, Lewis. *Grand Old Party: A History of the Republicans*. New York: Random House, 2003. Provides a comprehensive history of the Republican Party, including information about the Stalwarts.

Karabell, Zachary, and Arthur M. Schlesinger. *Chester Alan Arthur*. New York: Times Books, 2004. Analyzes Arthur's presidency and his single reform act, the signing of the Pendleton Civil Service Act.

King, Lester Snow. *Transformations in American Medicine: From Benjamin Rush to William Osler*. Baltimore, MD: Johns Hopkins University Press, 1991. Discusses the changes in the practice of American medicine from the eighteenth to the nineteenth century.

Leech, Margaret, and Harry J. Brown, *The Garfield Orbit*. New York: Harper & Row, 1978. Describes Garfield's relationships with his early mentors and women that portray Garfield as a rather ruthless and pragmatic politician.

Melanson, Philip H. *The Secret Service: The Hidden History of an Enigmatic Agency*. New York: Carroll & Graf, 2005. Traces the history of the U.S.

Secret Service from its inception in 1865 through the early part of the twenty-first century.

Peskin, Allan. *Garfield: A Biography*. Kent, OH: Kent State University Press, 1978. Part three of this outstanding biography of Garfield is devoted to his assassination.

Rosenbloom, David H. *Centenary Issues of the Pendleton Act of 1883: The Problematic Legacy of Civil Service Reform*. New York: Marcel Dekher, Inc., 1982. Analyzes the effects of the civil service reform Pendleton Act of 1883.

Rutkow, Ira. *James A. Garfield*. New York: Times Books, 2006. Written by a clinical professor of surgery, this work provides an indictment of the medical treatment that President Garfield received for his wounds, even taking into account late nineteenth-century medical equipment and knowledge.

Vowell, Sarah. *Assassination Vacation*. New York: Simon & Schuster, 2006. National Public Radio commentator Vowell traveled to the monuments and other places dedicated to three assassinated presidents—Lincoln, Garfield, and McKinley—and provides plenty of history surrounding each tragic event.

World Wide Web

"Alexander Graham Bell and the Garfield Assassination." http://www.history buff.com/library/refgarfield.html. Contains a description of the attempt by Alexander Graham Bell to use his metal detector to find the bullet still located in Garfield's body.

"Backgrounder on the Pendleton Act." http://exchanges.state.gov/EDUCA TION/ENGTEACHING/PUBS/AmLnC/br28.htm . Provides the legislative history outlining the reasons why the Pendleton Civil Service Reform Act was enacted by Congress after Garfield was assassinated.

"From Quackery to Bacteriology: The Emergence of Modern Medicine in 19th Century America." http://www.geocities.com/healthbase/anti_quack _sites.html. This excellent site gives an overview of the typical medical practices and treatments during the time Garfield lived.

"Garfield Assassinated!" http://memory.loc.gov/ammem/today/jul02.html. Provides the full text of various comments by Guiteau, a period illustration of the attack, speeches by Guiteau, and other period primary sources.

"Inaugural Address—James A. Garfield." http://www.americanpresidents.org/ inaugural/20.asp. Provides the full text of the address, which also sheds light on what Garfield's legacy may have been had he lived to implement some of his plans.

"James Garfield: How Alexander Graham Bell Helped Kill the President." http://
home.nycap.rr.com/useless/garfield/index.html. Provides a summary of
the incompetent treatment Garfield received at the hands of his physicians.

"The United States Secret Service History." http://clinton4.nara.gov/WH/
kids/inside/html/spring98-2.html. Gives a brief overview of the
final decision to use the U.S. Secret Service to protect the lives of U.S.
presidents.

Multimedia Sources

Insanity on Trial. Alexandria, VA: PBS Home Video, 1990. 1 videocassette. 58
minutes. Combines documentary sequences and dramatic recreations
based on court transcripts and first-hand accounts of Guiteau's trial to
shed light on nineteenth-century understanding of mental illness and
medicine.

"Why Did Garfield Not Become a Great President"? http://www.millercenter
.virginia.edu/index.php/scripps/digitalarchive/forumDetail/1102. Contains an audio interview with historian and Garfield expert Alan Peskin
concerning the reasons why Garfield would never have become a great
president, despite being assassinated.

83. Wyatt Earp and the Gunfight at the O.K. Corral (1881)

The legend of the western gunfighter has become an enduring part of
American popular culture. Glamorized in Hollywood films, serialized on
television, and popularized in western novels, the image of a gun-toting
outlaw meeting his match at high noon with a law-abiding sheriff is part
of nineteenth-century western lore. In 1881, a real gunfight occurred
between the Earp brothers and Doc Holliday and the McLaury and
Clanton brothers at the O.K. Corral in Tombstone, Arizona. The gunfight became the symbol for the idea of an untamed and lawless West.
The truth of what happened on that day is still in dispute. Virgil, Morgan,
and Wyatt Earp had several run-ins with the McLaurys and Clantons, a
loosely organized gang known as the "cowboys." The cowboys believed
that the Earps were behind much of the crime in Tombstone and were
trying to eliminate them as witnesses. After an altercation with Ike
Clanton, who publicly threatened to kill the Earps, Virgil Earp, as city

marshal, deputized his brothers and Doc Holliday. They met the McLaurys and Clantons, ostensibly to disarm them at the end of town, but a ferocious gunfight broke out between the two groups. When it was over, Billy Clanton and Frank and Tom McLaury lay dead. Virgil and Morgan Earp and Doc Holliday were wounded. Within days, Wyatt Earp and Doc Holliday were charged with murder. Justice of the Peace Wells Spicer and a grand jury both ruled that there was insufficient evidence to indict them. A few weeks later, Virgil Earp was shot by hidden assassins and Morgan was murdered by them. Wyatt Earp went on a killing spree to avenge their deaths and eventually fled the Arizona Territory.

TERM PAPER SUGGESTIONS

1. Research the long-standing feud that Wyatt Earp and his brothers had with the McLaurys and Clantons over the Earps' belief that the McLaurys and Clantons were rustlers and stagecoach robbers.

2. Investigate the court testimony that the "cowboys" were armed versus unarmed, and evaluate it for accuracy and reliability.

3. Many historians believe that Wyatt and Doc Holliday should have been charged with at least manslaughter. Analyze the legal issues involved in the event with regard to this charge.

4. Read period newspaper articles and trial testimony to determine whether the Earps deliberately provoked the "cowboys" to instigate a shootout.

5. Refer to the facts in this case and draw conclusions about the civic dangers of barnyard justice.

6. This event has been used by fiction writers and Hollywood and television writers to paint a picture of the Old West, filled with bandits and cattle rustlers, that was utterly lawless. Research the era and discuss the validity of this portrait.

ALTERNATIVE TERM PAPER SUGGESTIONS

1. Use and cite clips from some of the documentaries and well-known films about the shootout and create a two-minute iMovie that accurately depicts one encounter that the Earps had with the McLaurys and Clantons prior to the shootout.

2. Design an online biographical sketch replete with explanatory hyperlinks of Wyatt Earp, including information about what he did prior to and after the shootout.

SUGGESTED SOURCES

Primary Sources

Clum, John. *Apache Days and Tombstone Nights: John Clum's Autobiography, 1877–1887.* Silver City, NM: High Lonesome Books, 1997. John Clum, a close friend of the Earps, was mayor of Tombstone during the time of the shootout at the O.K. Corral.

Earp, Josephine Sarah Marcus. *I Married Wyatt Earp: The Recollections of Josephine Sarah Marcus Earp.* Tucson, AZ: University of Arizona Press, 1976. This memoir, as related to family friend Glenn Boyer, attempts to set the record straight concerning the life and times of Wyatt Earp.

Secondary Sources

Barra, Allen. *Inventing Wyatt Earp: His Life and Many Legends.* New York: Carroll & Graf, 1998. Provides an accurate and reliable analysis of the shootout at the O.K. Corral.

Blake, Michael F. *Hollywood and the O.K. Corral: Portrayals of the Gunfight and Wyatt Earp.* Jefferson, NC: McFarland and Company, 2006. Compares all of the film versions of Wyatt Earp and how each film altered the facts in order to maintain a high entertainment value.

Burns, Walter Noble. *Tombstone: An Iliad of the Southwest.* Reprint. Albuquerque, NM: University of New Mexico Press, 1999. Provides the blend of fact and fiction that was used to create many of the myths surrounding the shootout at the O.K. Corral and the myth about Wyatt Earp.

Gatto, Steve. *The Real Wyatt Earp: A Documentary Biography.* Silver City, NM: High Lonesome Books, 2000. Uses primary source documents to exempt the Earps from accusations of murder.

Lake, Stuart. *Wyatt Earp: Frontier Marshal.* New York: Pocket Books, 1994. Lake interviewed Earp in 1928 for this book that recounts his life and times.

Lubet, Steven. *Murder in Tombstone: The Forgotten Trial of Wyatt Earp.* New Haven, CT: Yale University Press, 2006. This outstanding academic work analyzes the events and trial from a legal perspective and explores the issues of guilt or innocence from both the Earps and cowboy gang sides.

McCool, Grace. *Gunsmoke: The True Story of Old Tombstone.* Tucson, AZ: Treasure Chest Publications, 1990. Describes the town of Tombstone and the events that led to the gunfight between the Earps and the "cowboys."

Marks, Paula Mitchell. *And Die in the West: The Story of the O.K. Corral Gunfight.* New York: Morrow, 1989. This scholarly work examines how the myth of the gunslinger and law-abiding sheriff was created with the gunfight at the O.K. Corral.

Roberts, Gary L. *Doc Holliday: The Life and Legend*. New York: Wiley, 2006. Attempts to find out the real facts behind the myth of Doc Holliday and his role during the shootout at the O.K. Corral.

Tanner, Karen Holliday. *Doc Holliday: A Family Portrait*. Norman, OK: University of Oklahoma Press, 2001. A distant cousin to Doc Holliday uses primary source documents to separate the man and the myth, and to describe Holliday's role at the shootout at the O.K. Corral.

Tefertiller, Casey. *Wyatt Earp: The Life Behind the Legend*. New York: John Wiley and Sons, 1997. Discusses the moral and legal issues surrounding the gunfight at the O.K. Corral.

World Wide Web

"Daily Nugget, Coroner's Inquest, Oct. 30, 1881." http://www.tombstone 1880.com/archives/nugget.htm. Provides the full text of the Coroner's inquest that was held to determine the cause of death for the McLaury brothers and Billy Clanton.

"Famous Trials: Wyatt Earp." http://www.lawbuzz.com/famous_trials/wyatt _earp/wyatt_earp_ch9.htm. Contains primary source trial documents and a description of the events surrounding the shootout at the O.K. Corral.

"The O.K. Corral Shootout!" http://www.angelfire.com/tx2/peacemaker/ corral.html. Provides an interactive forensic-like diagram of the shootout replete with an annotated version of the thirty seconds that it took to occur.

"Tombstone History Archives." http://home.earthlink.net/~knuthco1/index2 .html. Furnishes the full texts of period newspaper articles reporting the event, Judge Spicer's decision, first-person accounts, interviews with witnesses, and depositions taken from various participants.

"Wyatt Earp." http://www.geocities.com/zybt/earp.htm. Provides a biographical sketch of Wyatt Earp, including several useful resource links to additional material.

"Wyatt Earp Biography." http://riri.essortment.com/wyattearpbiogr_rnmg.htm. Presents a biographical sketch of Earp and the role he played in the gunfight at the O.K. Corral.

"Wyatt Earp Historical Homepage." http://www.oldwesthistory.net/old west2.html/. Supplies a variety of excellent resource links to primary sources and information about the gunfight between the Earps and the "cowboys."

Multimedia Sources

Biography—The Earp Brothers: Lawmen of the West. New York: A&E Home
Entertainment Video Network, 2006. 1 DVD. 50 minutes. This documentary recounts the life and times of the Earp brothers and their
involvement in the famous shootout.

84. Chinese Exclusion Act (1882)

Despite the Nativist Movement and formation of the Know-Nothing
Party, the United States never acted on its xenophobic tendencies until
1882 when it passed the Chinese Exclusion Act. The panic of 1873 had
caused a significant depression, and people living on the West Coast were
susceptible to blaming declining wages and other economic problems
on Chinese workers who comprised only 0.002 percent of the country's
population. In San Francisco, Chinese were forbidden to use local hospitals, and their children were allowed to attend public schools only if White
parents permitted it. Riots against Chinese, beatings, and destruction of
their property became commonplace in Seattle, Los Angeles, and even
Rock Springs (then Wyoming Territory). In San Francisco, Dennis
Kearney, ironically an Irish immigrant, formed the Workingmen's Party
of California and escalated the problem into a national issue. Congress
responded to the pressure of this party by passing an exclusion act that
attempted to limit Chinese immigration for twenty years, but President
Rutherford B. Hayes vetoed it. As more pressure was placed on legislators
and the executive branch by the Workingmen's Party, which claimed the
future of American labor was in danger, newly elected President Chester
Arthur signed a bill that suspended Chinese immigration for ten years
and declared the Chinese ineligible for citizenship. This law was not
rescinded until 1943.

TERM PAPER SUGGESTIONS

1. The United States attempted to close the door on Chinese immigration as
   early as 1850 when Chinese came to California for the gold rush. Research
   and discuss the discriminatory laws that the California legislature enacted to
   prevent additional immigration and assimilation by the Chinese.
2. Discuss the economic and social reasons for such gross discrimination against
   the Chinese.

3. One of the charges leveled against the Chinese was their refusal to assimilate and adopt western ways. Examine how California's laws and the nation's exclusion act made it almost impossible for the Chinese to assimilate.

4. The Chinese challenged the constitutionality of the exclusion act, but their efforts failed. Discuss the Constitutional Amendments on which their arguments rested and the reasons for their failure to get the act rescinded.

5. Investigate the role that the Workingmen's Party, under the leadership of Dennis Kearney, had in inciting riots and hatred toward the Chinese.

6. Discuss how the passage of the Chinese Exclusion Act of 1882 led to passage of additional immigration bills that discriminated against specific classes of immigrants from other foreign countries.

ALTERNATIVE TERM PAPER SUGGESTIONS

1. You are a reporter for a neutral, national newspaper. Describe the basic facts surrounding the massacres of the Chinese in Seattle, San Francisco, Los Angeles, and Rock Springs in Wyoming territory prior to passage of the Exclusion Act.

2. You are a legislative aide to Representative Charles Joyce of Vermont, who is undecided about his vote on the Exclusion Act. Prepare a PowerPoint presentation outlining the pros and cons of the issue to help him reach a decision.

SUGGESTED SOURCES

Primary Sources

Yung, Judy. *Unbound Feet: A Social History of Chinese Women in San Francisco.* Berkeley, CA: University of California Press, 1995. Uses interviews and oral histories to trace the history of immigrant Chinese women during the nineteenth century.

Yung, Judy, et al. *Chinese American Voices: From the Gold Rush to the Present.* Berkeley, CA: University of California Press, 2006. Contains primary sources in the form of letters, speeches, memoirs, oral histories, and testimonies that document the experiences of hundreds of Chinese immigrants from all walks of life from the nineteenth through the twenty-first centuries.

Secondary Sources

Barth, Gunther. *Bitter Strength: A History of the Chinese in the United States, 1850–1870.* Cambridge, MA: Harvard University Press, 1964. Provides a background history of all the previous attempts by Californians to discriminate against the Chinese up until 1870.

Chan, Sucheng, Ed. *Entry Denied: Exclusion and the Chinese Community in America, 1882–1943.* Philadelphia, PA: Temple University Press, 1991. Examines the legal issues surrounding the passage of the Exclusion Act and the effect it had on Chinese who remained in the United States.

Chang, Iris. *The Chinese in America: A Narrative History.* New York: Penguin, 2004. Traces the history of the Chinese attempt to assimilate and survive in America from the time of the gold rush through the passage of the Exclusion Acts.

Lau, Estelle. *Paper Families: Identity, Immigration Administration, and Chinese Exclusion.* Durham, NC: Duke University Press, 2006. Analyzes the effect that the Exclusion Act of 1882 had on the Chinese community and the role it played in making America a discriminating gatekeeper nation.

Lee, Erika. *At America's Gates: Chinese Immigration during the Exclusion Era, 1882–1943.* Chapel Hill, NC: University of North Carolina, 2007. Discusses the legacy of the Chinese Exclusion Act and how it changed America into a discriminating nation regarding immigrants from specific countries.

LeMay, Michael C. *From Open Door to Dutch Door: An Analysis of U.S. Immigration Policy Since 1820.* Westport, CT: Praeger Publishers, 1987. Examines the economic and racial causes of the anti-immigration movement in the United States since 1820.

Miller, Stuart Creighton. *The Unwelcome Immigrant: The American Image of the Chinese, 1885–1882.* Berkeley, CA: University of California Press, 1969. Provides a contradictory analysis for the arguments that racism was one of the main causes of the discrimination against the Chinese.

Peffer, George Anthony. *If They Don't Bring Women Here: Chinese Female Immigration Before Exclusion.* Urbana, IL: University of Illinois Press, 1999. This academic work examines the problems faced by female Chinese immigrants prior to the passage of the Exclusion Act.

Pfaelzer, Jean. *Driven Out: The Forgotten War Against Chinese Americans.* New York: Random House, 2007. Furnishes an exciting narrative history of the discrimination against the Chinese, including pogroms in the Pacific Northwest and passage of numerous Exclusion Acts.

Takaki, Ronald. *Strangers from a Different Shore: A History of Asian Americans.* Boston, MA: Little, Brown, 1998. Chapter 3 is devoted to a history of Chinese immigration to America.

Teitelbaum, Michael. *Chinese Immigrants.* New York: Facts on File, 2004. Written for secondary school students, this work gives a brief overview of the issues surrounding the Chinese immigration problem beginning in the nineteenth century.

World Wide Web

"Chinese Exclusion Act (1882)." http://www.ourdocuments.gov/doc.php?flash =true&doc=47. Furnishes a brief overview of the Chinese Exclusion Act and provides links to additional information at the National Archives site.

"The Chinese Exclusion Act." http://ocp.hul.harvard.edu/immigration/themes -exclusion.html. This outstanding collection of primary sources from Harvard University contains the full text of many nineteenth-century books and periodical articles about the Chinese Exclusion Act of 1882.

"Chinese Exclusion Act; May 6, 1882." http://www.yale.edu/lawweb/avalon/ statutes/chinese_exclusion_act.htm. Provides the full text of the Chinese Exclusion Act of 1882.

"Chinese Massacre at Rock Springs, Wyoming Territory." http://ocp.hul .harvard.edu/immigration/outsidelink.html/http://nrs.harvard.edu/urn-3 :FHCL:899981. Presents an 1886 book describing the massacre of the Chinese at Rock Springs, Wyoming Territory.

"The Chinese Question." http://pds.lib.harvard.edu/pds/view/4581431 ?n=2&s=4. Contains an 1881 example of the type of racist reasoning that was used to discriminate against the Chinese and rationalize passage of the Exclusion Act of 1882.

"The Chinese Question: Report of the Special Committee on Assembly Bill No. 13. Sacramento, California, 1870." http://ocp.hul.harvard.edu/ immigration/outsidelink.html/http://nrs.harvard.edu/urn-3:FHCL:884 323. Furnishes the full text of a discriminatory bill against the Chinese that provides evidence of racism on the part of California legislators prior to the Chinese Exclusion Act of 1882.

"Library of Congress—Exclusion." http://memory.loc.gov/learn/features/ immig/chinese6.html. Contains an overview of the history of discrimination against the Chinese, primary source photographs, and information about the deleterious effect that the Exclusion Act had on their families and communities.

Multimedia Sources

Becoming American: The Chinese Experience. Princeton, NJ: Films for the Humanities, 2003. 1 DVD. 85 minutes. Program 1, *Golden Mountain Dreams,* features interviews with historians, descendants, and recent immigrants. It traces the history and experiences of Chinese in the United States from the gold rush in California and the building of the Transcontinental Railroad, to the 1882 Chinese Exclusion Act, which barred their entry into the country.

19th Century Turning Points in U.S. History. New York: Ambrose Video Publishing, 2002. 1 videocassette. 25 minutes. Episode 8, 1882–1900, contains background material about the Chinese Exclusion Act of 1882 and its impact on American and Chinese societies.

85. First Skyscraper Built (1883)

As American cities began expanding upward and outward, the cost of land in their economic centers skyrocketed, challenging architects to design buildings that were taller so that space was utilized more efficiently. All of them faced a problem with weight load, water pressure, and stairs. Buildings could not rise more than five or six stories because customers did not wish to climb beyond five sets of stairs. As each story was added, the walls needed to be thicker because of the additional weight bearing down on the exterior walls. Builders also had to devise pumps and storage tanks for water at higher levels. In 1881, architect William Le Baron Jenney (1832–1907) solved the problem by discovering that a thin steel frame could support the building as safely as thick exterior walls. He designed a steel skeleton consisting of vertical columns and horizontal I beams that rendered the exterior part of the building nonessential to its survival. The exterior part of the building could then be used as a façade that could contain more windows, thus permitting air flow throughout the seasons. Using this new innovative design, he began work on the Home Insurance Building in Chicago, Illinois. City officials were so dubious about the design that work ceased in 1883 so that they could assess the building's safety. Finished in 1885, at a height of ten stories or 138 feet, the design of the Home Insurance Building revolutionized commercial urban construction, and the building became known as the world's first skyscraper.

TERM PAPER SUGGESTIONS

1. Research and discuss Sir Henry Bessemer's contribution to America's first skyscraper.
2. Analyze the formidable barriers that architects faced in designing a nineteenth-century skyscraper, including no air conditioning, water pressure

problems, weight load, and too many stairs, and explain how they overcame them.

3. Examine the role that William Le Baron Jenney played in discovering how to build the world's first skyscraper.

4. Chicago architect Louis Sullivan was more concerned with the aesthetics of skyscrapers. Describe and discuss his contribution to architectural skyscraper history, including his design of the Chicago window.

5. Urban critics describe skyscraper cities as concrete canyons that diminish people, rendering them insignificant and anonymous. Examine the negative effect that skyscrapers can have on quality of life for city residents and visitors.

6. Examine the influence on and legacy of the skyscraper in architectural history.

ALTERNATIVE TERM PAPER SUGGESTIONS

1. Assume you are a nineteenth-century urban planner who has been hired by a medium-sized city's historic preservation society. Present before and after photographs and panoramic illustrations showing how the addition of skyscraper buildings will change the aesthetics of their city.

2. Assume you are a nineteenth-century urban planner. Design a Web site showing members of the chamber of commerce how building skyscrapers will cause the development of suburbs, require additional mass transit, and create the need for additional businesses.

SUGGESTED SOURCES

Primary Sources

Burnham, Daniel, and Edward Bennett. *Plan of Chicago*. Chicago, IL: University of Chicago Press, 2006. This outstanding reprint provides a plan for the growth and development of Chicago that was used as a blueprint for the present-day city. Part two is devoted to a history of the growth and development of cities worldwide.

Sullivan, Louis Henry. *Autobiography of an Idea*. New York: Dover Publications, 1956. Contains Sullivan's ideas and inspiration for his architectural contribution to the world of skyscrapers.

Secondary Sources

Bascomb, Neal. *Higher: A Historic Race to the Sky and the Making of a City*. New York: Broadway, 2004. Discusses the competition and race to building

even taller skyscrapers and how the landscape of New York was forever
altered by their construction.

Bennett, David. *Skyscrapers: Form and Function.* New York: Simon & Schuster,
1995. Provides an outstanding overview of the history of skyscrapers
and the contribution that Jenney and Sullivan made to their growth
and development.

Douglas, George H. *Skyscrapers: A Social History of the Very Tall Building in
America.* Jefferson, NC: McFarland, 2004. Discusses the influence and
legacy of the skyscraper on American history and culture and includes
information on the construction problems it presented in the nineteenth
century.

Hudson, Leslie A. *Chicago Skyscrapers.* Mount Pleasant, SC: Arcadia, 2004.
Using two hundred vintage postcards of late nineteenth- and early
twentieth-century Chicago, this work presents a photographic history
of the construction of Chicago's skyscrapers, including the Home Insurance Building.

Lepik, Andres. *Skyscrapers.* New York: Prestel Publishing, 2004. Focuses upon the
history of fifty of the world's most influential skyscrapers, including several in Chicago.

Morrison, Hugh. *Louis Sullivan: Prophet of Modern Architecture.* Rev. ed. New
York: W. W. Norton, 2001. Examines the life and contribution of architect Louis Sullivan to the world of skyscrapers.

Moudry, Roberta. *The American Skyscraper: Cultural Histories.* New York: Cambridge University Press, 2005. Investigates the social, political, cultural,
and architectural influence that the skyscraper had on Chicago and
New York.

Sabbagh, Karl. *Skyscraper: The Making of a Building.* New York: Penguin, 1991.
Accompanies a PBS program about the financing and construction of a
modern-day skyscraper.

Shepherd, Roger. *Skyscraper: The Search for an American Style 1891–1941.* New
York: McGraw-Hill, 2002. Contains reviews from architectural journals
of skyscrapers and their effects on the public from the seventeenth
through the early twentieth centuries.

Van Zanten, David. *Sullivan's City: The Meaning of Ornament for Louis Sullivan.*
Seattle, WA: Amazon Remainders Account, 2000. Describes the contributing role that Sullivan played with ornamentation of nineteenth-century
skyscrapers.

Wells, Matthew. *Skyscrapers: Structure and Design.* New Haven, CT: Yale University Press, 2005. Examines the structural and engineering challenges
faced by architects when designing skyscrapers, including some of the
tallest ones that are susceptible to wind and earthquakes.

World Wide Web

"All About Skyscrapers." http://www.allaboutskyscrapers.com/. Provides photographs of famous skyscrapers, articles about them, and the latest *Guinness Book of World Records*–like statistics concerning the tallest.

"Dankmar Adler and Adler Louis Sullivan and Co. 19th Century Chicago Architects." http://patsabin.com/illinois/AdlerSullivan.htm. Presents an overview of the contribution of Dankmar Adler, a partner in the Louis Sullivan architectural firm.

"Leiber-Meister Louis Sullivan the Architect and His Work." http://www.geo cities.com/soho/1469/sullivan.html. Furnishes an extensive overview of the life and times of Louis Sullivan, famous architect of skyscrapers and their exterior ornamentation.

"Skyscraper Museum." http://www.skyscraper.org/home_flash.htm. Contains photographs and panoramic views of modern-day skyscrapers and information about the architectural impact they have had on various cities.

"Skyscrapers." http://www.pbs.org/wgbh/buildingbig/skyscraper/index.html. This outstanding site provides a loads laboratory with information about design challenges, a glossary of architectural terms, and specific overviews of famous skyscrapers, including the Home Insurance Building in Chicago.

"William LeBaron Jenney." http://library.thinkquest.org/J002846/a_jenney.htm. Gives an overview of Jenney's architectural career and the legacy he left, particularly for Chicago urban architecture.

"William Le Baron Jenney: 19th Century Chicago Architect." http://www .patsabin.com/illinois/jenney.htm. Furnishes an overview of the life of William Jenney, including a virtual tour of the Chicago skyscraper buildings that he designed.

Multimedia Sources

Building Big: Skyscrapers. Boston, MA: WGBH Boston Video, 2000. 1 DVD. 65 minutes. This documentary, hosted by children's writer and illustrator David Macaulay, discusses the history and current state of skyscraper design and construction.

86. Mark Twain and *The Adventures of Huckleberry Finn* (1884)

For more than one hundred years Mark Twain's *The Adventures of Huckleberry Finn* has been one of America's most beloved and banned books.

Many literary critics and historians consider it a brilliant satire against racism, while others believe that it does nothing but reinforce stereotypes. Mark Twain began writing a sequel to *The Adventures of Tom Sawyer* in a series of fits and starts in 1876 and finally completed it in 1884. *Huckleberry Finn* was unlike *Tom Sawyer* in that it featured the unrefined, colloquial dialect of a backwoods boy and it dealt with that peculiar institution, slavery. The plot consists of the adventures of two runaways floating down the Mississippi River together on a raft. Huckleberry Finn is trying to escape an abusive father and Jim being sold away from his family. Initially the book received excellent reviews for its depiction of river boat communities and satirical humor. In March 1855, however, the Concord (MA) Public Library banned it for its coarse humor, unsuitable behavior of many of the characters, and poor diction. Educators criticized it for the poor role model it fostered because Huck drank, smoked, and was continually truant from school. In 1957, the National Association for the Advancement of Colored People (NAACP) judged it racially offensive because the "n word" was used two hundred times and Jim is stereotyped as a plantation slave. Despite all of the criticism, *The Adventures of Huckleberry Finn* has sold more than fifteen million copies and is definitely considered part of the pantheon of great American literature.

TERM PAPER SUGGESTIONS

1. Trace the history of censorship of *The Adventures of Huckleberry Finn* since its first banning in 1855 by the Concord Public Library.

2. Analyze how the offensive content in *The Adventures of Huckleberry Finn* evolved over the years from one of poor role modeling to one of racial insensitivity.

3. Historians have recently discovered an earlier manuscript of *The Adventures of Huckleberry Finn* that Mark Twain chose to edit and rework. Compare this recently discovered manuscript with the published version and analyze the possible reasons for Twain's editorial changes.

4. Research the life and times of Mark Twain and discuss their influence on Twain's writing of *The Adventures of Huckleberry Finn*.

5. Investigate the events, life, speech, and mannerisms of Mississippi River communities during the 1840s. What would the actual conditions have been like for Huck and Jim as they floated down the river on a raft? Discuss Twain's accuracy of Mississippi River boat life from a nineteenth-century viewpoint.

6. Twain's novel begins in Hannibal, Missouri, in the 1840s. Research what the conditions were like for the character Jim during those times and the

dangers he faced traveling through the states that allowed slavery in that time period.

ALTERNATIVE TERM PAPER SUGGESTIONS

1. Assume you are a school board member who has been asked to hear a request to censor *The Adventures of Huckleberry Finn* by a parent who considers the book racially insensitive. Provide a written decision that takes into account the latest criticisms balanced against First Amendment free speech issues.

2. Assume that *Huckleberry Finn* has just been published and you have been asked to review it for National Public Radio. Prepare a podcast review that listeners can hear at their convenience.

SUGGESTED SOURCES

Primary Sources

Twain, Mark. *The Adventures of Huckleberry Finn,* edited by Thomas Cooley. 3rd ed. New York: W. W. Norton, 2001. Contains Twain's original manuscript, Edward Kemble's original illustrations, early reviews, critical essays, and a timeline.

Twain, Mark, and Charles Neider. *The Autobiography of Mark Twain.* New York: Harpers, 2000. Written when Mark Twain was in his sunset years, this book sheds light on the author's thoughts concerning slavery and race in America within the context of the nineteenth century.

Twain, Mark, Susan K. Harris, ed., and Lyrae Vanclief-Stefanon, ed. *The Adventures of Huckleberry Finn: Complete Text with Introduction, Historical Contexts, Critical Essays.* Boston, MA: Houghton Mifflin & Company, 2005. Contains the recently discovered manuscript of Twain's original *The Adventures of Huckleberry Finn,* and shows how Twain continually had to stop himself from writing a darker, more confrontational novel.

Secondary Sources

Brooks, Van Wyck. *The Ordeal of Mark Twain.* Rev. ed. New York: E. P. Dutton, 2000. Provides an important critique of Mark Twain's writing that incorporates some of Bernard DeVoto's criticism.

Chadwick-Joshua, Jocelyn. *The Jim Dilemma: Reading Race in "Huckleberry Finn."* Jackson, MS: University of Mississippi Press, 1998. Furnishes an African American scholar's defense of Twain's book as being an antiracist satire, and it presents Jim as a character of great strength.

DeVoto, Bernard. *Mark Twain's America.* Lincoln, NE: Bison Books, 1997. First published in 1932, this work describes the nineteenth-century events that influenced Twain and his writing of *The Adventures of Huckleberry Finn.*

Doyno, Victor. *Writing Huck Finn: Twain's Creative Process.* Philadelphia, PA: University of Pennsylvania Press, 1993. Gives a thorough analysis of the writing of *The Adventures of Huckleberry Finn.*

Kaplan, Fred. *The Singular Mark Twain: A Biography.* New York: Doubleday, 2003. Provides a psychobiography of the life of Mark Twain that helps shed light on his landmark novel about race relations, *The Adventures of Huckleberry Finn.*

Kaplan, Justin. *Born to Trouble: One hundred years of Huckleberry Finn.* Washington, DC: Library of Congress, 1985. Traces the history of the continuing controversy over Mark Twain's publication of *The Adventures of Huckleberry Finn.*

Leonard, James S., et al., eds. *Satire or Evasion? Black Perspectives on "Huckleberry Finn."* Durham, NC: Duke University Press, 1992. Contains a collection of essays by African American scholars about the controversy concerning the publication of *The Adventures of Huckleberry Finn.*

Powers, Ron. *Dangerous Water: A Biography of the Boy Who Became Mark Twain.* New York: Da Capo Press, 2001. Discusses Mark Twain's childhood and its influence on his writing of several books, including *The Adventures of Huckleberry Finn.*

Powers, Ron. *Mark Twain: A Life.* New York: Free Press, 2006. Furnishes an outstanding biography of the life and times of Mark Twain, including the nineteenth-century events that influenced his writing of *The Adventures of Huckleberry Finn.*

Rasmussen, R. Kent. *Critical Companion to Mark Twain: A Literary Reference of His Life and Work.* New York: Facts on File, 2007. Provides more than forty thousand words of material on *The Adventures of Huckleberry Finn,* along with a lengthy summary and recent criticism of the work.

Sattelmeyer, Robert, and Donald J. Crowley, eds. *One Hundred Years of "Huckleberry Finn": The Boy, His Book and American Culture.* Columbia, MO: University of Missouri Press, 1985. Contains twenty-four essays that discuss various aspects of *The Adventures of Huckleberry Finn* and how the book is an integral part of the American literary canon.

World Wide Web

"Culture Shock Mark Twain's Adventures of Huckleberry Finn." http://www.pbs.org/wgbh/cultureshock/flashpoints/literature/huck.html. Provides an overview of the debate between those who wish to censor Twain's book and those who consider it a great work that is truly representative of the American literary canon.

"Expelling 'Huck Finn,'" http://www.jewishworldreview.com/cols/hentoff
    112999.asp. Famous First Amendment author and authority Nat Hen-
    toff gives his opinion on the NAACP's request to remove *The Adventures
    of Huckleberry Finn* from the curriculum.

"Huck Finn and the Power of Words." http://interact.uoregon.edu/medialit/
    JCP/articles_mlr/walsh/Huck_Finn_Power_Words.html. Secondary
    school English teacher and author Bill Walsh relates how he used *The
    Adventures of Huckleberry Finn* to initiate a discussion about the power
    of words. The site also provides a brief overview of the controversy con-
    cerning the book.

"Huckleberry Finn, Alive at 100." http://www.nytimes.com/books/98/05/10/
    specials/mailer-finn.html. Furnishes author Norman Mailer's famous
    centenary essay that celebrates *The Adventures of Huckleberry Finn* as
    one of the great works of literature.

"Is Huck Finn a Racist Book?" http://www.salwen.com/mtrace.html. Proffers a
    defense of Twain's book as being nonracist.

"Random house for High School Teachers—*Adventures of Huckleberry Finn.*"
    http://www.randomhouse.com/highschool/catalog/display.pperl?isbn
    =9780553210798&view=tg. Provides a teacher's guide in the form of
    provocative questions that could be used for term paper topics concern-
    ing the publication of Twain's *The Adventures of Huckleberry Finn.*

"Say It Ain't So, Huck: Second Thoughts on Mark Twain's 'Masterpiece,' by Jane
    Smiley." http://www.fhs.fuhsd.org/~dclarke/AM_LIT_H/READINGS/
    UNIT_2/finn_smiley_abbr.pdf. Contains a thorough analysis of the
    controversy surrounding Mark Twain's *The Adventures of Huckleberry
    Finn* and concludes that other books should be taught in its place.

Multimedia Sources

Born to Trouble: Adventures of Huckleberry Finn. Alexandria, VA: PBS Home
    Video, 1999. 1 VHS tape. 90 minutes. Provides information about the
    continual controversy concerning the publication of *The Adventures of
    Huckleberry Finn.*

87. Founding of the American Federation of Labor (1886)

During the late nineteenth century the U.S. economy underwent an
unprecedented period of growth as inventions such as the telephone,
elevator, electricity, adding machines, and typewriters paved the way for

a different type of work environment. Gone were the days when a worker could simply walk into an owner's office and request a raise or day off. Industries such as railroad, coal, steel, and oil consolidated into trusts and monopolies, and off-site chief executive officers were dictating wage cuts and long hours in unsafe conditions to millions of employees. A second wave of immigration occurred, and thousands of immigrants needing work were willing to accept low wages and unsafe working conditions just to survive. The Noble Order of the Knights of Labor founded in 1869 was the first national workers organization that focused on these problems, but it did not believe in the strike as a tool for securing equity for their members. They also opposed the formation of trade unions. The Knights of Labor promoted equality of all workers including women, skilled versus unskilled, and minorities. In 1886, under the leadership of Samuel Gompers, an alliance of trade unions convened calling themselves the American Federation of Labor (AFL). The AFL gave skilled workers a national voice to express their desires for a shorter work week, decent wages, and safer working conditions. The union weathered the great depression of 1897 with 265,000 members and continued to dominate the labor movement well into the twentieth century.

TERM PAPER SUGGESTIONS

1. Describe the economic conditions in 1886 that helped give rise to the AFL. Be sure to include the inability of individual workers to obtain higher wages, shorter work hours, and safer working conditions.

2. Although the Knights of Labor was a powerful national labor organization, it was soon eclipsed by the AFL because of major philosophical differences regarding how members should be organized, who could be members, and what methods should be used to seek redress of grievances over wages and the like. Analyze these differences and discuss why the AFL became the dominant nineteenth-century labor union.

3. Discuss the role that Samuel Gompers played from 1886 until 1924 in developing the AFL. How do you account for his longevity?

4. Unlike other unions that formally participated in the political process, AFL unions were involved more indirectly. Discuss the pros and cons of this labor philosophy.

5. While the Knights of Labor was an egalitarian social movement dedicated to the advancement of all workers regardless of ethnicity and gender, the AFL was committed to "business unionism" that was designed to primarily

advance the economic interests of their members. Most of these members were white and male. Analyze why the Knights of Labor failed and the AFL succeeded.

6. Under the leadership of Samuel Gompers, the AFL unions initiated collective bargaining procedures with employers that directly advanced the economic interests of their membership. Examine why this system worked so effectively.

ALTERNATIVE TERM PAPER SUGGESTIONS

1. Many AFL unions excluded minority and female workers from membership. Prepare a podcast speech describing why this practice will undermine the overall strength of the labor movement in the years to come.

2. Assume you are a nineteenth-century AFL union organizer. Design a union plan that will appeal to a majority of workers in a recently established cigar-making factory.

SUGGESTED SOURCES

Primary Sources

Gompers, Samuel. *The Samuel Gompers Papers.* 9 volumes to date. Urbana, IL: University of Illinois, 1986–2003. Provides all important correspondence of Gompers on behalf of the American Federation of Labor.

Gompers, Samuel. *Seventy Years of Life and Labor: An Autobiography.* Reprint. Ithaca, NY: Cornell University Press, 1984. Provides primary sources in the form of speeches, letters, and recollections of Samuel Gompers who led the AFL from 1886 until his death in 1924.

Secondary Sources

Buhle, Paul. *Taking Care of Business: Samuel Gompers, George Meaney, Lane Kirkland, and the Tragedy of American Labor.* New York: Monthly Review Press, 1999. Asserts that all of these labor leaders allied themselves closely to corporations instead of representing their union members.

Fink, Leon. *In Search of the Working Class: Essays in American Labor History and Political Culture.* Urbana, IL: University of Illinois Press, 1994. Furnishes an outstanding overview of the history of the American Labor Movement.

Foner, Philip S. *History of the Labor Movement in the United States: From the Founding of the American Federation of Labor to the Emergence of American Imperialism.* Vol. 2. New York: International Publishers, 1974. Is considered the definitive history of the American Federation of Labor.

Foner, Philip S. *Women and the American Labor Movement: From the First Trade Unions to the Present.* New York: Free Press, 1979. Investigates the roles that women played in the growth and development of unions.

Greene, Julie. *Pure and Simple Politics: The American Federation of Labor and Political Activism, 1881–1917.* New York: Cambridge University Press, 1998. Studies the extent that the AFL engaged in the political process under the leadership of Samuel Gompers.

Laurie, Bruce. *Artisans into Workers: Labor in Nineteenth Century America.* New York: Hill and Wang, 1989. Explores how work changed as a result of the rise of vertically integrated industries and manufacturing processes in the nineteenth century.

Mandel, Bernard. *Samuel Gompers: A Biography.* Yellow Springs, OH: Antioch Press, 1963. Provides a comprehensive biography of the life and times of Samuel Gompers.

Meltzer, Milton. *Bread and Roses: The Struggle of American Labor, 1865–1915.* New York: Facts on File, 1991. Gives a thorough history of the labor movement and the organizing challenges it faced, particularly during the nineteenth century.

Taft, Philip. *The A.F. of L. in the Time of Gompers.* New York: Harper & Brothers, 1957. Is considered the definitive history of the AFL during Gomper's leadership.

Voss, Kim. *The Making of American Exceptionalism: The Knights of Labor and Class Formation in the Nineteenth Century.* Ithaca, NY: Cornell University Press, 1993. Provides an outstanding history of the Knights of Labor and their attempts to form a social, political movement not just a trade union federation.

Yellowitz, Irwin. *Industrialization and the American Labor Movement, 1850–1900.* Port Washington, NY: Kennikat Press, 1977. Studies the relationship between the rise of monopolistic industries and the responding growth and development of organized labor.

World Wide Web

"AFL-CIO." http://www.aflcio.org/aboutus/history/history/index.cfm. Contains the home page of the current AFL-CIO labor union that includes labor history links, a labor history timeline, and a description of key events in the labor movement.

"A Curriculum of United States Labor History for Teachers." http://www.kentlaw.edu/ilhs/curricul.htm. Provides lesson plans and an extensive set of labor history links that includes information about the AFL.

"Leonora Barry's Report to the Knights of Labor, 1887." http://www.scc.rutgers.edu/njwomenshistory/Period_4/barry.htm. Furnishes the full text of a

report by a woman organizer for the Knights of Labor on the employment conditions of women working in New Jersey mill towns.

"Making of America." http://cdl.library.cornell.edu/moa/. Cornell University
provides a digital collection of primary sources about the social history
of nineteenth-century America that sheds light on the economic conditions that helped give rise to the American Labor Movement.

"Samuel Gompers, 1850–1924." http://www.kentlaw.edu/ilhs/gompers.htm.
Provides an overview of the life of Samuel Gompers, along with several
exploratory questions that could serve as term paper topics.

"The Samuel Gompers Papers." http://www.history.umd.edu/Gompers/
index.htm. Sponsored by the University of Maryland, this outstanding
site features a biographical sketch of Gompers, a timeline of AFL events,
information about the Knights of Labor, full text labor history documents, and labor history resource links.

"Women Working, 1800–1930." http://ocp.hul.harvard.edu/ww/. Harvard
University provides a digital collection of the history of women working
in a variety of jobs during the nineteenth century that includes letters,
diary entries, and other correspondence.

Multimedia Sources

Organizing America: The History of Trade Unions. Charleston, WV: Cambridge
Educational Corp., 2003. 1 DVD. 38 minutes. Narrates the formation
of U.S. trade unions, including the American Federation of Labor.

Rise of Industrial America. Chicago, IL: Encyclopaedia Britannica, 1969.
1 videocassette. 30 minutes. Traces the history of the American Labor
Movement from the 1800s to the present, the effects of early strikes in
altering governmental attitudes toward labor, and the founding of the
American Federation of Labor.

88. Haymarket Square Riot (1886)

There were many victims of the tragic Haymarket Square Riot, which
took place on a square on Randolph Street, Chicago, May 4, 1886. The
event was a sympathy rally in protest to a violent strike and riot that took
place the day before at the McCormick Reaper Works in which several
workers were killed by the police. Albert Parsons, Samuel Fielden, and
August Spies, unionists and anarchists, spoke to the crowd, calling them
to arms. Rain poured down and the police requested that the remaining
three hundred people disperse. As they were leaving peaceably, someone

threw a bomb, killing seven policemen and injuring twenty-seven others. In addition to the three speakers, five other anarchists were indicted for conspiracy. After a sensational trial with no evidence produced that any of them threw the bomb, seven were sentenced to death and one to life imprisonment. Ultimately four were hanged and one committed suicide in prison. In 1893, Illinois Governor John Peter Altgeld pardoned the three who were still in prison, at the cost of his reelection. Unions such as the Knights of Labor that had gained the public's support for an eight-hour day were associated with the anarchist movement and totally discredited. By 1890, their membership had fallen to one hundred thousand from seven hundred thousand members. The public fear of anarchists continued and set the stage for further Red scares in the future.

TERM PAPER SUGGESTIONS

1. Many journalists reported that unionism was becoming synonymous with anarchism. Describe the typical working environment of an employee at a Chicago meat-packing plant or railroad yard. Discuss the reasons why anarchism rather than unionism might appeal to them.

2. Explore the damage that the Haymarket Square Riot did to the American Labor Movement, particularly to the Knights of Labor.

3. Samuel Gompers, head of the newly founded American Federation of Labor (AFL) defended those charged with conspiracy, calling their executions "judicial murder." Examine how the trial was a serious miscarriage of justice.

4. Analyze how the bombing was a godsend to enemies of the burgeoning American Labor Movement. Discuss how they capitalized on the event in period newspaper and magazine articles to discredit unions.

5. Anarchism was an offshoot of socialism within the American Labor Movement. It had roots in Europe, particularly among the followers of Karl Marx and Friedrich Engels. Discuss how anarchist leaders such as August Spies and Samuel Fielden translated their ideas to their followers in newspaper articles and speeches. How did the anarchists' views threaten those held by capitalists?

6. Prosecutor Julius Grinnell argued the state's case against the anarchists. Examine how he was able to obtain a conviction for all of them without producing any evidence linking them to throwing the bomb.

ALTERNATIVE TERM PAPER SUGGESTIONS

1. Assume you are an aide to Illinois Governor John Peter Altgeld. He has asked you to draw up an annotated list of reasons why Michael Schwab, Samuel

Fielden, and Oscar Neebe should be pardoned. He has also asked for an assessment of how his decision to pardon the anarchists will affect his reelection campaign.

2. Prepare an online chronology including relevant images of the Haymarket Square Riot beginning with the May 1, eight-hour work week solidarity marches nationwide and ending with Governor Altgeld's pardon of the surviving anarchists.

SUGGESTED SOURCES

Primary Sources

Foner, Philip S., ed. *Autobiographies of the Haymarket Martyrs*. New York: Anchor Books, 1969. Still in print, this work contains the testimony and life histories of several of the accused anarchists.

Marx, Eleanor, et al. *The Working-Class Movement in America*. New York: Humanity Books, 2000. This 1886 reprint of a best-selling book by Karl Marx's daughter accurately depicts the state of the working man in nineteenth-century America and the status of the American Labor Movement at that time.

Secondary Sources

Avrich, Paul. *The Haymarket Tragedy*. Princeton, NJ: Princeton University Press, 1986. This scholarly work discusses and analyzes the events of the Haymarket Affair.

Brexel, Bernadette. *The Knights of Labor and the Haymarket Riot: The Fight for an Eight-Hour Workday*. New York: Rosen Books, 2005. Written for secondary school students, this work shows how the Knights of Labor union was permanently affected by the Haymarket Square Riot.

Burgan, Michael. *The Haymarket Square Tragedy*. Minneapolis, MN: Compass Books, 2005. Written for secondary school students, this book furnishes an excellent overview of the background, events, and aftermath of the Haymarket Square Riot.

Clark, Christopher, et al. *Who Built America?: Working People and the Nation's Economy, Politics, Culture, and Society*. New York: Worth Publishers, 2000. Traces the evolution of work from the time of slavery to the factory worker, showing how their low-paid work really built the country and made it rich.

David, Henry. *History of the Haymarket Affair*. New York: Macmillan, 2000. Filled with information about socialism and the anarchist movement, this book discusses how it related to the Haymarket Square Riot of 1886.

Debouzy, Marianne. *In the Shadow Statue Liberty: Immigrants, Workers, and Citizens in the American Republic Liberty, 1880–1920*. Urbana, IL: University of Illinois Press, 1992. Describes the working conditions for immigrants and employees of meat-packing plants, railroad yards, and other manufacturing jobs in the nineteenth century before unions won them any benefits.

Green, James. *Death in the Haymarket: A Story of Chicago, the First Labor Movement, and the Bombing That Divided Gilded Age America*. New York: Pantheon Books, 2006. Provides an outstanding narrative history of the Haymarket Square Riot, including the temporary damage it did to the American Labor Movement.

McClellan, Jim R. *Historical Moments: Changing Interpretations of America's Past, Volume 2*. New York: McGraw-Hill, 1999. Contains an overview of the Haymarket Square Riot and its impact on American labor history.

Nelson, Bruce C. *Beyond the Martyrs: A Social History of Chicago's Anarchists, 1870–1900*. New Brunswick, NJ: Rutgers University Press, 1988. Provides an excellent narrative history of the anarchist movement in Chicago during the time of the Haymarket Riot of 1886.

Shore, Elliott. *The German-American Radical Press: The Shaping of a Left Political Culture, 1850–1940*. Urbana, IL: University of Illinois Press, 1992. Provides a history of the anarchist movement as conducted in radical period newspapers by followers of Marx and Engels.

Smith, Carl. *Urban Disorder and the Shape of Belief: The Great Chicago Fire, the Haymarket Bomb, and the Model Town of Pullman*. Chicago, IL: University of Chicago Press, 1996. Traces the history of these three events and how they related to people thinking that cities were places of great disorder.

World Wide Web

"Anarchist Archives: The Haymarket Massacre Archive." http://dwardmac.pitzer.edu/ANARCHIST_ARCHIVES/haymarket/Haymarket.html. Contains biographical sketches of all of the anarchists, commentary about the event, period illustrations from magazines, a history of the event, and bibliography.

"Chicago Anarchists on Trial: Evidence from the Haymarket Affair." http://memory.loc.gov/ammem/award98/ichihtml/haybuild.html. Provides primary sources in the form of the trial transcript and eyewitness testimony of the Haymarket Affair.

"Death in the Haymarket: A Story of Chicago, the First Labor Movement, and the Bombing that Divided Gilded Age America." http://www.iht.com/articles/2006/05/14/news/booklun.php. Provides a lengthy book review of James Green's recent book about the Haymarket Riot.

"The Dramas of Haymarket." http://www.chicagohistory.org/dramas/. This part
    of the Chicago Historical Society's collection attempts to place the Hay-
    market Square affair within the historical context of the period.
"The Haymarket Affair Digital Collection." http://www.chicagohs.org/hadc/.
    Contains primary sources in the form of first-person accounts, a chronol-
    ogy of events, summary of the event, and more.
"The Haymarket Massacre, 1886." http://recollectionbooks.com/anow/history/
    haymarket.html. Provides an excellent set of resource links concerning
    the Haymarket Square Riot.
"Inspector John Bonfield Report to Frederick Ebersold, General Superintendent
    of Police, 1886 May 30." http://www.chicagohs.org/hadc/manuscripts/
    m03/M03P160.htm. Contains the full text of the report to the general
    superintendent of police concerning the events surrounding the Haymar-
    ket Square bomb explosion.

Multimedia Sources

Chicago: City of the Century. Alexandria, VA: PBS Home Video, 2003. 4 DVDs.
    270 minutes. This excellent documentary devotes part of its coverage to
    nineteenth-century labor unrest in Chicago, including information
    about the Haymarket Square Riot of 1886.
John Peter Altgeld: The Eagle Remembered. DeKalb, IL: Northern Illinois Univer-
    sity Press, 2000. 1 videocassette. 59 minutes. Narrates the heroic story
    of Governor Altgeld and his decision to pardon some of the accused
    Haymarket Square rioters at the price of his reelection.
The Road to Haymarket. Chicago, IL: Committee for Labor Access, 1987.
    1 videocassette. 30 minutes. Re-creates the incidents that led to the Hay-
    market Square Riot that resulted in the death of several policemen.

89. Oklahoma Land Rush (1889)

There had been other land rushes in U.S. history when the government
made land available on a first come first serve basis, but nothing in
present-day Iowa or other parts of Oklahoma equaled the one in 1889. It
should have been called the "Oklahoma stampede" for at high noon on
April 22, more than two hundred thousand people along the northern border of Texas and southern boundary of Kansas poured into Oklahoma
Territory when a bugle sounded. Arriving in wagons, on horseback, on
bicycles, by jumping off trains, and by sprinting, settlers raced to stake
out their claims to the last frontier land left in nineteenth-century United

States. Within nine hours of the bugle's signal, almost two million acres of Oklahoma territory were claimed and settled. Between noon and sundown, twelve thousand people claimed and staked out the town of Guthrie. The excitement that cheap land engendered ignored the price that was paid by the American Indian. For when the sun set on this newly claimed acreage, thousands of Indians belonging to twenty-two tribes had lost their ancestral lands and were being herded onto useless reservations to a way of life that was totally foreign to them. The territory that eventually became the forty-sixth state in 1907 mushroomed overnight to a population of fifty thousand settlers.

TERM PAPER SUGGESTIONS

1. Examine some of the people and industries that had a vested interest in settling the Oklahoma Territory including railroad owners, land speculators, and so-called "Boomers" themselves.

2. Research the role that President Rutherford B. Hayes played in renegotiating treaties with the Creek and Seminole Indians for the purpose of settling their lands.

3. Although Congress failed to establish any form of government, they did send U.S. Marshals to ensure that no one crossed into the territory until noon on April 22, 1889. Instead, however, many marshals used their positions to take prior claim of land parcels. Research the illegality of their actions and implications for lawlessness in the Oklahoma Territory.

4. Settlers soon found themselves covered in a fine, red dust from sandy soil that held little moisture. Research the amount of yearly rainfall, type of soil, and other relevant climactic conditions of the Oklahoma Territory. What were the implications for the "Dust Bowl" of the 1930s?

5. Many Boomers were extremely poor people who had failed at farming in Kansas. Analyze what basic nineteenth-century supplies they would have needed to succeed in farming or ranching in Oklahoma. Explore the government's lack of requirements and responsibility toward them.

6. Within hours, the town of Guthrie, consisting of twelve thousand persons, was mapped out and claimed. Research why and how this town, unlike Oklahoma City, became such a target for settlement.

ALTERNATIVE TERM PAPER SUGGESTIONS

1. Assume you are a reporter for a national, nineteenth-century periodical. Write several articles, replete with human interest stories, describing the excitement and chaos of this wild stampede for cheap land.

2. Draw or research a series of pre- and postmaps showing the displacement of several major Indian tribes. Research the condition of the reservations that they ended up living on in terms of the availability of wild game, buffalo, clean water, and the like.

SUGGESTED SOURCES

Primary Sources

McGuire, Lloyd H. *Birth of Guthrie: Oklahoma's Run of 1889 and Life in Guthrie in 1889 and the 1890's, 2nd edition*. San Diego, CA: L. H. McGuire, 2000. This self-published work contains then and now photographs and first-person accounts of the settlement of Guthrie, Oklahoma, during the Great Land Rush of 1889.

Wayman, Phil. *Daughter of the Cherokee Strip*. Victoria, BC: Trafford Publishing, 2006. Relates eyewitness testimony by a young girl who, with her family, was part of the Oklahoma Land Rush of 1889.

Secondary Sources

Baldwin, Kathlyn. *The 89ers: Oklahoma Land Rush of 1889*. Oklahoma City, OK: Western Heritage Books, 1981. Furnishes an exciting history of the people who settled present-day Oklahoma as part of the Land Rush.

Dubois, Muriel L. *Indians & the Oklahoma Land Rush*. Armonk, NY: Owl Publications, 2002. This packet of materials contains facsimiles of the posters advertising the sale of federal land, eyewitness testimony of the event, maps showing the area designated for sale, and the dispositions of various Indian tribes as a result of the rush.

Flanders, Stephen A. *Atlas of American Migration*. New York: Facts on File, 1998. Provides a chapter on the forced migration of the American Indian, including maps that reveal movement caused by the Indian Removal Act, major battles, and population figures from 1890 to 1990.

Flores, Dan L. *Horizontal Yellow: Nature and History in the Near Southwest*. Albuquerque, NM: University of New Mexico Press, 1999. Furnishes a history of the ecology of the region encompassing Oklahoma and the flora and fauna that settlers would have encountered in 1889.

Hoig, Stan. *The Oklahoma Land Rush of 1889*. Oklahoma City, OK: Oklahoma Historical Society, 1984. Provides a narrative history of the Great Oklahoma Land Rush that includes descriptions of claim jumpers, land speculators, and the trials and tribulations of various settlers.

Issacs, Sally Senzell. *The Great Land Rush*. Chicago, IL: Heinemann, 2003. Written for secondary school students, this work furnishes a short overview of the events surrounding the last land rush in America.

Oklahoma, the Beautiful Land. Oklahoma City, OK: 89er Society, 1990. Gives a history of Oklahoma starting with the 1889 Land Rush.

Russell, Sheldon. *Dreams to Dust: A Tale of the Oklahoma Land Rush*. Norman, OK: University of Oklahoma Press, 2006. Winner of the Langum Prize for legal history, this work of historical fiction is patterned after actual persons who experienced the Oklahoma Land Rush.

Speer, Bonnie. *Cleveland County the Pride of the Promised Land: An Illustrated History*. Norman, OK: Reliance Press, 1988. Provides a history of one of the counties created by the Oklahoma Land Rush of 1889.

Sprague, Donovan Arleigh. *Choctaw Nation of Oklahoma*. Chicago, IL: Arcadia Publishing, 2007. Provides a short history of the Choctaw nation who occupied the Oklahoma Territory until the Land Rush of 1889.

Sturm, Circe Dawn. *Blood Politics: Race, Culture, and Identity in the Cherokee Nation of Oklahoma*. Berkeley, CA: University of California Press, 2002. Traces the history of the Cherokee tribe and their attempts to assimilate into American society in the eighteenth and nineteenth centuries, despite loss of their lands in Oklahoma.

World Wide Web

"Boomer Movement." http://digital.library.okstate.edu/encyclopedia/entries/B/ BO011.html. Presents a synopsis of the boom (hence the name "boomers") to unsettled areas of the United States, including the Oklahoma Territory.

"Immigration—Native American." http://memory.loc.gov/learn/features/ immig/native_american6.html. This Library of Congress site discusses all the Congressional Acts that were used to remove the American Indians from Oklahoma Territory and paved the way for the Land Rush of 1889. There is also a settler's description of the violent clash between many settlers and American Indians as the latter group fought to keep their lands.

"Land Run of 1889." http://digital.library.okstate.edu/encyclopedia/entries/L/ LA014.html. Supplies an outstanding hyperlinked overview of the Oklahoma Land Rush.

"Oklahoma Land Openings 1889–1907." http://marti.rootsweb.com/land/ oklands.html. This outstanding megasite features primary sources in the form of period maps, census data, first-person accounts, and details concerning the growth and development of all the counties that were designated as part of the acreage included in the Land Rush.

"Oklahoma Land Rush Images." http://www.hanksville.org/sand/realprop/gof
.html. Provides many primary source images of soldiers, settlers, trains,
covered wagons, and other sights surrounding the Land Rush of 1889.

"The Rush to Oklahoma." http://www.library.cornell.edu/Reps/DOCS/
landrush.htm. Contains the full text of a May 18, 1889, *Harper's Weekly*
article by a reporter who attended and observed the Oklahoma Land
Rush, including the overnight settlement of the town of Guthrie.

"Settlement Patterns." http://digital.library.okstate.edu/encyclopedia/entries/S/
SE024.html. Gives an overview of the settlement patterns before and
after the Oklahoma Land Rush, including those of the American Indian.

Multimedia Sources

Cheyenne Autumn. Burbank, CA: Warner Home Video, 1964. 1 videocassette.
155 minutes. Hollywood film directed by John Ford and starring
Richard Widmark dramatizes the plight of the Cheyenne as they decide
to leave the reservation during the nineteenth century and fight once
more for their ancestral lands in what is Oklahoma Territory.

19th Century Turning Points in U.S. History. New York: Ambrose Video
Publishing, 2002. 1 videocassette. 25 minutes. Episode 8, 1882–1890,
narrates and describes the significance of pivotal events in U.S. history,
including the Oklahoma Land Rush of 1889.

Rutherford B. Hayes Presidential Center. *Rutherford B. Hayes: Citizen, Soldier,
President* (CD-ROM). Chicago, IL: Legacy Publications, 1999. This
1,200-page CD-ROM provides an engrossing biography of the life and
times of Rutherford B. Hayes, including his role in negotiating with various Indian tribes and support for the Oklahoma Land Rush of 1889.

90. Nellie Bly, Journalist Extraordinaire

Nellie Bly was the pen name for journalist Elizabeth Jane Cochrane
Seaman (1864–1922). It was the expectation of the day that female journalists publish under a pen name, and her editor at the *Pittsburgh Dispatch*
bestowed the name on her when she was hired. Nellie obtained the job
after writing a feminist response to a sexist column in the paper. Initially
she tackled articles that featured the lot of working women in factories,
but she was soon shunted off to cover typical women's areas such as style,
society, and gardening for those sections of the paper. Disgruntled and
disappointed, she left the *Pittsburgh Dispatch* and went to work for the
New York World run by Joseph Pulitzer. One of her first assignments was

to go undercover for ten days, masquerading as a mental patient in an insane asylum. Her articles, later compiled into a book entitled *Ten Days in a Mad-House,* were groundbreaking and brought her the recognition that she truly deserved. In 1888, she decided to challenge the circumnavigation record in Jules Verne's book, *Around the World in Eighty Days.* Traveling solo by steamer, train, rickshaw, and sampan, Nellie Bly successfully circled the globe in seventy-two days and returned to New York to welcoming gun salutes. She had beaten Verne's record, had kept her readers tantalized with articles about her progress, and had become a role model for independent women everywhere.

TERM PAPER SUGGESTIONS

1. The article in the *Pittsburgh Dispatch* that so infuriated Nellie Bly was entitled, "What Girls are Good For." Discuss the essence of the piece and why a woman such as Nellie Bly in 1888 would have been so enraged by its contents and tone.

2. Nellie Bly was one of the first women foreign correspondents. Investigate and describe her reportage from Mexico that resulted in a book she wrote entitled, *Six Months in Mexico,* and why she was almost arrested by the Mexican government.

3. Nellie Bly is considered one of the muckraking journalists. She believed that newspapers played an essential role in serving as attorneys for the poor and the damned. Examine her contribution to the field of mental health after she published articles and her book on the mentally ill entitled, *Ten Days in a Mad-House.*

4. Bly also knew how to sell newspapers. Analyze how her challenge to circumnavigate the globe in less than 180 days sold thousands of copies of the *New York World.*

5. In 1894 Bly married a wealthy manufacturer of steel containers. After his death she assumed responsibility for the company. Discuss the obstacles and challenges that she would have faced as a nineteenth-century businesswoman.

6. Analyze how Nellie Bly served as role model for women who wished to live and work independently in the nineteenth century. Describe how many taboos she broke as a female journalist.

ALTERNATIVE TERM PAPER SUGGESTIONS

1. Using nineteenth-century style reportage, write several online articles in the style of Nellie Bly about why a woman should be the next president of the United States.

2. Assume that Nellie Bly is being inducted into an online Women's Hall of Fame. Design a hyperlinked Web site of no more than four screens that highlight the significant parts of her life and times.

SUGGESTED SOURCES

Primary Sources

Bly, Nellie. *Around the World in Seventy-Two Days.* http://www.gutenberg.org/browse/authors/b#a9648. The full text of Bly's book is available online at Project Gutenberg.

Bly, Nellie. *Ten Days in a Mad-House.* http://www.gutenberg.org/browse/authors/b#a9648. The full text of Bly's famous exposé about the plight of the mentally ill is available online at Project Gutenberg.

Secondary Sources

Bedford, Barbara. *Brilliant Bylines: A Biographical Anthology of Notable Newspaper-Women in American.* New York: Columbia University Press, 1988. Chapter 8 is devoted to Nellie Bly's contribution to journalism and the pioneering role she played in breaking the glass ceiling in the newspaper business.

Berson, Robin Kadison. *Young Heroes in World History.* Westport, CT: Greenwood Publishing Group, 1999. Nellie Bly's courage in going undercover and her exposé of the abusive treatment of the mentally ill are lauded in this work.

Brian, Denis. *Pulitzer: A Life.* New York: Wiley, 2001. Chapter 11 is devoted to a discussion of Nellie Bly's undercover work in an insane asylum and her trip around the world in seventy-two days.

Davidson, Sue. *Getting the Real Story: Nellie Bly and Ida B. Wells.* Seattle, WA: Seal Press, 1992. Written for secondary students, this work gives an excellent overview of the life, times, and contributions of Nellie Bly and African American journalist Ida B. Wells.

Douglas, George H. *The Golden Age of the Newspaper.* Westport, CT: Greenwood Publishing Group, 1999. Chapter 13 is devoted to women such as Nellie Bly who broke barriers with their reportage of events other than the typical domestic issues to which they were historically assigned.

Gale, Robert L. *The Gay Nineties in America: A Cultural Dictionary of the 1890s.* Westport, CT: Greenwood Press, 1992. Discusses the life and times of Nellie Bly within the context of the period in which she lived.

Kroeger, Brooke. *Nellie Bly: Daredevil, Reporter, Feminist.* New York: Crown Books, 1994. Considered the definitive work on Bly, this work gives an excellent account of her life and career.

Marks, Jason. *Around the World in 72 Days*. 2nd ed. Pittsburgh, PA: Sterling-house Publishers, 1999. Relies upon the journals and articles of Nellie Bly to recount her tale of circumnavigating the globe in a record-breaking seventy-two days.

Marzolf, Marion. *Up from the Footnote: A History of Women Journalists*. New York: Hastings House, 1977. Discusses Nellie Bly's groundbreaking role as a nineteenth-century woman journalist, along with other women's contributions.

Ross, Donald, and James J. Schramer, eds. *American Travel Writers, 1850–1915*. Detroit, MI: Gale, 1998. Provides a description of the life and legacy of travel writer Nellie Bly.

Schilpp, Madelon Golden. *Great Women of the Press*. Carbondale, IL: Southern Illinois University Press, 1983. Chapter 13 is devoted to describing the life and legacy of Nellie Bly to the world of journalism.

World Wide Web

"Elizabeth Jane Cochrane: Nellie Bly—Pioneer Woman Investigative Journalist." http://home.att.net/~gapehenry/NellieBly.html. Gives a brief overview of her life and details about how aspects of her life were incorporated into a Victorian parlor game and trading cards during the 1890s.

"Jules Verne: Nellie Bly (1864–1922)." http://www.julesverne.ca/nelliebly.html. Contains a biographical sketch of Nellie Bly, information about the Victorian parlor game and trading cards associated with her trip around the world, a copy of Stephen Foster's song "Nellie Bly," and a bibliography of additional print resources.

"The Lost World of Joseph Pulitzer." http://www.slate.com/id/2126420/. Provides an interesting article about the typical articles in Joseph Pulitzer's *New York World* and the role that one of his top investigative reporters, Nellie Bly, played in it. The article also contains images from different issues of the *New York World*.

"Nellie Bly 1864–1922." http://www.library.csi.cuny.edu/dept/history/lavender/386/nellie.html. Furnishes an overview of the life and times of feminist and journalist Nellie Bly.

"Nellie Bly Spartacus Educational Biography." http://www.spartacus.schoolnet.co.uk/USAWbly.htm. Contains a forty-six page biographical portrait of Nellie Bly, including excerpts from her book *Ten Days in a Mad-House*.

"New York World." http://www.spartacus.schoolnet.co.uk/USAnyworld.htm. Describes Joseph Pulitzer and his newspaper, which was associated with sensationalistic journalism, and the role that Nellie Bly played in furthering it.

"People and Events—Nellie Bly." http://www.pbs.org/wgbh/amex/world/peopleevents/pande01.html. Provides an overview of the life and times of journalist and feminist Nellie Bly.

Multimedia Sources

American Experience—Around the World in 72 Days. Alexandria, VA: PBS Home Video, 1997. 1 videocassette. 60 minutes. This documentary captures the excitement generated by Nellie Bly's articles sent back to the *New York World* as she circumnavigated the globe in a successful attempt to beat Verne's record in his best-selling book, *Around the World in Eighty Days.*

91. New Immigration Wave (1890s)

In the two decades from 1881 to 1900, well over nine million immigrants entered the United States. While two million were from Germany and one million from Great Britain and Ireland, the remainder came from Scandinavia and eastern and southern Europe. They were considered "new immigrants" because overall they did not speak English or share the common Anglo Saxon backgrounds that had enabled "old immigrants" to integrate themselves into American society. Unlike other immigrant groups that could take advantage of cheap land to begin homesteading, U.S. agriculture was in a depression caused by railroads that established freight prices, manufacturing monopolies that set the price of farm machinery, and banks that controlled credit. American farmers were selling their lands and immigrating to the city to take jobs in factories and encountering significant numbers of immigrants who had left similar situations in their home countries only to experience them in America. New industrial technology had reduced the need for skilled labor, so Americans and new immigrants found themselves vying for jobs that did not pay well, causing them to take up residence in tenements and slums in big cities such as New York, Chicago, Detroit, Boston, and Cleveland. It was no wonder that there was a backlash against new immigrants who spoke little or no English, ate different foods, practiced different religions, held no basic trust in the democratic process, and even looked different from Americans. Cries for quotas continued throughout the 1890s until Congress finally set some in 1924. By then, most of the new immigrants had assimilated into American society and left the urban ghettos and slums.

TERM PAPER SUGGESTIONS

1. Examine how improved means of transportation in Europe served as an impetus for this new immigration wave.

2. Describe the agricultural economies of the Mediterranean and Slavic countries and how their circumstances generated significant numbers of immigrants to the United States in the 1890s.

3. Analyze how a dramatic population increase in central and southern European countries was a major factor in people emigrating to the United States. Discuss how the United States served as a safety valve for this area of Europe's discontented, discriminated against, and unemployed populations.

4. America did not become a melting pot during this immigration wave. Instead, immigrants relied upon the advice and advanced knowledge of friends and relatives who had immigrated before them. Choose one émigré country and research how its social, economic, and employment network worked to help immigrants survive in the United States.

5. As usual, there emerged nativists who believed that this wave of new immigrants, who did not share an Anglo Saxon heritage, would create a permanent underclass. Research the role that the Reverend Dr. Josiah Strong played in this area with his anti-immigrant book, *Our Country* (published in 1885).

6. Most immigrants chose to live in large cities such as New York, Cleveland, Chicago, Boston, and Detroit because the American agricultural economy was in shambles. Examine the effects of the Populist Movement on new immigrants and their ability to continue farming as they had done in their countries of origin.

ALTERNATIVE TERM PAPER SUGGESTIONS

1. Assume that you are a skilled, Swedish potter who has decided to emigrate to the United States. Exchange four letters with a cousin who has already arrived concerning the potential for skilled employment, wage structures, working conditions, cost of living, and the like.

2. Assume you are a public relations specialist for a railroad company servicing the Great Plains area. It is imperative that your company attract immigrants to the Great Plains to ensure a continual profit in passenger and freight traffic. Design a series of brochures and/or broadsides that may induce immigrants to leave the cities and try their hand at farming or running a business in a small town. Feel free to exaggerate descriptions of opportunities as they did during this period.

SUGGESTED SOURCES

Primary Sources

Baicker, Karen. *Immigration (Primary Sources Teaching Kit, Grades 4–8)*. New York: Scholastic Inc. Teaching Resources, 2003. Contains a series of reproducible facsimiles of primary sources about immigration, including oral histories, statistics, photographs, and more.

Brownstone, David, et al., eds. *Island of Hope, Island of Tears*. New York: Penguin Books, 1986. Contains interviews with immigrants who went through Ellis Island as members of the new immigrant wave, along with photographs.

Dublin, Thomas, ed. *Immigrant Voices: New Lives in America, 1773–1986*. Urbana, IL: University of Illinois Press, 1993. Provides primary sources in the form of first-person accounts of immigrants' experiences in the United States. The book is divided evenly between male and female experiences.

Secondary Sources

Bodnar, John. *The Transplanted: A History of Immigrants in Urban America*. Bloomington, IN: Indiana University Press, 1987. This excellent source provides a history of the social and economic conditions that drove so many southern and central Europeans to immigrate to the United States and the tremendous challenges that they overcame just to survive once they arrived.

Daniels, Roger. *Coming to America: A History of Immigration and Ethnicity in American Life*. New York: Harper Collins, 2002. Presents statistics concerning how various ethnic groups fared during the initial immigration period.

Daniels, Roger. *Guarding the Golden Door: American Immigration Policy and Immigrants since 1882*. New York: Hill and Wang, 2004. Beginning with the Chinese Exclusion Act of 1882, this book traces the history of attempts by Congress and various activist groups to set limits on immigration using rhetoric that concealed their racist intentions.

Gabaccia, Donna R. *Immigration and American Diversity: A Social and Cultural History*. Malden, MA: Blackwell, 2002. Provides a survey of immigration history from the mid 1800s to the early 1900s. It focuses on cultural and social trends with an emphasis on ethnic conflicts, nativist movements, and racial theories.

Greene, Victor R. *Singing Ambivalence: American Immigrants Between Old World and New, 1830–1930*. Kent, OH: Kent State University Press, 2004. Compares the challenges and struggles faced by the following respective immigrant groups: the Irish, Germans, Scandinavians and Finns, eastern European Jews, Italians, Poles and Hungarians, Chinese, and Mexicans.

Handlin, Oscar. *The Uprooted: The Epic Story of the Great Migrations That Made the American People*. Reprint. Philadelphia, PA: University of Pennsylvania Press, 2002. Written by the "father of immigration history," this classic work depicts the epic struggle that immigrants endured to survive and thrive in the United States.

Higham, John. *Strangers in the Land: Patterns of American Nativism, 1860–1925*. Reprint. New Brunswick, NJ: Rutgers University Press, 2002. Gives a history of the various nativist movements in the United States that eventually led to immigration restrictions and quotas

Meltzer, Milton. *Bound for America: The Story of European Immigrants*. New York: Benchmark Books, 2001. Written for secondary school students, this work features an overview-type history of European immigration during the nineteenth century.

Reimers, David. *Still the Golden Door: The Third World Comes to America*. New York: Columbia University Press, 1985. Gives a history of twentieth-century immigration to the United States and contrasts its similarities to nineteenth-century immigration history.

Sandler, Martin. *Island of Hope: The Journey to America and the Ellis Island Experience*. New York: Scholastic, 2004. Written for secondary school students, this work traces the history of the immigrant process through first-person accounts from the Library of Congress Immigration Studies Collection.

Wepman, Dennis. *Immigration: From the Founding of Virginia to the Closing of Ellis Island*. New York: Facts on File, 2002. Presents a history of immigration from the colonial era through the mid 1950s, including many primary source excerpts in the form of statistics and first-person accounts.

World Wide Web

"Center for Immigration." http://www.cis.org/. Click on the link "immigration history" to retrieve online resources about new immigrants during the 1890s period.

"Ellis Island." http://www.ellisislandrecords.org/. Click on the link "Ellis Island" to retrieve a set of resources concerning Ellis Island history, a timeline, the Ellis Island experience for a typical immigrant, and photo albums.

"Immigration to the United States, 1789–1930." http://ocp.hul.harvard.edu/immigration/. This outstanding collection from Harvard University features the full text of 1,800 books and pamphlets, 9,000 photographs,

200 maps, and 13,000 manuscript pages about the history of immigration to America.

"Internet Lesson Plan Activities Immigration." http://www.libsci.sc.edu/miller/
EllisIsland.htm. Contains lesson plans, term paper questions, and hundreds of resource links to full text online materials about immigration
history.

"Library of Congress Learning Page: The Rise of Industrial America, 1876–
1900." http://memory.loc.gov/ammem/ndlpedu/features/timeline/
riseind/riseof.html. Two sections of this excellent site are devoted to the
new immigrant wave of the late 1800s. The site also contains descriptions of rural and urban life during that time.

"Lower East Side Tenement Museum." http://www.wnet.org/tenement/. Features photographs and text about life in a typical lower East Side New
York City tenement during the time of the new immigrant wave.

"Yearbook of Immigration Statistics." http://www.dhs.gov/ximgtn/statistics/
data/index.shtm. Provides statistics on the countries of origin for immigrants to the United States from 1820 to the present year.

Multimedia Sources

Ellis Island: The Immigrant Experience. Alexandria, VA: PBS Home Video, 2004.
1 DVD. 150 minutes. Through oral histories and interviews with former
immigrants, this documentary recounts the experiences of new immigrants beginning in 1892 when Ellis Island was designated as the point
of entry for most of Europe's immigrants.

92. *How the Other Half Lives* (1890)

Known as the "Great Emancipator of the Slums," muckraking journalist
Jacob Riis was a tireless campaigner for freedom from poverty. His main
focus was the tenements of New York City, which teemed with disease,
filth, and despair. He sought to eradicate them by publishing books and
articles as a reporter for the *New York Tribune* and the *Evening Sun* that
pulled at one's heartstrings. They depicted the life of the poor, especially
their children, in living quarters that not even a family pet would tolerate.
Riis emigrated to the United States from Denmark in 1870 to seek work
as a carpenter. Arriving during a huge wave of immigration, when jobs were
scarce, he spent many nights in police-operated alms houses that were unfit
for human habitation. In 1889, *Scribner's Magazine* published a series of
photographic essays that in 1890 became Riis's most important book,

How the Other Half Lives. It caused such a sensation that Commissioner of Police Theodore Roosevelt, and soon-to-be President of the United States, shut down the houses and befriended Riis for life. It was Roosevelt who coined the term "muckraking journalism" to describe Riis's efforts on behalf of the poor and downtrodden. Riis was one of the first journalists to use flash powder to take pictures of the darkened rooms and the slums at night. His pictures were worth a thousand words and revealed a world of poverty to his readers that they could have only imagined through his prose. Although Riis went on to publish more than twelve other books about life in the tenements and slums of New York City, it is this text that definitely earned him the sobriquet the "Great Emancipator of the Slums."

TERM PAPER SUGGESTIONS

1. During the Gilded Age, many people believed that poor people were lazy, shiftless, and totally responsible for their lot in life. Discuss how Riis's work upended this theory and exposed the environmental causes of poverty.

2. During the late nineteenth century, New York City was undergoing rapid demographic shifts in population as the wealthy fled certain parts of the city when tenements were established. Analyze the main causes for this shift in demographics.

3. New York City has been called a "melting pot." Read several chapters from the book *How the Other Half Lives* about various ethnic groups living in the city. Would you agree or disagree with this statement? Why?

4. Refer to some of Riis's photographs of slums and tenements, and analyze the impact that photographic essays had on his readers.

5. Although Riis's legacy is a fine one with regard to his exposés of urban poverty, his writings also reveal someone who was sexist and even prejudiced toward some immigrant groups. How do you account for this hypocrisy in his character?

6. Research the impact of the waves of immigration during the 1880s and 1890s on New York City. Discuss what the city should or could have done to alleviate some of the poverty and poor living conditions that so many people were forced to endure.

ALTERNATIVE TERM PAPER SUGGESTIONS

1. This option is for two students. One should assume the role of a reporter for the *New York Tribune,* and the other should take on the role of a "recent immigrant" described in Riis's book *How the Other Half Lives.* The "reporter"

should interview the "recent immigrant" and ask the person to describe the living and working conditions in a tenement in Hell's Kitchen.

2. Assume you have been asked by the mayor of New York City to chair a committee to outline reforms for the city's slums. Prepare a PowerPoint presentation complete with nineteenth-century images of tenements, poor children, and slums that outlines things you would do immediately to improve conditions. What things would you do in five years? Be sure to address issues of landlord profits, rent control, and the eradication of rats and other pests.

SUGGESTED SOURCES

Primary Sources

Riis, Jacob. *The Battle with the Slum.* New York: Dover Publications, 1998. Provides a sequel to *How the Other Half Lives.*

Riis, Jacob A. *How the Other Half Lives.* http://www.yale.edu/amstud/inforev/ riis/title.html. Contains the full text of Riis's seminal work about the shame of New York City's tenements and slums.

Riis, Jacob. http://www.gutenberg.org/author/Riis+Jacob+A. Project Gutenberg contains the full text of other books written by Jacob Riis, including *Children of the Tenements* and *The Making of an American.*

Secondary Sources

Bial, Raymond. *Tenement: Immigrant Life on the Lower East Side.* Boston, MA: Houghton Mifflin, 2002. Similar to Riis's work, this book contains photographic essays of the tenements and slums of New York City during the 1880s and 1890s.

Bremner, Robert. *From the Depths: The Discovery of Poverty in the United States.* New York: New York University Press, 1972. This classic work discusses the history of American poverty, including the development of large urban slums and tenements in the late nineteenth century.

Fried, Lewis. *Makers of the City.* Amherst, MA: University of Massachusetts Press, 1990. Discusses immigrants' contribution to the growth and development of cities as an important legacy.

Gale, Robert L. *The Gay Nineties in America: A Cultural Dictionary of the 1890s.* Westport, CT: Greenwood Press, 1974. Provides a cultural reference for other events, trends, beliefs, and practices that helped contribute to New York City's slums and tenements.

Gandal, Keith. *The Virtues of the Vicious: Jacob Riis, Stephen Crane, and the Spectacle of the Slum.* New York: Oxford University Press, 1997. Discusses how groundbreaking the Riis book was because of the use of its accompanying photographs.

Hopkinson, Deborah. *Shutting Out the Sky: Life in the Tenements of New York, 1880–1924*. New York: Orchard Books, 2003. Written for secondary school students, this work relates first-person accounts of various immigrants' struggles to survive in America during a time of massive emigration from eastern and southern Europe.

Kraut, Alan M. *Silent Travelers: Germs, Genes, and the Immigrant Menace*. Baltimore, MD: Johns Hopkins University Press, 1995. Argues that the need for cheap labor created the abysmal living conditions that in turn spawned diseases such as cholera, dysentery, and tuberculosis among immigrant populations living in tenements and slums.

Lane, James B. *Jacob A. Riis and the American City*. New York: Harper Collins, 1975. Presents a biography of Jacob Riis and his legacy of photographic essays about the poverty of nineteenth-century New York City.

Lubove, Roy. *The Progressives and the Slums: Tenement House Reform in New York City, 1890–1917*. Westport, CT: Greenwood Press, 1974. Recounts the attempts by the nineteenth-century Progressive Party to reform New York City's slums and tenement houses.

Riis, Jacob A. *Theodore Roosevelt, the Citizen*. Seattle, WA: Adamant Media Corporation, 2005. Jacob Riis was a lifelong admirer of President Theodore Roosevelt because he championed the cause of the poor. This is Riis's admittedly positive biography of Roosevelt.

Yochelsem, Bonnie. *Jacob Riis (55)*. New York: Phaidon Press, 2001. Features fifty-five of Jacob Riis's most famous photographs of poor children, tenements, and slums.

World Wide Web

"Jacob Riis." http://xroads.virginia.edu/~MA01/Davis/photography/riis/riis.html. Furnishes a biographical sketch of Riis, together with samples of his photographs and an analysis of them and their impact on Gilded Age society.

"Jacob Riis Page from the Open Collections Program at Harvard University. Immigration to the United States, 1789–1930 Collection." http://ocp.hul.harvard.edu/immigration/people_riis.html. Contains a biographical sketch of Jacob Riis, the full texts of ten of his books about poverty, tenements, and slums, and a webography of online nineteenth-century, subject related books.

"Jacob Riis Photographs." http://xroads.virginia.edu/~ma01/davis/photography/images/riisphotos/slideshow1.html. Contains hundreds of labeled pictures taken by Jacob Riis for his photographic essays regarding the slums and tenements of New York City.

"Muckrakers." http://www.digisys.net/users/benwood/progressivism/web doc3.htm. Provides information concerning the origin of the term that is attributed to President Theodore Roosevelt, Riis's contribution to the muckraking movement, and how it fit within the movement of progressivism in the United States.

"Riis, Jacob." http://www.rleggat.com/photohistory/history/riis.htm. Describes Riis's deployment of flash powder to illuminate his photo object and how dangerous it was to use during the nineteenth century.

"Teaching History Online." http://www.spartacus.schoolnet.co.uk/USAriis.htm. Provides a biographical sketch of Riis plus excerpts from his books accompanied by relevant photographs of slums, poor children, and tenement life.

"What Do the World and People Deserve." http://www.lenbernstein.com/Pages/RiisArticle.html. Provides a lengthy article on the life and legacy of Jacob Riis, replete with some of his most famous photographs.

Multimedia Sources

American Visions. Alexandria, VA: PBS Home Video, 1999. 1 videocassette. 58 minutes. Part II, documented by Jacob Riis's photographs, discusses the tremendous wave of immigration that helped precipitate the tenements and slums in large American cities during the nineteenth century.

The Other Half Revisited. New York: Cinema Guild, 1996. 1 videocassette. 59 minutes. Combines Riis's original photographs with the social vision of contemporary photographers, including Margaret Morton, Eli Reed, and Fred Conrad, and explores the similarities between the 1890s and 1990s.

93. "Yellow Peril" Campaign Against the Japanese (1892)

In 1890 there were only two thousand Japanese living and working in California and the Pacific Northwest. Hawaii's population was more than 40 percent Japanese, but it was not yet a state. Both areas, however, became the focus of serious Japanese hate campaigns that were conducted in the press. They led to the formation of anti-Japanese societies similar to the Ku Klux Klan and to boycotts against Japanese merchants and anyone who hired them as workers. Many labor unions, including the American Federation of Labor, urged quotas on Japanese immigration and went on record against their employment. The Japanese, who had labored tirelessly in Hawaii's sugar cane fields and built the connecting railroad line between Tacoma and Seattle for Alaska's gold rush miners, responded to this racism by settling into ethnic enclaves called Japantowns. In these communities, they educated their children in their native language and customs and felt somewhat safe from the outright hostilities that they had experienced living among White people. Despite this withdrawal from American life, pressure continued through legislators to limit Japanese immigration to the United States. In 1894, Japan signed a treaty with the United States that gave both governments the power to limit immigration. Anti-Japanese sentiment continued throughout the nineteenth century and into the twentieth. As protests continued, Japan agreed to a voluntary program to limit Japanese immigration to the United States. The "yellow peril" campaign, which began in the press in 1892, surfaced again after the attack on Pearl Harbor and resulted in the internment of thousands of innocent Japanese Americans during World War II.

TERM PAPER SUGGESTIONS

1. Research how the employment of the Japanese to break a coal miner's strike in British Columbia may have been a contributing factor in the anti-Japanese campaign throughout California and the Pacific Northwest.

2. Discuss the powerful impact that anti-Japanese editorials in the *San Francisco Bulletin* and the *San Francisco Chronicle* had on readers' perceptions of Japanese immigration. How may the editorials have prejudiced readers?

3. Describe the work and the economic contribution that the Japanese made in building the Tacoma to Seattle railroad connection and in growing Hawaii's sugar cane crop.

4. Some historians believe that anti-Japanese prejudice was a psychological form of projection. Whites saw what they hated in their own lives: hard and under-paid work, long hours, and poor living conditions. They made the Japanese their scapegoats because of their similarities rather than their differences. Research the work and living conditions of unskilled White workers during this time period and compare them to those of the Japanese. Note the similarities.

5. Research how the anti-Japanese campaign was conducted in Hawaii, including the ban on children attending Japanese schools to learn their own language and history.

6. Trace the role of organized labor and that of politicians in discriminating against the Japanese, including the San Francisco Building Trades Council

resolution and the American Federation of Labor's urging of exclusion and, if necessary, "force of arms" to keep the Japanese out of America.

ALTERNATIVE TERM PAPER SUGGESTIONS

1. Assume that you are a recent Japanese immigrant living in a racially mixed neighborhood. You and your family have just received a death threat from an anti-Japanese group. Discuss the pros and cons of your decision to move your family to a Japantown.

2. Assume you are a reporter for a neutral California newspaper. Write three editorials rebutting the charges that have been made against the Japanese. Be sure to include information about the contribution that they are making to the local economy and society.

SUGGESTED SOURCES

Primary Sources

Center for Oral History. *Koloa: An Oral History of a Kauai Community.* Honolulu, HI: University of Hawaii Press, 1987. Provides primary sources in the form of first-person accounts of Japanese immigrants who worked in Hawaii during the nineteenth century.

Tamura, Linda. *The Hood River Issei: An Oral History of Japanese Settlers in Oregon's Hood River Valley.* Urbana, IL: University of Illinois Press, 1993. Presents oral histories of Japanese immigrants who lived and worked in the Hood River Valley during the late nineteenth century.

Secondary Sources

Asato, Noriko. *Teaching Mikadoism: The Attack on Japanese Language Schools in Hawaii, California, and Washington, 1919–1927.* Honolulu, HI: University of Hawaii Press, 2005. Discusses the history of the conflict surrounding Japanese schools in Hawaii, California, and the Pacific Northwest and how the anti-Japanese movement labeled them anti-American.

Daniels, Roger. *Asian America: Chinese and Japanese in the United States Since 1850.* Seattle, WA: University of Washington Press, 1990. Presents a scholarly account of the immigrant experiences of the Chinese and Japanese in America during the nineteenth century.

Daniels, Roger. *The Politics of Prejudice: The Anti-Japanese Movement in California and the Struggle for Japanese Exclusion.* Berkeley, CA: University of California Press, 1999. This scholarly work traces the history of racism against the Japanese from the nineteenth through twentieth centuries and demonstrates how it set the stage for the internment of Japanese Americans during World War II.

Gulick, Sidney Lewis. *The American Japanese Problem; a Study of the Racial Relations of the East and the West.* Reprint. New York: J. S. Ozer, 1971. This classic work discusses the history of American and Japanese race relations within a nineteenth-century context.

McWilliams, Carey. *Prejudice: Japanese-Americans, Symbol of Racial Intolerance.* Reprint. Hamden, CT: Archon Books, 1971. Includes a complete history of anti-Japanese prejudice and discrimination up to World War II.

Okihiro, Gary. *Cane Fires: Anti-Japanese Movement in Hawaii, 1865–1945.* Philadelphia, PA: Temple University Press, 1992. Traces the history of the anti-Japanese campaign in Hawaii and the attempt to stop the Japanese from educating their children in their native language and culture.

Takaki, Ronald. *Iron Cages: Race and Culture in 19th-Century America.* New York: Oxford University Press, 2000. Presents an academic history of race relations between White Americans and Asians, including the Japanese, in the nineteenth century.

Takaki, Ronald. *Strangers from a Different Shore: A History of Asian Americans.* Boston, MA: Little, Brown and Company, 1998. Gives an outstanding overview of the immigration of all Asian nationalities to the United States and how they tended to fare regarding employment and settlement.

Ward, Peter W. *White Canada Forever: Popular Attitudes and Public Policy Toward Orientals in British Columbia.* 3rd ed. Montreal, CN: McGill-Queen's University Press, 2002. Contains a thorough history of how Asians, including the Japanese, were treated in Canada from the nineteenth through twentieth centuries.

Wilson, Robert A., and Bill Hosokawa. *East to America: A History of the Japanese in the United States.* New York: William Morrow, 1980. Furnishes an excellent overview of Japanese immigration and settlement in the United States.

Zurlo, Tony. *Immigrants in America—Japanese-Americans.* San Diego, CA: Lucent Books, 2003. Written for secondary school students, this work presents a history of the type of work done by many Japanese during the nineteenth century and the contribution that they made to the American economy and society.

World Wide Web

"Eating Bitterness: The Impact of Asian-Pacific Migration on United States Immigration Policy." http://www.ilw.com/articles/2004,0602-Campi .shtm. Provides an overview of Japanese nineteenth-century immigration to Hawaii, California, and the Pacific Northwest.

"For Further Reference." http://asianamericanmedia.org/picturebride/bib.html. Contains an extensive bibliography of books about the experience of Japanese immigrants in the United States during the nineteenth and early twentieth centuries.

"Immigration: The Japanese Journey to America." http://library.thinkquest.org/20619/Japanese.html. Provides an excellent history of Japanese immigration to America and also Hawaii.

"Immigration to the United States, 1789–1930." http://ocp.hul.harvard.edu/immigration/. Provides access to 1,800 books and pamphlets and 9,000 photographs concerning immigration. Many feature primary sources in the form of diaries and letters written by Japanese immigrants.

"On Yellow Peril Thrillers." http://www.violetbooks.com/yellowperil.html. Provides an essay about nineteenth-century books that were designed to negatively stereotype Chinese and Japanese immigrants.

"Prostitutes and Picture Brides: Chinese and Japanese Immigration, Settlement, and American-Nation Building, 1870–1920." http://www.ccis-ucsd.org/publications/wrkg70.pdf. This forty-nine page paper examines the prejudice toward both Asian groups, including the fact that Chinese women were considered prostitutes while Japanese women were allowed to immigrate to the United States as picture brides.

"Receptions of Asians to the United States—Asian Immigration." http://science.jrank.org/pages/10966/Reception-Asians-United-States-Asian-Immigration.html. Provides a brief history of how the Japanese were perceived and treated by Americans when they first immigrated to the United States.

Multimedia Sources

Japanese Americans. Wynnewood, PA: Schlessinger Video Productions, 1993. 1 videocassette. 30 minutes. Celebrates the heritage of Japanese Americans by tracing the history of their immigration to North America.

94. Frederick Jackson Turner's Thesis of the American Frontier (1893)

The census of 1890 inspired Professor Frederick Jackson Turner to publish and publicize a thesis entitled "The Significance of the Frontier in American History." In 1890, the U.S. Census Bureau officially declared the "frontier" closed because there was no area of the country left that had fewer than two people per square mile. The Apache wars ceased in 1886 with the surrender of Geronimo. In 1890, Sioux Chief Sitting Bull was murdered in South Dakota, and in the same year the last battle with the Sioux was fought at Wounded Knee. Other than reservations, there was no longer any American Indian land that had not been either ceded to settlers or the U.S. government. Turner believed that the closing of the frontier represented the end of a historical epoch of westward advancement and settlement. He hypothesized that this westward expansion had uniquely shaped American character, political institutions, and our form of democracy. Turner saw the frontier as advancing through a series of stages: the explorer's frontier; the hunter's frontier; the fur trapper and trader; the miner; the frontier of the plantation owner and settler farmer. The final stage was the frontier of trade, manufacture, and organized government. He also saw the frontier as a safety valve for those who were unhappy with their current situation, discontented, or oppressed. Turner proposed that the frontier "promoted individualism, economic equality, freedom to rise, and democracy." His thesis dominated the study of American history until the 1930s when historians began to question different aspects of it.

TERM PAPER SUGGESTIONS

1. Turner believed that there were important differences among types of frontiers. Discusses how the agricultural frontier of the Midwest was different from the mining frontier of the Rocky Mountains and how the woodland frontier of the seventeenth and eighteenth centuries was different from the Great Plains frontier of the 1800s.

2. Examine how the frontier promoted a feeling of nationalism rather than sectionalism.

3. Many critics of Turner's thesis believe that he failed to take into account the development of small towns. Analyze the growth of small towns in the Great Plains during the mid-nineteenth century as a result of the expansion of the railroads. Explain how this pattern contradicts Turner's thesis.

4. Cite examples from U.S. history of how the frontier served as a safety valve for the discontented, adventurers, and economic failures from the East.

5. A tenet of Turner's thesis presumed the constant availability of cheap land through a series of Homestead Acts that offered land for $1.25 per acre. Land speculators, however, were almost always ahead of the farmer, purchasing prime property and reselling it to the homesteader at a premium. Research and describe this process and how it contradicted Turner's thesis.

6. Historians believe that the idea of a safety valve may have been psychological for many Americans. Workers believed that they could move to the frontier if their economic situation declined. Discuss how this misperception of possible future wealth and social status for themselves made radical social movements less appealing to Americans.

ALTERNATIVE TERM PAPER SUGGESTIONS

1. Several U.S. presidents referred to Turner's thesis in their public speeches. Assume you are a speech writer for a twenty-first century U.S. president. Write a speech for this president that incorporates some of the basic ideas expressed in Turner's thesis.

2. Assume that you are an historian of Native American history. Prepare an on-line montage of images and text from the period 1886–1890 to demonstrate how the Census of 1890 marked the end of the American Indian's way of life.

SUGGESTED SOURCES

Primary Sources

Jacobs, Wilbur R. *The Historical World of Frederick Jackson Turner, with Selections from His Correspondence.* New Haven, CT: Yale University Press, 1968. Provides an explication of Turner's constantly adjusted thesis together with correspondence concerning it.

Turner, Frederick Jackson. *The Frontier in American History.* Reprint. New York: Dover, 1996. Contains Turner's explanation of the thesis that he first proposed at a conference in 1893.

Secondary Sources

Axelrod, Alan. *Chronicle of the Indian Wars.* New York: Prentice-Hall, 1993. This reference work summarizes the many conflicts and wars that occurred between various American Indian tribes and the U.S. government as the Indians fought to retain their ancestral lands.

Billington, Ray Allen. *America's Frontier Heritage.* New York: Holt, Rinehart and Winston, 1966. Historian Billington was one of the first to see flaws in Turner's thesis. In this work, he examines the nature of the frontier experience and how it uniquely affected the American character.

Bogue, Allan G. *Frederick Jackson Turner: Strange Roads Going Down.* Norman, OK: University of Oklahoma Press, 1998. This academic biography of Turner provides evidence of why he should remain one of America's foremost historians.

Calloway, Coin G. *The World Turned Upside-Down: Indian Voices from Early America*. Boston, MA: St. Martin's Press, 1994. Contains primary sources in the form of speeches and quotations of various American Indian leaders about the loss of their ancestral lands and way of life because of the expansion of the frontier.

Delbanco, Andrew. *The Real American Dream: A Meditation on Hope*. Cambridge, MA: Harvard University Press, 2000. Discusses the safety valve idea of the American dream throughout American history and how Americans use it as a means of providing themselves with a sense of hope that things will get better.

Jacobs, Wilbur R. *On Turner's Trail: 100 Years of Writing Western History*. Lawrence, KS: University Press of Kansas, 1994. Contains first-person accounts of the small towns in Kansas that were almost devastated by the Dust Bowl of the 1930s. This work disputes Turner's thesis about the development of nationalism because it was local government that saved the small towns from extinction.

Lewis, Archibald R., and Thomas F. McGann, eds. *The New World Looks at Its History*. Austin, TX: University of Texas Press, 1963. Contains the proceedings of the Second International Congress of Historians of the United States and Mexico. The Congress stresses the thesis of the frontier in the growth and development of North America.

Parish, John Carl. *The Persistence of the Westward Movement and Other Essays*. Berkeley, CA: University of California Press, 1943. Provides nine essays proposing that the westward movement was not one movement, but many shifts in the population.

Paxson, Frederic Logan. *When the West Is Gone*. New York: Henry Holt, 1930. Contains three lectures delivered at Brown University that analyze Turner's thesis from the perspective of a shifting frontier rather than one occurring in a series of stages.

Utley, Robert M. *The Indian Frontier of the American West, 1846–1890*. Albuquerque, NM: University of New Mexico Press, 1984. Provides an overview of American Indian history during the mid-nineteenth century.

White, Richard, and Patricia Nelson Limerick. *The Frontier in American Culture*. Berkeley, CA: University of California Press, 1994. Applies Turner's thesis of the peaceful settlement of the frontier that placed the American Indian at the margins of civilization, to events that caused the Diaspora of thousands of American Indians and the loss of their land.

Wyman, Walker D., and Clifton B. Kroeber, eds. *The Frontier in Perspective*. Madison, WI: University of Wisconsin Press, 1957. Presents thirteen lectures delivered at the University of Wisconsin regarding various aspects of Turner's frontier thesis.

World Wide Web

"Frederick Jackson Turner." http://www.bgsu.edu/departments/acs/1890s/turner/turner.html. Furnishes a biographical sketch of Turner that discusses the influence of his thesis on the study of U.S. history. This site also contains a link to an excellent 1890s chronology.

"Frederick Jackson Turner (1861–1932)." http://www.pbs.org/weta/thewest/people/s_z/turner.htm. Presents a biographical sketch of Frederick Jackson Turner and a short discussion of the significance of his thesis to the study of U.S. history.

"Frederick Jackson Turner: An Examination of His Frontier Thesis and American History." http://www.bluecorncomics.com/markwibe.htm. Provides a useful analysis of Turner's thesis from a contemporary standpoint.

"The Frontier in American History." http://xroads.virginia.edu/~Hyper/TURNER/. Contains the full text of Turner's thesis about the American frontier.

"Geronimo: An American Indian Legend." http://www.tfaoi.com/aa/4aa/4aa494b.htm. Furnishes information about Geronimo and his capture and surrender to the U.S. military in August 1886.

"Library of Congress—Historical Analysis and Interpretation: Turner's Frontier Thesis and the "New Western History." http://memory.loc.gov/learn/collections/settlement/thinking4.html. Supplies a summary of Turner's thesis, with primary sources and questions about those sources that relate to Turner's thesis.

"The Wounded Knee Massacre December 29, 1890." http://www.bgsu.edu/departments/acs/1890s/woundedknee/WKIntro.html. Contains an overview of the Battle of Wounded Knee, in addition to many resource links to other informative sites.

Multimedia Sources

The First Measured Century. (Part 1) Alexandria, VA: PBS Home Video, 2005. 1 DVD. 84 minutes. Uses statistics to chart the salient sociological changes in the United States in the twentieth century and how it relates to Turner's thesis.

The West. Santa Monica, CA: PBS Home Video. 1996. 5 DVDs. 707 minutes. Disc 5 references Turner's thesis and visually documents the loss of ancestral lands by American Indians. Click on http://www.pbs.org/weta/thewest/program/ to obtain a multimedia guided tour of each episode in the series, along with selected documentary materials, archival images and commentary, and links to background information and other Internet resources.

95. Pullman Strike (1894)

The Pullman Strike resembled a labor dispute between two equals, but the Pullman Palace Car Company (PPCC) owned by inventor George Pullman, who invented the Pullman railroad car, was clearly favored by big business, the law, federal troops, and even President Grover Cleveland. After the panic of 1893, the country went into a severe depression. Pullman fired one-third of his workers and cut the wages of those remaining by 40 percent. Despite these cuts, however, his company still managed to pay an 8 percent dividend to the stockholders. Pullman's three thousand employees were living in a company town south of Chicago that he had built. The rents were designed to produce a return of 6 percent. When a grievance committee requested a reduction in the rent that corresponded with their wage cut, Pullman refused the reduction and fired three grievance committee members. The workers sought help from the American Railroad Union (ARU) under the leadership of Eugene V. Debs. When Pullman ignored pleas to negotiate, the ARU ceased to work on any trains that hauled a Pullman car. Within a month, fifty thousand workers were on strike throughout two-thirds of the country. Pullman allied with a union of railroad companies called the General Managers Association. Together they arranged for strikebreakers and positive articles in the press. Using mail stoppage as an excuse, they persuaded President Cleveland to invoke the Sherman Antitrust Act to stop the strike and send in federal troops to restore train service. Eugene Debs was jailed on a conspiracy charge and the strike was broken.

TERM PAPER SUGGESTIONS

1. Discuss how the imposition of the Sherman Antitrust Act to prosecute workers established a precedent that impeded collective bargaining between unions and companies until 1914.

2. The town of Pullman seemed like a worker's paradise. Workers lived in fully equipped, company-owned houses, received free education, and had access to a public library and even a church. Investigate why workers living in Pullman were dissatisfied.

3. Initially Eugene Debs was ambivalent about the ARU strike. Research his reasons for opposing the strike and analyze if he was correct in his reservations.

4. Examine why the ARU was unable to obtain support from the railroad brotherhoods, African American railroad workers, and the American Federation of Labor. Assess whether their additional help might have turned the tide in the union's favor.

5. Explain how the General Manager's Association (GMA) and PPCC crushed the strike. Be sure to include how they influenced President Cleveland, appointed a sympathetic Attorney General, created public discontent regarding the strike, and used other union-busting techniques.

6. Research the aftermath of the strike concerning the number of people killed and wounded, property damage, loss of jobs, and the like. Assess whether the strike was inevitable or avoidable.

ALTERNATIVE TERM PAPER SUGGESTIONS

1. Eugene Debs was jailed on a charge of conspiracy to obstruct the mail. He was defended by legendary attorney, Clarence Darrow. Assume you have been asked to assist Darrow with Debs's defense. What arguments would you make in favor of Debs?

2. Assume you are an ARU employee who is paid to solicit support for the strike. Prepare a series of podcasts that outline workers' specific grievances against wage cuts, working conditions, the tyranny of company towns, and stockholders' dividends.

SUGGESTED SOURCES

Primary Sources

Addams, Jane. *A Modern Lear: Jane Addams' Response to the Pullman Strike of 1894*. Chicago, IL: Jane Addams Hull-House Museum, 1994. Provides the famous social worker's sympathetic reaction and response on the worker's behalf to the Pullman Strike.

Darrow, Clarence. *The Story of My Life*. New York: Da Capo Press, 1996. Contains Darrow's life story as well as how he conducted some of his famous defenses, including that of Eugene V. Debs.

Levendecker, Liston E. *Palace Car Prince: A Biography of George Mortimer Pullman*. Niwot, CO: University Press of Colorado, 1992. Contains primary sources in the form of speeches and other correspondence of George Pullman, inventor of the Pullman car and creator of the company that was struck by the ARU in 1894.

Wright, Carroll Davidson. *Report on the Chicago Strike of June–July 1894 by the United States Strike Commission*. Chicago, IL: A. M. Kelley, 1972. Provides the government report that discusses the use of the Sherman

Antitrust Act to break the strike, the authorization of federal troops, and other strike-related documents.

Secondary Sources

Brommel, Bernard J. *Eugene V. Debs, Spokesman for Labor and Socialism.* Chicago, IL: Kerr, 1978. Provides a scholarly account of Deb's life and the key role that he played in the Pullman Car Strike of 1894.

Darrow, Clarence. *Attorney for Damned: Clarence Darrow in the Courtroom.* Chicago, IL: University of Chicago Press, 1989. Darrow discusses some of his most famous defenses, including that of Debs in the Pullman Strike.

Ginger, Ray. *The Bending Cross: A Biography of Eugene V. Debs.* Reprint. Kirksville, MO: Thomas Jefferson University Press, 1992. Is still considered the most definitive biography of Debs and contains a great deal of information about his role in the Pullman Car Strike.

Hirsch, Susan Eleanor. *After the Strike: A Century of Labor Struggle at Pullman.* Urbana, IL: University of Illinois Press, 2003. This fascinating work discusses the aftermath of the strike and the effect it had on labor relations at a local and national level.

Laughlin, Rosemary. *The Pullman Strike of 1894: American Labor Comes of Age.* Greensboro, NC: Morgan Reynolds Publishing, 1999. Provides a succinct overview of the Pullman Strike.

Lindsey, Almont. *The Pullman Strike: The Story of a Unique Experiment and of a Great Labor Upheaval.* Chicago, IL: University of Chicago Press, 1994. Provides a narrative history of the Pullman Strike that evokes the economic and social climate of the times.

Papke, David Ray. *The Pullman Case: The Clash of Labor and Capital in Industrial America.* Lawrence, KS: University Press of Kansas, 1999. Analyzes the Pullman Strike as being a titanic struggle between capital and labor.

Potter, David M. *The Chicago Strike of 1894: Industrial Labor in the Nineteenth Century.* New York: Holt, Rinehart and Winston, 1963. Features an excellent overview of the economic and social forces that precipitated the strike.

Schneirov, Richard, et al., eds. *The Pullman Strike and the Crisis of the 1890s: Essays on Labor and Politics.* Urbana, IL: University of Illinois Press, 1999. Contains a series of essays that analyze the Pullman Strike from economic, labor, and social perspectives.

Smith, Carl S. *Urban Disorder and the Shape of Belief: The Great Chicago Fire, the Haymarket Bomb, and the Model Town of Pullman.* Chicago, IL: University of Chicago Press, 1995. Furnishes a great deal of information about the pros and cons of life in the company town owned by George Pullman.

Stein, R. Conrad. *The Pullman Strike and the Labor Movement in American History.* Berkeley Heights, NJ: Enslow Publishers, 2001. Written for secondary school students, this work traces the rise of unions and the economic conditions that generated them as well as the basic events surrounding the Pullman Strike of 1894.

Warne, Colston E., ed. *The Pullman Boycott of 1894: The Problem of Federal Intervention.* Boston, MA: D. C. Heath, 1955. Gives the opinions of all the major participants about their decision to invoke the Sherman Antitrust Act to stop the Pullman Car Strike.

World Wide Web

"1894: The Pullman Strike." http://www.chipublib.org/004chicago/disasters/pullman_strike.html. Provides a brief overview of the strike and a bibliography of sources.

"The Homestead and Pullman Strikes." http://projects.vassar.edu/1896/strikes.html. Contains summaries of both strikes, accompanied by images and illustrations, and an analysis of their significance to the American Labor Movement.

"Pullman Strike." http://www.spartacus.schoolnet.co.uk/USApullman.htm. Contains the full text of a letter by American Federation of Labor President Samuel Gompers to Judge Peter Grossup concerning the imprisonment of Eugene Debs during the Pullman Strike.

"The Pullman Strike." http://dig.lib.niu.edu/gildedage/pullman/events4.html. Discusses the role of Eugene Debs in the Pullman Strike.

"The Pullman Strike." http://www.kentlaw.edu/ilhs/pullman.htm. Provides a summary of the strike, together with links to information about George Pullman and Eugene Debs. It also includes an address to the American Railroad Union workers at their 1894 convention by Jeanne Curtis, leader of the women's local unit of striking Pullman shop workers.

"The Pullman Strike of 1894." http://www.oah.org/pubs/magazine/labor/bassett.pdf. This outstanding site provides primary sources in the form of financial data about the Pullman Company, testimony by Pullman before the Strike Commission, and a series of lesson plans that involve role-playing some of the events that took place during the strike.

"Sherman Antitrust Act." http://www.infoplease.com/ce6/history/A0844878.html. Provides an overview of the Sherman Antitrust Act and what the intention of Congress was in creating it.

Multimedia Sources

A Nation in Turmoil. Wynnewood, PA: Schlessinger Media, 2003. 1 videocassette. 30 minutes. Examines the period of industrialization in the late nineteenth century, including all of the causes, events, and aftermath of the Pullman Strike.

The Pullman Strike. Culver City, CA: Zenger Video, 1985. 1 videocassette. 20 minutes. Narrates the events of the Pullman Strike.

96. Booker T. Washington's Atlanta Compromise Speech (1895)

African American educator Booker T. Washington's Atlanta speech must be considered within the context of the times. Between 1882 and 1901, more than one hundred African Americans were lynched every year. In the South, Jim Crow laws had taken away their civil rights, including the right to vote, and opportunities for an equal education. Booker T. Washington believed that accommodation was the key to progress for African Americans. His methods were successful too. Washington courted the financial assistance of Standard Oil magnate Henry Huttleston Rogers and Sears, Roebuck and Company president, Julius Rosenwald. From his position as head of Tuskegee Institute, an educational facility that provided occupational and technical training to African Americans, he established 4,977 secondary schools, 217 teacher's homes, and 163 businesses. In 1895 he was invited to deliver the keynote address at the Atlanta Cotton State and International Exposition that was highlighting recent developments in southern agriculture. Using a parable of a ship lost at sea, Washington stressed that African Americans must become economically self-reliant and accept this reward in exchange for civil and political rights that might come in the future. Washington received praise for the speech in the press and even a congratulatory note from President Grover Cleveland. African Americans, however, believed that he had squandered a precious opportunity to press for civil equality and political power in a time of increasing racism.

TERM PAPER SUGGESTIONS

1. Psychologists theorize that people are the products of their upbringing and environment. Research Washington's upbringing and environment. How

may it have shaped his decision to advocate accommodation rather than direct opposition to overt racism?

2. Washington's most strident critic was W. E. B. Du Bois, founder of the National Association for the Advancement of Colored People (NAACP). He labeled Washington, "The Great Accommodator." Discuss how Du Bois's views about progress for African Americans differed from those of Washington.

3. During the time that Washington was urging patience and resignation to Jim Crow laws, Ida B. Wells was documenting and speaking out against systematic lynchings of African Americans throughout the South. Compare her approach with that of Booker T. Washington.

4. In Washington's Atlanta speech he said, "The wisest among my race understand that the agitation of questions of social equality is the extremest of folly . . . ." Discuss why this part of the speech was greeted so enthusiastically by so many White people, including former Georgia Governor Rufus Bullock and President Grover Cleveland.

5. During Washington's tenure as head of the Tuskegee Institute, education consisted of technical and occupational training. Explore how this type of education matched many of the views Washington expressed in his Atlanta speech and other writings.

6. Describe the social, economic, and political environment of the South during the 1890s. What were conditions like for African Americans? Analyze how the lack of civil rights, lynchings, poverty, and the lack of education for African Americans may have contributed to Washington's belief in accommodation rather than confrontation.

ALTERNATIVE TERM PAPER SUGGESTIONS

1. Assume that Booker T. Washington and W. E. B. Du Bois are going to hold a debate concerning their views about how African Americans could best attain equality and economic freedom. Write a series of cue cards for each person that captures their views on issues such as education, franchisement, lynching, and economic opportunity.

2. Booker T. Washington's views on economic self-reliance for African Americans still resonate as a worthy African American value. Write a speech for Washington that expresses his view on this subject.

SUGGESTED SOURCES

Primary Sources

Washington, Booker T. *Up From Slavery.* Reprint. Rocky Mount, NC: Gardner's Books, 2007. Chapters 13 and 14 are devoted to a discussion of the events leading up to his Atlanta speech. It also contains the entire address and presents the reactions to it.

Wells, Ida B., and Afreda M. Duster, eds. *Crusade for Justice: The Autobiography of Ida B. Wells.* Urbana, IL: University of Illinois, 1991. Provides the autobiography of the "woman who killed Judge Lynch" by writing articles, keeping statistics of lynchings, and giving speeches against it.

Wells-Barnett, Ida B. *On Lynchings.* Amherst, NY: Humanity Books, 2002. Contains three primary sources: "Southern Horrors," "Mob Rule in New Orleans," and the "Red Record." All were pamphlets that Ida B. Wells published to document the terrible lynchings of innocent African Americans that were occurring mainly in the South from 1882 to 1901.

Secondary Sources

Baker, Houston A., Jr. *Turning South Again: Re-Thinking Modernism/Re-Reading Booker T. Washington.* Durham, NC: Duke University Press, 2001. Criticizes Washington's fear that confrontation with White people would lead to less power for African Americans and his Tuskegee Institute curriculum, which only trained African Americans for technical occupations rather than professions.

Bontemps, Arno. *Young Booker: Booker T. Washington's Early Days.* New York: Dodd Mead, 1972. This famous African American poet and art critic provides a history of Washington's life from his humble beginnings to his Atlanta speech in 1895.

Brundage, Fitzhugh, ed. *Booker T. Washington and Black Progress: "Up From Slavery" One Hundred Years Later.* Gainesville, FL: University Press of Florida, 2003. Contains a series of essays that examine Washington's autobiography from different viewpoints. Some of the essays place Washington's rationale for his accommodating theory within a nineteenth-century economic perspective.

Carroll, Rebecca. *Uncle Tom or New Negro? African Americans Reflect on Booker T. Washington and Up from Slavery One Hundred Years Later.* New York: Broadway Books, 2006. Twenty contributors discuss and assess the controversial position and actions of Booker T. Washington and his Atlanta Compromise speech.

Du Bois, W. E. B. *The Souls of Black Folk.* Reprint. New York: Pocket Books, 2005. Chapter 3 of Du Bois's observations about African American life is devoted to a criticism of the ideas Washington expressed in his Atlanta speech.

Franklin, John Hope, and Alfred A. Moss Jr. *From Slavery to Freedom: A History of African Americans.* 8th ed. Boston, MA: McGraw-Hill, 2000. Chapter 14 of this classic African American history discusses Washington's philosophy and its critics.

Harlan, Louis R. *Booker T. Washington: The Making of a Black Leader, 1865–1901.* New York: Oxford University Press, 1972. The first volume of this two-volume set discusses the effect of Washington's Atlanta compromise speech.

Harlan, Louis R. "The Secret Life of Booker T. Washington," *Journal of Southern History* 37 (August 1971): 393–416. (Available in JSTOR.) Washington's biographer reveals that Washington secretly financed and directed litigation against disenfranchisement and segregation.

McMurray, Linda O. *To Keep the Waters Troubled: The Life of Ida B. Wells.* New York: Oxford University Press, 2000. Provides an exciting and scholarly account of the life and times of Ida B. Wells.

Marable, Manning. *W. E. B. Du Bois: Black Radical Democrat.* Boston, MA: Twayne Publishers, 2005. Provides a biography of the life and times of W.E.B. Du Bois, critic of Booker T. Washington and founder of the NAACP.

Verney, Kevern. *The Art of the Possible: Booker T. Washington and Black Leadership in the United States, 1881–1925.* New York: Routledge, 2001. Compares Washington with other great African American leaders and reformers: Frederick Douglass and Marcus Garvey. It also discusses his reaction to segregation and his philosophy of responding to it.

World Wide Web

"Booker T. Washington's West Virginia Boyhood." http://www.wvculture.org/history/journal_wvh/wvh32-1.html. Contains an excellent overview of Booker T. Washington's formative years in West Virginia.

"Booker T. Washington National Monument Homepage." http://www.nps.gov/bowa/home.htm. Furnishes a biographical sketch of Washington and other subject-related resource links.

"The Booker T. Washington Papers." http://www.historycooperative.org/btw/Vol.10/html/122.html. Contains the full text of Booker T. Washington's voluminous correspondence to donors, newspapers, and others concerning African American matters.

"Booker T. Washington's Atlanta Compromise Speech." http://www.crm-essentials.com/Atlanta_Compromise.pdf. Provides the full text of Washington's famous Atlanta speech for which he was so praised and eventually criticized.

"Books by Booker T. Washington in Project Gutenberg." http://www.gutenberg.org/author/Booker+T.+Washington. Provides the full text of

Washington's autobiography, *Up From Slavery, The Negro Problem,* and *A Negro Explorer at the North Pole.*

"Legends of Tuskegee." http://www.nps.gov/history/museum/exhibits/tuskegee/ intro.htm. Includes a biographical sketch of Washington and a selected bibliography of additional resources.

"Library of Congress—Biography—Booker T. Washington." http://memory .loc.gov/ammem/aap/bookert.html. Furnishes a biographical sketch of Washington and an audio excerpt link to his Atlanta address, plus a report on education at the Tuskegee Institute.

"Library of Congress—Booker T. Washington Era." http://memory.loc.gov/ ammem/aaohtml/exhibit/aopart6.html. Provides a history of the times in which Booker T. Washington lived from an African American perspective.

Multimedia Sources

Black Americans of Achievement: Booker T. Washington. Wynnewood, PA: Schlessinger Media, 1992. 1 videocassette. 30 minutes. This documentary gives an overview of the life and times of Booker T. Washington.

Booker T. Washington the Life and Legacy. Huntsville, TX: Educational Video Network, 2005. 1 videocassette. 32 minutes. Booker T. Washington was a controversial figure in his own time. This film depicts him in a positive light and shows his commitment to educating African Americans and helping them find a means to a better life.

97. *Plessy v. Ferguson* (1896)

After the end of the Civil War, many southern states passed new laws known as "Black Codes." They restricted African Americans' right to vote, to own property, and to seek gainful employment. In response, Congress passed the Thirteenth, Fourteenth, and Fifteenth Amendments, and the Civil Rights Act of 1875. The latter act tried to extend the Fourteenth Amendment's legal protection to private places and acts. In 1883, the Civil Rights Act of 1875 was ruled unconstitutional. Seven years later the Louisiana legislature enacted a Separate Car Bill that required separate train cars for Whites and African Americans. A group of outraged New Orleans citizens formed the Committee to Test the Constitutionality of the Separate Car Law and sought the help of a French-speaking cobbler who was one-eighth African American. His name was Homer Adolph

Plessy. He courageously purchased a first class ticket for a train trip and took a seat in a car reserved for Whites. He was arrested immediately. Plessy took his case all the way to the Supreme Court where it ruled by a 7–1 vote that separate but equal facilities did not violate the Thirteenth or Fourteenth Amendments. This momentous Supreme Court decision opened the floodgates for a series of segregation laws, also known as "Jim Crow laws," that created separate waiting rooms, factory entrances, water fountains, theatre seating, and even schools. The idea of equal facilities was cast aside and education of African Americans suffered grievously. Some states never provided African Americans with high schools until well into the twentieth century.

TERM PAPER SUGGESTIONS

1. Initially the Separate Car Bill was blocked by eighteen African American legislators and railroad officials. Discuss the economic consequences of providing two or more passenger coaches for each passenger train to accommodate segregated seating and a possible boycott by African American riders.

2. Examine why the Citizens Committee to Test the Constitutionality of the Separate Car Law chose Homer Plessy, a French-speaking cobbler who was only one-eighth African American.

3. Justice John Marshall Harlan was the sole dissenting Supreme Court Justice. He compared the disastrous decision by the court to the *Dred Scott* case. Discuss whether the two cases were that similar.

4. Suppose a railroad conductor had seated a White rider in a designated African American car. If this rider were to bring a lawsuit seeking damages for this situation, how do you think the court would rule?

5. Discuss the degree to which the *Plessy v. Ferguson* case legalized racial segregation in all aspects of public education, transportation, recreation, and accommodations.

6. Albion Winegar Tourgee argued the case before the Supreme Court on behalf of Plessy. What arguments did he make and which ones do you find most persuasive?

ALTERNATIVE TERM PAPER SUGGESTIONS

1. Assume you are representing Homer Plessy in the mid 1950s. How would you try to convince the Supreme Court that the original 1896 decision should be overturned?

2. Design an annotated online chronology complete with nineteenth-century cartoons, illustrations, and images from the time of the Emancipation Proclamation and ending with *Plessy v. Ferguson*. Be sure to include information about the Black Codes, Reconstruction Amendments, Civil Rights Act of 1875.

SUGGESTED SOURCES

Primary Sources

"Plessy v. Ferguson, 163 U.S. 537 (1896)." http://www.law.cornell.edu/supct/html/historics/USSC_CR_0163_0537_ZS.html. Provides the full text of the *Plessy v. Ferguson* case.

"Plessy versus Ferguson—1896." http://www.multied.com/Documents/PlesseyvsFerguson.html. Furnishes the sole dissenting opinion by Justice Harlan in the *Plessy v. Ferguson* case.

Secondary Sources

Aaseng, Nathan. *Plessy v. Ferguson*. San Diego, CA: Lucent Books, 2003. Written for secondary school students, this work provides an easy-to-understand overview of the Plessy case.

Anderson, Wayne. *Plessy v. Ferguson: Legalizing Segregation*. New York: Rosen, 2003. Targeted to secondary school students, it contains primary sources in the form of excerpts from the trial decision and arguments by the lawyers both for and against Plessy.

Ayers, Edward. L. *Southern Crossing: A History of the American South, 1877–1906*. New York: Oxford University Press, 1994. This brilliantly written and prize-winning book provides a history of African American political, social, and cultural life during the time of the Jim Crow laws and *Plessy v. Ferguson*.

Fireside, Harvey. *Separate and Unequal: Homer Plessy and the Supreme Court Decision That Legalized Racism*. New York: Carroll & Graf, 2004. Provides a scholarly account of the impact of segregation that the *Plessy v. Ferguson* decision had on African American society.

Lofgren, Charles A. *The Plessy Case: A Legal-Historical Interpretation*. New York: Oxford University Press, 1987. The author's thesis is that the transportation law did not result in Jim Crow laws, but simply affirmed preexisting racial discrimination.

Medley, Keith Weldon. *We as Freemen: Plessy v. Ferguson*. Gretna, LA: Pelican Publishing Company, 2003. Presents a compelling narrative history of the history and events surrounding the *Plessy v. Ferguson* case.

Packard, Jerrold M. *American Nightmare: The History of Jim Crow.* New York: St. Martin's Press, 2004. Traces segregation laws back to before slavery and then details how the *Plessy v. Ferguson* decision institutionalized racism throughout the country.

Thomas, Brook. *Plessy v. Ferguson.* New York: St. Martin's Press, 1996. Provides an excellent overview and legal analysis of the case.

Woodward, C. Vann. *American Counterpoint: Slavery and Racism in the North-South Dialogue.* Boston, MA: Little, Brown, 1971. Analyzes the irony of Justices Brown's and Harlan's opposing positions, given their backgrounds.

Woodward, C. Vann, and William S. McFeely. *The Strange Career of Jim Crow.* New York: Oxford University Press, 2001. This classic work documents Jim Crow laws up through the 1880s.

Wormser, Richard. *The Rise and Fall of Jim Crow.* New York: St. Martin's Press, 2004. Provides an accompaniment to the PBS series by the same name that is sited under Multimedia Sources. It gives an overview of the beginning and the end to segregation laws regarding almost every aspect of African American life up until 1954.

World Wide Web

"From Plessy v. Ferguson to Brown v. Board of Education: The Supreme Court Rules on School Desegregation." http://www.yale.edu/ynhti/curriculum/units/1982/3/82.03.06.x.html. Scroll down to week two of this site to access a short synopsis and analysis of the *Plessy v. Ferguson* decision

"Plessy v. Ferguson." http://www.kawvalley.k12.ks.us/brown_v_board/plessy_v_ferguson.htm. Presents a short synopsis of the Plessy Case, including case-related documents, the opinion, and other useful information about the *Brown v. Board of Education* case, which overturned *Plessy v. Ferguson.*

"Plessy v. Ferguson." http://www.watson.org/~lisa/blackhistory/post-civilwar/plessy.html. Provides an overview of the case along with links to the *Dred Scott* and *Brown v. Board of Education* decisions.

"Plessy v. Ferguson (1896)." http://www.landmarkcases.org/plessy/home.html. This excellent site provides both concurring and dissenting opinions, background about the case, a discussion of its impact and legacy, and additional questions suitable for term papers.

"The Rise and Fall of Jim Crow." http://www.pbs.org/wnet/jimcrow/stories_events_plessy.html. This Web site accompanies the PBS documentary cited under Multimedia Sources. It supplies images and actual photographs depicting Jim Crow laws, maps, lesson plans, and more.

"Separate but Equal, *Plessy v. Ferguson,* 1896." http://www.lawbuzz.com/can _you/plessy/plessy.htm. Furnishes a reaction to the case plus a brief analysis with links to the dissenting opinion by Justice Harlan.

"A Voice Against Segregation, Albion Tourgee." http://www.aaregistry.com/ african_american_history/2863/A_voice_against_segregation_Albion _Tourgee. Supplies an informative biographical sketch of Albion Tourgee, who argued the case on behalf of Homer Plessy before the U.S. Supreme Court in 1986.

Multimedia Sources

Plessy V. Ferguson Today. Washington, DC: Public Affairs Video Archives, 1996. 1 videocassette. 121 minutes. Panelists from a variety of disciplines discuss the current ramifications of *Plessy v. Ferguson.*

Rise and Fall of Jim Crow. Alexandria, VA: PBS Home Video, 2002. 4 videocassettes. 240 minutes. This outstanding documentary traces the history of segregation from the end of the Civil War through the modern Civil Rights Movement. It includes information about the *Plessy v. Ferguson* case.

98. *United States v. Wong Kim Ark* (1898)

The Reconstruction Amendments were passed after the Civil War to not only legally end slavery but also unequivocally bestow citizenship on newly freed slaves and protect their rights from any infringement by state governments. The Fourteenth Amendment's first sentence states that "all persons born or naturalized in the United States and subject to the jurisdiction thereof, are citizens of the United States and of the State wherein they reside." However, the Fourteenth Amendment did not legally end racial discrimination or legislative discriminatory acts. When racism broke out against the Chinese in California and the Pacific Northwest, Congress, from 1882 through 1894, passed a series of Exclusion Acts that were specifically written to keep persons of Chinese ancestry from entering the United States. The laws targeted low-skilled Chinese laborers who were thought to be taking jobs away from Americans because they would work for lower wages. Wong Kim Ark was born in San Francisco, California, in 1873 to Chinese parents who were lawful resident aliens. In 1890, when they returned to China, Wong, who was employed as a cook, went to visit them. He successfully returned and went back to work. In 1894 after a second visit, Wong was denied readmission to the United States on the grounds that he was not a citizen. Wong sued because his rights were violated under the Fourteenth Amendment. The Supreme Court ruled in 1898 that Wong was indeed a citizen because he had been born in the United States.

TERM PAPER SUGGESTIONS

1. Most European countries followed the Roman law under which children of resident aliens assumed the citizenship of their parents. The U.S. government argued that this practice should be followed in this country. Discuss the implications of such a practice.

2. Discuss how the diversity of America would have been affected if the views of dissenting Justices Fuller and Harlan had been the controlling decision.

3. Do you think that the drafters of the relevant part of the Fourteenth Amendment envisioned the children of undocumented aliens, when their primary focus was on the children born to slaves?

4. Discuss how *United States v. Wong Kim Ark* resolved the conflict between the Fourteenth Amendment and the Chinese Exclusion Acts.

5. Explore whether Justices Fuller and Harlan would have made the same argument if the Exclusionary Acts had been applied to the children of European or African ancestry.

6. Investigate how Chief Justice Fuller used Chinese citizenship laws and treaties between the United States and China to justify the constitutionality of the Chinese Exclusion Acts.

ALTERNATIVE TERM PAPER SUGGESTIONS

1. Under the rationale of the Wong Kim Ark decision, it has been assumed that the children of undocumented aliens who are born in the United States are eligible for U.S. citizenship. Imagine that Congress has passed a law denying U.S. citizenship to the children of undocumented aliens born within the United States. Prepare a legal brief arguing that such a statute would not be invalid under the rationale of the Wong Kim Ark decision.

2. Suppose that Congress enacted a law restricting employment rights of children born to undocumented aliens in the United States. Prepare an argument supporting or challenging the constitutionality of such a law.

SUGGESTED SOURCES

Primary Sources

Kingston, Maxine Hong. *Chinamen.* New York: Alfred A. Knopf, 1980. Contains oral histories and memoirs from Kingston's relatives about the discrimination they faced in nineteenth-century America. Chapter 3, entitled "Laws," is devoted to a discussion of the Chinese Exclusion Acts and refers to the case of *United States v. Wong Kim Ark.*

"United States v. Wong Kim Ark." http://www.oyez.org/cases/1851-1900/1896/1896_132/. Presents the full text of the case as it was argued before the Supreme Court, including basic facts and the concurring and dissenting opinions.

Secondary Sources

Barth, Gunther. *Bitter Strength: A History of the Chinese in the United States, 1850–1870.* Cambridge, MA: Harvard University Press, 1964. Provides a background history of all the previous attempts by Californians to discriminate against the Chinese up until 1870.

Chan, Sucheng. *Entry Denied: Exclusion and the Chinese Community in America, 1882–1943.* Philadelphia, PA: Temple University Press, 1991. Provides a thorough analysis of the legal and economic effects of the Chinese Exclusion Acts.

Coolidge, Mary Roberts. *Chinese Immigration.* Reprint. New York: Arno Press, 1969. Argues that the Exclusion Act was essential to stop unchecked Chinese immigration to the United States and the destruction of the economy.

Gyory, Andrew. *Closing the Gate: Race, Politics, and the Chinese Exclusion.* Chapel Hill, NC: University of North Carolina Press, 1998. Documents the systematic legal efforts on behalf of state and the national government to deny Chinese Americans their rights as citizens.

Lee, Erika. "Wong Kim Ark: Chinese American Citizens and the U.S. Exclusion Laws, 1882–1943." In *The Human Tradition in California,* edited by Clark Davis and David Igler. Wilmington, DE: Scholarly Resources, 2002. Explores the history of Chinese Americans in California and the deleterious effect that the Exclusion Laws had upon them.

LeMay, Michael C. *From Open Door to Dutch Door: An Analysis of U.S. Immigration Policy Since 1820.* Westport, CT: Praeger Publishers, 1987. Examines the economic and racial causes of the anti-immigration movement in the United States since 1820.

McKenzie, Robert Duncan. *Oriental Exclusion: The Effect of American Immigration Laws, Regulations, and Judicial Decisions upon the Chinese and*

Japanese on the American Pacific Coast, 1885–1940. New York: J. S. Ozer, 1971. Presents information about the discrimination against the Chinese and Japanese so that readers can emotionally understand the negative impact it had on them economically, socially, and educationally.

Pfaelzer, Jean. *Driven Out: The Forgotten War Against Chinese Americans.* New York: Random House, 2007. Documents how Chinese American filed more than seven thousand lawsuits after the Exclusion Acts were passed, most of which were successful.

Salyer, Lucy E. *Laws Harsh as Tigers: Chinese Immigrants and the Shaping of Modern Immigration Law.* Chapel Hill, NC: University of North Carolina Press, 1995. Contains an impressive history of immigration law regarding Chinese Americans and documents their consistent and courageous legal battles for citizenship, including that of Wong Kim Ark.

Takaki, Ronald. *Strangers from a Different Shore: A History of Asian Americans.* Boston, MA: Little, Brown, 1998. Chapter 3 is devoted to a history of Chinese immigration to America.

Thomas, Brook. "China Men, United States v. Wong Kim Ark, and the Question of Citizenship." *American Quarterly* 50 (December 1998): 689–717. (Available in JSTOR.) Describes the legal battle that not only Wong had to endure but also other Chinese Americans.

White, Sherwin. *The Roman Citizenship.* London: Oxford University Press, 1973. Furnishes a complete history of the idea of Roman citizenship and how it became the standard measurement for access in many European countries with the exception of Great Britain.

World Wide Web

"The Chinese and the Chinese Question by James A. Whitney (New York: Tibbals Book Company, 1888)." http://pds.lib.harvard.edu/pds/view/4286014?n=11&s=4. Contains the full text of a racist book devoted to negatively stereotyping Chinese Americans.

"Chinese Exclusion Act." http://ocp.hul.harvard.edu/immigration/themes-exclusion.html. Furnishes an excellent overview of the Act plus a lengthy bibliography of books and resource links about the immigration problems that Chinese Americans faced in America during the nineteenth century.

"Documents on Anti-Chinese Immigration Policy." http://www.pbs.org/weta/thewest/resources/archives/seven/chinxact.htm. Presents the full text of the Chinese Exclusion Act of 1882 and the Chinese Exclusion Treaty of 1880 that limited immigration to the United States by the Chinese.

"The Legacy of *US v. Wong Kim Ark.*" http://library.uchastings.edu/library/Library%20Collections/Displays/wkadisplay/index.htm. This outstanding site from Hastings College of Law features an introduction to the case, the full text of the case, a legal analysis, and a discussion of its legacy regarding future issues of citizenship.

Library of Congress—Chapter XXIX: The Chinese Massacre of 1871." http://memory.loc.gov/cgi-bin/query/r?ammem/calbk:@field(DOCID+@lit (calbk023div37)). Furnishes Harris Newmark's eyewitness account of the massacre of the Chinese in the Los Angeles area in 1871.

"Library of Congress—The Chinese in California." http://memory.loc.gov/ammem/award99/cubhtml/cichome.html. Provides first-person accounts by Chinese Americans of their lives in the United States during a period of intense discrimination, a historical timeline, and a list of related resources.

"The Progeny of Citizen Wong." http://www.sfweekly.com/1998-11-04/news/the-progeny-of-citizen-wong/. Describes the reaction of Alice Wong, granddaughter of Wong Kim Ark, upon learning how her grandfather was denied his rights of citizenship and detained until his case was heard before the U.S. Supreme Court.

Multimedia Sources

Gold Mountain Dreams. (Program 1) Princeton, NJ: Films for the Humanities, 2000. 1 videocassette. 85 minutes. Uses interviews with historians, descendants, and recent immigrants to trace the history and experiences of the Chinese in the United States from the California gold rush to the 1882 Chinese Exclusion Act, which banned their entry into the country.

19th Century Turning Points in U.S. History Episode 8, 1882–1900. New York: Ambrose Video Publishing, 2002. 1 videocassette. 25 minutes. Refers to the legal status of and laws passed against Chinese Americans.

99. Spanish-American War (1898)

Called a "splendid little war" by Secretary of State John Hay, the Spanish-American War lasted all of fourth months, but, as predicted by former Senator Carl Schurz, it left the United States with a taste for more confrontations around the globe. The initial cause was a revolution against the Spanish government that controlled Cuba, which was bloody and deadly. Between 1896 and 1898 about one hundred thousand Cubans died either while fighting for their freedom or while imprisoned in concentration camps erected by the Spanish. Presidents Grover Cleveland and William

McKinley were under great pressure to aid the Cubans, and finally President McKinley succumbed to sensationalistic newspaper articles, Senator Henry Cabot Lodge's dreams of an empire, and business interests that relied on Cuba for a source of sugar. President McKinley sent the battleship *Maine* into Havana Harbor on an ostensibly friendly visit where it exploded, killing more than two hundred troops. It was the spark for a war that catapulted Assistant Secretary of the Navy Theodore Roosevelt to fame as head of a group of volunteers and Ivy League students called the Rough Riders. The fighting did not go smoothly in Cuba, but eventually the United States prevailed. Almost simultaneously, Commodore George Dewey captured the entire Spanish fleet in the Philippines. All told, more than five thousand Americans lost their lives in Cuba and another five thousand died in an insurgency in the Philippines. The United States took possession of Cuba, Guam, Wake Island, Puerto Rico, and the Philippines and paid Spain $20 million in compensation.

TERM PAPER SUGGESTIONS

1. Research and explain at what point the Spanish-American War was no longer viewed as a crusade to make part of the world safe for democracy.

2. Between 1892 and 1898, trade between the United States and Cuba, mainly in the form of sugar, fell from $79 million to $15 million. Examine why businessmen and their political representatives such as Senators Mark Hanna, Nelson W. Aldrich, and Orville H. Platt were opposed to the war on trade grounds.

3. Former Missouri Senator Carl Schurz argued that "the more such enterprises there are, the greater will be the dangers of new wars, with all their demoralizing effects upon our Democratic government." Discuss the self-fulfilling prophecy of his words with regard to wars the United States engaged in after 1898.

4. Describe the military and political role that then Assistant Secretary of the Navy Theodore Roosevelt played in the war and how it helped propel him to the White House.

5. Investigate the roles that Senator Henry Cabot Lodge and naval strategist Alfred Thayer Mann played in urging the country and President McKinley to wage war on Spain.

6. The "splendid little war" ended up costing the lives of more than five thousand Americans in Cuba and another five thousand in the Philippines. Discuss whether it was justified given the lack of threat that the situation in Cuba was to America.

ALTERNATIVE TERM PAPER SUGGESTIONS

1. Assume that you are a U.S. general who has been asked to prepare a postwar report assessing the troops' performance in battle, inadequacies of supplies, and general preparedness for war. Be sure to include information about the explosion of the *Maine*, soldiers sickened by tainted beef from the Armour Company, and other military and supply debacles.

2. Create a map of America's new possessions after the war including Wake Island, Guam, Cuba, Puerto Rico, and the Philippines. Choose any two possessions and trace our relations with them up to the present day.

SUGGESTED SOURCES

Primary Sources

Offner, John L. *An Unwanted War: The Diplomacy of the United States and Spain over Cuba, 1895–1898*. Chapel Hill, NC: University of North Carolina Press, 1992. Cites primary sources in the form of communiqués, letters, and former treaties to show how both countries started on the road to war.

Roosevelt, Theodore. *Theodore Roosevelt: The Rough Riders/An Autobiography*. New York: Library of America, 2004. President Roosevelt was an exciting writer, and his autobiography of his role in the Spanish-American War is one of the most captivating primary sources an historian could have for research purposes.

Secondary Sources

Brands, H. W. *The Reckless Decade: America in the 1890s*. Chicago, IL: University of Chicago Press, 2002. Provides a historical backdrop for the Spanish-American War that enables it to be studied within a nineteenth-century context.

Campbell, W. Joseph. *Yellow Journalism: Puncturing the Myths, Defining the Legacies*. Westport, CT: Praeger Publishers, 2003. Provides a thorough history of the role that William Randolph Hearst's newspapers played in inciting the United States to war with Spain.

Cosmas, Graham A. *An Army for Empire: The United States in the Spanish-American War*. Columbia, MO: University of Missouri Press, 1971. Provides an academic account of the Spanish-American War that is highly readable.

Gould, Lewis L. *The Spanish-American War and President McKinley*. Lawrence, KS: University Press of Kansas, 1982. Furnishes information concerning McKinley's initial reservations about waging war and then details the role that he played in ensuring victory for the United States.

Karp, Walter. *The Politics of War: The Story of Two Wars which Altered Forever the Political Life of the American Republic 1890–1920*. New York: Harper & Row, 2003. Analyzes the Spanish-American War and World War I as two wars where powerful men were acting out of self-interest.

Morgan, H. Wayne. *America's Road to Empire: The War with Spain and Overall Expansion*. New York: John Wiley & Sons, 1965. Justifies McKinley's decision to go to war with Spain and discusses its consequences.

O'Toole, G. J. A. *The Spanish War: An American Epic—1898*. New York: W. W. Norton, 1986. Provides a narrative history of all of the events, people, and battles surrounding the Spanish-American War.

Phillips, Kevin. *William McKinley*. New York: Times Books, 2003. Explores President McKinley's short term as president and his intention to turn the United States into a global power.

Smith, Joseph. *The Spanish-American War: Conflict in the Caribbean and the Pacific, 1895–1902*. New York: Longman, 1994. Provides an outstanding military analysis of the Spanish-American war along with an overview of its causes and consequences.

Trask, David F. *The War with Spain in 1898*. New York: Macmillan, 1981. Provides the definitive treatment of the war and discusses its military and strategic significance to the United States.

Traxel, David. *1898: The Birth of the American Century*. New York: A. A. Knopf, 1998. Examines the most salient aspects of the war and shows how it resulted in America developing into a formidable global power.

World Wide Web

"Buffalo Soldiers at San Juan Hill, 1 July 1898." http://www.army.mil/cmh/documents/spanam/BSSJH/BS-SJH.htm. Furnishes a study of how heroically the first and tenth African American cavalry regiments performed during the Spanish-American War, including action reports. The report also disputes the heroic role that former President Theodore Roosevelt wrote about in his autobiography.

"1898–1998, Centennial of the Spanish-American War." http://www.zpub.com/cpp/saw.html. Presents a history of the war replete with period images and illustrations plus a discussion of it from a twentieth-century viewpoint.

"Emergence to World Power, 1898–1902." http://www.army.mil/cmh/books/AMH/AMH-15.htm. Provides the full text of Chapter 15 of Matloff's, *American Military History* that provides an introduction to the Spanish-American War and how it spurred America's rise to become a global power.

"The Impact of the 'Disaster' of 1898 on the Spanish Army." http://www.army
.mil/cmh/documents/spanam/WS-SpARmy.htm. This paper, delivered
in 1998, discusses how unprepared the United States was to wage war
and the disastrous effect the war had on the Spanish forces.
"Library of Congress—The World of 1989—The Spanish-American War." http://
www.loc.gov/rr/hispanic/1898/index.html. This superb site provides an
introduction to the war, a chronology, literary responses to it, additional
online resources, personal narratives, and a selected bibliography.
"Spain to Use Privateers." http://www.nytimes.com/learning/general/onthisday/
big/0424.html#article. Provides the full text of a period *New York Times*
article where Spain published its rules for engagement in the coming war,
including their intention to use privateers.
"War of 98—the Spanish-American War." http://forum.stirpes.net/modern
-contemporary-history/2576-memoriam-heroes-cuba-phillipines.html.
Gives a history of the Spanish-American War from a Spanish perspective.

Multimedia Sources

Biography: Theodore Roosevelt: Roughrider to Rushmore. New York: A&E Home
Entertainment, 2002. 1 DVD. 50 minutes. Discusses and shows the life
and times of President Theodore Roosevelt, including the military role
he played in the Spanish-American War.
The Spanish-American War: Birth of a Nation. New York: A&E Home Entertainment, 2002. 1 DVD. 50 minutes. This documentary presents information about the Spanish-American War and the role that William
Randolph Hearst and his newspaper played in fanning the flames to
ignite it.
The Spanish-American War: First Intervention. New York: A&E Home Entertainment, 2002. 1 DVD. 141 minutes. Supplies information about the
Spanish-American War that depicts it as America's first real intervention
into an area outside of our borders, and discusses the consequences of
such an action.

100. Scott Joplin and Ragtime Music (1899)

When Americans either White or Black first heard the syncopated rhythm
of Scott Joplin's song "Maple Leaf Rag" played on the piano, it set their feet
tapping and many rose spontaneously to dance. Joplin, an African American composer, was not the first to compose a rag, but "Maple Leaf Rag"
was the first to sell more than a million copies of sheet music in the United

States in 1899. Joplin moved to St. Louis in the 1880s because the red-light district could provide him with employment as a pianist. Fortuitously, the George R. Smith College for Negroes in Sedalia, Missouri, had opened nearby. Joplin enrolled and began to study music theory and notation. By chance, John Stark, owner of a sheet music company, heard Joplin perform one of his piano rags at the Maple Leaf Club. After two other publishers had rejected it, he agreed to publish it, and the success brought Joplin instant fame and a steady income for the rest of his life. Joplin was a prolific composer of more than thirty rags, and he collaborated on at least seven others. His music became so wildly popular that it became associated with an historical era that was characterized by a sense of optimism and innocence. Joplin's music also served as a cultural bridge between Blacks and Whites because people responded to it so positively that they neglected to note the race of the composer or player. Historians also agree that his music presaged jazz, especially with the use of the piano, and that it made a lasting contribution to the development of American culture.

TERM PAPER SUGGESTIONS

1. Discuss how Joplin's access to formal music lessons enabled him to create a "classical" form of rag.

2. Describe how Joplin's form of music became so wildly popular throughout America that it formed a cultural bridge between African American and White communities.

3. Explain the musicality of ragtime music and analyze why it is definitely considered a form of music that was unique to nineteenth-century America.

4. Examine how ragtime music contributed to the development of jazz, especially through the inclusion of the piano.

5. Moral critics of ragtime music emerged, decrying that it would corrupt the morals of youth. Compare these critics to twentieth-century critics who wrote similar criticism about jazz and rock 'n' roll.

6. Ragtime music also defined an historical era between 1899 and the 1920s. Describe the time politically and socially, in terms of its innocence and optimism.

ALTERNATIVE TERM PAPER SUGGESTIONS

1. Draw ten cover sheets in the style of John Stark and Sons, the publisher of Joplin's rags, that illustrate the contents and historical times in which they were composed.

2. Listen to a compact disc of some of Joplin's rags. Prepare a podcast that cites and incorporates some of his rags, and explain why the beat was so infectious that it captured America's heart and soul. Tell listeners of Joplin's legacy to American culture and history.

SUGGESTED SOURCES

Primary Sources

Berlin, Edward A. *King of Ragtime: Scott Joplin and His Era.* New York: Oxford University Press, 1994. This extensive biography contains primary sources in the form of photographs, information from archives and period newspapers, and a comprehensive listing of all of Joplin's compositions.

Joplin, Scott. *The Best of Scott Joplin.* Fort Lauderdale, FL: FJH Music Company, 1999. Contains seven original rags as composed by Scott Joplin.

Secondary Sources

Bankston, John. *The Life and Times of Scott Joplin.* Hockessin, DE: Mitchell Lane, 2004. Written for secondary school students, this work projects the life of Joplin against the backdrop of what the times were like for an African American living in post-Reconstruction America.

Berlin, Edward A. *Ragtime: A Musical and Cultural History.* Reprint. Berkeley, CA: University of California Press, 1980. Analyzes the cultural and musical influences on ragtime that includes examples of other forms of music.

Blesh, Rudi, and Harriet Janis. *They All Played Ragtime.* New York: Oak, 1971. This definitive work includes information about all the players of rag, their compositions, and the impact they had on music history.

Curtis, Susan. *Dancing to a Black Man's Tune: A Life of Scott Joplin.* Columbia, MO: University of Missouri Press, 1994. Provides an academic account of the life and times of Scott Joplin and how his music characterized an historical era.

Doctorow, E. L. *Ragtime: A Novel.* New York: Random House, 2007. Although this work is fictional, Doctorow is noted for his historical accuracy. This work captures an historical era that was typified by ragtime.

Gammond, Peter. *Scott Joplin and the Ragtime Era.* New York: St. Martin's Press, 1975. Juxtaposes chapters on Joplin's life with chapters about the era in which he was composing and publishing his music.

Hasse, John Edward, ed. *Ragtime: Its History, Composers and Music.* New York: Schirmer Books, 1985. Contains a broad collection of essays about the influence of ragtime on early country music, other ragtime composers, woman ragtime artists, and reasons for its popularity.

Jasen, David A. *Ragtime: An Encyclopedia, Discography, and Sheetography.* New York: Routledge, 2007. This comprehensive work, by foremost ragtime specialist Jasen, features a complete listing of all ragtime composers and their works, as well as rare photographs of sheet music and other ragtime artifacts.

Jasen, David A., and Gene Jones. *That American Rag: The Story of Ragtime in the United States.* New York: Schirmer Books, 2000. This reference work provides a comprehensive history of ragtime and how it developed as a unique music form in the United States.

Schafer, William J., and Johannes Riedel. *The Art of Ragtime.* Baton Rouge, LA: Louisiana State University Press, 1973. Furnishes a scholarly account of the growth and development of rag, and analyzes its legacy to American culture and history.

Waldo, Terry. *This Is Ragtime.* New York: Hawthorn Books, 1976. Using a decade approach, this work traces the beginnings of ragtime through its resurgence in the 1970s.

World Wide Web

"A Biography of Scott Joplin (c. 1867–1917)." http://www.scottjoplin.org/biography.htm. Provides a long biographical sketch of Joplin with an illustration of the cover sheet from the John Stark and Sons Company that published "Maple Leaf Rag."

"Library of Congress—Ragtime." http://lcweb2.loc.gov/diglib/ihas/html/ragtime/ragtime-home.html. This outstanding site contains essays about the contribution of rag to American history and culture, copies of sheet music, audios, and conversations with various ragtime composers.

"100 Years of Maple Leaf Rag." http://music.minnesota.publicradio.org/features/9905_ragtime/index.shtml. Features a biographical sketch of Joplin that is interspersed with descriptions of his music and audio links so that listeners can hear it being played. "Maple Leaf Rag" is one of the selections. The site also relates how and why Joplin's music was so wildly popular.

"Scott Joplin." http://www.famoustexans.com/scottjoplin.htm. Features a short biographical sketch of Joplin.

"Scott Joplin: A Brief Biographical Sketch." http://www.edwardaberlin.com/work4.htm. This sketch is quite long compared to other Joplin Web sites. It is particularly useful because it is framed by a series of cover sheets to various rags that Joplin published during his lifetime.

"Scott Joplin: King of Ragtime." http://www.carolinaclassical.com/joplin/index.html. Presents a lengthy biographical sketch of Joplin, together with several of his compositions that can be listened to online, followed by a listing of many published ragtime pieces.

"What Is Ragtime, Stride and Novelty Piano?" http://www.johnroachemusic. com/ragtime.html. Features a short history of ragtime music. Click on the icons to hear examples of the syncopated beat that characterized Joplin's music.

Multimedia Sources

"Library of Congress Presents Music, Theatre and Dance—Ragtime." http:// lcweb2.loc.gov/diglib/ihas/search?query=memberOf:Ragtime&format =video+recording&view=thumbnail. Contains thumbnail sketch videos of interviews with famous pianists and other musicians who discuss the influence of rag on other forms of music and composition.

Scott Joplin. Milburn, NJ: Meet the Musicians, 1999. 1 videocassette. 55 minutes. Tells the extraordinary story of an African American musical genius whose music genre helped break down racial barriers.

Scott Joplin. Universal, CA: Universal Pictures, 2001. 1 videocassette. 95 minutes. This nondocumentary, starring Billy Dee Williams as Scott Joplin, brings him to life, including his music and the times he lived in.

Index

About the Author

KATHLEEN W. CRAVER, Ph.D., is Head Librarian at National Cathedral School in Washington, D.C. She is the author of a number of Greenwood Press reference books, including *School Library Media Centers in the 21st Century* (1994), *Teaching Electronic Literacy* (1997), *Using Internet Primary Sources to Teach Critical Thinking Skills in History* (1999), and *Creating Cyber Libraries: An Instructional Guide for School Library Media Specialists* (2002).